FIGHTING ON ALL FRONTS

Popular Resistance in the Second World War

Edited by Donny Gluckstein

ABOUT THE AUTHORS

Kieran Allen is a lecturer in sociology in University College Dublin. His books include *Marx and the Alternative to Capitalism* and *The Politics of James Connolly*.

Kaye Broadbent is a senior lecturer in industrial relations at Griffith University, Brisbane, Australia. She has published on women, insecure work and unions in Japan and Korea.

William Crane has been an active socialist campaigner and writer in the USA and Britain, and a researcher on nationalism, labour and the left in South Asia. He is currently working on a PhD in Migration Studies at the University of Sussex.

Donny Gluckstein is a lecturer in history at Edinburgh College and a member of the Socialist Workers Party. His previous publications include *The Nazis, Capitalism and the Working Class* and *A People's History of the Second World War: Resistance Versus Empire*, the predecessor to *Fighting on All Fronts*.

Ben Hillier is an editor of *Red Flag*, a socialist newspaper in Australia.

Mark Kilian is deputy editor of the Dutch monthly paper *De Socialist*, and the grandson of a communist partisan, Peter van Sloten, who was executed on 7 March 1945 in Haarlem. He is preparing a people's history of the Dutch empire in the Second World War.

Tom O'Lincoln has been active as a Marxist since 1966 in Germany, the USA and Australia. He is the author and/or editor of eight books including *Australia's Pacific War* and *The Neighbour from Hell: Two Centuries of Australian Imperialism*.

Frank Renken contributes regularly to *Marx21*, a socialist magazine in Germany. He has worked and lived in North Africa. His books include *Frankreich im Schatten des Algerienkrieges*.

Janey Stone has written and presented on resistance to the Nazis during the Second World War in Germany, Poland and by Jews. Her mother, who migrated to Australia from Poland in 1938, lost a large part of her family in the Holocaust. As an anti-Zionist Jew, Janey has written about Jewish resistance to anti-Semitism and about the radical Jewish tradition.

Tomáš Tengely-Evans is a journalist on *Socialist Worker* and a socialist activist in east London.

FIGHTING ON ALL FRONTS

Popular Resistance in the Second World War

Edited by Donny Gluckstein

Bookmarks Publications

Fighting On All Fronts: Popular Resistance in the Second World War
Edited by Donny Gluckstein
Published 2015 by Bookmarks Publications
c/o 1 Bloomsbury Street, London WC1B 3QE
© Bookmarks Publications
Designed and typeset by Peter Robinson
Printed by the Russell Press
Cover picture: Jewish partisans near Vilna, just after the liberation
ISBN print edition: 978 1 909026 92 6
ISBN kindle: 978 1 909026 93 3
ISBN ePub: 978 1 909026 94 0
ISBN PDF: 978 1 909026 95 7

Contents

Introduction

Understanding the Second World War: practice and theory

Donny Gluckstein

Seventy years separate the end of the Second World War from 2015 and yet the issues it raised remain fundamental to our understanding of the world today.

It was supposed to be the moment when the dark days of the Depression were set aside and the forces of fascism and dictatorship that fed on them were definitively overcome. But the 1929 Wall Street Crash that sparked the Depression has its counterpart in the collapse of Lehman Brothers and the persistent economic crisis since 2008. In the 1930s the establishment diverted attention from the crisis-ridden nature of capitalism by targeting ethnic minorities, and the Nazis and other racists reaped the benefits. Nowadays the European extreme right—from the populist United Kingdom Independence Party (UKIP) to the outright fascist Front National in France or Jobbik in Hungary—is again gaining in confidence. International tensions, always present when there is a system of competing capitalist states, reached a new intensity in the 1930s, culminating in world war. Today imperialist rivalries that were supposed to have been banished by the fall of the so-called communist regimes of Eastern Europe in 1989 and "The End of History"[1] are reviving.

At the same time the Second World War showed that there could be a different trajectory. It ushered in huge mass movements that tore down the colonial empires that dominated the globe, defied and destroyed fascist dictatorships and authoritarian rule and drove forward the development of welfare states. These too have their parallels today, whether it be in the challenge to the established political parties witnessed in places like Spain and Greece, the Arab revolutions or mass struggles against austerity, privatisation, oppression and exploitation.

The impact of the Second World War was so profound and so widespread that for a long time it was difficult to achieve the sense of distance and perspective needed for an effective analysis. On the whole only the surface phenomena—the military campaigns, the biographies of individual leaders and suchlike—have received attention. This book is an attempt to go beyond that. Understanding the complex political and social processes of the Second World War is important not only so that we can establish the truth about a major past event but also to furnish lessons for today.

This book covers a wide range of countries and situations from major protagonists, such as Japan and Russia, to colonies like the Philippines and Burma, to the sub-imperialism of Australia. It also looks at European resistance, the Jews, and even a neutral country, Ireland. However, the global reach of the Second World War means that even these numerous examples cannot provide a full picture. To achieve a broader overview the rest of this chapter provides a point of comparison for the various situations discussed in the book by considering the pattern of events in centres of resistance not otherwise covered here. It then offers a theoretical framework within which the conflict can be set.

The road to war

Contrary to later claims of anti-fascist intentions on the part of Allied governments, the Second World War began as a naked conflict between the haves and have-nots of imperialism. Britain and France had appeased Hitler when he seized Austria and Czechoslovak territory because they wished to enjoy the fruits of their empires in peace. This desire to maintain class domination (and consequent fear of communism) led Britain's ambassador to Berlin to publicly applaud Hitler for "gigantic progress in the military, industrial and moral reorganisation of Germany". Furthermore, the ambassador warned against war with Nazism because "Moscow's chief aim was to embroil Germany and the Western Powers in a common ruin".[2]

As a backbench MP Churchill criticised appeasement because he saw German expansion as the greater threat to Britain's empire. But he had no principled objection to fascism, telling Mussolini in 1927: "if I had been an Italian, I am sure I should have been with you from start to finish in your triumphant struggle...against Leninism".[3] When Hitler invaded France in May 1940 its commander-in-chief feared armed resistance might unleash "anarchy and revolution". He was ready to capitulate once he could be "sure the Germans would leave me the forces necessary for maintaining order".[4] For its part Russia signed up to the Hitler-Stalin pact in August 1939, cynically agreeing to secret clauses that would partition Poland with Germany and give it the Baltic states.

The minor Allied states adopted a similarly unprincipled point of view. Poland's authoritarian regime signed a pact with Hitler in 1934, its leader having stated: "I would like [Hitler] to remain in power as long as possible".[5] This ran alongside a pre-existing pact with Stalin. The Yugoslav government also negotiated between Axis and Allies. As one British official put it: "Rumour has it that several Yugoslav generals have built themselves villas with money supplied by the Germans. Perhaps we could help them to add wings?"[6] Greece's fascist dictator was perplexed that his country became an Axis target, complaining: "if Hitler and Mussolini were really fighting for the ideology they preach, they should be supporting Greece with all their forces".[7] In the 1930s Albania was dominated by Italy but when still greater control was demanded King Zog replied to Mussolini: "The King is devoted. The people are grateful. Why do you want anything more?"[8] To general disgust, he abandoned his countrymen when the invasion began.

The step-by-step descent into all-out conflict showed how one government after another only opposed the Axis when there was no alternative to opposing the new contenders for imperialist dominance. Britain was compelled to declare war when Germany left it no choice by invading Poland in September 1939. Even then what ensued was a "phoney war" (Britain), *drôle de guerre* (joke war, France), or *"Sitzkrieg"* (sitting war, Germany). London's bombing raids consisted mainly of dropping propaganda leaflets. By contrast, the British and French governments showed much greater enthusiasm for aiding Finland, a future Axis satellite, against Russia's offensive. This "winter war" ended before help could be provided. Russia's war began after Hitler reneged on a non-aggression pact in the summer of 1941 and attacked. The US entered the fray after Japan's raid on Pearl Harbor in December 1941.

Ordinary people found the outbreak of war equally unwelcome but for very different reasons. In Paris "the mood, despite the rhetoric with which the newspapers were filled, was sombre, resigned, serious; there were too many memories of the enthusiasms of July 1914 and the terrible rolls of the dead".[9] In Britain at the outbreak of war one of the team of Mass Observers gauging popular moods remarked: "There is no gushing, sweeping-away dynamo of 'patriotism'".[10] Another noticed how many were "equating the employer with the friend of Fascism".[11] If there was to be war it must "put right first...the things that went wrong last time... Chief among these is certainty of a job, and then certainty of a decent house to live in".[12]

Given years of propaganda glorifying armed combat and the militarisation of Axis societies one might have expected a different response there. Yet according to Hitler's munitions minister, the population of Germany in September 1939 was:

> Noticeably depressed... None of the regiments marched off to war decorated with flowers as they had done at the beginning of the First World War. The streets remained empty. There was no crowd on the Wilhelmsplatz shouting for Hitler... Not a soul on the street took notice of this historic event: Hitler driving off to the war he had staged.[13]

Mussolini's decision to join Hitler in June 1940 was even more unpopular. As Spriano explains:

> Above all there was a general mood of aversion to Italy's entering the war...exemplified by innumerable individual testimonies... The Italian secret police reported with a single voice, unanimously and spontaneously, from September 1939 virtually right until June 1940, Italy did not want the war.[14]

Resistance in the west

Yet something extraordinary happened as the war progressed. Instead of the usual waning of militaristic ardour after initial euphoria, and despite millions killed and maimed at levels unprecedented in human history, backing for the fight against the Axis grew. Opinion polls in the US showed rising approval for the war and President Roosevelt while support for peace initiatives declined.[15] In Britain Mass Observers noted the same phenomenon. Since there had been little sympathy for imperialist war, this mood must have had a different source. Between 1939 and 1945 the meaning and character of the conflict had been transformed in the minds of many ordinary people. The way this happened varied from place to place according to the circumstances.

At its height the Nazi regime encompassed around 350 million people, from Norway to Crete. Although this fell short of the 450 million under the British Crown, it was still a considerable number. Bloody though the history of the British and French empires was, they had been built up over a considerable period and configured for long-term plunder of resources and provision of markets for goods. The Nazi empire by contrast was formed in the midst of all-out world war and, whatever the long-term ambitions of Hitler's "thousand-year Reich", its victims were expected to sustain that effort immediately and wholeheartedly. The pillage was naked and immediate. German policy was to seize labour (by 1945 there were some 11 million slave labourers in the Reich) and resources from invaded territories. For those who remained "the costs of occupying a given area are to be borne by the area itself" by what was euphemistically termed making a "contribution for military protection".[16] As one historian explains:

> These financial tributes soon exceeded the total peacetime budgets of the countries in question, usually by more than 100 percent and in the second half of the war by more than 200 percent.[17]

Apart from the extreme violence meted out to those conquered, the consequences of this economic policy showed up in appalling famines. In the Netherlands some 4.5 million people were affected. In Greece 250,000 died (out of a total population of 7 million). Although these figures fell short of the Bengal famine produced by British wartime policy,[18] Axis occupation provoked resistance movements in country after country.

These were politically differentiated from their official governments for several reasons. The pre-war period had been dominated by the Depression during which governments everywhere pursued economic policies of austerity leaving a vast gulf between rich and poor. This was often accompanied by repression to crush any possible opposition. For example, in Yugoslavia parliament was abolished in 1929. The Metaxas dictatorship in Greece was established in 1936 and immediately arrested 50,000 communists. While formal democracy limped on in France, when the war began hundreds of communist-controlled councils were suspended and seven communist parliamentary deputies were condemned to death.[19] If ordinary people had reason to distrust their erstwhile governments, these in turn were unwilling to wholeheartedly back domestic resistance. Whatever resentment the establishment felt towards the Axis for usurping their right to exploit, they dared not endanger that system by arming their own people.

That is not to say there were no supporters of governments-in-exile (or in the case of France of a segment of the old ruling class) in Axis-occupied lands. "Official" resistance movements included the Chetniks led by Mihailovich in Yugoslavia, the EDES (National Republican Greek League) in Greece and de Gaulle's Secret Army in France. They were well supplied by the Allies but made little progress. The aim might be to rid the country of Axis control but this must not put the rule of the establishment at risk. Two things followed: the arms they held could not be distributed to ordinary people and any serious military challenge against the Axis must await the arrival of Allied armies with enough strength to guarantee restoration of the old regime. This latter tendency has been called "attentism".

These constraints largely condemned the official resistance movements to impotence or worse. In Yugoslavia and to a lesser extent in Greece, they even collaborated with the enemy against left wing resistance movements. The Chetnik leader, for example, declared that: "His main enemies were the partisans...and only when he had dealt with them would he turn his attention to the Germans and Italians".[20] The Axis appreciated this stance and not only supplied the Chetniks with weapons but coordinated operations with them.[21]

The mass popular resistance movements had quite a different purpose. Liberated from the pressure of their own ruling classes and backed by popular hatred of the Axis invader, they were able to draw huge numbers behind them in spite of appallingly difficult circumstances. Largely denied arms by the Allies and threatened by the Gestapo, Wehrmacht and the full weight of Axis imperialism, they achieved significant results at a terrible personal cost.

In Yugoslavia Tito's partisans held down 200,000 Germans and 160,000 auxiliaries, suffering 300,000 dead and 400,000 wounded.[22] In Greece EAM-ELAS (National Liberation Front–National Popular Liberation Army) killed 19,000 German soldiers and tied up significant Wehrmacht strength.[23] In France a wide variety of radical resistance bodies launched large-scale heroic struggles. To assist the Allies with the D-Day landings the French resistance took on 12 German divisions and shortly afterwards liberated Paris against Wehrmacht opposition. Italy's resistance mobilised some 200,000 to 300,000 partisans, kept some 25 Wehrmacht divisions occupied and cost them tens of thousands of soldiers.[24]

It was not just the impressive scale of the popular resistance that differentiated it from the official Allied war effort. While the latter wanted restoration of pre-war conditions (including all the repression and exploitation this entailed), the former wanted economic, political and social liberation. Tito, whose forces withstood not only the full force of German, Italian and quisling Croat forces (the Ustashi) but deadly Chetnik attacks and years of indifference from the Allies (including London, Washington and Moscow), wrote:

> Our struggle would not be so stubborn and so successful if the Yugoslav peoples did not see in it not only victory over fascism but also victory

over all those who have oppressed and are still trying to oppress the Yugoslav peoples...if it did not have the aim of bringing freedom, equality of rights and brotherhood to all the peoples of Yugoslavia...[25]

In Greece's EAM-ELAS the same motivations were present. One female resistance fighter, speaking in the 1990s, recalled that during the struggle "we women were, socially, in a better position, at a higher level than now... Our organisation and our own [resistance] government... gave so many rights to women that only much later, decades later we were given".[26]

The French resistance had many currents but, as one study puts it, they were "virtually unanimous in predicting and declaring revolution".[27] The tone of the resistance press, which attained a daily circulation of 600,000 despite the Gestapo, was captured by this article: "the masses will not act unless they know what the aim is, and it needs to be an ideal that will justify their efforts and great enough to encourage supreme sacrifice".[28] This went far beyond driving out the Nazis and involved:

Liberation from material servitude: hunger, squalor, the machine
Liberation from economic servitude: the unfair distribution of wealth,
   crisis and unemployment
Liberation from social servitude: money, prejudice, religious intolerance
And the selfishness of the oppressors.[29]

The Italian resistance developed in a situation where the population had had to endure decades of fascism (from 1922 onwards) while the economy was far weaker than in Germany. During the conflict living standards collapsed and malnutrition stalked the working population. In the winter of 1942-1943 mass strikes swept the industrial north and this, combined with the Allies landing in Sicily, led the king and Fascist Grand Council to depose Mussolini in the hope of extricating itself from the war. This failed as the Germans proceeded to occupy the north and reimpose the Duce through the puppet Republic of Salò. The Italian resistance for obvious reasons therefore had no allegiance to its pre-war government and its economic system. Although dominated by the communists, even the Catholic segment adopted a radical tone:

the age of capitalism that has produced astronomical wealth and led to unspeakable misery, is in its death throes. A soulless regime encouraged the spread of poverty that was beyond belief, sabotaged the productive efforts of the people and deliberately provoked man's inhumanity to man... From the final convulsions of this age a new era is being born, the era of the working classes...[30]

Even in Britain, which was not under occupation (the Channel Islands excepted), there was enthusiasm for victory which, as Mass Observers noted, was indissolubly linked with the idea of a welfare state, a concept approved by 90 percent of people in polls.[31]

There were exceptions to this pattern, of course. For example, in Poland, a country which lost more people per head of population than any other but early on suffered the brutality of German occupation in the west and Russian occupation in the east, the resistance movement took a less radical form. Poland's extensive "underground state" encompassed a range of viewpoints from left to right and included both the "official" form of resistance discussed above and more rebellious elements. In 1944 it was the pressure of the latter that compelled the former to give up waiting for the Allies and to launch the Warsaw uprising. In Latvia the sheer weight of the opposing imperialist forces was such that any hopes of meaningful resistance were extinguished. The 1940 Russian occupation was followed a year later by a German invasion. This was generally welcomed by the population and there was even a locally generated Holocaust of 70,000 Jews which pre-dated the German Holocaust.

Anti-colonial resistance

The rhythm of popular resistance to imperialism in the Asian colonies differed from Europe. Here the Second World War had not initiated an era of foreign invasion but was a continuation of it. The British in India, the French in Vietnam and Dutch in Indonesia already operated with repressive brutality against subject populations. For example, India in 1919 suffered the Amritsar massacre during which some 1,000 non-violent protesters were butchered. In 1926 and 1927 Indonesian communists were arrested in their thousands and many were killed. In 1930 the French reacted to a Vietnamese nationalist attack on the Yen Bay garrison by executing many rebels and bombing villages indiscriminately.

The Japanese offensive that launched open inter-imperialist struggle in the East did not immediately change this dynamic. In India, for example, a local army was raised to fight to preserve the chains holding the sub-continent in subjugation. The burden of feeding this force pitched Bengal into a famine costing around 2.5 million lives. India's Congress Party had offered to assist London's fight against the Axis in return for a promise of independence at the conclusion of war. When its offer was spurned and repression stepped up once again, the Congress Party took the road of resistance, inaugurating a "Quit India" movement in 1942. Gandhi intended to keep action within the frame of non-violent civil disobedience but after mass arrests of Congress leaders it soon escaped these confines, becoming a mass movement from below. Leadership fell to J P Narayan of the Congress Socialist Party who explained:

> India's fight for freedom is at once anti-imperialist (and therefore anti-fascist for Imperialism is the parent of Fascism)… We work for the defeat of both Imperialism and Fascism by the common people of the world and by our struggle we show the way to the ending of wars and the liberation of the black, white and yellow".[32]

Britain quelled the Quit India movement but to do so it arrested 100,000 people and fired on protesters no less than 538 times, killing several thousand.

This proved to be only a temporary solution as war severely weakened the European colonisers with France and the Netherlands occupied and Britain under attack. Taking advantage of this situation, Tokyo rapidly supplanted former colonial masters in much of south east Asia.

In such conditions the resistance tended to be pulled in two directions. As the Quit India movement showed, some hoped that Allied rhetoric about fighting for freedom and democracy could be converted into national independence. Others, such as the Indonesian nationalist leader Sukarno and Subhas Bose, leader of the Indian National Army (INA), swallowed Japan's claim that it was campaigning to rid Asia of white racist domination. The former worked uncritically with the Japanese till the very end of the war. Bose organised Indian army prisoners of war (POWs) into a force which invaded India alongside Japan's army, though without success. In Vietnam, France continued to be formally in control for most of the war, though it collaborated closely with Japan. So, despite Ho Chi Minh's efforts to cultivate links with the Allies, the resistance had no choice but to oppose both camps. Alas, it was too weak to prevent a famine, again created by wartime conditions, that cost 2 million lives in Tonkin in 1945.

Rulers and masses interact: phase 1

While the Second World War began as an inter-imperialist struggle, it is clear that as it progressed popular movements also developed with their own goals. Both elements were involved in combat, but shared little beyond having a common foe (although even here there were exceptions such as the INA). An important question is therefore how the two currents interacted.

Once again certain rhythms can be detected. In Europe there was cooperation between Allied imperialism and resistance at the outset in the joint enterprise of defeating the Axis. The sheer weight of the Axis offensive left the Allied imperialists no choice but to call on all possible forces to oppose it and if resistance movements could challenge the Axis behind the lines this was welcome. The Allies were keenest to support the "respectable" resistance movements tied politically to governments-in-exile (often based in London) but since these tended to attentism, others might be considered.

The first European resistance movement to be recognised by the Allies was the Chetniks of Yugoslavia. At that point France had been defeated, the Soviet Union and the US were still to enter combat. The British state stood alone and unable to fight on the Continent. Churchill therefore decided to back forces which could "set Europe ablaze" and to establish the Special Operations Executive (SOE) to liaise with them. At this stage Western Allied governments were prepared to work with a wide variety of movements including those dominated by communists, such as in Italy, France and Greece. However, politics remained paramount since the point, in government eyes, was to assist the inter-imperialist struggle and nothing more.

Since many of the resistance movements were led by communists one might have expected major assistance from Moscow. Russia was so involved battling for its survival until the turn of fortunes in Stalingrad (February 1943) that military aid was unlikely but political support could have been made available. It was not. Stalin's attitude was demonstrated graphically when the Communist International was dissolved in the same year. For him Russia's need to work closely with other Allied governments to defeat Hitler took precedence. In its dissolution statement the Communist International declared:

> the sacred duty of the broadest masses of the people, and first and foremost of progressive workers, is to support in every way the war efforts of the governments of [Allied] countries for the sake of the speediest destruction of the Hitlerite bloc…irrespective of party or religion.[33]

As the war progressed there was a cooling of relations between Allied governments and resistance movements. By the end Allied governments frequently acted with outright hostility as the ultimate purpose of the war came into focus for each side.

The case of Poland showed the role of Allied political calculations clearly. Although Hitler's invasion was the official reason for Britain entering the war, while the struggle was in the balance London's attitude was generally influenced by Moscow which, following the Hitler-Stalin pact, regarded the country as its to conquer. So Western aid to the resistance was limited. Although by late 1944 the Polish resistance had killed eight times more German troops than the Greek resistance and at least 15 times more than the French, it received respectively just 10 percent and 5.6 percent of the supplies committed to these countries.[34]

In the Far East resistance movements were unlikely to receive support from Allied powers either because those powers were themselves already defeated (such as France or the Netherlands) or because a strong resistance movement would be able to throw off the shackles of colonialism once the war ended. Only the US, which had yet to establish formal political influence in the area, dabbled with the resistance movements in places like China and Vietnam. Ho Chi Minh was even temporarily counted as a US agent! But Washington concluded before long that its interests lay in bolstering the former colonial masters rather than forces opposed to foreign control in general.

In Greece, Britain initially backed both EAM-ELAS and the attentist EDES movement, a famous example of this being the destruction of the strategically important Gorgopotamus viaduct by a combination of British secret agents and fighters from both Greek groups. However, this ran against the political grain, which was to favour the more right wing tendencies. In France de Gaulle's Secret Army received favourable treatment over other more radical groups. In Yugoslavia, in the words of one British official, Mihailovich's Chetniks should be favoured by London over communist-led partisans: "independently of whether or not he continues to refuse to take a more active part in resisting and attacking Axis forces".[35] It required incontrovertible proof of Chetnik collaboration with the enemy to shift support to Tito's partisans.

Rulers and masses interact: phase 2

The official war aims of the Allies were supposed to be expressed in the Atlantic Charter of 14 August 1941 upholding "the right of all peoples to choose the form of government under which they will live".[36] But this was a sham designed to draw in the masses. The real stance of these governments was developed at the various meetings of the Big Three (Stalin, Roosevelt and Churchill). One famous encounter between Churchill and Stalin in the Kremlin in October 1944 took decisions which Churchill himself described as "crude, and even callous". Churchill's account of the notorious "percentages agreement" goes as follows:

> The moment was apt for business, so I said...how would it do for you to have ninety percent predominance in Roumania, for us to have ninety percent of the say in Greece, and go fifty-fifty about Yougoslavia?... It was all settled in no more time than it takes to set down...[37]

In Europe therefore the usefulness of resistance movements to Allied governments decreased in direct relation to the declining power of Axis forces and the increasing possibility of imposing an imperialist peace. There was a tipping point, discernible almost everywhere, when the imperialists concluded that the benefits of popular national movements confronting the Axis were outweighed by the disadvantages of potential democratic interference in their plans. The transition from one phase to another was brilliantly expressed by a British brigadier writing about Greece. He argued for public disapproval of EAM-ELAS as follows:

> we can expect them to be anti-British. Military considerations, however, demand that we should give maximum support...thus bolstering up EAM. Although these two policies appear to be diametrically opposed, this is not the case, as it is solely a question of timing. Our immediate policy should be the purely military one of giving support to the guerrilla organisations to enable them to assist us in liberating their country... This should give way to the political policy of no support to EAM as soon as liberation is achieved.[38]

This policy was followed meticulously. Germany was allowed to withdraw without interference from the Greek islands to the mainland so that the resistance could not gain control before the British were ready. When the Germans left Greece (a little too early for London's liking) Britain rushed troops to Athens to destroy EAM-ELAS. They arrived on 14 October 1944 with the following orders from Churchill: "Do not hesitate to fire... Act as if you were in a conquered city where a local rebellion was in progress".[39] Wholesale Royal Air Force (RAF) bombing of working class residential districts in Athens followed. By the end of December 50,000 Greeks had been killed. Thereafter Nazi-trained Greek battalions were mobilised to pursue a civil war which ultimately cost 158,000 lives.

In Poland, Stalin achieved the same effect by letting the Germans do the dirty work. On 1 August 1944, as the Red Army approached Warsaw, the poorly armed resistance there launched an urban insurrection against Nazi occupation that was the largest of the war. Although it only had arms for one week of fighting it fully expected imminent Russian assistance. But Stalin's attitude was immediately hostile. The rising, he wrote, "does not inspire confidence" and was "a reckless and terrible adventure".[40] Not only did the Red Army halt its advance but Russia put obstacles in the way of a British-US airlift of supplies for the rebels, refusing refuelling rights to their planes.

In Italy the change in Allied policy also occurred in late 1944. An Anglo-American army had control in the south but Germany held the north. Since the summer of 1944 it faced what the Wehrmacht commander Kesselring called "unlimited guerrilla warfare". The partisans fought 218 pitched battles and destroyed hundreds of locomotives and bridges.[41] Fifteen republics were established in liberated areas at the same time. Yet on 10 November the Commander of the Allied Forces announced on open airwaves that the resistance should stand down and go home.[42] To publicly disassociate itself in the very midst of battle amounted, in the words of a prominent resistance leader, to "an attempt on the part of the Allied command to eliminate the Italian liberation movement".[43]

The critical moment for France had occurred a little earlier. Inspired by the Allied D-Day landing in June 1944, the resistance, backed by waves of strikes, intensified the pressure on the German forces occupying Paris. By August, Germany was losing control of the capital. At that moment the officially recognised leader of the Free French in London, General de Gaulle, ordered Parisians to: "Return to work immediately and maintain order until the Allies arrive".[44] This threw the Germans a lifeline and an enraged resistance fighter commented: "It was impossible to imagine a greater divorce between the action sustained by the masses and the coterie which had positioned itself between them and the enemy".[45]

The case of Yugoslavia was an exception to this pattern. In the situations considered so far there was only one wing of the Allies decisively involved militarily with each particular resistance movement. For Greece, Italy and France this meant the Western Allies. With Poland it was Russia. In the case of Yugoslavia, Tito managed to balance the Western Allies and Russia by using imperialist rivalry between them. Britain and the US had belatedly supplied Tito while the Red Army was involved in the liberation of Belgrade. For one wing to have openly sabotaged the resistance would have given political advantage to the other.

As we have seen, resistance movements in the Far East lacked Allied patronage and so there was no period of cooperation, only hostility. With the exception of the crushing of Quit India there was little the Allies could do practically as long as the Axis ruled the territories in which they operated. This situation changed in August 1945. In Vietnam the collapse of Japan opened the way to a mass uprising which the Viet Minh came to head. The revolution swept all before it in the north, partly because here China's weak and corrupt Kuomintang government had been allocated responsibility by the Allies and was in no position to exercise control. However, Britain was assigned the south and General Gracey described his arrival in these terms: "I was welcomed on arrival by the Viet Minh who said 'Welcome' and all that sort of thing. It was a very unpleasant situation, and I promptly kicked them out. They were obviously Communists".[46] Using British troops, a ragbag of forces including Vichy and even Waffen SS soldiers, the revolutionary movement was blocked and the country prepared for the return of the French.

In Indonesia resistance was late to develop. The Japanese promised Indonesian independence in the future and under Sukarno's leadership the nationalist movement cooperated passively. Tokyo's defeat ended these hopes and under considerable pressure from a revolutionary movement of youth, the Pemuda, he was forced to declare independence. In 1945 the Dutch were in no position to retake their colony and turned to Britain to accomplish this. Britain, however, found itself overstretched. To bolster its fighting strength Japanese forces were enlisted! There followed a concerted attempt to crush Indonesian independence. Thousands were killed in pitched battles such as at Semarang where the Japanese fought and Surabaya where the British attacked the population.

Outcomes

Although by 1945 the Axis was defeated that did not mean a return to pre-war conditions. In this, the greatest of all total wars, Allied success had relied on the energy of the mass of the people not just in resistance movements but in official armies and on the home front in places like Britain and the US. Where the Axis occupied, official rule had been disrupted and the vacuum filled by unofficial resistance organisations. Therefore the idea that establishment rule was inevitable and there was no alternative to capitalism was questioned. In two broad arcs stretching from Beijing through Hanoi to Jakarta and Delhi and then from Athens through Belgrade to northern Italy and Paris the masses, many of them armed, were challenging for control.

Resistance movements by necessity could not arise using conventional organisational methods or routine bureaucracy. But in conditions of secrecy and illegality no leader could conjure up a movement by decree. When the Gestapo and SS were hunting down all opposition ruthlessly, self-motivated initiatives from below based on improvisation, rank-and-file commitment, courage and self-sacrifice were vitally necessary components. However, if by definition these were an almost classic expression of spontaneity, it was equally true that military effectiveness required centralised leadership. Individual heroism was no substitute for unified organised operations.

Spontaneity and leadership, decentralisation and centralism, which to an anarchist or autonomist appear to be inimical, were absolutely complementary and absolutely necessary. The historical record confirms this. Those resistance movements that failed to engage the masses through democratic participation and radical programmes withered on the vine. The Chetniks in Yugoslavia and EDES in Greece were good examples. Conversely, despite the deeply democratic methods employed by resistance movements (such as election of officers, no special pay for higher ranks, the overlap of civilian and soldier roles, involvement and equality for women), every one had a defined leadership. The actions of this group became critical at the end of the war when the ultimate meaning and outcome of years of titanic struggle were to be determined.

In many cases (such as Greece, Italy, Vietnam and Yugoslavia) Communist Parties (CPs) were the most influential. Their predominance had been earned before the war when they had opposed the establishment and proposed radical change, often at very high personal risk. Through deep working class roots that could articulate the popular mood, a strong sense of discipline, organisation, cohesive ideology and personal commitment, the CPs possessed invaluable tools for developing the underground activities of wartime resistance.

The CPs' Achilles' heel, however, was their devotion to Stalin's Russia. In the mistaken belief that this regime represented "actually existing socialism", CP leaders acted as tools of Russian foreign policy at the very same time as at the domestic level their members were championing grassroots resistance. This contradiction could remain unresolved while the fighting continued. When the war ended the situation became untenable. Either CPs accepted the spheres of influence drawn up in "crude and even callous" arrangements such as the percentages agreement or they broke with Russia.

A particularly sharp example of the problem was seen in Italy when CP leader Togliatti executed the so-called "Salerno turn" in April 1944. He insisted that the Italian CP "must abandon the position of opposition and criticism which it occupied in the past"[47] and enter a southern Italian cabinet led by a prominent fascist and the same king who had appointed Mussolini. Both were seeking left cover in an attempt to remain in power after ditching the discredited Duce. Since Stalin assigned Italy to Western imperialism its CP must assist in this quest. The Greek CP had the strength to see off Churchill's challenge but under Russian pressure it made fatal concessions which doomed it to defeat in a civil war. In France de Gaulle was able to dissolve the resistance almost overnight due to CP quiescence there. There were exceptions to this pattern where various circumstances, such as individuals exhibiting greater autonomy from Russia or balanced spheres of influence (such as for Yugoslavia where Stalin and Churchill went "fifty-fifty") helped resistance movement goals to find greater expression. China, Vietnam and Yugoslavia were examples of this.

Despite these obstacles the very existence of mass popular resistance meant the outcome of the war was not the one planned by the imperialists. The masses made their demands felt in a number of ways. India, Indonesia and Vietnam all achieved independence as a result of processes unleashed by the war.

In Europe the people were determined that they had not suffered and fought just to benefit one imperialist camp over another. They remembered the misery of the Depression that had followed the First World War. The ruling class were also very aware that the 1914-1918 war had sparked an unprecedented wave of revolutions that came close to destroying capitalism altogether. As one British MP famously put it in 1943: "If we don't give them reform, they will give us revolution".[48]

In Western Europe the ideas of social justice and social solidarity encouraged state provision of welfare, nationalisation of some industry and economic policies designed to avoid unemployment and so on. So the eventual outcome of the Second World War was deeply ambiguous. While the contours of imperialism were redrawn in favour of two new superpowers (the US and the Soviet Union), the break-up of traditional empires and an apparent "social democratic consensus" set a new pattern in many Western countries.

The context

If the first casualty of war is truth, the second is critical analysis. The conventional view of the Second World War subordinates everything to a struggle between nations with fascists on one side and democrats on the other. That is both the starting point and the end point, and the meaning of terms like "war", "fascism", "democracy" or "nation" is treated as self-evident. However, a proper understanding of the 1939-1945 period requires this scenario to be stood on its head. The fighting, the states involved, their ideologies and political institutions need to be rooted in their social context—the system of capitalism.

Capitalism is a system torn by two central antagonisms. One is between capitalists themselves who compete to survive and accumulate. From this vantage point the formation of hostile blocs and the outbreak of the Second World War emerge as a clash between ruling classes advancing their own interests. However, this was also a total war which drew entire populations into its gaping maw. The masses were not passive tools and their relations with the rulers, both Axis and Allied, were shaped by the second key contradiction of capitalism—between exploiters and exploited.

The key institution mediating these twin contradictions was the state. It is through the state that capitalists collectively enforce their internal and external goals. Exploitation within a state's territory is maintained by the carrot or the stick, democracy being an example of the former and fascism an example of the latter. It was therefore secondary that some of the leading Allied powers were parliamentary democracies while their opponents were fascist. Thus Stalinist Russia and Greece, both dictatorships, fought with the Allies while Finland, a member of the Axis coalition, remained a parliamentary democracy throughout the war.

When capitalist states use their power to further capitalist interests externally, to gain control of resources and people beyond their borders for the purpose of exploitation, this constitutes imperialism. During 1939-1945 the Axis powers found that in a world where there was virtually no "free" territory left achieving this goal involved the elimination of rival capitalist entities. So the Second World War was initiated by the most powerful capitalist state machines which fought each other. As such, it was not a battle of nations (if that term is used in the sense of the people in general) but of imperialist blocs.

What of the smaller states that fell victim to Axis expansion? They claimed a common "national" interest linking government, capitalists and the people. However, in practice more often than not the needs of exploitation took precedence over any hostility that these ruling classes felt towards imperialism. Therefore rather than consistently throw their lot in with the people and maintain independence from imperialist influence, the capitalists relied on one or other of the imperialist camps.

For ordinary people the continuation of capitalist drives from the top opened a gap between official propaganda and the lived reality of wartime conditions. Consequently the masses developed a host of activities from below through which they strove for their own interests in opposition to the top of society. Imperialism and exploitation engendered anti-imperialism and radical resistance. The concept of national interest was tested to destruction by mass struggles for justice, democracy and equality.

The rival blocs

Unlike their enemies, the major Allied powers such as Britain, France and the Soviet Union had a long history of imperialist activity. Before 1939 Britain, France and the Soviet Union controlled more than half of the globe's land mass: the British Empire encompassed a quarter of the world, France's possessions gave it almost a tenth and Stalin controlled a sixth. Up to that point the US state relied less on external state action, the focus having been internal expansion across the North American continent and exploitation of an imported labour force, many being slaves.

The Allies claimed to be acting in self-defence during the Second World War and this seemed plausible as their rivals could only build empires of their own by seizing land from the established plunderers. Moreover Allied governments could don the mantle of democracy. Their gradual accretion of colonies and the fact that it often involved overcoming economically weak areas meant that domestic populations did not have to be directly harnessed to achieve external expansion. There could thus be a relative separation between politics at home (which might take parliamentary form) and imperialist foreign policy dressed up in benign clothing such as a civilising Christian mission or in the case of Russia "actually existing socialism". When MPs at Westminster accused Churchill of endangering Britain's colonies by signing up to the democratic principles of the Atlantic Charter he replied that it did "not qualify in any way...the British Empire" and only applied to "the states and nations of Europe now under the Nazi yoke".[49]

By contrast the chief Axis powers were late starters in the imperial race. Japan's Meiji Restoration took place in 1867 while Italy and Germany only unified in 1870 and 1871 respectively. The first two gained nothing from their efforts in the First World War while Germany lost what little it had grabbed. This humiliation was compounded by internal crises during the inter-war years ranging from Japan's 1918 rice riots, to Italy's "Two Red Years" (1919-1921) and the German Revolution (1918-1923). Social upheaval threatened the ruling classes who turned to counter-revolutionary forces such as militarism, Italian fascism and Nazism to resolve both internal and external difficulties.

Their extreme right ideology wiped out domestic opposition (trade unions and political parties) and liquidated democratic rights. With the working class largely silenced, Axis governments aimed to make the respective populations obedient instruments of totalitarian, racist and aggressive imperialist expansion. Hitler's *Mein Kampf*, with chapters on "The Struggle against the Red Front" at home and "The Eastern Orientation" of conquest, encapsulated this strategy perfectly. Though the underlying process was the same, what had taken the Allies decades even centuries to achieve, the Axis felt they needed to consolidate in months, years at the most, and this lent a peculiarly sharp edge to their policies.

Nor was the turn to authoritarianism unique to the leading Axis powers. In 1920 most European countries had some form of parliamentary democracy. But the threat posed by communist revolution in the early 1920s and the impact of the 1929 Wall Street Crash meant that by 1939 this had disappeared everywhere except for the Western fringe of the Continent. The cancer was systemic.

While the rhetoric employed by Axis and Allies differed, the underlying substance of their imperialisms did not. For the ruling classes of Europe there was no principled distinction drawn between democracy and fascism since these were merely varieties of domination. For example, during the Spanish Civil War, Italy and Germany actively contributed to Franco's smashing of the Republic. Although Britain and France feigned neutrality, they ensured the Republic received no assistance. Meanwhile the US turned a profit supplying oil to both sides. The British and French establishments had no qualms about appeasing Hitler, Mussolini or Hirohito in the 1930s and only turned to war when Axis expansion became a clear threat to their hegemony. Russia had opposed appeasement but in 1939 Stalin concluded a pact with Hitler that included the seizure of the Baltic states and the partitioning of Poland with Germany. This was the green light the Führer needed to unleash the war which began two weeks later.

When appeasement failed and it came to blows these were on lines set out in 1932 by Stanley Baldwin: "you have to kill more women and children more quickly than the enemy…when the next war comes".[50] True to this strategy, the RAF conducted "area bombing" which killed 600,000 German civilians culminating in the Dresden firestorm in February 1945 which cost some 40,000 lives.

For their part the Nazis foresaw a *Grossraumwirtschaft* (macroeconomic space) in Eastern Europe. Planners deemed "a third of the [Polish] population…surplus to requirements" and "a barrier to capital formation".[51] Millions were to be slaughtered. In the Far East, Japan's Co-Prosperity Sphere meant shocking exploitation and violence across a vast swathe of territory.

Capitalist ruling classes that fell victim to the Axis responded on a strictly profit and loss basis. The French establishment concluded after brief resistance that it would be better to collaborate and accept occupation of the majority of the country than risk revolution by arming its workers. Some ruling classes enthusiastically sided with the Axis such as in Austria; some split between the two camps (as was the case initially in Yugoslavia); while yet others formed governments-in-exile and waited for Allied armies to restore their property and rights. Where temporary marriages of convenience between Allied governments and resistance movements had been arranged, they were repudiated as soon as the defeat of the Axis made divorce decently possible.

The war ended with Washington deploying nuclear weapons. Previously on the US western seaboard the entire population of Japanese ethnic origin (including US citizens) was thrown into concentration camps because "the Occidental eye cannot readily distinguish one Japanese resident from another" and some could be spies. In Japan itself the US sought to kill "the enemy wherever he or she is in the greatest possible numbers in the shortest possible time. For us there are no civilians in Japan".[52] By 1945 Tokyo was suing for peace behind the scenes. Nonetheless atomic bombs were dropped on Hiroshima and Nagasaki. These were deliberately selected as areas to experiment with the new weapon because they were "closely surrounded by workers' houses".[53]

For the capitalists the Second World War was about imperialist rivalry through and through.

The People's War

So far we have focused on the motivations of the tiny capitalist minority. To grasp the role of the vast majority it is useful to compare the Second

World War with the 1914-1918 war. Between 1914 and 1918 fighting was more geographically restricted, relatively static and often bogged down in trench warfare. There was little change to the status quo in terms of who exploited resources and people within national borders. With little success to show on either side, one aspect of imperialism—the merciless battle between capitalist rivals—became salient. Luxemburg exposed this clearly when she wrote:

> The cannon fodder loaded onto trains in August and September is moldering in the killing fields of Belgium, the Vosges, and Masurian Lakes where the profits are springing up like weeds. Violated, dishonoured, wading in blood, dripping filth—there stands bourgeois society...the ravening beast, the witches' sabbath of anarchy, a plague to culture and humanity. Thus it reveals itself in its true, its naked form.[54]

Pointless mass slaughter remained the First World War's most prominent feature and on the military plane it ended as an "armistice" rather than outright victory for either bloc.

When the propaganda of "national salvation" was exposed as a hollow lie, slogans such as the one issued in Germany by Karl Liebknecht, "The enemy is at home", or Lenin's appeal for "revolutionary defeatism", gained wide popularity despite initial support given to the war by the Second International socialist parties. A mass determination that the fighting must stop led to revolutions that finally ended the conflict. Class war ended imperialist war.

The course of the Second World War was different for a number of reasons. Instead of trenches the Axis used tanks, warplanes and Blitzkrieg tactics to achieve large-scale territorial gains in the early period. Berlin and Tokyo not only broke the states of their rival capitalist competitors; they moved on to exploit subjugated populations using brutal repression justified through racist ideology. This produced a far more complex situation than during the First World War.

In European areas of Axis occupation the invaders initially succeeded in both eliminating local ruling class competition and exploiting their populations. If local rulers chose exile in response, for the mass of people the chief enemy "at home" was Berlin or Tokyo. Where the establishment collaborated with the invader in the hope of being a junior partner in exploitation, there was now a dual enemy "at home".

For the colonies the severe weakening of the European masters by Axis forces removed imperialist domination of one sort but brought another in the form of Japan's army.

Many in the Allied heartlands of Britain, the US and the Soviet Union could see that their ruling class's sole interest in the fight remained the securing of continued domination at home and abroad but they also distinguished between this "normal" system of exploitation and a new threat of untrammelled fascist dictatorship.

Whichever situation applied, the First World War's precise sequence of working class movement collapse at the outset and outright class war at the end was not replicated in the Second. Instead there was, during the conflict itself, something called "people's war", a phenomenon which could mean very different things from place to place. For example, even within the Axis countries where the crippling impact of Nazism, fascism and militarism had been most pronounced, resistance never entirely ceased. Eventual defeat by the Allies created possibilities for a large-scale revival of movements from below which were seized upon but frustrated in Italy and stifled in Germany.

The term "people's war" is correct but problematic. The phrase was common during the 1939-1945 period and corresponded to the resistance movements, anti-colonial liberation struggles and a host of popular activities which the masses injected into the war process to express their aspiration for an end to oppression and exploitation.

However, the Communist International (Comintern) gave it a peculiar twist to justify Stalinist policy. After Hitler repudiated his pact with Stalin and invaded Russia, Moscow linked itself to London and Washington claiming that Allied governments and masses were waging a "people's war" against the Axis. Pretending that "we are all in this together" airbrushed away the imperialist motives of those in power.

While the fight against the Axis could mask these tensions temporarily, the fiction of unity was short-lived. Movements from below collided with the aims of Allied governments, who, in their turn, frequently forgot and forgave their erstwhile Axis enemies in order to suppress the masses.

To conclude, the Second World War began as a struggle between rival imperialisms to dominate the globe. It retained this character throughout and no sooner had the struggle between the Axis and the Allies been decided than the Cold War, a new imperialist competition, followed. But if the stamp of imperialism is therefore indelibly marked on this period, so too was its opposite. The people's war, often in spite of the intentions of those who led it, amounted to a rejection of capitalist imperialism and imperialist capitalism. It represented the struggle of masses of ordinary people for a different, better world.

How the book is organised

Fighting On All Fronts is organised around national studies divided between the struggles against the Axis in the West and in the East. It begins with a chapter on Algeria which asks whether the Second World War was a war of liberation or a war of domination between competing imperialist powers. The US spearheaded a landing in North Africa to help it in a vicious game involving the British and both anti-Nazi and collaborationist French forces. In the turmoil the opportunity for real liberation driven by the oppressed population of the colony was born. With the announcement of victory over the Axis in Europe, the contested nature of the Second World War was put to the test: Algerians celebrating the defeat of the Axis as the prelude to freedom were gunned down by the French authorities.

Southern Ireland is the only country in this collection to have remained neutral during the Second World War but this did not mean peace. The Irish Republican Army (IRA) launched a bombing campaign to finally expel the British from the whole island. The Irish government did not want its compromise with London disturbed and repressed the IRA. At the same time left wing forces such as the Communist Party wanted Ireland to fight on the British side. The argument put was that the Axis represented imperialist aggression, which was true enough but ignored the imperialist aggression of the Allies. Ireland may have been technically neutral but it was nonetheless drawn into the politics that the conflict reflected.

The chapter on Jews looks at Eastern Europe. Millions fell victim to Nazism but their history has fallen victim to the Zionist project of the Israeli state. This portrays them as surrounded by hostile compatriots and passively submitting to the Holocaust (the sub-text being Jews today must oppress Palestinians to survive). Jews were not a homogenous isolated group; they were internally divided by class and externally linked to class interests. Jewish resistance both fought the Nazis and opposed Jewish Council collaborators. One peak was the Warsaw Ghetto uprising. In Minsk a peak of a different sort saw a united Jewish and non-Jewish resistance under communist leadership (later repressed by Stalin). The author concludes that: "Jews did not go simply as sheep to the slaughter. They fought back against overwhelming odds and in the face of mass extermination. And they did not do this alone."

The Netherlands demonstrate how a ruling class, caught between Germany and Britain, worked to balance between the contending forces, its various wings maintaining good relations with both. After the Nazis invaded this was summed up by the announcement that: "the authorities would strive, in the interest of the population, to continue performing as good a job as possible under the changed circumstances." While several groups fought occupation, the domestic government sought "business as usual" and the government-in-exile encouraged only limited resistance. Both wings looked to a restoration of the pre-war set-up including Dutch colonies and especially Indonesia.

The Soviet Union proved to be the decisive factor in the defeat of Hitler. Stalin is usually credited with making this possible even if subject to partial criticism. This chapter argues that Stalin's regime acted like all the other imperialist contenders. His campaigns were as much directed at the survival of the regime through crushing internal opposition as fighting Germany's invasion of 1941. That the Soviet Union eventually triumphed was due to the heroic efforts of ordinary people and often despite the policies of Stalin. Yet this has been hidden from history. The state's repressive apparatus was effective in distorting the true story of the Second World War and inventing the powerful myth of Stalin's greatness.

The final chapter in the Western section traces complex manoeuvres surrounding the Slovak National Uprising. While for ordinary people hatred of home grown fascism and the Nazis encouraged resistance, various competing wings of the Czechoslovak ruling class looked to staying in power through an independent Slovakia or restoring the unitary Czechoslovak state. They were split over whether to collaborate with the Axis or to defy it by relying on London (with its history of appeasement) or Moscow. The latter had its own designs and tried to manipulate these struggles to its advantage. In the maelstrom of competing interests the popular energy of the masses was dissipated in what the author describes as "one of the largest—and shortest—incidents of armed insurrection against Nazi occupation".

The section on the war in the East begins with Australia. While discussions of the Second World War usually focus on the major powers that headed the Allied and Axis blocs, this chapter looks at the development of an Allied sub-imperialism. It shows that weaker Allied ruling classes shared the same racism, ruthlessness and belligerence as the major powers. War was an opportunity to advance self-interest through colonial expansion and exploitation at home just as much in Australia as it was in Britain, Germany, Japan or the US. This did not go unchallenged. The Australian working class fought back, with women often in the lead. In the armed forces resentment at "brass-hatted stupidity" and support for anti-colonialism presented an alternative worldview to the imperialist aspirations of the rulers.

Events in Burma destroy the conventional narrative of the good democratic Allies versus the evil dictatorial Axis. Divisions between the former imperialist power, Britain, and the up-coming imperialism, Japan, were used by Aung San to forge an independent country at the expense of both. Initially his Burmese Independence Army worked with the Japanese to disrupt British rule and then switched sides when Japan headed for defeat. The complications this manoeuvring presented for the left, with anti-imperialists and/or leftists supporting different sides at the same time, and the contradictions of nationalism in an ethnically diverse country like Burma are explored in this chapter.

China's experience in the Second World War was unlike that of every other country dealt with in this book because it was superimposed on a pre-existing process of revolutionary transformation which began in 1911 and only ended in 1948 with the victory of the Chinese Communist Party. When the Japanese attempted to seize the whole of China in 1937 they found a society already riven by war which set the tiny forces of Mao's Red Army against the forces of Nationalist leader Chiang Kai-Shek. This three-cornered territorial and social struggle therefore bore many of the features of war from above and below seen elsewhere but incorporated them into what Trotsky called "permanent revolution".

The chapter on Japan explodes many myths. Japanese involvement in the Second World War was part of the inter-imperialist struggle in which the USA played as much of a role in provoking conflict as any of the various governments. At the same time the author debunks the notion of Japanese blind obedience to the emperor and passive submission to the government war drive. Despite government repression, industrial struggles, sabotage, mass absenteeism, peasant disturbances, even resistance among kamikaze pilots were witnessed. There were even anti-war demonstrations and defections to independence movements such as those in China and Indonesia.

The final chapter sets the story of the Huk wartime resistance movement in the context of Filipino history. The Huk movement was driven from below and therefore reflects both opposition to Japanese occupation and the social and economic aspirations of urban workers and the peasantry. Although US forces and the Filipino ruling class found it advantageous to use the Huk movement during the war, its radical features made it unpalatable to the establishment post-war. A wave of repression followed while many Japanese collaborators were welcomed into positions of authority.

NOTES

1 F Fukuyama, *The End of History and the Last Man* (Free Press, 1992).
2 N Henderson, *Failure of a Mission* (London, 1940), p247.
3 Press statement by Churchill in 1927, Churchill Papers, CHAR 9/82B.
4 Quoted in C de Gaulle, *The Complete War Memoirs* (New York, 1998, p55).
5 Pilsudski, quoted in P Hehn, *A Low, Dishonest Decade* (A & C Black, London, 2005), p76.
6 H Williams, *Parachutes, Patriots and Partisans* (London, 2003), p27.
7 Quoted in C Tsoucalas, *The Greek Tragedy* (Harmondsworth, 1969), p55.
8 Quoted in Bernd J Fischer, *Albania at War 1939-1945* (Hurst and Company, London, 1999), p14.
9 D C Watt, *How War Came* (Heinemann, London, 1989), p595.
10 Mass Observation, FR89, April 1940.
11 Mass Observation, FR600, March 1941, p17.
12 Mass Observation, FR 2067, p7.
13 A Speer, *Inside the Third Reich* (Phoenix, London, 1995), pp240-241.
14 P Spriano, *Storia della partita comunista italiano*, vol 4 (Turin, 1976), pp3-4.
15 H Cantril, *The Human Dimension: Experiences in Policy Research* (New Jersey, 1967), p48.
16 G Aly, *Hitler's Beneficiaries* (Verso, London, 2007), p76.
17 G Aly, 2007, p7.
18 See D Gluckstein, *A People's History of the Second World War* (Pluto, London, 2012), pp163-165.
19 Y Durand, *La France dans la deuxieme guerre mandible* (Paris, 1939), p13.
20 Quoted in Williams, p110.
21 K Ford, *OSS and the Yugoslav Resistance 1943-1945* (Texas, 1992), p55.
22 P Auty, *Tito: A Biography* (Harmondsworth, 1974), pp256, 258; Ford, p66.
23 S Serafis, *ELAS, Greek Resistance Army* (London, 1980), p427.
24 L Lewis, *Echoes of Resistance: British Involvement with the Italian Partisans* (Tunbridge Wells, 1985), p25.
25 Tito, quoted in A Donlagic, Z Atanackovic and D Plenca, *Yugoslavia and the Second World War* (Belgrade, 1967), p138.
26 J Hart, *New Voices in the Nation: Women and the Greek Resistance* (Ithaca,1996) p24.
27 H Michel and B Mirkine-Guetzevich, *Les idees politiques et social de la Resistance* (Paris, 1954) p52.
28 Michel and Mirkine-Guetzevich, p156.
29 Michel and Mirkine-Guetzevich, p157.
30 R Battaglia, *The Story of the Italian Resistance* (London), p186.
31 A Calder, *The People's War* (London, 1971), p609.
32 J P Narayan, *Selected Works*, vol 3 (New Delhi, 2003), p131.
33 www.marxists.org/history/international/comintern/dissolution.htm.
34 W Borodziej, *The Warsaw Uprising of 1944* (Madison, 2007), pp33-34.
35 B Davidson, *Scenes from the Anti-Nazi War* (New York, 1970), p106.
36 Atlantic Charter, p4.
37 W Churchill, *The Second World War*, vol 4 (London, 1954), p198.
38 Quoted in W Deakin, E Barker and J Chadwick (eds), *British Political and Military Strategy in Central, Eastern and Southern Europe in 1944* (Houndmills, 1988), pp131-132.
39 P Auty and R Clogg (eds), *British Policy Towards Wartime Resistance in Yugoslavia and Greece* (London, 1975), p187.
40 Churchill, vol 6, pp115-116 and p118.
41 Lewis, p25.
42 T Behan, *The Italian Resistance* (London, 2009), p211.
43 L Longo, *Sulla via dell'insurrezione nazionale* (Rome, 1971), p25.
44 Quoted in C Tillon, *Les FTP* (Paris, 1962), p318.
45 Tillon, p348.

46 Quoted in J Springhall, "Kicking out the Vietminh", in *Journal of Contemporary History*, vol 40, no 1, January 2005, p119.
47 Quoted in D Sassoon, *The Strategy of the Italian Communist Party* (London, 1981), p22.
48 Q Hogg, Hansard, 17 February 1943.
49 Quoted in *The Times*, 10 September 1941.
50 M Hastings, *Bomber Command* (London, 1979), p116.
51 G Aly, "The Planning Intelligentsia and the "Final Solution", M Burleigh (ed), *Confronting the Nazi Past* (London, 1996), pp145, 147.
52 R Schaffer, *Wings of Judgment* (Oxford, 1985), p147.
53 Quoted in B J Bernstein, "Truman and the A-Bomb", *Journal of Military History*, vol 62, no 3, July 1998, p559.
54 www.marxists.org/archive/luxemburg/1915/junius/ch01.htm

Part One

WAR IN THE WEST

1

Algeria: Victory but not liberation

Frank Renken

The most usual perception of the US Army's contribution to the War in Europe brings to mind images of the Normandy Landings in 1944. After landing on the beaches of France, American soldiers, with the support of the Western Allies, then pushed on against German troops until they finally shook hands with Soviet soldiers at the River Elbe near Torgau on 25 April 1945, a scene which more than any other symbolises the myth of the anti-Hitler coalition.

Practically absent from historical memory is the landing of Allied troops in North Africa. This is despite the fact that it took place one and a half years earlier, and was the springboard for US intervention in the European theatre of war. On 8 November 1942 American and British troops under the code name "Operation Torch" invaded Morocco and Algeria. At the time Algeria was under occupation by France's Vichy regime, which was collaborating with the Nazis. Were the Allies about to bring down the symbols of fascist domination, as they did later in 1945 when they blew up the Nazi swastikas in Germany? Would they assert the right of peoples to self-determination?

On 14 August 1941, before the US had entered the war, President Roosevelt and prime minister Churchill proclaimed the Atlantic Charter. The Charter laid out the Allies' goals for the end of the war, and designated not only Hitler's regime in Germany a "danger to world civilisation" but also its "associated governments", for example the Vichy regime in France. The prospective victors announced they would "respect the right of all peoples to choose the form of government under which they will live; and they wish to see sovereign rights and self-government restored to those who have been forcibly deprived of them".[1]

The hopes of the oppressed in Algeria and the other French colonies in North Africa ran high. They were under the control of a government in league with Hitler and which denied them any rights to national independence. But the Allies did not come as liberators. When the war finally came to an end on 8 May 1945, it wasn't a moment of great joy for the people of Algeria. Instead the war ended with a barbaric massacre of the Algerian Muslim population. How could this have happened?

Vichy, de Gaulle and the colonial empire

Algeria was France's oldest colony on the African continent. Nowhere else was the penetration of a conquered country and the destruction of domestic society more thorough. In contrast to its neighbours Tunisia and Morocco, which as "protectorates" were dominated only indirectly via local regents, Algeria was ruled by a governor-general appointed by the government in Paris. Formally Algeria was simply an extension of metropolitan France on the other side of the Mediterranean, divided as France proper into "Départements" with French prefects at their head. It was a settler colony—a set up similar to the apartheid regime of South Africa—with almost a million Algerian French of European descent confronted by approximately 8.5 million Arab and Berber Muslims.

From 1830, when the French soldiers first set foot on Algerian soil, the "Algerian French"—which included naturalised Spaniards, Italians and Maltese—grabbed large swathes of fertile land. However, by 1939 a large majority of Algerian French did not own any land but lived in the towns. The standard of living of these "petits blancs" (small whites) was lower than that of workers in metropolitan France, although this did little to challenge the rampant racism of many petits blancs towards Muslims, who had no citizen rights at all and were systematically discriminated against in the economic sphere.[2]

Algeria's fortunes during the Second World War were closely tied to those of metropolitan France, which had suffered a traumatic defeat at the hands of Nazi Germany in the summer of 1940. The government of Marshal Philippe Pétain capitulated on 17 June and signed a truce whose terms included the occupation of Northern and Western France by German troops. The South East of France retained formal independence under Pétain, who governed from his seat in Vichy. His regime remained nominally neutral during the war, but sought close cooperation with Hitler and at home installed a dictatorship in the name of a "National Revolution", effectively establishing a military regime under which a mass fascist movement which advocated entering the war on Germany's side rapidly developed.

When the war ended the French ruling class did its best to downplay the rampant anti-Semitism of the Vichy regime, pretending that the policies of the National Revolution had been forced on it by Nazi Germany.

Yet Robert Paxton's seminal research gives the lie to this narrative, proving conclusively that the Vichy governments under Laval and Darlan actively and unsolicitedly sought cooperation with Hitler.[3] The regime was hoping to compensate for its loss of power on the European continent by expanding its colonial empire at the expense of Great Britain, which was militarily isolated between 1940 and 1941 before the US's entry into the war and as long as the Hitler-Stalin pact remained in vigour. Vichy was speculating on a speedy military defeat of Great Britain in its war with Germany.

The first military confrontations between France and Great Britain were soon to play out. British warships attacked the French naval base in Algerian Mers el-Kebir on 3 July 1940. One thousand three hundred and eighty French sailors died in the course of the battle, generating a wave of anti-British feeling in France and Algeria which made the signing of a truce with Germany more palatable. An attempted landing by British forces in West African Dakar in September 1940 was fiercely beaten back by forces loyal to the Vichy government.

Against this background the Nazi leadership shelved its plans for a joint intervention in North Africa together with Italian forces. Addressing the Italian dictator Mussolini, who was claiming Tunisia as well as Constantine in Eastern Algeria for himself, Hitler said that "the best solution was for France to defend French Africa herself. This evolution gave some substance to the Vichy gamble that order was best maintained in the empire with Germany rather than against her".[4]

Charles de Gaulle, who as junior government minister had fled to London during the chaotic days of June 1940 and urged, on the BBC, for a continuation of the war against Germany, turned the argument round. He said that French domination over its colonial empire must indeed be defended, but in alliance with Great Britain, not Germany. The colonies were to be a springboard for the fight against the German armed forces and the reconquest of metropolitan France. In his first broadcast on 18 June de Gaulle argued: "Is the defeat final? No! Because France is not alone!... It has a vast empire backing it. It can form a bloc with the British Empire, which controls the seas and is continuing the fight".[5]

De Gaulle's strategy was to attempt to win over the governor-generals and leading officers in the colonies and get them to carry on the war on Great Britain's side. "Gaullism" was initially a spontaneous reaction of a tiny minority in the officer corps of the defeated French army who rejected collaboration with Germany.[6] It wasn't out of democratic conviction that this group rebelled against Pétain's line. Indeed, as a group it initially had no specific politics at all. De Gaulle himself had had disagreements with his military superiors and Pétain in the 1930s because of their military-strategic conservatism, but at the same time shared their aversion towards the communist-supported Popular Front government of 1936 and towards the parliamentary system of the Third Republic in general: a system whose instability aroused fears of social revolution among the conservative middle classes and more particularly in the officer corps.

This protracted conflict, from June 1940 until November 1942, between the Vichy regime and the "Free French" forces under de Gaulle over who controlled the colonies set the scene in Algeria and other overseas territories. In 1940 the balance of forces was clear-cut. The Free French had indeed managed by the end of the year to win over the governors and colonial troops in Chad, Congo-Brazzaville, Cameroon and finally Gabon, but North and West Africa and the other colonies remained firmly under Vichy's control.

This led to a paradoxical situation as the empire carried on while metropolitan France was under foreign domination. The Vichy regime installed a new governor-general in Algiers in July 1940 who ensured Vichy laws were implemented in Algeria, intensifying the persecution of Jews, Communists, Free Masons and Algerian nationalists. Day-to-day life for the Muslim majority and the barracked troops, on the other hand, changed very little. The governor ruled on just as if France had never capitulated to the Nazis.

Underneath the surface, however, nervousness gripped ruling circles. They were worried that any sign of weakness might encourage the Arabs to revolt. They hadn't forgotten 1871, when, following France's defeat by Prussia, over 250 tribes, a third of the whole Algerian population of the time, revolted against colonial rule. The jumpiness of the weakened French colonial masters became obvious when the Vichy government, in the spring of 1941, agreed to German armistice inspection teams visiting neighbouring Morocco. They insisted that the Germans keep a low profile: "Once there, they were kept under surveillance and required to remain in civilian clothes. Their Arab contacts were arrested and even shot by French police. The natives must not be allowed to see the victors in uniform".[7]

The De Gaulle-Churchill tug of war over colonial possessions

Gaullism wasn't able to really take root as a political current in Algeria until after the Allied landing. US diplomat Kenneth Pendar claimed:

"when our State Department asked André Philip [in 1942], the Head of de Gaulle's underground, if he could put us in touch with Gaullist groups in North Africa, Philip was forced to answer that they did not have a single 'cell' there".[8] One of the reasons was the relentless pursuit of dissidents, another the prevailing anti-British sentiment. Just listening to BBC radio, over which de Gaulle's speeches were broadcast, was made a punishable offence. The local newspapers were full of spite, the *Echo d'Oran*, for example, painting de Gaulle as a "miserable creature, traitor and assassin".[9]

When in May 1941 the police came across an anti-German conspiracy centred around the officers Léon Faye, André Beauffre and Georges Loustaunau-Lacau, Algerian papers were quick to blame the Free French. In reality Loustaunau-Lacau emanated from an anti-communist secret society and in the 1930s entertained ties with the fascist Parti Populaire Français. In German occupied France he cooperated with the British secret service, but separately from de Gaulle. As for Beauffre and Faye they had been conspiring with the Americans for several months already. They were concerned about a possible German invasion from Spain, against which they hoped to be able to organise a revolt in the French African army with the help of the Americans. So they shared de Gaulle's aim of entering the war on the side of the Allies, without, however, entertaining any contact with him.[10]

Equating de Gaulle with the British enemy was a mainstay of Vichy propaganda aiming to immunise the French troops against the Free French. But how would Vichy's officers and soldiers react if given the opportunity to defect?

The test case occurred not in North Africa but in the Middle East. On 1 April 1941 British controlled Iraq was the site of an anti-colonial uprising. Hitler reckoned this would be a golden opportunity to weaken the British enemy and was planning to support the insurgents from the air. He invited Admiral Darlan to Berchtesgaden to discuss the use of airports in French dominated Syria.

The Iraqi uprising eventually collapsed, but Churchill remained alarmed. The German Wehrmacht had been supporting their Italian allies in North Africa since January 1941 and occupied Greece in April and Crete in May. In view of Vichy's control of the Syrian-Lebanese mandated territory, he feared the complete encirclement of the remaining British positions in Egypt and the Middle East and losing access to the oilfields of Iraq and Iran. This prompted Churchill to attack Vichy troops in Syria and Lebanon. In a short but fierce campaign the British troops, with the support of 6,000 foot soldiers of the Free French under General Legentilhomme, managed to beat the troops of Vichy's General Dentz.

De Gaulle now expected to be recompensed by being given control over the French mandated territory and the 30,000 soldiers of the defeated Vichy army being transferred to his National Committee. But his hopes were dashed. The Free French were kept out of the negotiations, concluded on 14 July, between the representatives of Vichy and London. François Kersaudy summarised the results:

[O]nly the immediate interests of British diplomacy and of the British High Command had been safeguarded, while the Vichy troops were being treated more than generously...they would be concentrated under the orders of their leaders, and those who did not wish to join the Allied Corps would be repatriated by units—thus rendering any free choice almost impossible; their equipment would be handed over to the British only; moreover, the Special Troops of the Levant, made up of Syrian and Lebanese volunteers, would purely and simply be placed under British command; there was no reference at all to Free France.

To make things worse the negotiators signed a secret protocol "under which it was agreed that no contact should be permitted between the Free French and the Vichy French".[11]

Churchill shielded Vichy soldiers from the Free French, hoping in return to be given a footing in the French colonial territories. De Gaulle was furious. He commented in retrospect: "In fact the text of the agreement was equivalent to a transfer, lock, stock and barrel, of Syria and Lebanon into the hands of the British".[12] He came to the conclusion that London was aiming at first to make the Levant into a "condominium", and then to grab it for the British with the help of money, foodstuffs and military power.

It appeared that the alliance between de Gaulle and his host, the British government headed by Churchill, was more fragile than it at first seemed. Indeed, it had never been based on democratic principles, but on their mutual weakness in their struggle against Hitler's troops. Their first military successes immediately generated renewed tension along the boundaries of their respective zones of influence.

The conflict between de Gaulle and Churchill over Syria and Lebanon carried on right to the end of the war.[13] In September 1942 relations almost came to a complete break. US consul general Gwynn informed Churchill that de Gaulle had in his presence even threatened to "declare war" on the British.[14] Churchill compared de Gaulle's demeanour to that of the German foreign minister Ribbentrop.[15] What in the end kept the alliance alive were developments in metropolitan France, where de Gaulle successfully sought to unite the growing resistance under his leadership. In the autumn of 1942 British foreign secretary Anthony Eden drew Churchill's attention to the fact that invading France without de Gaulle would mean the Allies having to deal with the Communists on their own, since they were the ones who had mobilised most of the Résistance fighters.

But in North Africa de Gaulle's services were not needed, neither in preparation for the landing nor in setting up the post-war regime. The Free French were kept out of all decisions in the run-up to Allied Operation Torch.

US foreign policy bets on Vichy

The landing of the Allied troops on 8 November 1942 in Morocco and Algeria was a US-led affair. It was America's first step towards realising its war aims in Europe. Roosevelt was hoping to use North Africa as a springboard from which to seize Italy, France and finally Germany. According to his plans France was to be treated much like other occupied territories and placed under the control of the planned Allied Military Government for Occupied Territories (AMGOT). The objective was to establish American influence in Europe on a permanent basis, and prevent the emergence of revolutionary movements or the establishment of left wing governments. The appointment of an Allied Military Government in France clashed head-on with de Gaulle's politics, so the US looked to establishing good relations with Vichy, hoping that Pétain's regime would sooner or later break with Germany and collaborate instead with the US.

As for the weak Vichy regime, it was eager to exploit the cracks between the hostile blocs. While its internal policies increasingly followed in the footsteps of its Italian and German models, at the international level it pursued a see-saw policy between Berlin and Washington. It opened full diplomatic relations with the US, accrediting the American ambassador Admiral Leahy in Vichy in January 1941. That was followed up in February by a trade agreement between the two countries, signed by US diplomat Robert Murphy and Maxime Weygand, Vichy's Delegate General for French Africa, which stated that the United States would provide North Africa with materials such as coal, cotton goods, medicines and petroleum.[16]

In return the US government was permitted to establish a consulate, thus enabling Washington to place a number of Office of Strategic Services (OSS) secret agents in North Africa. Hence Robert Murphy set himself up as consul general in Algiers, a whole eighteen months before the start of Operation Torch. There he functioned as Roosevelt's personal agent, responsible for locating French forces willing to lead a putsch to install a pro-Allies government in Algeria. The putsch would prepare for a landing, which would meet the least possible resistance, in the areas under Vichy control.

Prospective US partners were conspirational anti-German groups of the Franco-Algerian youth, which included quite a few Jews with leanings towards de Gaulle.[17] These loosely organised networks defined themselves as French patriots, which precluded any common ground with Algerian nationalism. The largest of these was formed in Algiers around the medical student José Aboulker from an established Jewish family. This group did regular physical training and engaged in open fights with the youth organisation of the Legionary Security Service (SOL)—a fascist street army that hounded Communists, Jews and BBC listeners.

Aboulker's cousin Roger Carcassonne set up another conspirational circle in Oran. Coming from a family of industrialists he had connections with members of the state apparatus, such as Henri d'Astier de la Vigerie, whose brothers had already openly sided with de Gaulle in 1940. Henri, however, had joined Vichy's youth organisation Les Chantiers de la Jeunesse before taking a leading position in the police apparatus of the regime in Algiers.

These patriotic groups represented a dissident, pro-Allies current of the French-Algerian middle classes. Murphy kept in contact with them but never became close. According to him these groups consisted of

> restless and even dangerous men and women, most of them anti-Nazi, but also many other things... What would these mixed-up people do if French Africa should become a battleground? The answer, it seemed to me, was that only French administrators already familiar with the complexities of these variegated local situations could possibly maintain the order in French Africa which an Allied Expedition Force would require.[18]

US secret diplomacy instead placed its bets on those superior officers who were in control of the troops, among whom was General Alphonse Juin, commander of the French armies in North Africa. Murphy was on the look-out for influential individuals who might convince Juin not to oppose an Allied landing in North Africa. Only people who had an interest in maintaining the Vichy system qualified for the job—businessmen, high officials, and the senior and middle ranks of the armed forces.

By the autumn of 1942 Murphy had got his conspirational group together. Its members included Jacques Lemaigre-Dubreuil, a businessman with fascist leanings, Jacques Tarbé de Saint-Hardouin, secretary in Vichy's General Delegation for North Africa and erstwhile member of a secret society with royalist leanings, Colonel Van Hecke, leader of the Chantiers de la Jeunesse, Generals Charles Mast and Émile Béthouart, and Colonel Jean Chrétien, Chief of Army Secret Service under Commander-in-Chief Juin. Then there was police officer Henri d'Astier, who maintained contact with the activists of Aboulker's and Carcassonne's networks.

But who would prove capable of holding such a motley group of putschists together? Murphy needed someone who could commit a kind of regicide: a leading figure of the Vichy regime prepared to break with Pétain and at the same time capable of securing the loyalty of the rest of the colonial apparatus for collaboration with the US military. US leaders chose none other than Admiral Darlan, the former head of the Vichy government, for this role in the remaining weeks leading up to Operation Torch.

While this narrative has been disputed by a number of French historians, what is certain is that after the landing of the troops in Algiers Darlan took charge of government affairs with the express approval of the US government—the story told is that he just happened to be in the country at the time for family reasons and the US government could not simply ignore him.[19] Anthony Verrier's research based on US documents establishes Murphy's conspirational dealings with Darlan a full four weeks before the landing. His advice to the US government was to "encourage Darlan", advice which was readily taken up since on 17 October Murphy was given full authorisation to enter into any arrangement with Admiral Darlan. Roosevelt ordered Murphy to offer Darlan "rewards that would entrench him in North Africa—prospectively in France—and enable anti-Vichy opposition to be eliminated".[20]

But there was another highly placed person who seemed a good pick for cooperation with the US military in North Africa and who also enjoyed the trust of Vichy officials, General Henri Giraud. He had one advantage since, having spent some time in German captivity, he was less compromised than Darlan. However, this did not make him an opponent of Pétain. On the contrary, upon his return to Vichy territory in

April 1942 he signed an oath of allegiance to Pétain. Giraud was about to play a prominent role in US plans next to Darlan.

US policies in North Africa in the run-up to 8 November had two main aims: preparation for a bloodless landing of American troops, and ousting de Gaulle. A third aim was to win the French troops over to the side of the Allied forces against the Nazis. Vichy had eight barracked army divisions in North Africa, a total of 250,000 soldiers, mostly Muslims. The forces of the Free French were substantially weaker, numbering 35,000 spread over a wide operations area.[21]

The US plan was, however, quite risky. The dynamic which the invasion of the Allied troops in North Africa would unleash could not be foreseen. There were fears that the Muslim population might harbour hopes for an improvement of their situation or even an end to colonial rule. According to Washington's plans the French African Army's role was to prevent the "Arab problem" from bogging down the US troops. General Patton, commander-in-chief of the US landing force in Casablanca, figured that for Morocco alone "it would take sixty thousand Allied forces to hold the tribes quiet".[22]

A further risk was the conspirational group's composition. Murphy sought his potential candidates for the establishment of a US-friendly putsch government not among those individuals who wanted to fight the Nazis out of conviction, but instead among those elements who were responsible for suppressing the anti-fascists in North Africa. This complicated things, inasmuch as the conspirators were only tending their own interests and could not therefore be fully relied on. The US government became aware of this only after the landing of their troops.

The Vichy regime lives on

While Murphy's buddies remained in the background during the night of 8 November 1942, Aboulker's network went into action in Algiers. Aboulker was in close touch with the British secret service, which operated separately and independently of the American services in North Africa. At the agreed upon signal and expecting the immediate arrival of the Allied troops, these young people cut telephone lines, occupied post offices, police stations and government buildings and arrested Vichy officials. Three hundred and fifteen of the 377 fighters participating in these operations were Jewish.[23]

From a military point of view their operations were a success. Unlike further west near Oran and along the Atlantic coast, the French chain of command broke down in the capital city, thus allowing the American troops to land near Algiers without meeting any resistance. However, the insurgents were left to fight it out alone in the capital itself, the American troops moving onto the scene only after a 36-hour delay. Aboulker's group had embarked on a chaotic undertaking without knowing who was going to fill the ensuing power vacuum after the removal of the governor-general. They were completely reliant on the Allied forces, for whom they were preparing the terrain, little knowing that the American leaders were simultaneously conspiring with the very same people they were attempting to arrest—not altogether unsuccessfully by the way, since General Juin was among those temporarily taken prisoner.

The time slot granted by the Americans permitted Darlan to take the initiative and organise a successful counter-coup. The pro-Allies uprising was already collapsing during the morning of 8 November. By the time a US advance unit had entered Algiers in the evening, Darlan was the strongman of the city. The US troops didn't take him prisoner; instead they made him their negotiating partner.

Major General Mark Clark, deputy commander-in-chief under General Eisenhower, led the negotiations for the US. He demanded a ceasefire. Darlan, however, moved to improve his bargaining position by ordering the French troops to continue resisting. As a result 1,500 soldiers on both sides met their death in a three-day long battle along the Moroccan coast. In the vicinity of Oran 750 men were killed or injured.

On 10 November Clark and Darlan finally reached an agreement which demanded practically no concessions from the French admiral. Darlan announced the ceasefire and in return was appointed High Commissioner for North Africa. Darlan declared: "I assume authority over North Africa in the name of the Marshal [Pétain]. The present senior officers retain their commands and the political and administrative organisations remain in force. No change will be made without fresh orders from me".[24] Darlan demanded from "everybody the strictest obedience".

In North Africa the Vichy regime lived on, albeit now in the shape of a US protectorate. This is confirmed by the personnel. The commanding heights remained firmly in the hands of those who had faithfully served Pétain. Giraud was appointed Chief-of-Staff of the Armed Forces. General Juin was happy to play second fiddle and retain operational command of the troops. On 24 November Darlan instituted an Imperial Council headed by himself and Giraud and which included the governor-generals of Algeria, Morocco and French West-Africa to secure control of the remaining colonial territories. Roosevelt was of the opinion that cooperation with Darlan would last for "a very long time...at least until the end of the war in Europe".[25]

Although having participated in Operation Torch, the British government was not pleased with the new ruler in Algiers. Initially it went along with Clark and his deal with Darlan because he had the necessary following amongst French officials throughout the region. But Darlan, who, as Commander-in-Chief of the French Navy, had been in direct military conflict with the British between 1940 and 1941, further provoked London. In various speeches he hinted that he would welcome anti-British revolts in Syria and even Egypt. The British government reacted by conniving to remove Darlan.

Fernand Bonnier, a young man from the entourage of the anti-German groups in Algiers, assassinated Darlan in his office on 24 December. He had obtained his gun during a two-week small arms and sabotage course organised by the British secret service. What Bonnier was not expecting was, mission completed, to be dropped by his sponsors. Eisenhower spread the word that Darlan had been killed by agents of the Axis powers and the British government kept quiet. A military tribunal was improvised and Bonnier executed two days later. The Allies didn't protest. Instead Allied troops mounted a guard of honour as Darlan, Hitler's former collaborator, lay in state, while General Consul Murphy and US Commander in Chief Eisenhower looked on.

The Imperial Council then nominated General Giraud, the Allies' second option after Darlan, as the new High Commissioner for North Africa. Roosevelt gave his assent just hours after Bonnier's execution. Giraud grasped the opportunity to arrest the Aboulker family. They, and many others who had actively assisted the Allied landing, were deported to a prisoners' camp in the desert.

On 19 January 1943 Marcel Peyrouton, none other than Vichy's first interior minister, who had Jews, Communists and Gaullists hunted down by his police, was appointed Governor-General of Algeria. His nomination too was approved by Murphy and Eisenhower, with blessings from the State Department and the White House. Eisenhower argued: "Abrupt, sweeping or radical changes, bringing into office little known or unqualified administrators, could create serious difficulties for us." He could not make decisions "on the basis of prejudice or past political affiliations in France".[26]

Were these liberators? Roosevelt displayed complete disinterest for the political regime in North Africa, as long as it remained stable and ensured an operational basis from which the Allies could carry on their war against the Axis Powers. The SOL kept marching on Algeria's streets and none of the Vichy laws were rescinded. Anti-fascists were still being condemned by military courts just as if the US Army had never landed in Algeria.

But US policies on the ground so openly contradicted the stated democratic ideals that the US and British press created a scandal. This was one of the reasons prompting the US government to put more pressure on Giraud. Another was the unsatisfactory military situation on the North African front. After having reached such a quick settlement in Algiers, Eisenhower was hoping to pre-empt German efforts to reinforce its positions in Tunisia. However, the Vichy-loyal officers' corps in East Algeria and Tunisia remained aloof if not openly hostile towards the Allies. General Barré, the French commanding general in Tunisia, was, at the end of 1942, definitely reported to be in negotiation with the German commander in Tunis. Thus the US plans to take Tunisia within six weeks following Operation Torch misfired.

Roosevelt took the decision to henceforth provide the French troops with weapons only in return for tangible political services. Giraud backed down, but only very reluctantly and in stages. Among the concessions he had to make was to ease the level of repression so as to give the US willingness to cooperate with the regime in Algiers greater legitimacy. At the beginning of February 27 Communist MPs of the dissolved French National Assembly, together with 300 other prisoners, among whom was the Aboulker family, were set free from the internment camp in the desert. On 14 March Giraud made a speech disputing the legitimacy of the ceasefire accord with the Nazis and hence the constitutional basis of the Vichy regime in its entirety. However, the institutional framework put into place by Vichy was only dismantled after de Gaulle succeeded in overcoming the resistance of the US leaders, and establishing a provisional government in Algiers under his own leadership in the latter half of the year. On 9 August 1943 all Vichy laws, decrees and treaties were annulled, and only a few days later, on 18 August, under increasing pressure from the Communists, a Cleansing Committee was installed. The Jews finally regained full citizen rights on 20 October, almost a year after the start of Operation Torch.

De Gaulle gets his way

For three whole months after the allied landing the Gaullists remained underground. Undeterred, de Gaulle continued issuing calls for support for the Allies in North Africa. He was banking on further developments working out to his benefit; which is exactly how things turned out. At a conference in Moroccan Anfa in January 1943 called by Roosevelt and Churchill, de Gaulle got permission for General Catroux to open a representation of the London Committee in Algiers.

This provided the hitherto illegal movement with an operational base. A Gaullist network grouped around the newspaper *Combat* covered the European quarters in Algerian cities with the Lorraine Cross, the symbol of Gaullist resistance. Other leading Gaullists such as Louis Joxe and René Capitant joined forces with Catroux. Their goal was to prepare the ground for de Gaulle to establish his headquarters in Algiers. Their main argument was: France needs a united army and a united leadership to take part in the war against Germany.

Several factors shaped the dynamics of the situation. The extension of Nazi occupation to the whole of France in November 1942 and the introduction of forced labour, the "Service du travail obligatoire", in February 1943 gave the Résistance an enormous boost which also affected Algeria. The defeat of the Wehrmacht at Stalingrad, on the other hand, raised hopes that Nazi Germany could be beaten after all. And finally the 8th British Army together with Gaullist troops were advancing from the east in the direction of Tunisia. The ensuing optimism increasingly constrained Giraud's room for manoeuvre. With his Vichy-critical speech on 14 March, meant only as a verbal concession, Giraud succeeded in further hastening the rot by infuriating the convinced Pétainists. He did get his weapons from the Americans, but the price he had to pay was growing isolation.[27]

The writing on the wall was there for all to see when de Gaulle arrived in Algiers on 31 May 1943 and Governor-General Peyrouton tendered his resignation, without even bothering to inform Giraud. The erstwhile collaborators sought leniency from the incoming champion. The Allied attempt to steer Algeria's political course and through it France's was falling apart.

On 3 June 1943 the Comité Français de la Libération Nationale (CFLN) was founded in Algiers and soon took on the contours of a provisional government. Due to Allied pressures it initially operated under the joint presidency of Giraud and de Gaulle. Washington was hoping to hem in de Gaulle's ascension. But from the start his supporters dominated the committee. Political developments combined with Giraud's dilettantism enabled de Gaulle to bolster his own position, eventually forcing Giraud to withdraw before the CFLN was officially declared Provisional Government of the French Republic in June 1944 with de Gaulle as sole president.

These developments were very much to the dismay of the US government. Washington had placed its bets on Vichy but not just out of tactical-military considerations. What was at stake was the post-war order in France proper. In summer 1943 when it became clear that de Gaulle wasn't going to be kettled by the CFLN, Roosevelt lost his temper and ordered Eisenhower to give "no arms to any military bodies not recognising the supremacy of his authority" and in future not to permit "any government or committee" to rule France over the Allied military government's head until such a time as the French people held elections.[28]

Events turned out very differently. Washington begrudgingly acknowledged de Gaulle's access to power in the summer of 1944 when he entered a jubilant Paris at the head of an unelected coalition government including leftists and the French Communist Party. This outcome cannot be explained on the basis of the military balance of forces. De Gaulle was able to browbeat Washington politically despite the US's overwhelming military might because the resistance against the Vichy regime, propelled by the desire to beat the Nazis, had unleashed a social dynamic first in Algeria then in France and finally within the ranks of the French Army, which frustrated all Washington's preferred options.

The People's War in Tunisia

The political struggle in Algeria was interwoven with what could, in part, be termed a people's war against the Nazis in Tunisia between November 1942 and May 1943. No sooner were the preparations for the Allied landing in North Africa under way than the opponents of the Vichy regime came up with the idea of creating a voluntary force so that "the Anglo-Saxon allies may not claim the glory of having liberated North Africa all to themselves".[29] Darlan and Giraud took up the idea. They saw the opportunity of ridding Algeria of Gaullists and other subversive elements, and preventing them at the same time from coming into contact with regular troops by packing them off to Tunisia in a separate unit.

Thus came into being the Corps Franc d'Afrique (CFA) under General Monsabert on 25 November 1942. According to Georges Elgozy's personal account this corps was composed of those Algerian French who wanted to rid themselves of their Pétainist past, plus Gaullists, Spanish Republicans, escapees from France's prison camps, but also Jews "originating from France or North Africa, who made up almost a third of the force...they were willing to die upright and free rather than passively submit to the bullying and atrocities meted out by the Germans or, even worse, by the French".[30]

Badly equipped, they engaged in their first battle on 2 February 1943 only to discover that their machine guns didn't work. Eventually, with better equipment provided by the Allies, the corps was able to raise its military effectiveness. Its willingness to fight despite all odds was quite extraordinary. Out of a total of 5,000 men only 2,000 were left when the CFA in advance of all other corps entered the strategic seaport Bizerte. There they met up with the Gaullist troops of the Second Armoured Division. The scene was radically different to what had happened in the summer of 1941 in Syria, when Vichy officers in collusion with the British army had succeeded in keeping the French soldiers apart from each other. This time more than half the CFA men went over to the Gaullist troops "delighted to have at last rid themselves of their 'Collabos'".[31]

But it wasn't just the CFA; the regular army in Tunisia too showed signs of disintegration. Young Algerian French were joining the armed forces in their droves to fight against Nazi Germany in Tunisia. Sixty five thousand soldiers under regular French command participated in the battle for Tunisia, which only came to an end after six months when the German army finally capitulated on 13 May. Eight thousand six hundred men had lost their lives, a further 7,500 wounded and 2,000 men temporarily taken into captivity.[32]

Politically it was a period of transition. In the armed forces led by General Juin, Jews, Communists and adherents of de Gaulle still had to keep their heads down. But for many the war represented an opportunity to quench their impatience until the day of reckoning with the Nazis and their collaborators would finally come. In the end military discipline was not enough to keep the regular troops together. The 4th Unit of the Spahis and the 7th Chasseurs d'Afrique, both predominantly of Muslim composition, went over to the Gaullist forces. The tide was turning. The military victory over the Wehrmacht in Tunisia helped de Gaulle to triumph politically over the regime set up by the US government in Algiers.

Muslim soldiers were to play an important role in the war against the Axis Powers both in Italy and in France, but were shown no gratitude in return. This was symbolised by their being kept away from liberating the French capital. Having got his way politically and having united all the French forces under his single command in the war against the Nazis, de Gaulle then made an agreement with Eisenhower providing for the participation of French soldiers in the battle for Paris. De Gaulle decided to field the 2nd Tank Division instead of an infantry division. The reason was their composition. The infantry was made up largely of North African troops, whereas in the tank division ethnic French served. Arabs as liberators along the Champs-Élysées? This was simply not on.[33]

Three sources of Algerian nationalism

The Second World War completely changed France's political landscape. It also changed colonial reality in Algeria, though in the course of a protracted, more complex and much bloodier process than the power struggle between Giraud and de Gaulle had been. The conflict between Algerian nationalists and France's new rulers in the years 1943 to 1945 did away with the illusion that an Allied victory over the Axis Powers and the reinstatement of bourgeois parliamentary democracy in France would open up a peaceful avenue to end colonialism. It was a political laboratory in which the three main currents of Algerian nationalism transformed themselves and their relations to each other.

The moderate wing had as its representative the pharmacist Ferhat Abbas. Finding his inspiration in the Young Turks who founded the Turkish republic after the First World War, he published a collection of essays in 1931 which struck a chord among the thin layer of Muslim-Algerian intellectuals. According to Charles-André Julien, his was a "courteous but firm criticism of French policies".[34]

1931 was marked by a giant colonial exhibition exalting France's empire, which attracted hundreds of thousands of admiring visitors. Abbas felt this was an attack on his self-esteem. As an Arab he was not granted equality with French citizens, something he had a right to in his view. In the context of the 1930s this made Abbas a reformer, but not an Algerian nationalist. In an often quoted passage he wrote: "Had I discovered the Algerian nation, I would be a nationalist... However, I will not die for the Algerian nation because it does not exist." At the same time he recognised that "without the emancipation of the indigenous population French Algeria will not last..."[35]

The second source of Algerian nationalism was the Association of Algerian Muslim Scholars, the Ulama, grouped around Abdelhamid Ben Badis. It was a current we today would label "political Islam". Although the colonialists branded them "Wahhabi", the Ulama in fact argued for a rapprochement between Sunni and other Islamic currents as well as between Arabs and Berbers, and to build a united bloc of Algerian Muslims against colonialism. Julien stressed: "It was the Ulama who awakened indigenous opinion from its lethargy... For they possessed a religious doctrine capable of serving as a basis for national aspirations".[36] While Ferhat Abbas denied the existence of an Algerian nation, the Ulama declared that "the Muslim nation has formed itself and exists".[37] It coined the slogan: "Islam is my religion, Arabic my language, Algeria my country."

The Ulama polemicised against the Marabouts and the brotherhoods, who practised a popular version of Islam. Fragmented in thousands of local towns and villages, these folksy clerics preached deference and submissiveness towards the colonial administration in return for a bit of flattery awards. They formed a part of those collaborators who were called by the derogatory name "Beni-Oui-Oui"—the "Yes-men". The main publication of the Ulama declared in 1937: "The Marabouts are colonialism's domestic beasts".[38] To fight the superstitions spread by the Marabouts and the general neglect of the hinterland by the French colonial state, the Ulama established over 200 schools which tried to combine teaching in Arabic with modern education.

The Ulama's successes were met by systematic repression on the part of the colonial administration. It instituted Consultative Councils of Cult which, as from 1933, were authorised to control who preached in the mosques. The administration hardly differentiated between Islamists and Communists. In February 1933 the prefect of Algiers ordered local government outposts to "monitor very closely communist agents and suspect Wahhabi Ulama who were attempting to do damage to the French cause".[39]

The third current of Algerian nationalism emanated from Muslim emigrants to France and was a child of the workers' movement. Hadj Ali Abdelkader, a leading figure in the French Communist Party (PCF), initiated the North African Star (ENA, "L'Etoile Nord-Africain") in March 1926. Under Messali Hadj's leadership the ENA rapidly gained influence. Practically exclusively concentrated in the factories in and around Paris, the organisation could claim a membership of 4,000 only three years after being launched.

With its unambiguous demand for Algerian independence and the whole of the Maghreb, the organisation was not only a political provocation in the general sense, but represented a concrete threat to army discipline long before the outbreak of the Second World War. Messali, like so many other Muslims of Algerian origin, had fought in the French Army during the First World War. In 1933 he was sentenced to prison for "instigating members of the military to disobedience and for incitement to murder for the purpose of anarchist propaganda".[40]

The ENA placed great hopes in the People's Front, a coalition government formed in 1936 and composed of the Socialist Party with bourgeois parties led by Socialist leader Léon Blum and supported by the Communist Party. At the time the ENA participated actively in the mass demonstrations of the French workers' movement. Its membership reached 11,000 and it was able to implant itself in Algeria. On 2 August, in a speech to 10,000 Muslims in the Algiers' municipal stadium, Messali demanded Algerian independence.

Under Stalin's influence and out of regard for its coalition with the Socialists and bourgeois parties, the PCF changed course. In the 1920s it had supported the Berber uprising in the Moroccan Rif Mountains, but by 1936 it had adopted an increasingly patriotic stance. This included bashful support for French imperialism and opposing the right to self-determination for the Algerian nation, arguing that Algeria was, in the words of its leader Maurice Thorez, in reality only in the process of "becoming a nation". Against demands for independence it limited its support to the very meagre proposals of the Blum government, which spoke of voting rights for a section of the Muslim population—a reform project which in any case was doomed to failure in view of the hysterical opposition of the colonial administrative machinery and the mighty settlers' lobby.

This stance brought the Communist Party into open opposition to the North African Star. In the autumn of 1936 the hitherto close contacts between the two organisations were severed and the PCF adopted an openly aggressive attitude towards the ENA, claiming that it was a "party in league with the fascist settlers". At the Communist Party Conference in January 1937 hundreds of Algerian Muslims were pushed out of the hall after they had sung an Algerian independence hymn. Two days later the Algerian governor-general appointed by Blum decreed the dissolution of the ENA on the grounds that its activities were "clearly directed against France".[41]

The breach between the Communists and the Algerian nationalists was to have fatal consequences for the struggle in Algeria, where it brought in its wake a breach between Muslims and the "petits blancs", the proletarian whites of European descent in Algeria's cities. The PCF alienated itself permanently from the Algerian Muslims so that its local offshoot, the Algerian Communist Party (PCA), despite all efforts hardly benefited from the upswing of the Algerian movement in the period after 1943. The Muslim struggle for independence, on the other hand, lost its specific class orientation to become, between 1954 and

1962, basically a minority guerrilla organisation substituting for the large majority of the population in its struggle against the state institutions—at times even bombing civilian targets.

1940-42: ferment below the surface

At the outbreak of the Second World War the colonial regime sat more firmly in the saddle than ever before. On 29 September 1939, long before the establishment of the Vichy regime, the Algerian People's Party, the Parti du Peuple Algérien (PPA), follow-up to the North African Star, was banned along with the Communist Party. However, the ban affected the two parties very differently. The Communists were already paralysed because of the Hitler-Stalin Pact, in whose wake the Kremlin declared Anglo-American capitalism was now the main enemy. This isolated the Moscow-faithful PCA not only from Anglophiles and BBC-listeners, but also disarmed them ideologically as they were faced with a regime that sought an alliance with Hitler just as Soviet Russia had done. The PCA was forced underground without putting up any significant resistance. Once there their lack of orientation persisted.

The PPA was initially equally badly hit by the repression. Several dozen party members were imprisoned, among them party leader Messali Hadj. In 1941 he was sentenced to 16 years' hard labour. The PPA had been effectively beheaded. However, the effects were short lived. In contrast to the PCA the PPA hadn't lost its bearings. On the contrary, repression strengthened the PPA's radical standing within the nationalist camp. Their analysis that the colonial state could not be reformed was confirmed by the experience of repression.

An important factor contributing to the resurgence of the PPA was the overall economic misery brought about by the Second World War. Within three years the production of citrus fruits fell by a fifth, that of cereal crops by two thirds. Semolina and bread had to be rationed. As a consequence of malnutrition many people succumbed to the terrible typhus epidemic that swept the country in 1941-42.

Rising unemployment and squalor forced untold numbers to flee a countryside plagued by lawless gangs, and migrate to the outskirts of the cities. So even if Algeria was largely spared direct warfare until 1942, the economic consequences of the war created mounting bitterness among large sections of the Muslim population and increased hatred of all Europeans. While the cattle of the large estate holders had plenty of fodder, many day labourers went hungry.

Economic misery and the displacement of such large numbers of people were preparing the ground for a revolution against the colonial administration. Police accounts at the time attest to the growing restlessness. The number of reported fist fights between members of different communities as well as of arson attacks in the woods in 1941 was on the increase. One police commissar reported having been the object of kids throwing stones while walking through an Arab quarter in Aumale.[42] Governor-General Weygand complained: "The Muslim population is proving to be undisciplined, impolite and at times downright insolent".[43]

Interior migration brought a new generation of impoverished country people into contact with the ideas of modern proletarian anti-colonialism in the suburbs. "These mostly young migrants—between the ages of 17 and 21—fear nothing and don't hesitate to defy the forces of repression." Among these young rural migrants many "read anything they can get hold of, they distribute leaflets, listen to the eldest and most eloquent political orators, for whom they constitute a choice audience".[44]

This enabled the PPA to rebuild its forces. Repression itself created new opportunities for organising. In May 1941 the party launched a solidarity campaign for their leader Messali, bringing in many new members. And the PPA wasn't alone. The Union of the Ulama also developed into an important wing of the resistance. After Ben Badis's death Bachir el-Ibrahim became its leader. Returning from Damascus he brought with him pan-Arab beliefs that were being discussed there in urban intellectual circles.

Regaining strength from 1941 onwards, both Ulama and the PPA changed their make-up. A new generation took over, shaped under conditions of sharpened repression and economic misery. In 1942 the medical doctor Lamine Debaghine became general secretary of the PPA. He stood for a new layer of nationalists, among whom young radicals such as Mohamed Belouizdad, who built a Youth Committee in the Belcourt suburb of Algiers which soon developed into an alternative pole of leadership to the old Messalists in the old city centre.

The rapid process of displacement, impoverishment and urbanisation at the same time undermined the support those sections of Muslims who actively collaborated with the colonial state had hitherto enjoyed. In those localities where it had no direct presence, the French state had local Qada ("leaders") in its pay. Corruption among these local leaders was generously tolerated by the colonial administration, so long as they could guarantee the maintenance of order.

The class stratification of Arab-Berber society was reproduced in the army. Muslims could attain the grade of captain, but all higher grades were reserved for Frenchmen from Algeria or the mother country. The limited opportunities for advancement did not impact on the loyalty of the Muslim minority which had managed to climb up to the middle ranks. A famous example of this phenomenon is Bachaga Boualam, who till this day is celebrated in nostalgic colonialist literature as proof of how successfully assimilation worked, and who himself contributed his own gushes of French patriotism to this literary genre.[45] The son of a gendarme, Boualam was the archetype of the patriotic French officer who owed his privileged position to the ancient and well-to-do family of Qada he named his own.

This stratification model suffered from a lack of elasticity. The layer of educated and enlightened Muslims was simply too thin and the retaliation of the hangers-on of "French Algeria" at even the slightest hint of any reform to the benefit of the Muslim majority too aggressive for this model to achieve any lasting stability. So long as the Qada remained in control, the Muslim population appeared to be undemanding and accepting of their fate. Apologists for French Algeria interpreted, and to this day still interpret, this sullen indifference as proof of loyalty towards France. In fact this apparent indifference could spontaneously flip into its opposite, into uncontrollable rage, as soon as the pressure that had built up through decades of humiliation exploded.

The first sign of growing resentment was the mutiny in the Maison-Carrée barracks in Algiers on 25 January 1941. The Muslim Spahi and Tirailleur units quartered there were to be sent off to Syria to reinforce the Vichy-loyal troops under General Dentz and so counterbalance the British. What triggered the mutiny was the constant harassment Muslims suffered which, among other things, prevented them from celebrating Islamic holidays. This insult made the absence of freedom acutely felt and united the troops in common hatred of their French superiors.

On 25 January, a Saturday, 800 soldiers broke the curfew and killed a captain and a dozen French corporals. They seized arms and munitions from the arsenal and made their way into the city, where they gave vent to their anger. European passers-by were killed and soldiers laid siege to the town hall and a cinema. Reaction was quick and relentless, but a number of Muslim soldiers managed to escape and go underground.

The Maison-Carrée mutiny was basically a local and isolated affair, but news travelled quickly and spread fear among French Algerians. "From this point on the settlers of the Mitidja [Plain] begin to arm themselves and [arms] traffic takes on quite vast proportions. Apprehension and a sense of insecurity gradually take hold".[46]

1943: The PCF makes the PCA toe the line

After the Nazi invasion of Russia in August 1941 the Algerian Communist Party faced a completely new situation. In tune with the PCF's about-turn in France, it too started on the road of opposition to the Vichy regime without being further hampered by the Hitler-Stalin pact. Great Britain and later on the US were no longer considered enemies, but rather part of the "Anti-Hitler coalition".

Unlike the PCF, however, the PCA initially went a step further and drew closer to the Algerian nationalists. In November 1941 some sections of the PCA for the first time took up the issue of Algerian independence. After hefty discussion the delegates at a clandestine party conference in December voted to appeal to the Algerian nationalists of the PPA to build a united resistance in order to achieve a "Free and independent People's Republic of Algeria united with a free France". This formula was a definite step in the direction of the PPA. At the same time it didn't specify what the position of the PCA would be should the PPA work towards national independence including a full break with France.

The message was clear enough, and the state took harsh measures. In March 1942 61 Communists were brought to court. Six of them were condemned to death and nine to life imprisonment. Eight prisoners eventually died due to the terrible prison conditions.

Repression decimated the PCA. Several months after the Allied invasion their cadres were still languishing in the prison camps of Colomb-Béchar and Djelfa in the inhospitable south, while others remained incarcerated in the Lambèse and Maison-Carrée gaols. This was reason enough for the PCF to lend support to its Algerian counterpart the PCA, the other reason being their concern over the growth of Algerian-Muslim nationalism. First Maurice Deloison was sent over as "instructor" with the assignment to propagate "Franco-Algerian unity against fascism". Finally André Marty took over the leadership of the PCA, receiving substantial help from many Communists in the mother country who came to Algeria after the Allied landing.

This gave the PCA a great boost. By 1943 it had 8,000 members. At the same time it developed its political line in close coordination with the "Colonial Section" of the PCF in Paris. The demand for Algerian independence disappeared from the Communist press, the *Alger République* and the weekly paper *Liberté*, which henceforth concentrated on French questions and the fight against the Nazis. The question of colonialism was reduced to that of removing social inequality between Muslims and Europeans.

Its renunciation of independence for Algeria was in accordance with Stalin's demand for subservience to the "progressive elements of the French Bourgeoisie", ie to de Gaulle. In January 1943 the PCF joined "Fighting France", as the National Committee based in London called itself at the time. In March 1944 the Communists François Billoux and Fernand Grenier entered the Provisional Government. De Gaulle was hoping that by incorporating the PCF he could avoid a possible Communist takeover after victory over Nazi Germany. He proved right. In the years 1944-45 the PCF tamed the revolutionary spirit of a lot of its supporters and pushed through the disarming of the anti-fascist partisans, or francs-tireurs, thus propping up French capitalism. It now unashamedly propagated the defence of the French Empire and endeavoured to make the Communist parties in the colonies follow suit.

That is not to say that the year-long factional dispute within the PCA simply dissipated without a fight. Those Communists who had come into direct contact with Algerian nationalism, the incarcerated of Maison-Carrée and others, continued to hold that the demand for independence was justified. And a number of Communists threw themselves heart and soul into the anti-colonial struggle. However, they were in no position to influence the party line. The leadership around Marty prevailed at the party conference held in Hussein-Dey in September 1943. The main resolution spoke out against "half-measures", stating that Algerian independence was a distraction and all efforts needed to be concentrated on the struggle against the Nazis in Europe and the liberation of France. The PCA even went so far as to shelve demands for inner reforms within the colonies. The formula chosen was: "Democracy in the colonies must come through the instalment of democracy in France... The colonies, in no position to exist independently economically, nor therefore as an independent nation, would risk falling under Anglo-Saxon domination. It is therefore in their interest to maintain their voluntary union with France".[47] Those Communists, especially in the region of Constantine, who criticised the PCA line as 'too French' were accused of opportunism and either ignored or expelled.[48]

Algerian nationalism united

The mere prospect of an Allied landing gave the Algerian nationalist movement an enormous boost. Contacts between the various currents had been intensifying since October 1942. The moderate Abbas, who remained a popular and influential figure, invited the leader of the PPA Lamine Debaghine to his home town. They agreed to cooperate.[49] A follow-up to their discussions was the publication of a manifesto with the working title *To whatever occupying power*. The final version, drawn up by Abbas and signed by the PPA and the Ulama, was published on 10 February 1943 under the title *Manifesto of the Algerian People*.[50]

The manifesto was enormously influential. It told a counter-history to the colonial myths and stressed the historical significance of systematic land grabbing. "An agrarian feudalism has implanted an imperialist and racist soul into this colonial society... Dispossessed, the indigenous people own nothing. Everything is in the hands of the European minority. Even their language is considered foreign. Their social fabric has vanished, creating a people of small peasants, white collar workers and a huge working class."

About the existing situation, Abbas observed that the Allied landing "has provoked among the Algerian French a veritable race for power. Republicans, Gaullists, Israelites, each group is vying to get its efforts at collaboration acknowledged by the Allies and to ensure the defence of their particular interests" while "everyone seems to ignore even the very existence of the eight and half million natives".

On the occasion of the official handover of the manifesto to Governor-General Peyrouton, the demand was raised for a new statute based on social justice before there could be any talk of the mass of Muslims joining the war against the Axis powers. This was less than the demand for independence, but in the logic of the colonial state nevertheless unfulfillable. But it served Abbas and his numerous moderate cosignatories as a bridge to reach out to more radical views.

A weakened Peyrouton played for time and instituted a commission made up of Muslim dignitaries with the task of elaborating a new statute book for Algeria. It was in this context that 25 PPA leaders were released from prison, among them Messali, who was allowed to present his case before the commission. But the governor-general was only procrastinating. When the commission's suggestions were not taken up, the Muslim negotiators were disappointed. In June they declared that the attainment of full French citizen rights was no longer their goal, but instead Algeria's recognition as a nation—precisely that nation whose existence Abbas had refused to recognise back in 1936. His radicalisation is representative of a whole layer of Algerian-Muslim intellectuals.

The Muslims and their representatives were not in any way involved in the power struggle between Giraud and de Gaulle. However, the cracks at the top of the colonial state created a space for mobilisation from below. And the question of participation in the Allied war became a trump card in the hand of the nationalists. Muslims were less and less willing to join the army. This became apparent when the reserves were called up in December 1942 and July 1943. In many communities up to half the draftees didn't turn up. The growing influence of the united nationalist movement found expression in this mass refusal, as not only the PPA, but also the moderate forces around Abbas opposed Muslims filling the ranks of an army whose victory only meant restoring the same colonial set-up. Abbas argued in July 1943: "So long as the Muslim people doesn't know what it is fighting for, it will refuse to be mobilised. If we don't reach an agreement with the government, it will descend onto the streets".[51]

De Gaulle, having won the power struggle, appointed Catroux as the new governor-general and tried to regain control by resorting to harsh measures interspersed with moments of leniency. He first had Ferhat Abbas and another moderate nationalist, Abdelkader Sayah, arrested. Then the governor-general, in consultation with de Gaulle, dug out the old reform ideas of the Popular Front Government of 1936 and decreed limited changes in the electoral law. Also 60,000 Muslims were to be granted full citizen rights, without, however, being allowed to hand these down to their children.

These policies won the approval solely of the Socialists and the Communists, who dreamt of democratising Algeria only to chain it all the more tightly to the French unitary state. The defenders of French Algeria, the main Franco-Algerian newspapers and the civil servants of the colonial state for their part rejected out of hand even the most modest reform, which in their view would only embolden the Muslims to demand more. For the nationalists on the other hand these plans were too little too late.

The message was clear: the demands of the manifesto could only be achieved through open struggle. Barely a week after the reforms were decreed, the Friends of the Manifesto and of Liberty (AML, "Amis du Manifeste et de la Liberté") was launched. It soon developed into the largest political coalition Algeria had ever seen, reflecting a new revolutionary mood in broad layers of society.

On the brink of social revolution

In 1943 the nationalist movement advanced enormously both in terms of unity and of dynamics. The more the war seemed to be drawing to a close, the more expectations rose that mobilisation might after all herald fundamental change. Hope for independence gripped more and more people and combined with the desire for far reaching social reform.

It was in this climate that the AML was launched on 14 March 1944. It was a united front made up of the PPA, Abbas's new party UPA, the Ulama, boy scouts and students' associations. Ferhat Abbas became its general secretary. The AML was tremendously successful. At the beginning of 1945 this front organisation claimed over 165 local groups and by April of the same year over 257.[52] Funds kept pouring in and according to Abbas up to 500,000 applications for membership reached the main offices in Algiers.[53] The AML had its own publication, *L'Égalité*, which had a print run of several tens of thousands. Abbas and others went on speaking tours visiting local groups. The leadership regularly issued circular letters and leaflets in an attempt to steer the AML organisationally and politically.

Gone were the days when the anti-colonial struggle had been tribal in character and based on the countryside. The AML was structured along the lines of the mass European parties. It grew rapidly and distinguished itself by its high level of activity. This included not just demonstrations. The AML also began to intervene in daily life. It organised boycotts of European businesses and estate owners in many localities and concealed harvest yields from landowners. The AML destroyed the networks of loyalty which bound the mass of ordinary Muslims to the Qada and had hitherto helped prop up the colonial administration. The demand for national liberation was placing social revolution on the agenda.

Gone were yesteryear's fears and with them the "apathy" of the Muslim population that apologists of colonialism so love to dwell on. Euphoria was universal. A French captain described the general atmosphere in these words:

> Cinemas, theatres, cafés everywhere are being invaded by natives taking the best seats, something they never did in the past. The indigenous population shows no desire to please, no deference towards military staff as they used to in the recent past... Even the douars [villages] are infected by politics. Political meetings are taking place practically non-stop. This is a new and disturbing symptom.[54]

The Communist Party and the CGT trade union it controlled both rejected the invitation to join the AML. By doing so they threw away a historic chance to overcome the chasm separating French from Algerian workers.[55] The PPA, on the other hand, used the AML as a roof under which to rebuild. The path it took was quite contradictory. Its leader, Messali, now under house arrest, had a charismatic personality and the party was disciplined and well organised. Three of its cadres were in the AML leadership. Thus they were in a position to steer the activities of mass organisations in many localities and to channel the influx of new members in their direction.

The gains made in such a short time raised new challenges. The PPA attracted radicalised youth, who quickly came into conflict with the old cadres around Messali Hadj. Putschist tendencies arose with little regard for a sober analysis of the balance of forces in Algeria and beyond. One example is the Comité de Jeunesse, mentioned above, which managed to recruit 1,500 young members in the Belcourt borough of the capital city. "Having received their political formation in the syndicalist milieu of the tramway workers they are now seriously preparing a large-scale revolutionary offensive to be kicked off with propaganda, a few spectacular actions, the seizure of arms, writing slogans on walls".[56]

Another example is the group around Mohamed Taleb, which started off amassing arms. On 30 September on the occasion of Eid al-Fitr, the last day of Ramadan, the group led the masses that were leaving the mosques after prayers to Government Square, and there staged a huge rally demanding Messali's, Abbas's and Sayah's release. The police intervened in force arresting scores of demonstrators.[57] Similar scenes took place in almost every city, putting the colonial government on the defensive and creating mounting tension.

The PPA did not remain unaffected. The group around Lamine Debaghine had been leading the organisation since mid-1944. Under the influence of the new activists it now began to prepare for armed struggle. But many questions remained unanswered. What was the relationship between mass struggle and armed struggle? How should the organisation prepare itself against state repression? Can the army be won over? The PPA leaders gave the impression of stumbling from one step to the next. Annie Rey-Goldzeiguer commented:

> The search for arms is on the agenda, in preparation for a revolutionary war which will at last give the people the means to express itself and take action... But in this struggle which promises to be merciless, they think it

is sufficient to simply launch the action for all obstacles to disappear. They mythologise political violence which gives them the opportunity to assert themselves, they give priority to tactics, because they can't envisage a long term strategy.[58]

Within a year the PPA was dominating the AML. This was proven conclusively by Ferhat Abbas's defeat at the AML congress held 2-4 March 1945 in Algiers. Thanks to rapid growth in membership the young radicals were able to outvote general secretary Abbas and the other moderate bourgeois intellectuals on all important motions. Boosted by this success, the PPA started putting its programme into practice. And the general mood was receptive. On 6 March there were hunger marches in Oran, and the next day in Tlemcen. On 12 March in Orléansville (now Chlef) Qada were pelted with stones by a crowd of 200. The military secret service was alarmed. Ever since September 1944 it had been warning of the danger of an "insurrectionary movement". The tragedy was that the general situation was indeed ripe for social revolution, but not the PPA. Its leadership failed to develop an adequate strategy. From its purely nationalist viewpoint the revolt could be nothing other than armed action taken by a minority acting on behalf of the masses. It had no class strategy and for them the masses had no independent role to play in the revolutionary situation. They were reduced to being bystanders looking on at the activities of the party leadership.

The voluntarist wing of the PPA around Lamine Debaghine and Hocine Asselah, who now dominated the party, reverted to spectacular actions at the end of the war in Europe in order to attract the attention of the Allied victors to the demands of the Algerians for independence. In April 1945 Debaghine and Asselah visited Messali, wanting to convince him of the necessity for armed insurrection.[59] The latter surreptitiously embarked on an inspection tour on 16 April to see for himself what preparations were under way. He came back the next day completely shattered. He had discovered neither weapons nor trained partisans and nowhere anything resembling serious preparation, absolutely nothing to justify a venture which could easily annihilate all the political work the AML had invested. It was thanks to Messali's opposition that the plans for insurgency were ditched.

The massacre

While the great majority of party members and also of the population at large had no idea of these goings-on, the colonial army had started military manoeuvres in preparation for the inevitable confrontation. The colonial government, however, still needed to find the right man to translate the discontent and impatience of the rightist forces into concrete action. The Socialist Yves Chataigneau, since September 1944 governor-general appointed by de Gaulle, seemed much too liberal in their eyes. Things changed when Pierre-René Gazagne was installed as General Secretary of the General Government. Gazagne originated from Algeria and had close connections with influential circles in French Algeria. On arrival he immediately took measures over Chataigneau's head to hasten and heat up the conflict with the Algerian nationalists.

Informed by the secret services of the dissent within the PPA leadership, Gazagne and his retinue of colonial officers saw their time to liquidate the PPA together with all the other Algerian nationalist organisations had come. The General Secretary of Algiers Prefecture, Francis Rey, put it thus: "We have allowed the abscess to ripen so as to more easily puncture it".[60] At the beginning of April, Gazagne ordered the subprefectures across the country to stage provocations to be used as an excuse for arrests and so weaken the leading ranks of the PPA. Within a month around 50 cadres had been thus "neutralised". Then Gazagne ordered Messali's arrest, who on 21 April was carried off by the security forces to an unknown destination and subsequently deported to the Congo.[61]

The PPA, having dropped its plans for insurrection, was caught completely unawares by this turn of events. On the occasion of the traditional 1 May demonstrations it called for celebrating the approaching victory over Nazi Germany. It gave the order to chant slogans demanding Messali's and others' release as well as Algerian independence and to carry the Algerian flag. But the colonial administration would have nothing of that. In Oran and Algiers, the two largest Algerian cities, the demonstrators, pouring into the city centres from the outskirts, were stopped by police barriers. The police fired shots into the crowd and arrested some of the "ringleaders".

The Communist Party, which had its own ministers in the French government, together with the leadership of the CGT trade union, sanctioned the repression, comparing the PPA with Nazis. A leaflet put out by the CGT on 3 May called for Algerian workers to foil the "manoeuvres" of the PPA, whose slogans were "the faithful expression of Radio Berlin". In another leaflet the PCA maintained that the PPA "receives its orders from Berlin, directly from Hitler...the PPA demonstrations, an expression of Messali's long tradition of divisive politics, are Hitlerian provocations". The leaflet's headline read: "Down with the provocateurs!"[62]

The French colonial machine set about implementing the PCA's demand with the most vicious efficiency. On the day of the capitulation of the Wehrmacht, the AML was planning its own marches with distinct symbols: strictly non-violent and disciplined, the participants were to hold up flags of the victorious Allies, including France, interspersed with Algerian flags. Thus peaceful marches gathered together in eastern Algerian Sétif, as well as in many other Algerian towns and cities. As the Muslim crowd reached the town centre they were faced with a police cordon and the demand to hand over the Algerian flags, which they refused to do. There ensued a scuffle. To this day it remains unclear who fired the first shot. What is undisputed is that the police and the army then began shooting directly into the crowd. People panicked and sought refuge in the suburbs. Disorientated and full of hatred they attacked Algerian French on their way. The day's record was 21 Europeans killed. How many Muslims were shot dead has never been investigated.

In the evening General Duval made an appearance in the Sétif area with the mandate to put down the "insurrection". The job was to be executed not by the army alone. Weapons were distributed to the European settlers' militia forces, who hunted down Muslims with complete impunity. The authorities distributed white armbands to Muslim civil servants. The rest were forbidden from walking the streets. An eyewitness report by a French officer explained that in the reaction to the European deaths, "we observe a large number of summary executions of dubious Muslims. Individual executions are tolerated. Right in the town centre a European comes upon an Arab without an armband, he kills him with one revolver shot. Nobody protests. In a garden a small boy is picking flowers, a sergeant passes by and kills him..."[63]

Whereas in Sétif the colonial administration in deploying the militia managed to get the situation under control, trouble spread to other parts of the countryside. Here the PPA and the AML had lost all authority over the various clans which now wrought vengeance on outposts of the colonial regime and isolated settlers and their families. As well as the militia now the French army was sent in. While the ground forces moved in, the air force bombed gatherings of people and even whole villages.

Colonial inequality applied even beyond death. Whereas the full names of all 102 Europeans killed during the events are known, no one knows the numbers of Muslims who met their death. The Algerian state today officially speaks of 45,000 deaths, an assertion which is not verifiable. What is certain is that the whole population of the Sétif region, measuring over 5,000 square kilometres, were subjected to a whole range of suppressive measures.

Then there was the town Guelma and its surroundings, the scene of similar violence on the evening of 8 May with one notable difference, namely that here a Gaullist subprefect André Achiary was directly responsible, the same individual who had played such a prominent role in the struggle for power in Algiers in 1943. He personally ordered the execution without trial and without verdict of nine AML members for "admitting to have initiated the movement on orders from Algiers".[64]

Repression was so vicious and widespread that the AML was completely wiped out, while the PPA split and went underground, where it spent the next ten years primarily infighting. Eventually out of the various faction struggles a new group calling itself National Liberation Front (FLN, "Front de Libération Nationale") emerged, which in 1954 engaged in a guerrilla war and eventually catalysed the complete demise of France's colonial empire in Africa.

Conclusion

Under the coalition government constituted by de Gaulle after the liberation of France and which included Socialists and Communists, colonial domination remained intact and unchanged. What had changed were the Algerians. Large numbers of Muslim soldiers had fought and died alongside the Allied forces in the battle for Monte Cassino in Italy and during the reconquest of France. Those who survived and returned to Algeria after the war were expecting changes which did not materialise. Instead they were confronted with tales of the horrors committed by the French. Whereas in France and the other allied countries on 8 May people euphorically celebrated victory and the end of hostilities, in Algeria this day stood for the continuation of the brutal reality of colonial repression—only even more terrible than before.

Edward Behr describes the political consequences: "Every one of the 'new wave' of Algerian nationalists prominent in the National Liberation Front traces his revolutionary determination back to May 1945... Each of them felt after May 1945 that some sort of armed uprising would sooner or later become necessary".[65]

Looking back, 8 May was for many the beginning of the coming war for national liberation. This was to last seven long years and claim hundreds of thousands of lives before Algeria finally became independent in 1962.

NOTES

1 www.nato.int/cps/en/natolive/official_texts_16912.htm
2 Labelling the various groups of the population in colonial Algeria is not easy. The Algerian French went alternately under the name "colonists", "Europeans" or "pieds-noirs" (black-feet), the latter still a common term but of unknown origin. In modern texts the local population are, retrospectively, referred to as "Algerians", though during the colonial period they were termed Arabs or "indigènes" (natives). All these various terms, however, only encompass a part of the historical reality. I have opted for the term Muslims to designate the nationally oppressed majority. This corresponds to their self-conception and self-denomination prevailing at the time. The French colonial administration used their religion to define the local population as "French subjects" (but not citizens)—a process which in turn bound them together.
3 Robert O Paxton, *Vichy France, Old Guard and New Order, 1940-1944* (London: Barrie and Jenkins, 1972). As vice-président du Conseil, Laval was effectively the government's strong man. He was prime minister from 1940 to 1944 with only a short break between December 1941 and April 1942, when Pierre-Étienne Flandin and Admiral François Darlan took over his functions. Field Marshal Pétain declared himself president as from July 1940, but did not intervene in the daily running of government affairs.
4 Paxton, 1972, p80.
5 Charles de Gaulle's speech on the BBC on 18 June 1940: www.charles-de-gaulle.org/pages/l-homme/dossiers-thematiques/1940-1944-la-seconde-guerre-mondiale/l-appel-du-18-juin/documents/l-appel-du-18-juin-1940.php
6 Just how tiny this minority was is demonstrated by one number: out of the 18,000 French sailors residing in Britain in June 1940 only 200 followed de Gaulle's appeal to remain in situ.
7 Paxton, 1972, p114. This situation formed the background to the Hollywood classic *Casablanca*, which mistakenly showed the German Armistice inspectors in uniform.
8 According to US diplomat Kenneth Pendar, in *Adventure in Diplomacy: The emergence of General de Gaulle in North Africa* (London: Cassel, 1966), p83.
9 L'Echo d'Oran in September 1942, quoted in Annie Rey-Goldzeiguer, *Aux origines de la guerre d'Algérie. De Mers-el-Kébir aux massacres du Nord-Constantinois, 1940-1945* (Découverte, 2002), p101.
10 Claude Paillat, "L'Echiquier d'Alger (Tome 1)" *Avantage à Vichy: Juin 1940-Novembre 1942* (Paris: Laffont, 1966), p247ff.
11 François Kersaudy, *Churchill and de Gaulle* (London: Fontana Press, 1981), p141.
12 Charles de Gaulle, *Mémoires de Guerre* (Tome 1), *L'Appel: 1940-1942* (Paris: Plon, 1954), p164.
13 The British-French conflict over the Levant came to a head at the end of the war in Europe. At the same time it opened up a space for the development of anti-colonial movements. In May 1945 the French army bombed Damascus, killing hundreds in retaliation to a wave of anti-colonial demonstrations. However, they were not able to crush the movement and Syria and Lebanon gained their independence the following year.
14 Peter Schunck, *Charles de Gaulle: Ein Leben für Frankreichs Größe* (Berlin: Propyläen, 1998), p212.
15 Kersaudy, 1981, p211.
16 Barnett Singer, *Maxime Weygand: A Biography of the French General in Two World Wars* (Jefferson N C: McFarland, 2008). General Weygand had been appointed supreme commander in May 1940 and as such was involved in the Armistice negotiations with the German Wehrmacht. In October he was appointed Delegate-General to French Africa as Pétain's personal representative. From July on he was at the same time governor-general in Algiers. He deported political prisoners to concentration camps in Algeria and the South of Morocco, which he had set up especially for that purpose. Weygand was one of the principal architects of the "National Revolution".
17 Jews, concentrated in the cities, made up 3 percent of the total population. The Crémieux

Bill, passed in 1870, granted Jews full citizen rights, whereas Muslims continued to be categorised as "French subjects". The bill was rescinded in October 1940. Vichy's minister of justice later upheld that this step was necessary to "protect the French organism from the microbe which was inducing mortal anaemia" (quoted in Michel Abitbol, *Les Juifs d'Afrique du Nord sous Vichy* (Maisonneuve et Larose, 1983), p61.

18 Robert Murphy, quoted in Anthony Verrier, *Assassination in Algiers: Roosevelt, Churchill, de Gaulle and the Murder of Admiral Darlan* (New York, 1990), p109.

19 This interpretation of events is taken up for instance by Jean-Louis Crémieux-Brilhac in "Jeux et enjeux d'Alger", in Jean-Pierre Azéma, François Bédarida (eds), *La France des années noires* (Tome 2) *De l'Occupation à la Libération* (Paris: Seuil, 2000), p205ff.

20 Verrier, 1990, p108, 118f.

21 Schunck, 1998, p214ff.

22 Verrier, 1990, p172.

23 Rey-Goldzeiguer, 2002, p140.

24 Quoted in Verrier, p167. In reality Pétain had nowhere along the line condoned Darlan's course of action. The latter's room for manoeuvre was, however, completely ruined after Hitler, on 11 November 1942, in reaction to Operation Torch, ordered the Wehrmacht to occupy the areas of France hitherto governed by Vichy.

25 Verrier, 1990, p26.

26 Quoted in Gabriel Kolko, *The Politics of War: The World and United States Foreign Policy: 1943-1945* (New York, Random House, 1990), p67f.

27 Pierre Ordioni, *Tout commence à Alger: 1940-1944* (Paris: Stock, 1972), p560.

28 Quoted in Kolko, 1990, p71.

29 Georges Elgozy, *La vérité sur mon Corps Franc d'Afrique* (Monaco: Rocher, 1985), p64.

30 Elgozy, 1985, p64.

31 Elgozy, 1985, p203.

32 Ordioni, 1971, p375. The Italian First Army capitulated one day later. Two hundred and fifty thousand soldiers of the Axis Powers were taken prisoner in Tunisia.

33 No more than the black troops of West Africa, who also played an important part in the fight to liberate France.

34 Charles-André Julien, *L'Afrique du Nord en marche. Algérie—Tunisie—Maroc, 1880-1952* (Omnibus, 2002), p99. This exceptional piece was first published in 1952, ie before the start of the armed liberation struggle in the Maghreb. Julien was in fact a moderate socialist, but quite open towards national liberation movements, which at the time were practically tabooed.

35 Ferhat Abbas, in the paper *L'Entente*, 23.2.1936, quoted in Julien, 2002, p100.

36 Julien, 2002, p101.

37 Ibid, p103f.

38 Ibid, p94.

39 Jules Michel's circular letter, February 1933, quoted in Julien, 2002, p104f.

40 Julien, 2002, p106.

41 The only political forces to speak out against the banning of ENA were the Trotskyists, a dissident current around Marceau Pivert within the French Socialist Party (SFIO), and the Parti Frontiste around Gaston Bergery, who at the time took a mid-position between the SFIO and the PCF.

42 Rey-Goldzeiguer, 2002, p55. Aumale is about 125 km south of Algiers.

43 Ibid, p55.

44 Ibid, p170.

45 Bachaga is the title of a higher Qa'id ("leader"). Boualam finally became an MP in the French National Assembly. His most famous work is *Mon pays, la France* (Paris: Editions France-Empire, 1962).

46 Rey-Goldzeiguer, 2002, p54.

47 Emmanuel Sivan, *Communisme et nationalisme en Algérie, 1920-1962*, (Paris: Les Presses de Sciences Po, 1976), p129ff.

48 Henri Alleg, *Mémoire algérienne* (Paris: Stock, 2005), p91.
49 Ben Khedda, *Les Origines du 1er novembre 1954* (Algier: Dahlab, 1989), p90.
50 For the full text see texturesdutemps.hypotheses.org/1458. See also Paul-Emile Sarrasin, *La crise algérienne* (Paris: Le Cerf, 1949), p176ff.
51 Christine Levisse-Touzé, *L'Afrique du Nord: recours ou secours? Septembre 1939-Juin 1943* (Thesis) (Paris-I Sorbonne, 1991), p892; also in Jacques Marseille, "L'Empire", in: Azéma, Bédarida, p298.
52 Charles-Robert Ageron, "Les troubles du Nord-Constantinois en mai 1945: une tentative insurrectionnelle?"; in Charles-Robert Ageron, *Genèse de l'Algérie algérienne* (Paris: Bouchène, Paris, 2005), p471.
53 Ferhat Abbas, *Guerre et révolution, I: La nuit coloniale* (Paris: Julliard, 1962), p152.
54 Report by Captain Fraisse, SHAT, 1H2887, quoted in Rey-Goldzeiguer, 2002, p242.
55 As a result the war of independence 1954-62, from the onset, involved very few Europeans. Instead it was fascist organisations which benefited as the conflict intensified, pouring yet more oil onto the flames so as to completely alienate the Europeans from the Muslims. By 1962 hate and mistrust had reached such dimensions that practically the whole European population fled Algeria out of their fear of independence.
56 M'hammed Yousfi, *L'Algérie en marche* (Tome 1) (Paris: Almarifa, 1983), p30.
57 Ibid, p40.
58 Rey-Goldzeiguer, 2002, p193f.
59 Mohammed Harbi, *Le FLN, mirage et réalité* (Paris: Jeunes Afrique, 1980), p28ff.
60 Quoted by Rey-Goldzeiguer, 2002, p238.
61 For a review of the diverging views on the circumstances of Messali's arrest see Roger Benmebarek, "De Gaulle et les événements du Constantinois du 8 mai 1945", at www.clan-r.org/portail/IMG/pdf/De_gaulle_et_le_8_mai_1945.pdf
62 Quoted by Rey-Goldzeiguer, 2002, p251.
63 Rapport Essplass, in Henri Alleg, *La guerre d'Algérie* (Tome 2) (Paris: Temps actuels, 1981), p265f.
64 See investigation report 22 May 1945, quoted in Rey-Goldzeiguer, 2002, p284.
65 Edward Behr, *The Algerian Problem* (Penguin, 1961).

2

Ireland: They called it 'The Emergency'

Kieran Allen

The former provost of Trinity College, FSL Lyons, once compared the population of Ireland during the Second World War to those "condemned to live in Plato's cave, with their backs to the fire of life and deriving their only knowledge of what went on outside from the flickering shadows thrown on the wall".[1] It was a condescending remark that stuck for decades afterwards. Writers like Max Hastings who extolled Britain's war effort also took up the theme of an isolated and misguided people. He complained that "many lives and much tonnage were lost in consequence of the fanatical loathing of the Irish Prime Minister Eamon de Valera for his British neighbours".[2] This charge echoed that of Winston Churchill who contrasted de Valera's stab in the back with the manner in which Northern Ireland "made good in blood its pledge to stand by Britain".[3]

To this day Irish neutrality is a significant obstacle to those who want the country to join in imperialist campaigns, often fought under the guise of "humanitarian interventions". The former German chancellor has described it as an "irrational policy"[4] while many home-grown opponents denounce it as a "sacred cow" in need of slaughter.[5] Yet despite the denunciations, 78 percent of people in a recent poll continue to support a policy of Irish neutrality.[6]

The concept of Irish neutrality was first mooted during the First World War when James Connolly, the famous Irish socialist, constructed a broad front to oppose Irish support for Britain's war effort.[7] The leader of the Home Rule Party, John Redmond, supported Britain's war effort and urged members of the Irish Volunteer movement to enlist. In return for this support Redmond claimed that he had been promised an Irish parliament once the war was over. Connolly, however, rejected this argument and set up an Irish Neutrality League alongside more militant republicans. The impetus for the alliance came from the threat of conscription, but so big was the scale of popular opposition that the British authorities deferred it.

When the Second World War was declared on 1 September 1939, it was only 17 years since the Irish Free State had gained independence. In the previous two years the country had been subjected to a bitter colonial war, spearheaded by British auxiliary forces, colloquially known as the Black and Tans. These were the brainchild of Winston Churchill and were recruited from the ranks of demobbed soldiers for "a rough and dangerous task" of putting down the Irish Republic Army (IRA). Their brutality became legendary as they sacked and burnt towns such as Tuam, Trim, Balbriggan and Cork as collective reprisals for IRA activity. This recent memory meant that few people had any illusions about Churchill's role in fighting for the freedom of small nations.

Nor did the recent "economic war" endear the Irish population to Britain's pretensions as a freedom loving nation. In 1932 the Fianna Fail party had been elected to power on a militant programme of breaking from Ireland's neocolonial relationship with its former master and undoing a humiliating treaty that had ended the War of Independence in 1922. De Valera, the leader of the party, claimed that the country had become "an out garden of Britain" essentially supplying agricultural produce to feed its industries.[8] He tore up aspects of the original Anglo-Irish Treaty by appointing one of his own supporters to the office of governor-general and by refusing to pay land purchase annuities—which amounted to one eighth of his state's budget—to the British Exchequer. Britain responded by launching an "economic war" on the new republican government, imposing punitive tariffs on Irish imports. This effort at destabilisation failed and in 1938 Britain not only withdrew its demand for annuity payments (in return for a once-off down payment) but also handed back three main "Treaty ports" to the Irish authorities.

This then was the background for Fianna Fail's assertion of Irish independence from its old empire. Three main considerations lay behind the adoption of a neutrality policy.

The first and most frequently cited reason was the partition that had been imposed on Ireland as part of the Anglo-Irish treaty. Fianna Fail, and the population more generally, regarded the division of Ireland as a historic wrong. Their sympathies lay with the nationalist population in the North whom they regarded as being oppressed by the Unionist party and the Orange Order. Military support for a colonial power that had imposed partition was, therefore, unthinkable. Inside Fianna Fail there were those who wanted to peddle the nostrum that "England's difficulty is Ireland's opportunity". At the first Fianna Fail conference after the outbreak of the war there were calls from delegates to employ force to take back the six counties under British rule. The Fianna Fail minister and former IRA leader Frank Aiken was demoted because, it was suggested, he believed "that the army should be ready to march into Ulster at any time".[9]

The salience of the partition issue grew when a proposal to introduce conscription into Northern Ireland was mooted by James Craig, the Unionist prime minister of the province in April 1939. Craig, also known as Lord Craigavon, was an arch imperialist who secretly called on Churchill to overrun the South with soldiers drawn from Scottish regiments.[10] His motivation in calling for the conscription was to demonstrate how loyal and staunch little Ulster was. Nationalists, however, regarded conscription as a crime because it meant forcing those who disagreed with empire to fight for it. Memories of the 1918 mass movement against conscription were also still fresh in the collective memory. Therefore when Craig declared his intention to extend national service to the North, there was an explosion of anger on both sides of the border.

The Irish Catholic hierarchy came out strongly against conscription, even claiming that the population had a "moral right" to resist conscription to the British army.[11] Belfast trade union leaders also opposed it, reflecting not just nationalist opinion but the bitter experience many Protestant workers had in the First World War when thousands were sent to their death in the Somme. Such was the scale of the opposition that Basil Brooke, the Unionist minister responsible for recruitment, predicted that there would be significant opposition that would range from "passive resistance to actual rioting".[12] Given this anger, de Valera had little choice but to cancel a trip to New York and declare that the conscription of Irishmen in the province of Ulster would be regarded as "an act of aggression".[13] The level of all-Ireland opposition forced the British government and Unionist politicians to withdraw the threat.

The second—and in many ways more crucial—reason for neutrality was that the Irish ruling class feared that any other policy would have opened up deep divisions in their own society and undermined the stability of their rule. These divisions stemmed from the historic legacy of British colonial rule. Colonialists do not secure their domination simply by military intervention but by winning over a section of the population to becoming their allies. The manner in which Britain intervened in 1922 to split the republican movement and help foment a civil war is a testimony to this legacy. No wonder, then, that Frank Aiken, the minister responsible for the Coordination of Defensive Measures, noted that "it might very well be that we would have another civil war to decide the question as to which of the European belligerents we would declare war upon".[14]

There were also more pragmatic reasons for staying out of the conflict. Intervention on the side of Britain would have led to an outcry from the republican movement. If British troops landed in Ireland to repel a German invasion, there was little doubt that they would be subject to attacks not only from the IRA but also from sections of Fianna Fail itself. Similarly, if the Irish government showed any support for Nazi Germany there was little doubt they would be subject to British military intervention. The small size of the Irish army—which in May 1940 comprised a regular force of 14,000 and a reserve of 12,000—meant that it was not in a position to resist either imperial power.[15] Of even greater cause for concern for the ruling class than military defeat was a fear that leadership of the national movement might shift to more extreme republicans. In the event of a German invasion, for example, it was assumed that the Nazis would seek their own allies among the IRA and depose the official representatives of Irish nationalism. Any overt support for the British would unleash a more intense anti-imperialist movement against the Irish state itself. All of this explains why de Valera believed it would be "suicide" to abandon neutrality and why his representative in Washington thought it might even lead to "revolution".[16]

Thirdly, despite its repeated reference to the wrongs of partition, Fianna Fail's aim was to use "the emergency"—as they referred to the Second World War—as an opportunity to create a new identity between 26 county state and its population. In brief, to forge a new 26 county Little Ireland nationalism. As the writer Terrence Brown later noted, "neutrality and the experience of the war times years mobilised Irish opinion for the first time to consider the 26 county state as the primary unit of national loyalty".[17]

This project worked at many levels. Despite its rhetorical opposition to British imperialism, the Southern state engaged in covert cooperation with its neighbour. Meetings between the Irish police, the Gardai and the Royal Ulster Constabulary, began for the first time in 1940 and led to an exchange of intelligence.[18] The Southern state turned a blind eye to the widespread recruitment to the British army. It came to an agreement with the British government that a dump of civilian clothes be provided in Holyhead so that Irish citizens serving in the British forces could change out of uniform before returning home.[19] British pilots who crashed over Ireland and survived could quietly return to their own country while Germans were interned. The British naval attaché was allowed to travel around Ireland to inspect its coastal defences and de Valera secretly accepted that British warships could pursue and attack enemy submarines in Irish waters. Despite its anti-imperialist rhetoric, de Valera prepared for a long-term accommodation with his "old enemy".

During the period of the war the Fianna Fail government imposed a strict censorship that was mainly directed at opposition voices in its own society rather than reports from belligerent powers. It worked closely with the Catholic church to impose a deeply conservative, fundamentalist culture on its society. In 1943, for example, it appointed the Catholic Archbishop of Dublin to chair a committee on youth unemployment even though he refused to sit with any representatives of Protestant churches or accept representation from Protestant associations. In 1944 the minister for lands boasted that only 40 foreigners had purchased land in Ireland and "only one of them was a Jew".[20] It launched repeated attacks on British based trade unions—which had continued to operate in Ireland after independence—and sought to effectively render them illegal. It recruited massively to a local defence force and used this to inculcate loyalty to the 26 county state. Its aim was to create a homogenous and parochial 26 county Catholic identity that covered over the class divisions in its midst. It hoped through this to bind workers to its own project of strengthening indigenous capital.

At an official level it was quite successful. Over the course of the war it effectively relegated Fine Gael—its former civil war enemy—to the status of second-rate opposition. Fine Gael's base was predominantly among the larger farmers who favoured retention of the neocolonial relationship with Britain. Between 1938 and 1943 its share of the national vote fell from a third to a quarter as Fianna Fail used the policy of neutrality to consolidate its hold. Fianna Fail was also successful in forging links with a section of the union bureaucracy, grouped around the Irish Transport and General Workers Union. Its opposition to British based unions and its call to rally round the Southern state in its hour of need found vocal supporters in these groupings. However, on both the North and South of the border the ruling class faced opposition from two major groups—the republican movement and militants in the unions.

Republican resistance

On 12 January 1939 the Army Council of the IRA addressed the British foreign secretary, Lord Halifax, demanding "the withdrawal of all British forces stationed in Ireland". When the deadline passed the IRA began to implement the S or Sabotage Plan that was a blueprint for the paralysis of English public utilities and transport infrastructure.[21] What followed was a low-key guerrilla campaign on three fronts.

In England itself the bombing began with explosions at seven major power plants and was followed up with other periodic targets. About 160 "outrages" followed in subsequent months, according to a report presented to the British cabinet.[22] Then on 25 August a city centre bomb in Coventry killed five people and injured dozens of others. A British crackdown ensued and IRA activists were quickly arrested. Two of them, Peter Barnes and James McCormack, were eventually executed for the Coventry bombing, even though they had taken no part in it. Soon afterwards the campaign in England fizzled out.

In the six counties of Northern Ireland there was a louder echo from this campaign. In 1938 the Belfast IRA had nearly 500 members but they had not planned a military campaign in the province.[23] Instead they resorted to tactics of militant civil disobedience and small-scale armed propaganda to undermine the British war effort. This meant a wider engagement with the nationalist section of the population who saw themselves as a discriminated minority. On the night of 1 to 2 September, when the first blackout was ordered in Belfast, a number of bonfires were lit in West Belfast. Gas masks were also collected from local houses and publicly burnt. Members of the Territorial Army were also attacked and relieved of their uniform.[24]

The Unionist government responded in time-honoured fashion and immediately introduced internment. Eight hundred republicans were eventually rounded up and were initially joined by a small number of communists, who at that time were arguing for a class war against imperialism. The republicans responded with prison riots demanding political status and these were accompanied by bombings and riots on the outside. Particular targets of the IRA were cinemas showing "offensive" British newsreels. They also infiltrated the British army camp in Ballykinlar and staged a daring arms raid to capture rifles. By 1942 the campaign had escalated to armed attacks with two Royal Ulster constables shot dead at the Easter Weekend in April. But while IRA activities provoked a wave of sympathy from the nationalist population, it did not lead to any major uprising against British rule. It was the wider mass opposition that helped force the authorities to give up on the idea of both military conscription and compulsory registration for labour. The Westminster authorities calculated that they could do without substantial social resistance in their colony while engaged in a war to supposedly free oppressed nations.

Ironically it was in Southern Ireland that the greatest level of confrontation took place between the IRA and the state. The IRA's very formal declaration of war on Britain arose from a peculiar piece of political theology. The IRA Council was, according to its own belief, the rightful government of Ireland as power was conferred on it by the First Dail of 1919-21, the elected democratic assembly that proclaimed itself the parliament of a united Ireland. De Valera's government regarded this as a piece of nonsense but took more seriously the IRA's declaration of war on Britain because it challenged its own rule. It responded by setting up a Special Court and a Military Tribunal to arrest and try republican suspects. When the war broke out supplies of guns to the IRA from the US began to dwindle and they in turn responded by staging an armed raid on the main arsenal of the Irish army. On 23 December 1939 they seized 13 lorry loads of ammunition, the bulk of the Irish army's reserve supply. The government responded with an Emergency Powers Act and this led to the internment of hundreds of republicans.

This set the scene for a brutal attempt by the de Valera government to finally crush the IRA. Just as in the North, the interned republicans demanded their right to political status and began a hunger strike. The Irish government ignored them and a riot broke out where imprisoned republicans were badly beaten. Two republicans then died on hunger strike and in response to further riots, soldiers opened fire without warning, shooting one prisoner in the back. This brutality led to a spate of IRA attacks on the Special Branch, the newly formed political police that Fianna Fail had recruited from their former republican comrades. The state in turn responded by executing two republicans, supposedly involved in shooting Special Branch officers.

There was some sympathy for the republicans but their activities were largely met with indifference. There was no mass opposition because de Valera was able to don the mantle of anti-imperialism, protecting a small country in its hour of need and standing up to the bullying tactics of Churchill. Even while he was smashing the IRA, de Valera continued his rhetorical republican attacks on perfidious Albion. He called for the lifting of the executions of republicans in the North and condemned the hangings of Barnes and McCormack—even though he would execute republicans himself. The double speak of de Valera was part of a wider strategy of detaching republican militants from the IRA and winning them to Fianna Fail. By and large de Valera was successful. In 1933 the IRA had 12,000 members but by 1938 it had shrunk to just 2,000.[25]

The decline of the IRA was the result of two factors. After a decade of isolation following their defeat in the civil war their former comrades in Fianna Fail appeared to be enjoying success in dismantling the Anglo-Irish Treaty and gaining popular support. Some of the IRA membership, therefore, drifted over to the constitutional road. Second, under attack from the Catholic church the IRA leadership turned on its left, who then split off to form the Republican Congress. This left a more militaristic hard core behind which was increasingly tempted to form alliances with Nazi Germany, especially at the start of the Second World War when their military victories appeared to augur a new era.

The link up with Germany was presented in purely instrumental terms. Sean Russell, who stayed in Germany for a period, claimed that "I am not a Nazi. I am not even pro-German. I am an Irishman fighting for the independence of Ireland. The British have been our enemies for hundreds of years. They are the enemy of Germany today. If it suits Germany to give us help to achieve independence, I am willing to accept it, but no more, and there must be no strings attached".[26] However, the "my enemy's enemy is my friend" argument disguised a significant drift rightwards in the IRA that had begun from the mid-1930s. The leadership promoted ideas about social credit and distributionism as an alternative to its left wing. It defined itself as anti-communist and so when its members were later interned they appealed to the Catholic cardinal to remove a known communist, Neil Gould Verschoyle, from their midst less he contaminate good Catholics. The cardinal naturally obliged by writing to de Valera who duly had him transferred.

Contacts between the IRA and the Nazis had begun in the US through the IRA support group, Clann Na Gael. This led to promises of financial support for the IRA bombing campaign in Britain. The IRA in turn responded by claiming that "if the German forces should land in Ireland, they will come as friends and liberators of the Irish people".[27] They praised Germany for helping to establish the Catholic government of Franco in Spain. The IRA's *War News* also occasionally engaged in anti-Semitic rhetoric, attacking the influx of Jewish refugees, claiming that they were "like the English, when they are strong—they bully and rule".[28]

The republican movement was rather a mixed bag and a few individuals produced publications like *War News* under illegal conditions. It is difficult to establish how much the IRA links with Nazi Germany went beyond a purely instrumental arrangement for fighting British imperialism or how far there had been a drift to more extreme right thinking. One thing is certain though. The movement was hooked on the dogma

of armed struggle and displayed no tactical sense. It was totally outma-
noeuvred by de Valera and had no viable strategy to undercut his
rhetorical anti-imperialism. By contrast, the resurgence of labour militancy proved more dangerous for the Southern state.

Union militancy

As soon as it came to power Fianna Fail embarked on a programme of
protectionism to foster native Irish capitalism. The strategy had limited
success and one of its by-products was a growing confidence among
workers. The Irish Transport and General Workers Union (ITGWU),
for example, grew by 120 percent between 1930 and 1938.[29] This newfound
confidence was soon in evidence as workers responded to price rises at
the start of the war. The government's call for an embargo on wage rises
was largely ignored as unions such as the National Union of Railwaymen
made substantial wage claims. A wave of strikes broke out at the end of
1939 and the start of 1940 with one major union figure declaring that
"there were strikes all over the place; there were pickets on every street in
Dublin".[30] Attempts to conscript the unemployed to labour camps modelled on the Construction Corps in the US also met with stiff resistance.
In Cork there was a riot after 300 unemployed men were called up to join
the scheme.[31]

Fianna Fail's initial response was to introduce anti-strike legislation
modelled on the British Trade Disputes and Trade Unions Act 1927 that
had followed the defeat of the General Strike. At the core of this was a
ban on strikes in essential services and fines for those who refused to
return to work. Sean McEntee, the minister responsible, drafted a memo
to his cabinet where he noted that strikers were normally "more reliant
upon physical strength than on mental process for the solution of difficulty" and had, therefore, to be subject to economic sanctions.[32]

However, vocal opposition from the ITGWU led the government to
a change of direction. Fianna Fail had been carefully cultivating the
union's leadership since the mid-1930s. Their main point of common
agreement was opposition to the presence of British-based unions in
Ireland. This stemmed from both a shared nationalist outlook and a
belief that British unions were not fully responsive to the needs of the
Irish state and might engage in militant action. The ITGWU leader,
William O'Brien, had tried to remove British unions through a voluntary
agreement in the wider labour movement but when this failed he turned
to Fianna Fail for legislative action.

When the Second World War broke out relations between the ITGWU and Fianna Fail grew even closer and the union was very explicit in its support for neutrality. The union president described the war as "an imperialist bloodlust"[33] and a key ideologue within the union, Cathal O'Shannon, wrote in Labour Party paper *The Torch*:

> Let no man tell us after these last shameful years that Chamberlain, Daladier and the capitalist and imperialist elements they serve are leading a crusade against Nazism and fascism and a holy war for democracy and liberty… No, the issue now in 1939 is not so very different from in 1914-1918. It is a clash of competing imperialisms.[34]

But while O'Shannon's language was left wing, a more accurate description of the ITGWU's approach emerged at a Labour Party conference in 1941 when a Trotskyist member proposed a motion seeking to combine neutrality with a more general internationalist championing of struggles against imperialism. The ITGWU representative rebuked him in terms that showed the union's real agenda, when he said that they did not want:

> A full time job worrying about the position of oppressed people in India and China…we are only a small island and should be better employed consolidating the labour movement. Surely we do not want a revival of the sufferings of 1916 and 1922, the days of the Fenian and Penal laws.[35]

The ITGWU had moved a long way since its foundation by the revolutionary socialist James Connolly. Its aim was to settle into a comfortable groove with close links to the Southern state and it saw its relationship to Fianna Fail as the way to bring this about. It only used occasional left rhetoric to wrong foot those socialists who took an uncritical view of Britain's role in the war. Its primary motivation for supporting neutrality was not a consistent anti-imperialism but a growing identification with an emerging 26 county national identity. Symbolically it gave a £50,000 loan to the government to help with "the Emergency".[36] Fianna Fail was also more than willing to respond to the union's entreaties. Instead of pressing ahead with its original legislation to impose sanctions on strikers it entered secret talks with William O'Brien and decided to play the nationalist card by dividing the labour movement. The result of these talks was the Trade Union Bill of 1941, which contained two major provisions. Unions who wished to gain immunities under the Trade Disputes Act had to first lodge a substantial deposit with the High

Court. The aim of this measure was, in the words of an internal circular, "the disappearance of small irresponsible unions".[37] The principal target here was the Workers Union of Ireland (WUI), a significant militant breakaway from the ITGWU led by the legendary Jim Larkin. The second provision was for a tribunal to establish sole negotiating rights for the union that had a majority of members in particular workplaces and industry. British-based unions were to be automatically excluded and so faced eventual extinction. These two measures cemented the alliance between the left and British-based unions in opposing the Fianna Fail/ITGWU axis.

However, Fianna Fail now made a tactical error. As well as trying to push through the Trade Union Bill they imposed a Wages Standstill Order to break the strike wave. The Dublin Council of Trade Unions—from which the ITGWU had withdrawn because of the presence of the WUI—responded by setting up the Council of Action and began to publish its own paper, *Workers Action*, to get around the censor. It denounced Fianna Fail's measures as the first step to "corporative organisation made up of workers and the employers under the control of the government".[38] This was a reference to the contemporary campaign promoted by the Catholic bishops to implement Catholic social teaching through such a form of organisation. In June 1941 the Council of Action organised a massive 20,000 strong demonstration and Larkin symbolically burnt the trade union bill from the platform.[39] Another huge demonstration took place in October. The scale of the opposition persuaded the Labour Party to come out strongly against both measures and they experienced a spurt of growth. In 1941 the Labour Party had 174 branches but by 1943 this had risen to 750.[40]

However, the growing links between the ITGWU and Fianna Fail meant that this massive display of opposition was not translated into industrial action. The result was a defeat for the unions as the Trade Union Act was pushed through with minor amendments and an extensive system of wage regulation was introduced via an Emergency Powers Order. In the immediate aftermath, however, the anger against these measures translated into electoral support for the Labour Party and a weakening of Fianna Fail's base in the Dublin working class. In 1942 Labour won many extra seats to become the majority party in Dublin Corporation. At the 1943 general election its share of the vote rose to 17 percent—a full ten points more than it had received at the start of the era of Fianna Fail dominance in 1932. Nationally, Fianna Fail's vote dropped from 51 percent to 41 percent.

The party responded by forging an alliance with the Catholic bishops and ITGWU bureaucrats to launch a Red Scare which one writer described as "the most effective in the state's history".[41] The *Catholic Standard*, a paper with a circulation of 80,000 at the time, spearheaded the campaign. Using its access to Special Branch files—undoubtedly supplied by Fianna Fail—the paper ran regular exposé articles against known communists.[42] A small number of Communist Party members had, in fact, joined the Labour Party after the Communist Party had voted to dissolve its Dublin branch in 1941. This led the Fianna Fail minister McEntee to denounce Labour leader William Norton, as "the Kerensky of the Labour Party" who was "preparing the way for the Red Shirts". The Labour Party leadership responded by promptly setting up a commission of inquiry and expelling a number of these individuals.

However, the real target of the campaign was not the tiny handful of Communist Party members but Larkinism. "Larkinism" was a term that summed up the popular sympathy which the Dublin working class had for Jim Larkin and his three sons, who played leading roles in the Workers Union of Ireland and who typified a militant approach to trade unionism and left wing politics. Larkin had also joined the Labour Party in 1941 and was elected to a Dail seat in 1943. The ITGWU attempted to block his nomination and, when that failed, they disaffiliated from the party. Seven members of the Dail (TDs) who were closely linked to them broke away to form the National Labour Party.

The formation of the anti-communist National Labour Party has sometimes been presented in terms of a long-standing personal feud between ITGWU leader William O'Brien and James Larkin, leader of the WUI. But while a personal animus no doubt existed, there was far more to it. Its real roots lay in the ITGWU's retreat from Connolly's revolutionary syndicalism. It had evolved to a position of embracing Catholic social teaching and attacking socialist ideas. This in turn was part of its wider journey to embracing the 26 county state, which was also using a form of Catholic fundamentalism to unite its population around it. The upsurge of militancy at the start of the Second World War and its political after-effects in the 1942 local and 1943 general election served, in fact, to crystallise all these tendencies. The result was the formation of an axis of anti-communist Catholic fundamentalism that united the ITGWU and the National Labour Party with the Catholic bishops and Fianna Fail.

One factor which helped this alliance gain considerable hegemony over workers was the approach that left wingers took to the Second

World War. The Communist Party was an insignificant force in the South but it was a different story in the North. Within two years of the invasion of the Soviet Union the party had grown to 1,000 members as it embraced "the patriotic war". The party had moved from being a subversive body to one where its pamphlets were distributed to thousands of households and its meetings even advertised in Unionist Party publications. Around the party was also grouped a looser alliance of left wing trade union officials principally in the Amalgamated Transport and General Workers Union (ATGWU), which was the main British-based union in Ireland.

The Northern Irish working class responded to the war in quite contradictory ways. In the largely Protestant section of the workforce support for the war effort was combined with deep seated plebeian cynicism about the elite leading it and a determination to maintain some control over their working lives. The Catholic section of the workforce was simply indifferent and sometimes downright hostile. This combination led to an occurrence of considerable "lack of discipline" in the workforce. The number of strikes—particularly in aircraft, engineering and shipbuilding—grew considerably. Although Northern Ireland accounted for only 2.5 percent of the insured UK workforce, it accounted for 10 percent of the working days lost.[43]

In October 1942 a strike at Short and Harland over Sunday working and overtime led to the sacking of two shop stewards. In response the Belfast Shop Stewards movement was formed to link together all the major factories in the city to spread the strike. The Communist Party, however, took a position that "a strike, no matter under what circumstances it takes place, cannot be supported by our party".[44] Naturally this met with considerable hostility from the workers. On 25 February 1944 the largest wartime strike took place when 3,000 workers at Harland and Wolff shipyard came out to demand a pay rise. By 24 March 20,000 workers were on strike as a solidarity movement spread across the city. The Belfast Shop Stewards movement again led the struggle and five of its leaders were jailed. This only led to further solidarity action and Belfast was soon in the grip of a virtual general strike. Once again throughout these struggles the Communist Party was implacably opposed to the strikes. It manoeuvred behind the scenes to defuse the conflict and the shop stewards were released on bail. The strikers, however, won a pay rise and more autonomy for their shop stewards.[45]

Communist Party opposition to strikes arose from their uncritical acceptance that Britain was fighting an anti-fascist war. This position also led them—and the wider left—to constantly challenge the neutrality of the South. The main forum for this occurred inside the Irish Trade Union Congress, a 32 county body that linked all unions together, and in the Labour Party to which many unions were affiliated. Communist Party officials from the North openly attacked neutrality and promoted the line of their Belfast party leader, Billy McCullough, that neutrality was "a matter of grave concern to democratic opinion" because it put Ireland "out of step with the rest of progressive mankind".[46] This view was echoed by the leader of the ATGWU, Sam Kyle, who spoke against neutrality at a Labour Party conference, claiming that Ireland "could not be indifferent to the national rights of France, Poland, Norway, Denmark, Belgium, Holland, Yugoslavia, Albania, Greece and Czechoslovakia".[47] The significant omission from this interesting list was countries such as India, which had been colonised by the British Empire and therefore excluded from the category of those with national rights.

O'Brien and the ITGWU aptly exploited this blind spot of the CP and the left Labourite union leaders, attacking the fact that the British Communist MP Willie Gallagher, for example, was willing to "shout and applaud for Churchill".[48] By laying claim to his own conservative version of Ireland's anti-colonial legacy, O'Brien gained a cover to cement his alliance with Fianna Fail. Soon after ITGWU-sponsored TDs split from the Labour Party, a split also took place in the trade union movement. A group of Irish-based unions, principally around the ITGWU, broke away from the Irish Trade Union Congress ostensibly over participation in an international event deemed a breach of Irish neutrality. Fianna Fail's strategy of dividing the labour movement on nationalist lines had borne fruit. They responded to the formation of the Council of Irish Unions— which was formed to oppose British imperialism, British-based unions and communist influence—with enthusiasm. An internal circular within the government stated that "it will be our policy to build up the Council of Irish Unions and to treat it as the most representative organ of Irish union opinion".[49]

Conclusion

The war years saw a considerable degree of class struggle on both sides of the Irish border, which led to a short spurt of growth in left wing parties organising in these respective areas. This level of class struggle is often hidden in conventional accounts of the era, which treats nations as one in their desire to line up on one or other side of geopolitical divides.

However, class struggle in itself does not always lead to political clarity on the left. The tragedy of the period is that a small left was clearer than nationalist and Unionist forces in seeing the danger of Hitlerite fascism, but it decided to take an uncritical stance about Britain's motive in fighting that war. In particular, the left ignored Britain's attempt to shore up its empire against its German rival and so played down the genuine grievances that the mass of people in Ireland—or India—had with colonialism.

This blind spot was used by Fianna Fail and the union allies to forge a hegemonic alliance, which tied the labour movement to the 26 county state for decades afterwards

NOTES

1   F S L Lyons, *Ireland Since the Famine* (Fontana, London, 1973), p558.
2   M Hastings, *All Hell Let Loose* (Harper, New York, 2011), p67.
3   R Fisk, *In Time of War* (Andre Deutsch, London, 1983), p470.
4   *Irish Independent*, 27 December 2013.
5   B Tonra, *Global Citizen and European Republic: Irish Foreign Policy in Transition* (Manchester University Press, Manchester, 2012), p154.
6   Red C Poll, 11 September 2013, www.pana.ie/download/Pana-Neutrality-Poll-September-2013-Pie-Charts.pdf
7   J Connolly, "Ireland and the War", *Irish Worker*, 17 October 2014, www.marxists.org/archive/connolly/1914/10/irewar.htm
8   Dail Debates, vol 35, col 478, 12 July 1928.
9   J Bowman, *De Valera and the Ulster Question* (Clarendon, Oxford, 1982), p209.
10 *Sunday Times*, 21 March 2010.
11 Fisk, 1983, p80.
12 Basil Brooke Diary, 24 May 1941, PRONI D/3004/D/32.
13 Fisk, 1983, p80.
14 "Neutrality, Censorship and democracy", State Papers Office, S11586A Aiken to Government.
15 JA Murphy, *Ireland in the Twentieth Century* (Gill and Macmillan, Dublin, 1975), p103.
16 Bowman, 1982, p208.
17 T Brown, *Ireland: A Cultural and Social History 1922-85* (Fontana, London, 1985), pp215-216.
18 P Ollerenshaw, *Northern Ireland in the Second World War* (Manchester University Press, Manchester, 2013), p145.
19 Fisk, 1983, p95.
20 Minutes of Fianna Fail Party parliamentary party meeting, 19 October 1944.
21 C Nic Daibhead, *Sean McBride: A Republican Life* (Liverpool University Press, Liverpool, 2011), p126.
22 P Ollerenshaw, 2013, p41.
23 J Boyer Bell, *The Secret Army: The IRA 1916-1979* (The Academy Press, Dublin, 1979), p177.
24 P Ollerenshaw, 2013, pp45-46.
25 B Hanley, "'Oh, Here's to Adolf Hitler': The IRA and the Nazis", *History Ireland*, no 3, May/June 2005.
26 A Hoar, *In Green and Red: The Lives of Frank Ryan* (Brandon, Dingle, 2004), p243.
27 Hanley, 2005.
28 Hanley, 2005.
29 ITGWU, *Fifty Years of Liberty Hall* (ITGWU, Dublin, 1959), p89.
30 Congress of Irish Unions, *Annual Report and Conference Proceedings* (1945), p54.
31 *Cork Echo*, 15 May 1941.
32 McEntee to Secretary, Department of Industry and Commerce, 17 March 1940, McEntee Papers, P67/229, University College Dublin archives.
33 ITGWU, *Conference Proceedings* (1940), p21.
34 *The Torch*, 2 September 1939.
35 Labour Party, *Conference Proceedings* (1941), p109.
36 E O'Connor, *A Labour History of Ireland 1824-1960* (Gill and Macmillan, Dublin, 1992), p146.
37 Memo, Department of Industry and Commerce, 28 April 1941, SPO file S11750, National Archives Dublin.
38 O'Connor, 1992, p145.
39 O'Connor, 1992, p144.
40 Labour Party, *Annual Reports* (1942 and 1943).
41 M Milotte, *Communism in Modern Ireland* (Gill and Macmillan, Dublin, 1984), p197.
42 McEntee speech, 4 June 1943, McEntee Papers P 67/364.

43 B Black, "A Triumph of Voluntarism? Industrial Relations and Strikes in Northern Ireland during World War Two", *Labour History Review*, vol 70, (April 2005), pp1-19.
44 Milotte, 1984, p204.
45 Milotte, 1984, p205.
46 Milotte, 1984, pp193-194.
47 Labour Party, *Annual Report* (1941), pp106-107.
48 ITUC, *Annual Report and Conference Proceedings* (1945), p157.
49 Minister for Industry and Commerce Instructions to all Departments, 23 May 1945, Department of Labour Files, W63, National Archives.

3

Jewish resistance in Eastern Europe: 'Never say there's only death for you'

Janey Stone

Never say there's only death for you.
Though leaden skies may be concealing days of blue—
Because the hour we have hungered for is near;
Beneath our tread the earth shall tremble: We are here![1]
—*Hersh Glik, song inspired by Warsaw Ghetto uprising*

Hitler's "Final Solution" meant genocide for Europe's Jewish population: 6 million Jews died in the Holocaust, 3 million of them in Poland. Only 5 percent of the Jewish population of Poland survived. Anti-Semitism could take no more dreadful form.

Following the Hitler-Stalin Pact in August 1939, Germany invaded Poland. Russia invaded two weeks later and it was all over by 27 September. Hitler gained control of 48 percent of the country which was then divided into two parts. The Nazis annexed outright the western part of Poland, which became a part of "greater Germany", and controlled the remainder of the occupied area through a regime called the General Government. Later a third region was added when Germany occupied the area previously occupied by Russia.

Immediately following the invasion Jews were subject to attacks and atrocities but following the Wannsee Conference in January 1942 the Nazis constructed the extermination camps at Auschwitz and Treblinka. From July 1942 Operation Reinhardt initiated the systematic annihilation of the Jewish population.

But we must not see the Jews simply as victims. There is a widespread misconception that the Jews went passively to the gas chambers.[2] Consider the following from Henri Michel, a historian of the Resistance in Europe:

Hundreds of thousands of Jews allowed themselves to be torn unprotestingly from their work and their homes, stripped of their possessions and taken they knew not where; finally they climbed docilely and apparently without fear into the trucks which took them to the door of the simulated "bath-houses"; when to their horror, they discovered the fearful truth that they were in a gas chamber, it was too late either to escape or to sell their lives dear.[3]

This chapter will prove that chilling and inhuman image wrong and outline the widespread resistance that did occur. It focuses on Poland as the epicentre of the Holocaust.

Class structure and politics of the Eastern European Jews

Yiddish speaking Jewish communities lived in Eastern Europe for hundreds of years among other populations which had not yet fully established modern nation states, creating a web of tensions and conflicts. Denied the legal right to own agricultural land until the 19th century, Jews concentrated in towns where exclusion from many economic fields led to a restricted range of occupations. The resulting competition laid the basis for hostility among ordinary people. At the top end of the class structure meanwhile, Jews historically played particularly important roles in finance and trade and owned between 60 and 90 percent of Poland's banks by the end of the 19th century.

With the urbanisation of the 19th and 20th centuries the primarily religious Jewish communities of the Middle Ages were secularised and exposed to the phenomena associated with the rise of capitalism—the mass market and the rise of the industrial proletariat. They organised into trade unions very early compared to other workers in the region, beginning in the 1890s in the Pale of Settlement.[4] In 1938 there were 98,000 members of Jewish trade unions in Poland. In the inter-war period half the workforce in Poland was made up of self-employed craftsmen such as tailors and watchmakers. Jewish industrialists on the other hand were reluctant to employ Jewish labour and put their class interests first even amid the increasing anti-Semitism and high unemployment of the late 1930s.[5]

Thus Jews in Eastern Europe were divided by class but the divisions were distorted by historical restrictions and repression. The relatively large proportion of the Jewish bourgeoisie in finance and trade appeared to the popular imagination as a global conspiracy. The relatively strong socialist and trade union ideas among the working class provided grist to anti-communist right wing nationalists.

In the 1920s there were approximately 2.8 million Jews in Poland, 10.5 percent of the population. There were three main political currents. On the right was Agudas Yisrael, the party of traditional orthodoxy, supported by about one third of the community.[6] They took the conventional position of loyalty to any regime that did not interfere with their religious activities. Although there were Jews in the Communist Party and the Polish Socialist Party, the main left wing Jewish party was the Jewish Labour Bund, numerically smaller than the Zionists until the mid-1930s, but dominant among the Jewish working class.[7] The third political current, Zionism, was strong enough to send representatives to parliament in Latvia, Lithuania and Poland. But its local base must be seen in the international context.

The Zionists have historically had a peculiar relationship with the imperialist powers. In the period before the Second World War most countries fell into one of two camps. On the one side were the major imperialist powers (the US, Britain and the Soviet Union) together with smaller imperialists and colonial settler states (Australia and South Africa). On the other side were countries which had been occupied as colonies in which anti-imperialist nationalist struggles occurred. Zionism was a political project without a national base but with nationalist aspirations. However, unlike the colonial based nationalist movements, and despite the position of Jews as an oppressed group in society, at no point did the Zionists side with the anti-imperialist camp. From the very beginning their strategic orientation was geared to winning support for their project of establishing a state from the major imperialist powers.

In the 19th and early 20th centuries they targeted the German Kaiser, the Russian Tsar, the Sultan of Turkey and the Austrian Habsburgs, despite their professed and active anti-Semitism. During the First World War most Zionists were pro-German[8] but established a major alliance with British imperialism in the form of the Balfour Declaration in 1917. Britain's nominal support for the establishment of a Jewish homeland in Palestine was purely propaganda; they had no power to act. But the Zionists were encouraged in their orientation to imperialist powers. Notoriously, Zionists offered themselves to the British as imperialist agents in the Middle East where they sought to form "an outpost of civilisation as opposed to barbarism".[9]

The Zionists soon found that support was only offered insofar as it suited the interests of imperialism. The period after Hitler came to power in 1933 was marked by increasingly virulent attacks on Jews. In 1938 US President Franklin Roosevelt initiated a conference at Evian-les-Bains,

France, supposedly to help Jewish refugees. At that time about 450,000 Jews had left Germany out of a total of 950,000. But the conference did nothing. The US delegates offered no place to settle Jews fleeing Hitler and passed the buck to the South American states. One by one the South Americans said no. The Australian representative announced: "as we have no real racial problem, we are not desirous of importing one".[10] Genocide against Aborigines and the "White Australia" immigration policies went unremarked.

The outbreak of war did not change the attitude of the imperialist powers. When Jan Karski, the Polish resistance fighter, escaped to the West, he brought detailed information about the situation under the Nazi occupation, including the Holocaust. Karski met political leaders including the UK foreign secretary Anthony Eden and President Roosevelt. None of the political leaders took him seriously. Roosevelt reportedly asked about the condition of horses in Poland but did not ask a single question about Jews.[11] Karski concluded that the Jews "were abandoned by all world governments".[12]

Beginning around March 1943 there were calls for the Allies to bomb the rails leading to the Auschwitz death camp. US military chiefs refused, arguing this would divert resources from the war effort and that the rails were hard to hit. Undersecretary of war John J McCloy fretted that such bombings might "provoke more vindictive actions by the Germans"—as if there was any worse fate than the death camps.[13] The tone was set in Allied refugee policy by the US but Britain followed closely behind, "putting self-interest first".[14]

Overall the Western governments displayed a shocking indifference to the fate of the Jews. Walter Laqueur concluded that, despite knowing about the "final solution" from an early date, the US, the UK and the Soviet Union showed no interest in the fate of the Jews.[15] US intelligence, for example, took an interest in the movements of forced labour teams because they were a factor in the German war effort. But according to Richard Breitman in *US Intelligence and the Nazis*, the CIA's predecessor organisation, the Office of Strategic Services (OSS), "does not seem to have taken much detailed interest in German camps as they concerned the extermination of Jews".[16] Michael Neufeld, introducing a collection of essays on prospects for bombing Auschwitz, concludes: "The Holocaust simply was not an important issue on the public or military agenda of World War II".[17]

Thus there was never a real prospect that the imperialist powers before the war or the Allies and the official war effort would help Jews.

Throughout the whole period, however, Zionism never swerved from its orientation to imperialism but continued basing strategies on the powers that be even when anti-Semitic. The revisionist wing of the Zionist movement had such active relations with the Italian Fascists in the 1930s that Mussolini praised them in 1935:

> For Zionism to succeed you need to have a Jewish state, with a Jewish flag and a Jewish language. The person who really understands that is your fascist, Jabotinsky.[18]

The German Zionists actively collaborated with the Nazis in the 1930s, breaking the international boycott on German goods and transferring capital to Palestine in a deal known as the "Ha'avera" (Transfer) Agreement. Some 60 percent of all capital invested in Palestine between 1933 and 1939 was channelled this way.[19]

Their fundamental orientation to imperialism critically weakened the Zionists once they were confronted with the Holocaust. They were used to accommodating local and international powers, not resisting them. They were accustomed to relying on others and on wheeling and dealing. They were experts at behind the scenes manoeuvres and manipulations. And they were practised at turning a blind eye to the anti-Semitic beliefs and actions of those with whom they were negotiating.

The focus for all Zionist factions was always the promotion of emigration to Palestine, not action to resist growing anti-Semitism. Consequently support for Zionism among Polish Jews declined during the 1930s. As the slogan of the right wingers and anti-Semites was "Kikes to Palestine", Zionists who made the same argument (although with more refined language) had some difficulty distinguishing their politics. Zionist politics was hamstrung both in fighting anti-Semitism in the 1930s and in the coming crisis of the Eastern European Jewish population.

"It burns! Brothers, it burns!"

In May 1926 Marshal Joseph Pilsudski took power in Poland through a military coup. Although a reactionary right winger, Pilsudski was not in fact a fascist nor was he an anti-Semite. Huge unemployment and increased social tensions brought anti-Semitism but while Pilsudki was in power the police in general suppressed pogroms.

After he died in 1935 conditions for Jews deteriorated considerably. There were boycotts of Jewish stores and street assaults and a form of segregated seating known as "ghetto benches" was introduced at universities.

A major wave of pogroms included one in March 1936 at Przytyk, a small town in central Poland, whose population was 90 percent Jewish. When fascists attacked Jewish stalls a Jewish self-defence group intervened. Two Jews and a Pole were killed, property was destroyed and more than 20 people were severely beaten.

This event inspired the Jewish folk poet and songwriter Mordecai Gebirtig to write *S'brent* (It burns). Using flames as a metaphor for the threat of fascist violence, the song was intended as a call to action. Widely known in Poland before the war, it was later sung in many ghettos and camps and inspired young people to take up arms against the Nazis.

> It burns! Brothers, it burns!
> And help can only be from you alone!
> If our shtetl[20] is dear to you,
> Grab the buckets, douse the fire!
> Douse it with your own blood
> Show us that you can![21]

The Jewish working class movement did fight back using all the means they had available. Although many groups and individuals participated, the main leadership was provided by the Jewish Labour Bund. Its goals were quite different to that of the Zionists:

> Today as always our slogan is still true: right here [in Poland] and not elsewhere—in a relentless fight for freedom, arm in arm with the working masses of Poland—lies our salvation.[22]

The Bund self-defence groups consisted of militias and 24-hour flying squads. Originally set up for the defence of the Bund itself, during the 1930s they broadened to the general defence of Jews: "Their livelihood, dignity, honour and often their very lives".[23]

One self-defence group was based on the Bund youth organisation *Tsukunft* ("Future"). The adult group (the *Ordenergruppe*) included Bundists and Jewish unionists and was allied with a Polish Socialist Party (*Polska Partia Socjalistyczna*, PPS) militia. A Bund leader declared their defiance at a 1937 rally:

> Today, the Jewish working class is saying to the fascist and anti-Semitic hoodlums: the time has passed when Jews could be subject to pogroms with impunity. There exist a mass of workers raised in the Bund tradition of struggle and self defense... Pogroms [will not] remain unpunished.[24]

The squads broke up anti-Semitic pickets at Jewish stores, patrolled areas at risk and responded to fascist assaults in the universities. Sometimes they arrived early in sufficient force to prevent an attack. At other times they carried out organised retaliations. Perhaps the most important battle occurred in the Saxonian Garden, a Warsaw park, in 1938. Bernard Goldstein, a leader of one of the Bund self-defence groups, described what happened:

> We organised a large group of resistance fighters which we concentrated around the large square near the Iron Gate. Our plan was to entice the hooligans to that square, which was closed off on three sides, and to block the fourth exit, and thus have them in a trap where we could give battle and teach them an appropriate lesson... When we had a fair number of Nara [fascist] hooligans in the square...we suddenly emerged from our hiding places, surrounding them from all sides...ambulances had to be called.[25]

Important as self-defence groups were, by necessity only relatively small numbers of committed and trained individuals could participate. The other critical component of the fightback was street mobilisations. Throughout the late 1930s there were numerous small demonstrations in the streets, many almost spontaneous. Frequently these were broken up by police. There were also large organised protests. In March 1936 a half-day general strike, originally called by the Bund to protest against the Przytyk pogrom, turned into a mass protest against anti-Semitic violence. The action was supported by the PPS, and some Polish workers—mostly socialists—joined in; much of Poland was shut down.

A year later a demonstration against the government's failure to punish those who had incited a pogrom at Breszcz resulted in a massive turnout. And in October 1937 a two-day general strike included a mass protest in Warsaw against the "ghetto benches" and the terror at the universities. This drew in not just the Jewish community, but also PPS unions, academics and many others. The participants drove off fascist attacks. A Jewish high school student wrote:

> The whole Jewish community chose to protest against this injustice... We know that after the university ghetto will come ghettos in other aspects of life... The streets were filled with [protesters]. Jewish stores were closed. The whole community showed its solidarity.[26]

The Bund could lead such impressive actions and mobilisations because it had a base in the working class built up over decades. These militant workers were ready to respond to the call to action and provided an organising base. They could mobilise the broader Jewish trade union movement and students. But alone these strengths would not have been sufficient. Crucially the Bund was able to draw on support from outside the Jewish community, in particular, Polish socialists. Through them they often received tip-offs about planned attacks and their support at the demonstrations was invaluable.

It is a widespread myth that Poles are inherently anti-Semitic and that deep hatred of Jews existed throughout Polish society and history. Anti-Semitism in Poland in this period was in fact primarily a ruling and middle class phenomenon. The bulk of the Polish working class supported the PPS which understood from the beginning that the fight against anti-Semitism and the fascists was its fight.[27]

The absence of anti-Semitism among the working class was acknowledged by Jacob Lestchinsky, a leading Zionist scholar:

> The Polish labour party may justly boast that it has successfully immunised the workers against the anti-Jewish virus, even in the poisoned atmosphere of Poland. Their stand on the subject has become almost traditional. Even in cities and districts that seem to have been thoroughly infected by the most revolting type of anti-Semitism the workers have not been contaminated.[28]

Facing the strong anti-Semitic currents at the universities was a layer of non-Jews who resisted. When segregated seating was first introduced at Lvov (present day L'viv, Ukraine) Polytechnic, Jewish students protested by standing rather than sitting in their places. They were joined in this action by some Polish students. When the ghetto benches were introduced throughout Poland in 1937 at least two university rectors resigned in protest and over 50 professors signed a petition against it. White Russian and Ukrainian students (also minorities in the Poland of the inter-war years) in Vilna and Lvov also joined the anti-ghetto actions.[29]

Peasants were divided in their attitude to anti-Semitism; it was most common among the richer ones. The Peasant Party recognised by 1937 that the anti-Semitic campaign was a ruse to divert attention from political issues relevant to them. In return Jews supported a mass ten-day general strike of peasants in August 1937 in which police killed 50 demonstrators. A Bundist youth leader reported: "During the strike you could see bearded Chassidim [religious Jews] on the picket lines together with peasants".[30]

Jewish confidence in the working class was demonstrated at the time of the Nazi invasion. According to the Labour Zionist Emmanuel Ringelblum, Jews tried desperately to find hiding places in the homes of workers:

> Polish workers had long before the war grasped the class aspect of anti-Semitism, the power-tool of the native bourgeoisie, and during the war they redoubled their efforts to fight anti-Semitism... There were only limited possibilities for workers to hide Jews in their home...[but] many Jews did find shelter in the flats of workers.[31]

"Driven out of the society of the human race"—Ghettos, defiance and resistance

The establishment of the ghettos was the first step in the Nazis' plans to annihilate the Jews. Descriptions of life in these hundreds of walled, isolated and tightly controlled communities defy the imagination. For example, in Minsk a living space of 1.5 square metres was allotted per adult; no space at all was allotted for children. The food ration was 400 calories a day. In Warsaw people returning home with their tiny bread ration had to ignore children dying in the street.

Jan Karski commented after a secret visit to the Warsaw Ghetto, "everything there seemed polluted by death, the stench of rotting corpses, filth and decay".[32] Marek Edelman, a leader of the Warsaw Ghetto uprising, described the terrible atmosphere:

> The Jews, beaten, stepped upon, slaughtered without the slightest cause—lived in constant fear. There was only one punishment for failure to obey regulations—death—while careful obedience...did not protect against a thousand and one fantastic degradations... [The] conviction that one was never treated as an individual human being caused a lack of self-confidence and stunted the desire to work... To overcome our own terrifying apathy, to fight against our own acceptance of the generally prevailing feeling of panic, even small tasks...required truly gigantic efforts on our part.[33]

Such an atmosphere is extremely corrupting. To obtain even the basic necessities of life the ordinary population had to bribe, steal or lie. With shortages of everything and survival at the centre of everyone's mind, some used their positions for additional personal advantage such as to avoid forced labour. The Jewish police were notorious for supporting the

Nazis in their actions and there are horrifying examples of Jews spying for the Gestapo.[34] But this was not only true of the Jewish population. They were divided like all others.

Concentrating the Jews in ghettos served the Nazis strategically but there was also an ideological function. In order to commit atrocities it is necessary to first dehumanise the victims, and the ghetto environment facilitated this process. After a visit to the Warsaw Ghetto the Nazi governor of Krakow commented: "A German would not be able to live under such conditions", because they were a civilised people with a high culture and the state of the children of the ghetto was due to Jews being a diseased race.[35] As Chaim Kaplan put it: "We are segregated and separated from the world...driven out of the society of the human race".[36]

In all ghettos the Nazis created a special body, the *Judenrat* (Jewish Council), to act as an intermediary.[37] The members were selected by the Nazis and naturally they chose people who would cooperate. The members of the *Judenräte* often saw their function as primarily welfare, running soup kitchens and so on.[38] But to the Nazis these activities were irrelevant. The Nazis used the *Judenrat* to control the population, to provide manpower for the slave labour factories and finally, and chillingly, to process deportations to death camps. More Zionists were chosen for this role than all other political groups combined.[39] The remainder were mostly the traditional conservative community leadership—rabbis and elders.

Jewish leaders who served in the *Judenräte* clearly did not cause the Holocaust; the brutality of the Nazis was beyond the control of anyone subject to it. But the one thing that Jews could take responsibility for was their own response. Would they submit or would they resist?

The responses of the *Judenräte* varied greatly. Many argued that compliance would limit the damage the Nazis did or that by making themselves economically useful at least some Jews would survive. They argued that resistance could not be successful so it was futile.

This is a much disputed field. Yehuda Bauer discusses the research of Aharon Weiss into the behaviour of the *Judenräte*. Weiss drew a "red line"—active collaboration "meant handing over Jews to the Germans at the latters' request".[40] An extreme example of this occurred in the Lodz Ghetto, where the head of the *Judenrat* Mordechai Rumkowski was, in Bauer's words, "without any doubt a brutal dictator",[41] who handed the children of the ghetto over to the Nazis and turned the ghetto into a slave labour camp. An example of a different kind is the notorious case of politically based collaboration known as the Kastner affair.[42]

Active collaboration is one thing. More significant for my general argument are the *Judenräte* who were not active collaborators but who failed to support the underground groupings and opposed active resistance to the Nazis. This was the case in several large and important ghettos such as Vilna, Bialystok and Warsaw. Their attitude affected the populations in the ghettos; it exacerbated the feeling of hopelessness and made the building of resistance organisations even more difficult.

Feelings of hopelessness are understandable. Militarily the situation *was* hopeless. Nehama Tec argues that there are five conditions upon which the possibility of successful armed resistance is predicated: time to prepare, a strategic base of operations, leadership, arms and allies.[43] Overwhelmingly these conditions were lacking. As Lucjan Dobroszycki put it: "Has anyone seen an army without arms; an army scattered over 200 isolated ghettos; an army of infants, old people, the sick; an army whose soldiers are denied the right even to surrender?"[44]

Yet there was resistance—and on a scale that has somehow disappeared from historical awareness. The Warsaw Ghetto uprising is not the only case; Jewish resistance occurred right across Nazi occupied Eastern Europe.[45]

Definitions of resistance tend to divide into two groups. The first group focuses on an active ideological component.

> [Resistance] could develop only from an active ideology which presented its holders in opposition to the existing circumstances and believed in the possibility of changing the cultural and political ecology. Therefore the resisters usually had a previous history as members of anti-establishment groups.[46]

This type of definition applies readily enough to members of formally structured resistance organisations. The political parties, and above all their youth groups, formed the core of the underground. Overwhelmingly it was young people who were able to recognise the true intentions of the Nazis and to organise against them, particularly Labour Zionists, the socialist Zionists Hashomer Hazair, the Bund youth group *Tsukunft* and communist youth groups.[47]

However, the Jewish population as a whole faced a situation where almost all normal activities were banned by an enemy determined to exterminate them. In such circumstances even staying alive is at least defiance and even efforts to hide or flee must be regarded as opposition. In this broader context the definition offered by Nehama Tec sits better:

"Activities motivated by the desire to thwart, limit, undermine, or end the exercise of oppression over the oppressed".[48]

Consider the case of the Jews in the small eastern Polish town of Biala Podlaska who gave bread to Soviet prisoners of war (POWs) marching through the town under guard in June 1941. Sent to Auschwitz they were among the first Jewish victims to perish there.[49] Ideology does not enter into such acts of courageous defiant humanity which occurred in everyday activities. Even simple survival activities such as soup kitchens required a defiant attitude. As one Vilna Ghetto inmate said: "the resistance of the anonymous masses must be affirmed in terms of how they held on to their humanity, of their manifestation of solidarity, of mutual help and self-sacrifice".[50]

Defiance can also be seen in the extraordinary range of cultural activities that occurred including music, theatre and art. I have used lines from songs as section headings to give an indication of their power. In addition "people kept their sense of humour, albeit grotesque, amidst the most appalling and unspeakable atrocities. We were always singing and telling vulgar jokes about our predicament." A song in one concentration camp sung every evening contained the lyrics: "It's already nine o'clock, All the camp is going to sleep, The latrines are locked up now, You're no longer allowed to shit."[51]

A very Jewish joke:

A Jewish teacher asks his pupil, 'Tell me Moshe, what would you like to be if you were Hitler's son?' 'An orphan', answers the pupil.[52]

The remainder of this chapter focuses on collective and organised active resistance within this wider context.[53]

Rising up against their destroyers

The most famous example of resistance by Jews is the Warsaw Ghetto uprising.[54]

Nearly 400,000 people were sealed into the Warsaw Ghetto in 1940. The *Judenrat* and much of the population tended to rationalise what was happening. But some of the Zionist youth groups recognised the Nazis' intentions as early as March 1942 and called for the creation of a self-defence organisation but without success.[55] The Nazis started mass deportations to Treblinka in July 1942 in the so-called *Gross-Aktion Warschau*. By then over 100,000 had already died due to starvation, disease or random killings. With another 250,000 to 300,000 people transported, the political groups finally faced up to the need for a united armed response.

Finally at the end of October 1942 three political groupings—the Bund, the Labour Zionists and the communists—formed the Jewish Fighting Organisation (*Żydowska Organizacja Bojowa*, ZOB) under the command of the Labour Zionist Mordechai Anielewicz.

When a second wave of deportations commenced on 18 January 1943, ZOB members fought back. The subsequent four days saw the first street fighting in occupied Poland. Despite the almost complete lack of arms and resources, the ghetto fighters were able to force the Nazis to retreat and to limit the number of deportations.

Marek Edelman, a member of the Bund and the five-person command group of the ZOB, wrote:

> For the first time German plans were frustrated. For the first time the halo of omnipotence and invincibility was torn from the Germans' heads. For the first time the Jew in the street realized that it was possible to do something against the Germans' will and power... [It was] a psychological turning point.[56]

The ZOB then took effective control of the ghetto. With a very different approach to the typical *Judenrat*, they executed Jewish police, Nazi agents and spies and prepared for military resistance. They also oversaw all aspects of ghetto life including the publication of newspapers and taxing wealthy residents.

On 19 April the German forces tried to resume deportations with a view to finally liquidating the ghetto. At this point the ZOB had some 220 fighters armed with some handguns (many barely functional), grenades and molotov cocktails, a few rifles, two land mines and a submachine gun. Also part of the uprising, but not operating under the direction of the ZOB, was the Jewish Military Union (*Żydowski Związek Wojskowy*, ZZW) with approximately 500 fighters consisting of former Jewish officers of the Polish army plus right wing Zionists.[57] The ZZW had somewhat better weapons due to their links with the Polish Home Army (*Armia Krajowa*).Together both groups could gather only 750 fighters.[58]

The German side consisted of more than 2,000 soldiers with heavy weapons including artillery, mine throwers and machine guns. With their overwhelming military superiority they anticipated an action of only three days. But the Nazi commander General Stroop was forced to report after a week: "The resistance put up by the Jews and bandits could be broken only by relentlessly using all our force and energy by day and night".[59]

The stories of personal bravery are inspiring and heartbreaking. Edelman describes a young boy, Dawid Hochberg, blocking a narrow passageway. Once killed by the Germans his wedged in body took some time to remove, allowing the escape of fighters and civilians.[60] A number of captured fighters—especially the women—threw hidden grenades or fired concealed handguns after surrendering, killing themselves with their captors. Some Polish resistance members fought with the Jews inside the ghetto. Polish resistance groups also engaged the Nazis at six different locations outside the ghetto walls to help divert the German forces.

The Nazis had to fight from building to building. Defeating the uprising took six weeks and necessitated setting fire to the ghetto. As Edelman says, the insurgents "were beaten by the flames, not the Germans".[61] Organised resistance was over by the end of April but localised resistance continued until June. Many people hid in bunkers and were only forced out by smoke bombs.

Anielewicz noted in his last letter: "What took place exceeded all expectations. In our opposition to the Germans we did more than our strength allowed".[62] Even Goebbels (unintentionally) paid the resistance tribute: "The Jews have actually succeeded in making a defensive position of the ghetto... It shows what is to be expected of Jews when they are in possession of arms. Unfortunately some of their weapons were good German ones".[63]

The ghetto uprising was a military failure. But as Yitzhak Zuckerman, second in command of the ZOB, said:

> I don't think there is any need to analyse the uprising in military terms... [N]o one doubted how it was likely to turn out... The really important things were...in the force shown by Jewish youths...to rise up against their destroyers and determine what death they would choose: Treblinka or Uprising[64]

The uprising had an enormous impact on the Polish population as well as the Jews and intensified resistance throughout the country. Many of the other uprisings were directly or indirectly inspired by the ghetto insurgents.

"We should have raised them in the spirit of revenge"

When the Nazis set up the Warsaw *Judenrat* in August 1939 it was argued that at least one Bund member should participate and Shmuel Zygelboym reluctantly joined. However, the demands of the position soon came into conflict with his politics. When the Nazis attempted to set up the ghetto in Warsaw in October of that year, Zygelboym refused to help. Instead he addressed Jews gathered outside the organisation's headquarters, and told them not to cooperate but to remain in their houses and make the Nazis take them by force. This single call for resistance succeeded in having the order to establish the ghetto cancelled for several months.[65]

The leader of the Warsaw *Judenrat*, Adam Czerniaków (a general Zionist), behaved differently. He carried out Nazi instructions, including providing lists of people to be deported, even though he knew their fate. In this he was supported by the Jewish police. Marek Edelman comments about a *Judenrat* meeting in July 1942 in response to the German demand that all "non-productive" Jews be deported in the *Gross-Aktion Warschau*:

> Not a single councilman stopped to consider the basic question— whether the Jewish Council should undertake to carry out the order at all... There was no debate on the implications of the order, only on the... procedure for its execution... Thus the Germans made the Jewish Council itself condemn over 300,000 ghetto inhabitants to death.[66]

The role of the youth in the creation of a fighting organisation was central. Immediately following the Nazi invasion of Poland most of the top leaders of the Zionist organisations left the country to go into exile, leaving secondary leaders and the youth groups to lead their response. Similarly the Bund leadership largely departed, leaving their youth group *Tsukunft* to play a leading role in the party's underground activities.[67]

Unfortunately the remaining Bund leaders were reluctant to unite in an underground organisation with the Zionists. They rejected the call for unity in March 1942 and only came to an agreement in October. For virtually their entire history they had (rightly) opposed Zionism. But the situation faced by the population of the ghetto was beyond normal political conflicts. The Nazis planned to annihilate Jews of all political currents and military action required unity with anyone who was prepared to take up arms. It took the efforts of the youth group, in particular its leader Abrasha Blum, to convince the adults of the Bund to join in a united fighting organisation.[68]

The Zionists in the ghetto on the other hand were hamstrung by their politics in a different way. In the first period even the youth groups mainly engaged in communal activities. Emmanuel Ringelblum described how Anielewicz regretted the delays and failure to face up to the necessity of armed resistance and felt that they "had wasted three war years on cultural and educational work".

We had not understood that new side of Hitler that is emerging, Mordechai lamented. We should have trained the youth in the use of live and cold ammunition. We should have raised them in the spirit of revenge against the greatest enemy of the Jews, of all mankind, and of all times.[69]

Yitzhak Zuckerman, a founder of the ZOB and later a major historian of the Warsaw uprising, stated baldly: "The Jewish Fighting Organisation arose without the parties and against the wish of the parties".[70]

The failure of the ZOB to unite with the ZZW may also have weakened them, although they did fight together. Politically the ZZW were associated with the right wing Revisionist Zionists to whom the ZOB remained hostile. Their role was played down by the post-war Polish government and their actual contribution remains contentious.

Underground organisation, uprisings and partisans

In June 1942 the head of the Jewish Social Relief Organization in Biala Podlaska expressed the views of many when he angrily asked: "How much longer will we go as sheep to the slaughter? Why do we keep quiet? Why is there no call to escape to the forests? No call to resist?"[71]

There was never going to be a general call to resist. But in spite of the almost hopeless situation, Jews did fight back against the Nazis far more extensively than is currently recognised. They did not go as sheep to the slaughter.

The Warsaw Ghetto uprising is well known but it was not the only expression of resistance. There were underground resistance movements in approximately 100 ghettos in Nazi-occupied Eastern Europe (about a quarter of all ghettos) and uprisings occurred in five major ghettos and 45 smaller ones. In addition there were uprisings in three extermination camps and 18 forced labour camps. Some 20,000 to 30,000 Jewish partisans fought in approximately 30 Jewish partisan groups and 21 mixed groups while some 10,000 people survived in family camps in the forest.[72]

There can be no strict division between the various means of resistance. Ghetto underground organisations communicated with partisans and provided them with information or supplies; carried out non-military sabotage; helped POWs and escapees; distributed illegal information and money; forged documents; and published newspapers and proclamations. Individuals and illegal groups helped Jews to find the necessities of life in the ghettos, to escape and to find arms.

One feature of this fragmented and dangerous activity was the thousands of couriers who worked to overcome the isolation of the ghettos at great risk to themselves. Often they were women because they could pass as non-Jews more easily (Jewish men were all circumcised). Tema Schneiderman, a courier for the Jewish underground in Bialystok, Vilna and Warsaw, secretly delivered news and ammunition. Ania Rud, a former member of the Bialystok Ghetto underground, lived outside the ghetto as a White Russian and acted as a contact between couriers, the local underground and forest partisans. Marylka Rozycka, a member of the Communist Party in Lodz, was Jewish but looked like a Polish peasant. She maintained contacts between the Communist Party and the ghetto underground and later joined the partisans in the forest.[73]

Major efforts went into collecting information and recording events. Krakow activist Gusta Draenger was arrested after a grenade attack on a Nazi coffee shop. She recorded the history of the Krakow underground on toilet paper while in prison. This document still exists. Bund member Zalmen Frydrych met escapees near Treblinka and obtained information about the death camps.[74]

"We will not offer our heads to the butcher like sheep"—the Ghetto underground and uprisings

The underground in Bialystok (Poland) began in late 1941 with the establishment of groups to help Russian POWs, who received appalling treatment from the Nazis. The activists, the majority of whom were young, established contacts with Polish supporters and were able to smuggle in some weapons.

In late 1942 the Warsaw ZOB decided to organise armed resistance in the other key ghettos and sent Mordechai Tenenbaum (Josef Tamaroff) to Bialystok. Under his leadership all political factions including the Communists, Bundists, Labour Zionists and other Zionists united and started to prepare for an uprising.[75]

The Bialystok *Judenrat*, on the other hand, was dominated by older people. Although the Zionist chairman Efraim Barasz was aware of the mass murders and destruction of communities, he refused to cooperate with the underground, arguing that because the ghetto was "productive" the Germans would leave it alone.[76] When the *Judenrat* handed 6,000 Jews over to the Nazis in February 1943 some underground groups put up armed resistance, including 20 young men led by Edek Borak. Others resisted with acid, axes, knives and boiling water.[77] Afterwards people searched for informers who had led Nazis to hideouts. "When a cry of 'traitor' was heard, crowds rushed to the scene. They would tear and claw at the suspect, and lynch him on the spot".[78] May Day 1943 saw a strike among the forced labourers in the factories. Protest demonstrations or absence from work were not possible. But the workers stood idle near their inactive machines, turning them on when they saw a German approaching and off the moment the German left.[79]

Strategically the underground activists in the ghettos faced a terrible dilemma. An armed uprising could not hope to achieve anything if it was isolated; it would require the support of a significant section of ghetto inhabitants. But the ghettos were full of children, old people and other non-combatants and arms were difficult to come by. The other option was escape, usually with an intention of joining the partisans. While this had a better chance of success for individuals or small groups, it meant leaving the rest of the population to its fate.

The situation in Bialystok illustrates the predicament. The underground met on the evening of 27 February 1943, believing the Germans planned to attempt liquidation of the ghetto the next day. Minutes of this meeting have survived. The leader Mordecai Tenenbaum commented: "It's a good thing that at least the mood is good. Unfortunately, the meeting won't be very cheerful... We must decide today what to do tomorrow". He went on:

> We can do two things: decide that when the first Jew is taken away from Bialystok now, we start our counter-Aktion... It is not impossible that after we have completed our task someone may by chance still be alive... We can also decide to get out into the forest... We must decide for ourselves now. Our daddies will not take care of us. This is an orphanage.[80]

In fact liquidation did not occur until later in the year. The planned attack and mass escape into the forest failed. The underground staged a heroic ten-day uprising from 16 August 1943 but having failed to previously win the support of the ghetto population it was isolated.

Vilna (Lithuania) was an important Jewish cultural centre. The underground United Partisan Organisation (Fareynikte Partizaner Organizatsye, FPO) was formed on 1 January 1942 when Abba Kovner spoke at a clandestine public meeting held in the soup kitchen. Also known as "The Avengers" they carried out many sabotage operations. In their first action Vitka Kempner and two companions blew up a Nazi military transport carrying 200 soldiers on the outskirts of the town.[81] Abba Kovner recorded:

Lithuanians did not do it, nor Poles, nor Russians. A Jewish woman did it, a woman who, after she did this, had no base to return to. She had to walk three days and nights with wounded legs and feet. She had to go back to the ghetto. Were she to have been captured, the whole ghetto might have been held responsible.[82]

The action was memorialised in a famous song by Hirsh Glik, *Still the Night Was Full of Starlight*.[83] Vitka became one of Kovner's chief lieutenants and was later involved in many acts of resistance. She died in February 2012.

Eighteen months later when the liquidation of the ghetto was imminent, the FPO issued a manifesto inspired by the Warsaw Ghetto uprising and called on the remaining Jews to resist deportation. It declared: "We will not offer our heads to the butcher like sheep. Jews defend yourselves with arms... Active resistance alone can save our lives and our honour".[84]

But the *Judenrat* opposed the call and refused cooperation, arguing that armed resistance would lead to destruction of the ghetto population. When the Nazis liquidated the ghetto virtually all of its inhabitants went to their deaths in forced labour camps, Sobibor death camp or were murdered directly. A few hundred members of the underground organisation including Kovner escaped to become partisans in the forest.[85]

In Kovno (Kaunus, central Lithuania) a large underground of 600 members was led by Chaim Yelin, a Jewish Communist who was able to unite the Communists and Zionist youth groups.[86] The *Judenrat* actively supported the underground as did a number of the ghetto's Jewish police. Among the Poles who helped the Jewish underground in Kovno was Dr Kutorghene. She explained why she risked her life in this way:

You gave me courage, you gave a new lease of life, encouraged me. I feel I am stronger when I am with you and do not want you to go even though we both risk our lives and lives of our family members...[87]

Ultimately there was no uprising but some 500 ghetto fighters escaped to join Jewish partisan groups. When the ghetto was liquidated the population refused to present themselves for deportation following an appeal from the underground. Many people went into hiding and hid as long as possible although the Nazis set the ghetto on fire.

Of the smaller ghettos Lachva (Belarus) was among the first to show resistance as a united community in August 1942, possibly because the *Judenrat* supported the underground.[88] The uprising started during the liquidation of the ghetto. People had no guns so they set fire to the ghetto and attacked the Nazis with axes, knives, iron bars, pitchforks and clubs:

> The fire and smoke, along with the spontaneous Jewish attack, created panic among the Germans. The Jews took the opportunity to break through the ghetto fences. Under heavy fire, hundreds of Jews ran towards the swamps in the forest. 600 people escaped...including elderly people, women and children.[89]

Approximately 150 people made it to the swamps and later joined the partisans.

"Culture of solidarity between Jews and non-Jews"—Minsk

Minsk deserves attention as the location of one of the most successful of the underground organisations.[90]

Minsk, in present day Belarus, had been part of the Soviet Union before the war. Their experience during the war was perhaps unique in that Jews and non-Jews were united in one communist-led underground organisation across the ghetto and the main city. Historian Barbara Epstein emphasises the "culture of solidarity between Jews and non-Jews" within the underground organisation but also points to personally based support and interaction outside the formal underground organisation.[91]

Formed in late 1941, the underground ran a clandestine press and smuggled Jewish children out of the ghetto to hide them in other parts of the city. Jews and non-Jews both engaged in sabotage within Nazi factories. For instance, shoemakers put nails into shoes to make them unwearable and tailors sewed left arms into right armholes of coats and vice versa.

Participation in the underground was very dangerous. One well known example is the case of Masha Bruskina, a 17-year-old Jewish member of a communist underground group located outside the ghetto who helped wounded Soviet POWs. Captured in October 1941, she was hanged with two other non-Jewish members of underground Krill Trus and Volodya Sherbateyvich, the first public execution of resisters.

Rather than armed uprising, the Minsk underground focused on flight, which their circumstances particularly favoured. A barbed wire fence (rather than the high wall found in other ghettos) and relatively lenient guards made access to the nearby dense and impenetrable forest dangerous but possible. A major factor was also the support from the first two *Judenräte* which were more closely intertwined with the underground than elsewhere. The courageous stand of the *Judenrat* members no doubt contributed very significantly to the high number of escapes but they paid a high price once exposed.

Led by child guides and helped by non-Jewish contacts, roughly 10,000 Jews made their way into the forests; most of them survived the war. This was the most successful ghetto resistance in terms of numbers saved and deserves to be as widely recognised as Warsaw Ghetto uprising.

The Minsk underground supported and sent supplies to the partisans and also carried out successful sabotage within the town. A letter in a German newspaper in June 1943 describes the situation:

> Partisans are everywhere, even in the city of Minsk. In the last months many Germans have been killed in the streets. You can't travel along the Vilna-Minsk highway. You can move in the direction of Baranovichi only escorted by tanks...a mine was planted in the city theatre...as a result more than 30 people were killed and about 100 were wounded. Then they blew up an electric power station and the steam tank at the dairy plant.[92]

The soldiers' cinema and hostel, a bakery and many vehicles were also targeted, many successfully.

The story of the fate of the surviving underground members after the war is a sorry one. Not only were they not treated as heroes by the Russian regime, but they were arrested and many spent years in prison or keeping their heads down.[93]

"Today partisans are going to beat the enemy"[94]

Partisan units were a feature of the northern forest area. The partisan groups were very disparate but Soviet POWs who had escaped from the horrendous Nazi POW camps figured large. In the early days the units tended to be anarchic, loose and disorganised and we should not romanticise the partisan movement. As Nehama Tec says: "few forest dwellers resembled the idealised image of the fearless, heroic fighter".[95] The life of a partisan was extremely difficult and conditions "inhuman".[96] Forest conditions where dirt, hunger, exhaustion, danger and fear were the daily experience naturally bred suspicion, hierarchy, internal conflict—and anti-Semitism. "In these jungle-like forests, a jungle-like culture emerged".[97]

Many partisans in Belarus were communists and later the units became more organised as Stalin implemented a programme of control over them with an eye on post-war Poland.[98] The partisan groups would very often only accept young men with arms whereas fleeing Jews often arrived without weapons or skills. Nonetheless approximately 20,000 to 30,000 Jews fought in about 30 Jewish partisan groups and 21 mixed groups; an estimated 80 percent died.[99]

In 1944 more than 159 Jewish partisans were active in the Parczew forest north of Lublin (Poland). They cooperated with the Soviet partisans in a number of engagements against the Nazis including the takeover of the city of Parczew in April 1994.[100] However, not all the partisans were Soviet controlled. When "The Avengers" from Vilna moved into the forest after the liquidation of the town, they destroyed the town power plant and the waterworks. In honour of International Women's Day, Gertie Boyarski and a friend—both in their teens—demolished a wooden bridge used by the Nazis.[101]

The dilemma of the ghettos also applied in the partisan setting. What were the many people who fled the ghettos but unarmed and unable to be fighters to do?

About 10,000 Jews survived in family camps which provided shelter and support for non-fighting people as well as armed partisans. The most famous, Bielski Otriad, focused on rescuing Jews and accepted anyone of any sex or age who could reach them.[102] Another non-military group was, astonishingly, a musical troupe based near the village of Sloboda in Belarus. The group of 25 included three Jews—Chana Pozner, her father Mordechai Pozner and Yehiel Borgin—and provided entertainment for the partisan units.[103]

"The crematorium was burning against a dark sky".

The horrors of life in concentration camps are notorious and the degradation and misery led to bitter and corrupt behaviour. In her diary Hanna Levy-Hass, a communist and inmate of Bergen-Belsen, describes her pain at the collaboration and servitude. But there were also many local and individual instances of resistance. Levy-Hass also describes how she represented 120 women who organised to demand more equitable food distribution.[104]

Underground organisations arose in many camps and there were uprisings in three of the six extermination camps and 18 work camps.

The name of Auschwitz is virtually synonymous with death camp. It was in fact much more than that. Auschwitz-Birkenau, situated near the Polish town of Oswiecim in south west Poland, consisted of three main sections including transit camps, labour camps, extermination ovens and 45 satellite camps.[105]

Resistance occurred in many areas at Auschwitz. The Union Factory (*Weichsel-Union-Metallwerke*), which was owned by Krupp, employed forced labourers who manufactured a range of explosives and armaments. Krupp had complete control over the production while punishment was "inflicted by the SS at Krupp's request". Workers, many of whom were Jews, carried out sabotage and participated in the uprising.[106]

The underground organisation at Auschwitz included Polish political prisoners, forced labourers and Jews from the *Sonderkommando*, the group responsible for dealing with the remains from the crematorium. The Auschwitz underground astonishingly published a newspaper and even transmitted by radio direct to London.[107] The group planned a revolt and prepared weapons using gunpowder smuggled out of the Union Factory by women forced labourers such as Rosa Robota.[108] Having heard that the *Sonderkommando* was about to be liquidated, on 7 October 1944 camp inmates attacked the guards with axes and knives while the SS responded with machine guns. The *Sonderkommando* members then blew up crematorium IV with grenades made from smuggled dynamite.[109]

> In no time the entire guard force of the camp was mobilised against the rebels. Bullets were flying all over the place. SS with dogs were chasing the...rebels, many of whom fell while trying to escape... When they realised that they had no chance of survival, they set the forest on fire... As the day was coming to an end Auschwitz was surrounded by guards and fires. The crematorium was burning against a dark sky, as were small forests on opposite sides of the camp. The ground was covered with dead bodies of the members of the *Sonderkommando*.[110]

A total of 250 prisoners died during the uprising and 200 were later shot. None escaped. Perhaps two or three Nazis died with approximately 12 wounded. Rosa Robota and three other women were hanged in Auschwitz the following January only three weeks before the camp was liberated by the Soviets. After the war the Krupp owned Union Factory received 2.5 million marks as reparation for the factory they lost at Auschwitz. The forced labourers received nothing; the allies agreed to postpone claims. The German Supreme Court barred claims from forced labourers. Finally in 1993 a group of 22 survivors sued the former factory, with back pay being awarded in 1997 to one of them only. The court determined that the others were sufficiently compensated by governmental reparations.[111]

The uprising in Sobibor concentration camp in eastern Poland was more successful. The underground leadership consisted of a Jew, Leon Feldhandler, and a Soviet POW, Sasha Pechersky. Having learned about the Warsaw Ghetto uprising from deportees from that city, they made their own plans. On 14 October 1943 the group lured SS officers into the storehouses and attacked them with axes and knives, killing 11 including the camp commander. The rebels then seized weapons and ammunition and set fire to the camp. Tomasz (Toivi) Blatt describes what followed:

> During the revolt prisoners streamed to one of the holes cut in the barbed-wire fence. They weren't about to wait in line; there were machine guns shooting at us. They climbed on the fence and just as I was half way through, it collapsed, trapping me underneath. This saved me...[as the] first ones through hit mines. When most were through, I slid out of my coat, which was hooked on the fence, and ran till I reached the forest.[112]

Ultimately 300 of the total of 600 prisoners escaped, of whom nearly 200 avoided recapture; some were hidden from the Nazis by Poles.[113]

The underground at Treblinka (north east Poland) was organised by a former Jewish captain of the Polish Army, Dr Julian Chorążycki. After months of preparations on 2 August 1943 they stole arms from a warehouse, killed the guards, set the camp on fire and destroyed the extermination area. They then helped prisoners to escape into the forest. All resistance leaders were killed as the Germans retaliated. Out of 1,500 prisoners in the camp, approximately 600 escaped, the majority of whom were recaptured. Some of the escapees were helped by the Polish Home Army or by Polish villagers.[114]

Despite the losses, these two uprisings resulted in the closure of the camps which must be regarded as an achievement.[115]

"None of us would have survived [without] help"[116]

Much is made of Polish collusion with the Nazi extermination of Jews. Yet even the post-war Israeli War Crimes Commission could only identify 7,000 collaborators out of a population of over 20 million ethnic Poles.[117]

Poland had the most draconian penalties in occupied Europe for helping Jews in any way. In places like France and Germany people attempting to help Jews certainly faced severe consequences. But in Poland not only the person but their whole family would be executed. Up to 50,000 Poles were executed for aiding Jews and thousands more were arrested and sent to labour or concentration camps.[118]

At the same time Poles were themselves subject to genocidal attacks from the Nazis. For Hitler all Poles were "more like animals than human beings" and ethnic cleansing known as "housecleaning" displaced 900,000 people. Over 3 million non-Jewish Poles died. The Nazi food rationing allowed 2,613 calories for Germans but 669 for Poles—barely above that allowed for Jews.[119]

Yet even in these conditions people did help Jews. It came in many forms and from both individuals and groups. Poland was the only country in occupied Europe with a secret organisation dedicated to helping Jews: the Council to Aid Jews (Rada Pomocy Żydom) known as Zegota which helped approximately half of the Polish Jews who survived the war (thus over 50,000).[120]

Zegota was founded in September 1942 by Zofia Kossak-Szczucka, a Catholic activist, and Wanda Krahelska-Filipowicz ("Alinka") who was a socialist. Members came from many of the left wing organisations which had opposed anti-Semitism in the 1930s, including the Polish Socialist Party, the Peasant Party and the Bund. But there were also Catholic activists and Polish nationalists, students, the scout association, the writers' union, medical and social workers and activists in the Polish underground.

The first chairman, Julian Grobelny, had actively helped Jews before he joined Zegota and headed an underground cell composed mainly of Socialist friends of the Bund. Because of his links to doctors and medical workers he was able to hide people in quarantine. And due to his long involvement in trade unions, in particular his contacts with railway workers, he was able to arrange transport for Jews out of Warsaw.

Zegota's headquarters was the home of a Polish Socialist (Eugenia Wasowska) who had worked closely with the Bund. The organisation held "office hours" twice each week at which time couriers went in and out. Despite the enormous number of people who knew its location, the headquarters were never raided by the Germans. One "branch office" was a fruit and vegetable kiosk operated by Ewa Brzuska, an old woman known to everybody as "Babcia" (Granny). Babcia hid papers and money under the sauerkraut and pickle barrels and always had sacks of potatoes ready to hide Jewish children.

The best known Zegota activist is Irene Sendler, head of the children's division. A social worker and a socialist, she grew up with close links to the Jewish community and could speak Yiddish. Sendler had protested against anti-Semitism in the 1930s: she deliberately sat with Jews in segregated university lecture halls and nearly got expelled. Irene Sendler saved 2,500 Jewish children by smuggling them out of the Warsaw

Ghetto, providing them with false documents and sheltering them in individual and group children's homes outside the ghetto.[121]

Zegota was not the only support group. What Gunnar Paulsson called a "secret city" operated in Warsaw as between 70,000 and 90,000 people helped an estimated 28,000 Jews to live outside the ghetto.[122]

The divided stand on anti-Semitism of pre-war political currents continued during the war. So while the right wing press contained anti-Semitic diatribes, the Polish Socialist Party and other left wing newspapers published information about atrocities and death camps, as did the organ of the Peasant Movement and those of the Catholic underground groups.[123] Importantly, the Polish Underground State took a stand against anti-Semitism. They proclaimed laws against anti-Semitism and executed perpetrators, with details published in their underground newspapers. In early 1943 the Underground State's official publication wrote that they viewed the murder of Jews with shock and horror and stated that Poles had a duty to help Jews, despite the death penalty awaiting any caught doing so.[124] One major contribution of the Polish underground was its pivotal role in conveying news of Nazi extermination policy to the West.[125]

Should the Poles have done more?

We often hear people say that the Poles or other non-Jewish nationalities should have or could have done more to help the Jews. For instance, historian Barbara Epstein:

> If non-Jewish organisations with substantial influence and resources had done what they could to help the Jews, more Jews would have escaped and survived.[126]

But Epstein herself points out that most Jews in Eastern Europe died when "the Germans were at the height of their power and when they were engaged in killing not only Jews but also Poles, Byelorussians, Ukrainians, and others".[127]

On this topic Stewart Steven concludes: "Maybe Poland could have done more for its Jewish population, but then so could every country of occupied Europe. The record shows that the Poles did more than most".[128]

Gunnar S Paulsson reviewed a large range of available material, and concluded that despite the much harsher conditions, Warsaw's Polish residents managed to support and conceal a similar percentage of Jews as residents of cities in safer, supposedly less anti-Semitic countries of Western Europe.[129] The official count of Polish Righteous (people recorded at the Yad Vashem Holocaust Centre in Israel as having helped Jews) is 6,266. This is the highest count for any country. Everyone acknowledges that the list is incomplete and no one doubts more should be officially recognised. Any estimate is fraught with difficulties.[130] But as Martin Gilbert says: "Poles who risked their own lives to save the Jews were indeed the exception. But they could be found throughout Poland, in every town and village".[131]

Paulsson suggests the following:

> How many people in Poland rescued Jews? Of those that meet Yad Vashem's criteria—perhaps 100,000. Of those that offered minor forms of help—perhaps two or three times as many. Of those who were passively protective—undoubtedly the majority of the population.[132]

Indisputably, anti-Semitism was rife in Poland and throughout the Nazi occupied areas and many non-Jews thought only to save themselves, or denounced and betrayed Jews. This is an undeniable feature of the Second World War. But there were anti-Semites and betrayals in all countries and populations. Jews were even victims of denunciations and betrayal from within their own community. The Poles should not be singled out as an inherently anti-Semitic nationality.

On the contrary. The Jews who created underground organisations, who carried out uprisings, who escaped from the ghettos and concentration camps or who survived the war in hiding did so overwhelmingly with the help of non-Jews. Jewish survival and resistance went hand in glove with resistance and help from non-Jews.

"Let this song go like a signal through the years"[133]

We have seen that before and during the war the Allies showed little concern about the fate of the Jews. This continued in the aftermath. At the Nuremberg Trials Jews were not even accorded the status of a distinct category.[134]

Arnold Paucker, historian of Jewish resistance in Germany, comments on the fact that the historiography of the resistance in general, and Jews in particular, was a neglected subject prior to 1970.[135] He traces this to the influence of the Cold War environment:

> The communist influence on the resistance was simply hard for many to stomach. Indeed, on this point we encounter a whole range of taboos and considerable self-censorship on the part of historians.[136]

In the Eastern Bloc, on the other hand, Soviet policy (and subsequently the policy of the post-war Polish regime) was to emphasise the role of their own citizens without mentioning the specific experiences of Jews. A prime example is the report on the massacre of nearly 34,000 Jews at Babi Yar in the Ukraine in 1941. In the draft report of 25 December 1943 we see this text:

> The Hitlerist bandits committed mass murder of the Jewish population. They announced that on September 29, 1941, all the Jews were required to arrive to the corner of Melnikov and Dokterev streets and bring their documents, money and valuables. The butchers marched them to Babi Yar, took away their belongings, then shot them.

The censored version, which appeared in February 1944, simply stated:

> The Hitlerist bandits brought thousands of civilians to the corner of Melnikov and Dokterev streets. The butchers marched them to Babi Yar, took away their belongings, then shot them.[137]

One reason why the role of the Poles in helping Jews is little known is because much of the information was suppressed by the post-war Soviet-backed regime.[138]

Jewish historians also participated in the neglect of the subject of resistance and perpetuated the myth of "going like a sheep to the slaughter". According to Arnold Paucker, Bruno Bettelheim "wrote on a number of occasions that German Jews had no backbone and persisted in a passive ghetto mentality". And Raul Hilberg, a major historian of the Holocaust, "constantly emphasised that, in the face of mass extermination, resistance [was] so minimal as to be practically insignificant".[139]

This type of argument serves Zionism very well. Zionism argues that Jews are always outsiders and anti-Semitism can never be defeated. Theodore Herzl, the founder of Zionism, wrote in 1895 that he "recognised the emptiness and futility of efforts to 'combat anti-Semitism.'"[140] In 1925 Jacob Klatzkin, the co-editor of the *Encyclopedia Judaica*, wrote:

> If we do not admit the rightfulness of anti-Semitism, we deny the rightfulness of our own nationalism... Instead of establishing societies for defence against the anti-Semites, who want to reduce our rights, we should establish societies for defence against our friends who desire to defend our rights.[141]

This kind of attitude underlay their failure to play any significant role in the fight against anti-Semitism in Poland in the 1930s. "Revisionist" (right wing) Zionists were planning a military invasion of Palestine and actually trained their youth group in the use of weapons. But they did not use their skills to join in the self-defence actions led by the Bund against attacks by anti-Semites. As one Revisionist leader put it:

> It is absolutely correct to say that only the Bund waged an organised fight against the anti-Semites. We did not consider we had to fight in Poland. We believed the way to ease the situation was to take the Jews out of Poland.[142]

But there is no way that Palestine could ever have been a solution for the poverty, oppression and anti-Semitism faced by the millions of European Jews. The Zionists themselves knew this and knew that their focus on Palestine meant leaving the bulk of the population to their fate. In fact they deemed the bulk of the European Jewish population as too tainted and not worth saving. Chaim Weizmann, leader of the World Zionist Organisation in the inter-war years, said in 1937:

> The old ones will pass; they will bear their fate, or they will not. They were dust, economic and moral dust, in a cruel world... Two millions, and perhaps less...only a remnant shall survive. We have to accept it.[143]

Many Zionist functionaries who survived persisted in later years in their stand against underground activities, condemning them as "a series of childish and irresponsible antics that had achieved nothing other than to harm and further imperil the lives of...a community of hostages".[144] However, one leading Zionist, Nahum Goldman, did change his mind after the war:

> But in this context success was irrelevant. What matters in a situation of this sort is a people's moral stance, its readiness to fight back instead of helplessly allowing itself to be massacred. We did not stand the test.[145]

In Bialystok and many other ghettos Zionist youth did join and even provide leadership in the underground. Their actions are to be praised. But their actions were undertaken in spite of Zionist ideology and their underground struggle had to be conducted mostly in opposition to the position taken by leading Zionists and the *Judenräte*. The Zionist youth groups in the ghettos separated themselves from adult organisations because of their unwillingness to follow their "cautious and conciliatory approach".[146]

Lenni Brenner makes a critical point about Mordechai Anielewicz, the Zionist leader of the Warsaw Ghetto uprising:

Mordechai Anielewicz's apotheosis to historical immortality is entirely justified, and no criticism of his strategy should be construed as attempting to detract from the lustre of his name ... However, the martyrdom of the 24-year-old Anielewicz can never absolve the Zionist movement of its pre-war failure to fight anti-Semitism—in Germany or in Poland—when there was still time.[147]

The real argument of the Zionists is not that resistance *in this case* was futile. Resistance was never part of their political agenda. As Brenner puts it:

Those Jews who had resisted pre-war Polish anti-Semitism were the first to resist the Nazis. Those who had done nothing continued to do nothing.[148]

It also suits Zionist ideology to emphasise that the Jews were on their own. Many historians, Jewish and others, place great weight on how isolated and without help the Jews were. And no doubt this is how it must have felt to many. But the fact is that, aside from the small number who were able to pass themselves off as non-Jewish, almost all who did survive in Eastern Europe did so because they received help.

Barbara Epstein suggests the reason the Minsk experience has received little recognition may be due to fact that the Warsaw Ghetto story, which emphasises Jews fighting virtually alone, suits Zionist myth making. The cooperation between Jews and non-Jews in Minsk is less suited to this:

The forest/partisan model of resistance was predicated on the view that Jews and non-Jews had a common interest in fighting the Nazis, and it involved fostering such alliances.[149]

The problem is not that this form of resistance [military uprisings] has been so extensively examined, but that a memory of the Holocaust has been constructed in which other forms of resistance barely exist.[150]

Epstein comments that: "Every political current...regarded armed struggle...as more important than saving lives" and concludes that had more underground organisation placed a higher value on escape, more Jews would have been saved.[151] Saving lives depended more on external help than did a heroic but doomed uprising.

Zionists in general and Israel in particular have sought to appropriate the Warsaw Ghetto uprising to their own political purposes to the extent of casting the establishment of the Jewish state as an extension of the uprising.[152] Marek Edelman, the only surviving member of the ZOB leadership, repudiated this. In a 2002 letter of solidarity to the

Palestinians he insisted they were the real modern inheritors of the heroic Warsaw struggle.[153]

Not only were the Jews supposedly completely alone—they were also supposedly surrounded by an immense sea of anti-Jewish hostility. There is no dispute that anti-Semitism was a significant and major trend in Poland and the region already before the war and that groups from the local populations joined with the Nazis in committing atrocities. We have seen, however, the class nature of pre-war anti-Semitism. Furthermore in the conditions of war personal anti-Semitism was not necessarily determinant. Zofia Kossak-Szczucka, who was one of the instigators of Zegota, had anti-Semitic views which she never repudiated. She nonetheless worked untiringly to assist Jews. The leader of the Warsaw Uprising in 1944, General Bor-Komorowski, also had anti-Semitic tendencies. Nonetheless, the uprising released Jewish prisoners from Gesiowska concentration camp. The Polish Home Army and Underground State included people of all political persuasions including anti-Semites.[154] But their formal position leaves no doubt. Operating underground, they enacted laws against anti-Semitism and executed perpetrators.

There remains the question of why the Warsaw Ghetto was the only large ghetto in which not only unity of the political factions was achieved but also the support of the bulk of the population. This may be partly due to the fact that the ZOB ran the ghetto for three months before the uprising and therefore had a little time in which to win over the population. Furthermore, by this time, most of the children and older people had gone from the ghetto. Another pointer comes from Vladka Meed, a participant in the uprising:

> Jewish armed resistance...when it came, did not spring from a sudden impulse; it was not an act of personal courage on the part of a few individuals or organised groups: it was the culmination of Jewish defiance, defiance that had existed from the advent of the ghetto.[155]

In fact, defiance pre-dated the advent of the ghetto. We saw how during the 1930s the fight against the rising tide of anti-Semitism had involved Jews and non-Jews in mass struggle. This occurred in many cities and towns throughout Poland but was centred in Warsaw. The alliances that were forged at that time continued through the Nazi occupation and underlay much of the network of help and support that the ghetto inhabitants received. The population who rose up in April 1943 had been mobilising on the streets only a few years earlier in 1938. The memory must still have been there.

Jews did not go simply as sheep to the slaughter. They fought back against overwhelming odds and in the face of mass extermination. And they did not do this alone.

Let Hersh Glik's song, with which I began, continue to be an inspiration to all of us.

We'll have the morning sun to set our day aglow,
And all our yesterdays shall vanish with the foe,
And if the time is long before the sun appears,
Then let this song go like a signal through the years.[156]

NOTES

1   Hersh Glik, the Jewish folk poet and resistance fighter from Vilna, was a Labour Zionist. Inspired by a partisan battle and the Warsaw Ghetto uprising, this song has been widely sung ever since. The phrase "We are here!" (*"Mir zaynen do!"*) also appears in the work of Shmerke Kaczerginski (see note 93) and stresses the idea of Jewish endurance often in a spirit of rebelliousness and defiance. Shirli Gilbert, *Music in the Holocaust: Confronting Life in the Nazi Ghettos and Camps* (Clarendon, 2005), p73, ht. Below is the most popular English version. I accessed it at Australian Memories of the Holocaust website www. holocaust.com.au/mm/j_song.htm

Zog nit keynmol (Never Say):

Never say there is only death for you.
Leaden skies may be concealing days of blue—
Because the hour we have hungered for is near;
Beneath our tread the earth shall tremble: We are here!

From land of palm-tree to the far-off land of snow,
We shall be coming with our torment and our woe.
And everywhere our blood has sunk into the earth.
Shall our bravery, our vigour blossom forth!

We'll have the morning sun to set our day aglow,
And all our yesterdays shall vanish with the foe,
And if the time is long before the sun appears,
Then let this song go like a signal through the years.

This song was written with our blood and not with lead;
It's not a song that birds sing overhead
It was a people, among toppling barricades,
That sang this song of ours with pistols and grenades.

So never say that there is only death for you.
Leaden skies may be concealing days of blue—
Yet the hour we have hungered for is near;
Beneath our tread the earth shall tremble: We are here!

2   A summary of this myth and its development can be found in Richard Middleton-Kaplan, "The myth of Jewish passivity" in Patrick Henry, *Jewish Resistance Against the Nazis* (Catholic University of America, 2014), p3.

3   Henri Michel, *The Shadow War: Resistance in Europe 1939-45* (Andre Deutsch, 1972), p177.

4   Most Jews of the Russian Empire were restricted to an area of about 20 percent of the territory of European Russia that included much of present day Lithuania, Belarus, Poland and Ukraine. Known and the Pale of Settlement; this ended only with the Russian Revolution in 1917.

5   This was partly because the Jewish workers did not work on Saturdays (the Jewish Sabbath) but also because they were more trade union orientated. Celia Heller, *On the Edge of Destruction: Jews of Poland Between the Two World Wars* (Wayne State University Press, 1980), p262. Adam Teller, "Economic Life", *YIVO Encyclopaedia of Jews in Eastern Europe*, www.yivoencyclopedia.org/article.aspx/Economic_Life.

6   Although membership figures for Poland are not available, electorally they were second to the Zionists. Gershon Bacon, "Agudas Yisroel", *YIVO Encyclopaedia of Jews in Eastern Europe*, www.yivoencyclopedia.org/article.aspx/Agudas_Yisroel.

7   The General Jewish Labour League of Lithuania, Poland and Russia (*Algemeyner Yidisher Arbeter Bund in Lite, Poyln un Rusland*) founded in 1897 was a socialist organisation based in the Jewish working class in countries within the Russian Empire. Generally just called the

Bund (Yiddish for "league"), their aim was a united Jewish socialist organisation allied with socialists of other national groupings. They played a major role in the early trade union formation among Jews.

8   Due to the extreme anti-Semitism of the Tsarist regime. Lenni Brenner, *Zionism in the Age of the Dictators* (On Our Own Authority! Publishing, 2014), p25.

9   Theodore Herzl, "The Jewish State", in Jackson Spielvogel (ed) *Western Civilization: Since 1300 Alternate Volume C* (Engage Learning, 2011), p754. Accessed online at books.google. com.au/books?id=IYeUtjFBaggC&pg=PT487&lpg=PT487&dq=%22an+outpost+of+ci vilization+as+opposed+to+barbarism%22&source=bl&ots=4M-8T1M38p&sig=_WNa_ M05906gJkrs5R6h8tO_HUU&hl=en&sa=X&ei=R_OtVIT1OKO5mwXxy4CQAg&ve d=0CCIQ6AEwAQ#v=onepage&q=%22an%20outpost%20of%20civilization%20as%20 opposed%20to%20barbarism%22&f=false.

10 Hilary Rubenstein, *The Jews in Australia 1788-1845*, vol 1 (Heinemann, 1991), p171.

11 Nigel Jones, "Story of a Secret State by Jan Karski: Review", *The Telegraph*, 4 May 2011; US Holocaust Memorial Museum; "Claude Lanzmann interview with Jan Karski", Claude Lanzmann, 4 May 2011; Stephen Spielberg Film and Video Archive, www.ushmm.org/ online/film/display/detail.php?file_num=4739.

12 Jan Karski, personal communication to Nehama Tec, December 1999, cited in Nehama Tec, *Resilience and Courage: Women, Men and the Holocaust* (Yale University Press, 2003), p262.

13 Cited in Peter Novick, *The Holocaust in American Life* (Haughton Mifflin, 2000), p578.

14 Louise London, *Whitehall and the Jews 1933-48: British Immigration Policy and the Holocaust* (Cambridge University Press, 2000), p1.

15 Laqueur actually argues that not only was no action taken but the information was actively suppressed. Walter Laqueur, *The Terrible Secret: Suppression of the Truth about Hitler's "Final Solution"* (Penguin, 1982), p202.

16 Richard Breitman, Norman Goda, Timothy Naftali and Robert Wolfe, *US Intelligence and the Nazis* (Cambridge University Press, 2005), p37.

17 Michael Neufeld, "Introduction" in *Bombing Auschwitz: Should the Allies Have Attempted it?* (St Martin's Press, 2000), p9.

18 Cited in Michael Bar-Zohar, *The Armed Prophet: A Biography of Ben-Gurion* (Arthur Barker, 1967), p49.

19 David Rosenthal, "Chaim Arlosoroff 40 Years Later", *Jewish Frontier*, August 1974, p23, cited in Brenner, 2014, p84.

20 "Shtetl" is the word for the small towns where many Jews lived.

21 Mordechai Gebirtig was born in Crakow in 1877 and murdered by the Nazis in June 1942. A member of both the Polish Socialist Party and the Bund, he wrote numerous songs and poems which were and remain highly popular in Jewish communities. It is false to think that in this song Gebirtig somehow predicted the Holocaust. It is clearly a call to fight against present dangers. The following translation is modified somewhat by Rachel Sztanski and myself from the version at the United States Holocaust Museum website www.ushmm.org/ wlc/en/media_so.php?MediaId=2621

It burns! Brothers, it burns!
Oh, our poor shtetl, brothers, burns!
Evil winds are fanning the wild flames
And furiously tearing,
Destroying and scattering everything.
All around, all is burning

(Refrain) And you just stand there staring
With your folded hands...
And you just stand there staring
While our shtetl burns.
It burns! Brothers, it burns!

Oh, our poor shtetl, brothers, burns!
Already tongues of fire
Have surrounded all our houses,
And the evil winds are howling—
All around us burns!

It burns! Brothers, it burns!
Oh, God forbid the moment,
That our shtetl, with us in it,
Turns to ashes in the flames,
So all remains, as after battle,
Will be bare black walls!

It burns! Brothers, it burns!
And help can only be from you alone!
If our shtetl is dear to you,
Grab the buckets, douse the fire!
Douse it with your own blood
Show us that you can!

(Final refrain) Don't just stand there staring
With your folded arms
Brothers, douse the fire!
our shtetl burns!

22 Cited in Heller, 1980, p282.
23 Cited in Heller, 1980, p288.
24 Leonard Rowe, "Jewish Self Defense. A Response to Violence", in Joshua A Fishman (ed), *Studies on Polish Jewry 1919-1939* (YIVO Institute, 1974), p106, cited in Heller, 1980, p290.
25 Leonard Rowe, 1974, p123, cited in Brenner, 1980, p217.
26 Cited in Heller, 1980, p286.
27 Brenner, 2014, p217.
28 Jacob Lestchinsky, "Night over Poland", *Jewish Frontier* (July 1936), pp11-12. Cited in Brenner, 2014, p218.
29 Brenner, 2014, p218.
30 Alexander Erlich et al, Solidarnosc, Polish Society and the Jews, p13, cited in Brenner, 2014, p219.
31 Emmanuel Ringelblum, *Polish-Jewish Relations During the Second World War* (Northwest University Press, 1992), pp199, 203.
32 Cited in Deborah Dwork and Robert van Pelt, *Holocaust: A History* (John Murray, 2002), p243.
33 Marek Edelman, *The Ghetto Fights: Warsaw 1941-43* (Bookmarks, 1990), pp36-37.
34 A ghetto inhabitant commented that the police were "already known for their terrible corruption, but reached the apogee of depravity at the time of the deportation". Antony Polonsky (ed), *A Cup of Tears: A Diary of the Warsw Ghetto by Abraham Lewin* (Blackwell, 1988), p288 note 159, cited in John Rose, introduction to Edelman, 1990, p22.
35 Cited in Dwork, 2002, p246.
36 Chaim Kaplan, *Scroll of Agony: The Warsaw Diary of Chaim A Kaplan* (Collier Books, 1973), p225. Cited in Dwork, 2002, p216.
37 The German term *Judenrat* (plural *Judenräte*) has been used throughout.
38 The confusion of roles was exacerbated by the fact that many *Judenräte* were created from pre-existing welfare bodies known as the *Kehilla* which the community were accustomed to looking up to. Warsaw Ghetto survivor Hillel Seidman, for example, repeatedly uses the term *Kehilla* when referring to the Nazi sponsored *Judenräte*. Hillel Seidman, *The Warsaw Ghetto Diaries* (Targum/Feldheim, 1997).

39 Brenner, 2014, p229.
40 Aharon Weiss, "Jewish leadership in occupied Poland: postures and attitudes", in Yisrael Gutman, (ed), *Yad Vashem Studies*, vol 12, 1977, pp335-365, cited in Yehuda Bauer, *Rethinking the Holocaust* (Yale University Press, 2001), pp128-130.
41 Bauer, 2001, p131.
42 When the Nazis invaded Hungary in March 1944 Jewish leaders already knew about the exterminations from Polish and Slovakian Jewish refugees. But Rudolph Kastner, a Labour Zionist leader, did a deal with Eichmann, whereby he kept silent in return for safe conduct to Switzerland for 1,700 Zionist functionaries and their families. Eichmann later said: "We negotiated entirely as equals... We were political opponents trying to arrive at a settlement and we trusted each other perfectly." Eichmann's motive was concern about potential Jewish resistance or escape attempts to Romania which by then was unwilling to hand Jews over to the Nazis.

   Kastner's collaboration helped the Nazis to murder 450,000 Hungarian Jews not long before the end of the war. Much has been written about this despicable act. An Israeli court ruled in 1958 that it was not collaboration and the judge stated that Kastner's actions were justified. The Israeli attorney general stated: "It has always been our Zionist tradition to select the few out of many in arranging the immigration to Palestine." Kastner himself said: "The Hungarian Jew was a branch which long ago dried up on the tree." Labour Zionists have never regarded him as a traitor. All information and quotes on the Kastner affair are from Brenner, 2014, pp283-291.
43 Nehama Tec, *Jewish Resistance: Facts, Omissions and Distortions* (Miles Lerman Center for the Study of Jewish Resistance, Holocaust Memorial Museum, 2001), pp15-17.
44 Lucjan Dobroszycki, "Polish Historiography on the Annihilation of the Jews of Poland in World War II: A Critical Evaluation", *East European Jewish Affairs*, vol 23, no 2 (1993), p47, cited in Tec, 2001, p18.
45 For a comprehensive listing of works relating to Jewish resistance (updated 2003) see the Working Bibliography developed by the Miles Lerman Center for the Study of Jewish Resistance at the Center for Holocaust Studies, United States Holocaust Memorial Museum, which can be downloaded from www.ushmm.org/research/the-center-for-advanced-holocaust-studies/miles-lerman-center-for-the-study-of-jewish-resistance/jewish-resistance-working-bibliography.
46 Eli Tzur, "From Moral Rejection to Armed Resistance", in Ruby Rohrlich (ed), *Resisting the Holocaust* (Oxford, 1998), p40, cited in Donny Gluckstein, *A People's History of the Second World War: Resistance Versus Empire* (Pluto Press, 2012), p118.
47 Tec, 2001, p8. Kurt Schilde, *Jugendopposition 1933-1945* (Lukas Verlag, 2007).
48 Nehama Tec, *Resilience and Courage: Women, Men and the Holocaust* (Yale University Press, 2003), p261.
49 Holocaust Education & Archive Research Team. "Biala Podlaska", Holocaust Research Project website, www.holocaustresearchproject.org/ghettos/bialapodlaska.html. One reason I have presented examples from Biala Podlaska here and in note 71 is because that is the town of origin of my mother, Rose Stone. She reached safety in Australia in 1938 but her parents and younger siblings died in the Holocaust as did all members of her extended family who had remained in Poland.
50 Tec, 2001, p20.
51 Hela Rosner, "Sister Sister", Australian Memories of the Holocaust website www.holocaust.com.au/mm/j_sister.htm. (Excerpt from Anna Rosner Blay, *Sister, Sister* (Hale & Iremonger, 1998), pp 106-138).
52 From the "Oneg Shabbat" archive from the Warsaw Ghetto, cited in "In the ghettos", Australian Memories of the Holocaust website, www.holocaust.com.au/mm/j_ghettos.htm.
53 Non-military Jewish opposition activities are often labelled "spiritual resistance". My argument is that all resistance by Jews to the Nazis was political whether armed or not and whether ideologically based or not. In fact the ideological basis of the Zionists did not assist

them or provide guidance as to how to fight the Nazis.

54 Two major sources for the Warsaw Ghetto uprising are Yitzhak Zuckerman, *A Surplus of Memory: Chronicle of the Warsaw Ghetto Uprising* (University of California Press, 1993), and Edelman, 1990.

55 For instance, the Labour Zionist youth group newspaper called for armed self-defence in March 1942. "Call to Armed Self-Defense, from an Underground Publication", Yad Vashem website, www.yadvashem.org/about_holocaust/documents/part2/doc125.html.

56 Edelman, 1990, p71.

57 The right-wing Zionists, led by Ze'ev Jabotinsky, known as the Revisionists, were organisationally isolated from mainstream Zionism in the 1930s and 40s.

58 Tec, *Resistance During the Holocaust*, p21.

59 Cited in Tec, *Resistance During the Holocaust*, p21. "Bandits" was the Nazi term for the non-Jewish Poles who fought alongside Jews in the uprising.

60 Edelman, 1990, p112.

61 "Marek Edelman", *The Telegraph*, 4 October 2009, www.telegraph.co.uk/news/obituaries/politics-obituaries/6259900/Marek-Edelman.html.

62 Cited in Tec, *Resistance During the Holocaust*, p20.

63 John Rose, "Marek Edelman: Last surviving leader of the 1943 Warsaw Ghetto uprising against the Nazis", *The Independent*, 17 October 2009, accessed on-line at www.independent.co.uk/news/obituaries/marek-edelman-last-surviving-leader-of-the-1943-warsaw-ghetto-uprising-against-the-nazis-1798644.html

64 Antony Polonsky, *The Jews in Poland and Russia*, vol III, 1914-2008 (Littman, 2010), p537, cited in Tec, 2001, p23.

65 Brenner, 2014, p233.

66 Edelman, 1990, p55.

67 Abraham Brumberg, "The Bund's last battles", *The Jewish Daily Forward*, 10 October 2003, online at forward.com/articles/8322/the-bund-s-last-battles (accessed 10/10/2014); Daniel Blatman, *For Our Freedom and Yours: The Jewish Labour Bund in Poland 1939-1949*, translated by Naftali Greenwood (Vallentine Mitchell, 2003).
      At a meeting in March 1942 Avrasha Blum from the Bund youth group was in favour of a joint fighting organisation but felt he had to defer to his senior Maurici Auzach who was against, and the ZOB was formed in July without the participation of the Bund. Nazi attacks in the meantime resulted in a very high attrition rate and by the time they joined in November only 20 to 25 members of the Bund were left. "Avrasha Blum—Activities of the Zukunft in the Warsaw Ghetto", *Organization of Partizans, Underground and Ghetto Fighters*, Jewish Resistance in the Holocaust website, c3.ort.org.il/Apps/WW/page.aspx?ws=496fe4b2-4d9a-4c28-a845-510b28b1e44b&page=5d675d48-68df-4fc3-833c-04a23648f70e&fol=e5b35888-e7db-4e50-9ce4-e132ae92de2e&box=3e0902e0-b315-412c-a5ec-927e5dab4302&_pstate=item&_item=7ef98fee-ea87-44cb-b2c1-0689e149e8b2.

68 Brumberg, "The Bund's last battles"; Daniel Blatman, *For Our Freedom and Yours*.

69 Emmanuel Ringelblum, "Comrade Mordechai: Mordechai Aniliewicz—Commander of the Warsaw Ghetto uprising", in Yuri Suhl (ed), *They Fought Back: The story of the Jewish Resistance in Nazi Europe* (Shocken, 1975), p102.

70 Yitzhak Zuckerman (in debate), *Jewish Resistance During the Holocaust*, p150, cited in Brenner, 2014, p234.

71 Holocaust Education & Archive Research Team. "Biala Podlaska". Holocaust Research Project website, www.holocaustresearchproject.org/ghettos/bialapodlaska.html.

72 United States Holocaust Memorial Museum. "Jewish uprisings in ghettos and camps, 1941-1944". *Holocaust Encyclopedia*, www.ushmm.org/wlc/en/article.php?ModuleId=10005407. "Killing center revolts", www.ushmm.org/outreach/en/article.php?ModuleId=10007747. Tec, *Resistance during the Holocaust*.

73 Fighters of the Bialystok Ghetto website www.zabludow.com/bialystokghettofighters.html. Tec, 2001, p10.

74 Yael Margolin Peled, "Gusta Dawidson Draenger 1917-1943". Jewish Women's Archive, jwa. org/encyclopedia/article/draenger-gusta-dawidson; Edelman, 1990, p57.

75 Fighters of the Bialystok Ghetto website www.zabludow.com/bialystokghettofighters.html. Aktion Reinhardt Camps Website, "Bialystok Ghetto", www.deathcamps.org/occupation/ bialystok%20ghetto.html.

76 Holocaust Research Project website. "Efraim Barasz. Chairman of the Bialystok Judenrat." www.holocaustresearchproject.org/ghettos/barasz.html.

77 Arnold Zable, *Jewels and Ashes* (Scribe, 2005), p146.

78 Zable, 2005, p151.

79 Szymon Datner, "The Fight and the Destruction of Ghetto Białystok", 1945. Landsmanschaft of Bialystok and the surround website www.zchor.org/bialystok/testimony.htm.

80 The Holocaust Resource Center, Yad Vashem website. "The Discussion on Fighting Aims by the Activists of the Bialystok Ghetto, February 27, 1943", www.yadvashem.org/odot_pdf/ Microsoft%20Word%20-%20573.pdf.

81 "Vitka Kempner", Jewish Partisan Educational Foundation website. www.jewishpartisans.org/t_switch.php?pageName=mini+bio+short+bio+1&fromSomeo ne=&parnum=40.

82 Cited in "Hirsh Glik" Aktion Reinhardt Camps Website, www.deathcamps.org/ occupation/glik.html.

83 Still the Night (Shtil, Di Nacht Iz Oysgeshternt):

The still night was full of starlight,
And the frost—was burning;
Do you remember how I taught you
To hold a revolver in your hand?

A girl, a sheepskin and a beret,
And in her hands she clutches a gun.
A girl with a face as smooth as velvet
Keeps an eye out for the enemy's caravan.

Aimed, shot, and right on target
Did the small pistol strike.
With one bullet she halted
A truck stacked with ammunition.

At dawn she crawled out of the woods,
With snowy garlands on her hair,
Encouraged by her little victory
For our new, free generation.

Milken Archive of Jewish Music website, www.milkenarchive.org/works/lyrics/717

84 Cited in Tec, *Resistance During the Holocaust*, p15.

85 Tec, *Resistance During the Holocaust*, p13.

86 Tec, *Resistance During the Holocaust*, p17. "Resistance in the Kovno ghetto". Miles Lerman Centre. Holocaust Memorial Museum, www.ushmm.org/research/the-center-for-advanced-holocaust-studies/miles-lerman-center-for-the-study-of-jewish-resistance/ medals-of-resistance-award/resistance-in-the-kovno-ghetto.

87 Chaim Yelin and Dimitri Ghelpernus, "The Gelpernus Diary: Resistance in the Kovno Ghetto", Holocaust Education & Archive Research Team, www.holocaustresearchproject. org/revolt/gelpernusdiary4.html.

88 Stephen Pallavicini and Avinoam Patt, "Lachwa", *Holocaust Encyclopedia*, www.ushmm.org/ wlc/en/article.php?ModuleId=10007233.

89 "Lachva—The revolt that saved the town", based on an account by Yitzhak Lichtenstein, Organization of Partizans Underground and Ghetto Fighters. Jewish resistance in the

Holocaust website. c3.ort.org.il/Apps/WW/page.aspx?ws=496fe4b2-4d9a-4c28-a845-510b28b1e44b&page=5d675d48-68df-4fc3-833c-04a23648f70e&fol=e5b35888-e7db-4e50-9ce4-e132ae92de2e&box=3e0902e0-b315-412c-a5ec-927e5dab4302&_pstate=item&_item=41d7228f-be22-4788-b02c-61dc1fc96eec.

90 All information on Minsk from Barbara Epstein, *The Minsk Ghetto 1941-1943: Jewish Resistance and Soviet Internationalism* (University of California Press, 2008), unless otherwise indicated.

91 Epstein, 2008, p18.

92 Cited in Epstein, 2008, p252.

93 Epstein, 2008, pp228-257. This was partly due to an assumption by the Soviets that anyone who came under Nazi rule and survived must have been a collaborator. The whole process was exacerbated by a local Communist who invented an account of a massive evacuation from Minsk in order to conceal the fact that he and his friends had fled. Those arrested were not exonerated until 1962.

94 *Partizaner-marsh* (Partisan march) by Shmerke Kaczerginski, a writer of revolutionary poems and songs who had worked with communist youth as a young man and participated in the formation of the FPO (United Underground) in the Vilna Ghetto. This song was written in August 1943 when many were going to the partisans.

Hey FPO!
We are here!
Boldly and with courage into battle.
Today partisans
Are going to beat the enemy,
In the struggle for workers' power.

Shirli Gilbert, *Music in the Holocaust: Confronting Life in the Nazi Ghettos and Camps* (Oxford Historical Monographs, Clarendon, 2005), p73, www.questia.com/read/120194534.

95 Tec, 2003, p284.

96 Comment by Eva Kracowski quoted in Tec, 2003, p309. "Bernard Druskin" Jewish Partisan Educational Foundation website, www.jewishpartisans.org/t_switch.php?pageName=mini+bio+short+bio+1&parnum=34

97 Tec, 2001, p11.

98 Tec, 2003, p283.

99 Shmuel Krakowski, *War of the Doomed: Jewish Armed Resistance in Poland 1942-1944* (Holmes & Meier Publishers Inc, 1984), p301, cited in Tec, 2001, p11.

100 Tec, *Resistance During the Holocaust*, p32.

101 "Gertrude Boyarski" Jewish Partisan Educational Foundation website, www.jewishpartisans.org/t_switch.php?pageName=mini+bio+short+bio+1&fromSomeone=&parnum=8

102 Tec, 2003, p300. A fascinating account of the Bielski brothers' partisan group can be found in Tec, *Defiance* (Oxford University Press, 1993).

103 "Songs and Dances". Jewish Resistance in the Holocaust webpage, c3.ort.org.il/Apps/WW/page.aspx?ws=496fe4b2-4d9a-4c28-a845-510b28b1e44b&page=5d675d48-68df-4fc3-833c-04a23648f70e&fol=fe71099d-270f-4c68-8def-25ee7cc7f81b&box=3e0902e0-b315-412c-a5ec-927e5dab4302&_pstate=item&_item=2ed434f9-7319-4c81-99bb-7a17a49c1685

104 Hanna Levy-Hass and Amira Hass, *Diary of Bergen-Belsen: 1944-1945* (Haymarket Books, 2009).

105 The experiences of Roma (gypsies) in many ways parallels that of the Jews. They were imprisoned in dedicated camps or sometimes Jewish ghettos and some participated in partisan activities or assisted underground activities. Approximately 20,000 Roma were herded into a "family camp" in Auschwitz where they lived in conditions appalling even by Auschwitz standards. On 15 May 1944 SS guards armed with machine guns surrounded them to transport the remaining 6,000 to the gas chambers. The Roma resisted with knives made from scraps of sheet metal, iron pipes, clubs and stones. The Nazis did not confront

them directly, but after removing work-capable adults, eventually murdered the remaining approximately 3,000 inmates in the gas chambers. The book of wider Roma resistance to the *Porajmos* (Romani Holocaust) is yet to be written.
Tec, *Resistance during the Holocaust*, pp28, 36. United States Holocaust Memorial Museum, Holocaust Encyclopedia, "Genocide of European Roma (gypsies), 1939-1945", www.ushmm.org/wlc/en/article.php?ModuleId=10005219, accessed 23/11/2014.

106 Lore Shelley, *The Union Kommando in Auschwitz* (University Press of America, 1996).

107 Witold Pilecki, a member of the underground Polish Home Army (AK), voluntarily smuggled himself into Auschwitz in 1940 and set up an underground organisation whose main purpose was to send information out of the camp. He escaped in 1943 after realising that the Allies did not intend to liberate the camp, "Witold Pilecki", Jewish Virtual Library website, www.jewishvirtuallibrary.org/jsource/biography/Witold_Pilecki.html; Witold Pilecki, *The Auschwitz Volunteer: Beyond Bravery* (Aquila Polonica, 2012), p168.

108 Those familiar with Slavic languages might think this is a nickname but it is in fact the real name of a woman who deserves recognition.

109 Tec, *Resistance During the Holocaust*; "The Revolt at Auschwitz-Birkenau", Jewish Virtual Library, www.jewishvirtuallibrary.org/jsource/Holocaust/aurevolt.html.

110 Tec, 2001, p14.

111 Shelley, 1996, p8. Klaus-Henning Rosen, "Eine Stadt zeigt Betroffenheit", *Vorwärts*, 1 June 1985, no 23, p8, cited in Shelley, 1996, p7. Mary Williams Walsh, "German Judge Awards Back Pay to WWII Slave Laborer", *Los Angeles Times*, 6 November 1997.

112 "Tomasz (Toivi) Blatt", *Holocaust Encyclopedia*, United States Holocaust Memorial Museum website, www.ushmm.org/wlc/en/idcard.php?ModuleId=10006539.

113 "Sobibor", *Holocaust Encyclopedia*, United States Holocaust Memorial Museum website, www.ushmm.org/wlc/en/article.php?ModuleId=10005192.

114 Tec, *Resistance During the Holocaust*, p26, en.wikipedia.org/wiki/Treblinka_extermination_camp#Treblinka_prisoner_uprising.

115 Tec, *Resistance During the Holocaust*, pp26-27.

116 Hanna Szper Cohen: "To this day I say—since Jews have bad feelings about Poles...we who survived, a small percentage though it be, none of us would have survived if in some moment he did not get help, usually without ulterior motives, from some Pole." Julian Cohen, "Escape from Belzec: Saved By a Pair of Heels", Holocaust Education & Archive Research Team website, www.savingjews.org/docs/clergy_rescue.pdf, www.holocaustresearchproject.org/ar/belzec/belzecescape.html.

117 Cited in Richard C Lukas, *Out of the Inferno: Poles Remember the Holocaust* (University Press of Kentucky, 1989), p13.

118 Lukas, 1989, p13.

119 Neal Ascherson, *The Struggles for Poland* (Channel 4 Books, 1987), pp96-100, cited in Rose, 2009, p20, and Gluckstein, 2012, p57.

120 Unless otherwise indicated, information on Zegota is from Irene Tomaszewski and Tecia Werbowski. Zegota (Price-Patterson, 1994), accessed online at Warsaw Uprising website, www.warsawuprising.com/zegota.htm.

121 Marjorie Wall Bingham, "Women and the Warsaw Ghetto: A Moment to Decide", World History Connected website, worldhistoryconnected.press.illinois.edu/6.2/bingham.html.

122 Gunnar S Paulsson, *Secret City: The Hidden Jews of Warsaw 1940-1945* (Yale University Press, c2002), pp123, 231.

123 Daniel Blatman and Renee Poznanski, "Jews and their social environment. Perspectives from the underground press in Poland and France", in Beate Kosmala and Georgi Verbeeck, *Facing the Catastrophe: Jews and Non-Jews in Europe During World War II* (Berg, 2001), pp182-183.

124 "Directorate for civil action. Response to acts of treason". Polish Greatness website. www.polishgreatness.com/directorateforcivilaction.html.

125 Laqueur, 1982, p200.

126 Epstein, 2008, p13.

127 Epstein, 2008, p13.

128 Stewart Steven, *The Poles* (Collins/Harvill, 1982), cited in Andrzej Slawinski, "Those who helped Jews during WWII", Polish Resistance in World War II website www. polishresistance-ak.org/10%20Article.htm

129 Paulsson, 2002, p230.

130 Depending on which author is consulted, estimates of the number of Jews rescued by Poles vary from around 100,000 up to 450,000 with the number of Poles involved in rescue as many as 3 million—Lukas, p13; Norman Davies, *Rising '44: the Battle for Warsaw* (Viking, 2003), p200.

131 Martin Gilbert, *The Righteous: The Unsung Heroes of the Holocaust* (Holt Paperbacks, 2004), p103.

132 Gunnar S Paulsson, "The Rescue of Jews by Non-Jews in Nazi-Occupied Poland", *The Journal of Holocaust Education*, vol 7, nos 1 & 2 (summer/autumn 1998), pp19-44, cited in Mark Paul (ed), *Wartime Rescue of Jews by the Polish Catholic Clergy: The Testimony of Survivors* (Polish Educational Foundation in North America, 2007), p287; www.savingjews. org/docs/clergy_rescue.pdf

133 See note 1.

134 Tec, 2003, p13.

135 Henri Michel, for instance, in 1972, devotes four out of 360 pages to Jewish resistance (which he suggests involved only "a few thousand") and one sentence to the Warsaw Ghetto uprising—Michel, pp177-180.

136 Arnold Paucker, *German Jews in the Resistance 1933-1945: The Facts and the Problems* (Gedenkstaette Deutsche Widerstand, 2012), p8.

137 Draft report by the Commission for Crimes Committed by the Nazis in Kiev from February 1944. Page 14 shows changes made by G F Aleksandrov, head of the Propaganda and Agitation Department, Central Committee of the Communist Party of the Soviet Union, cited at en.wikipedia.org/wiki/History_of_the_Jews_in_Russia#cite_note-54.

138 "Zapluty karzeł reakcji, czyli lekcja nienawiści" at the Wayback Machine (archived February 22, 2012) (The spittly dwarf of the Reaction, or the lesson in hate). Leksykon PRL, Telewizja Polska SA (Internet Archive), retrieved 30 August 2013, cited in en.wikipedia.org/wiki/ Rescue_of_Jews_by_Poles_during_the_Holocaust#cite_note-www-3.

139 Paucker, 2012, p67.

140 Raphael Patai (ed), *The Complete Diaries of Theodor Herzl*, vol 1 (Herzl Press and Thomas Yoseloff, 1960), p6.

141 Jacob Klatzkin, *Tehumim* (Spheres, 1925), cited in Jacob Agus, *The Meaning of Jewish History*, vol 11 (Abelard-Schuman, 1963), p425.

142 Lennie Brenner, interview with Shmuel Merlin, 16 September 1980, cited in Brenner, p225.

143 Chaim Weizmann, *The Letters and Papers of Chaim Weizmann: Series B, Papers, vol 11 December 1931 to April 1952* (Transaction Books, 1983), p286, accessed online at books. google.com.au/books?id=PsabNtx33VMC&pg=PA286&dq=%22the+old+ones+will+pas s%22&hl=en&sa=X&ei=DWa_VMCXNqW_mwXgoIHQDA&ved=0CCIQ6AEwAQ# v=onepage&q=%22the%20old%20ones%20will%20pass%22&f=false

144 Referring in this instance to the situation in Germany—Paucker, 2012, p40.

145 Nahum Goldmann, *Memories: The Autobiography of Nahum Goldmann* (Weidenfeld and Nicholson, 1970), p149.

146 Epstein, 2008, p268.

147 Brenner, 2014, p239.

148 Brenner, 2014, p232.

149 Epstein, 2008, p284.

150 Epstein, 2008, p285.

151 Epstein, 2008, p291.

152 This is a comment by Yad Vashem historian Israel Gutman, cited in Marci Shore, "The

Jewish hero history forgot", *The New York Times*, 18 April 2013, on-line version mobile. nytimes.com/2013/04/19/opinion/the-jewish-hero-history-forgot. html?pagewanted=all&_r=0.

153 Rose, 2009. Other ghetto and Holocaust survivors have also opposed Israel's oppression of Palestinians. Chavka Fulman-Raban, a ghetto survivor, recently denounced the Israeli occupation of Gaza. Amira Hass, daughter of two Holocaust survivors, is world famous for her stand including calling Palestinian stone-throwing, "the birthright and duty of anyone subject to foreign rule", Richard Silverstein, "Last of Warsaw Ghetto Survivors Calls for Rebellion Against Israeli Occupation", Tikun Olam website www.richardsilverstein. com/2013/04/09/last-of-warsaw-ghetto-survivors-calls-for-rebellion-against-israeli-occupation/. Amira Hass, "The inner syntax of Palestinian stone-throwing", *Haaretz*, 3 April 2013, www.haaretz.com/opinion/the-inner-syntax-of-palestinian-stone-throwing. premium-1.513131.

154 See "Poland's Warsaw Rising", in Gluckstein, pp55-69, for more information about the underground state apparatus set up during the Nazi occupation.

155 Vladka Meed, *On Both Sides of the Wall* (New York, Holocaust Library, 1979), cited in Tec, 2001, p10.

156 See note 1.

4

The Netherlands: War and Liberation

Mark Kilian

The predominant view of the Allied Forces' liberation of the Netherlands in May 1945 heralds it as a triumph. The advantages of post-war democracy compared to Nazi terror can hardly be doubted, but the return of pre-war "business as usual" was not what the majority wanted.

After the war business and political leaders realised they and their state were thoroughly discredited. Although the state administration, police, monarchy and big business were subject to criticism, they were restored to power and their crimes were whitewashed. Post-war trials of Nazi sympathisers and collaborators were conducted on an individual basis, trying individuals for their crimes and opportunism (and failed even at that). And for the vast majority "liberation" meant continued oppression, or even, in the case of Indonesia, new war.

Background

Sending thousands of Dutch soldiers to the front by bicycle to confront modern German tanks and warplanes, as happened in May 1940, may, in hindsight, seem ridiculous if not perfectly useless.[1] Yet it was an expression of the level of Dutch development. The Dutch navy had been definitively defeated by its British competitor in the 17th and 18th centuries and the country was occupied by France until 1813. With its economy focused on trade with the colonies, the Netherlands had been slow to industrialise.[2] Generations of bosses and politicians learned to be realistic about the position of the Netherlands in the world pecking order. By the 20th century it was a second-rate colonial power, stripped of much of its military muscle, though still extracting fortunes from Indonesia and the West Indies. While maintaining the empire depended upon British support, many of its exports went to Germany.[3] Being trapped between two great powers economically and geopolitically demanded policies that would allow the Netherlands to balance between them.

The Netherlands remained formally neutral in the First World War, though businesses and its state profited from the conflict. Simultaneously, "by the end of the war the condition of the workers, badly clothed, underfed, miserably housed, was desperate".[4] When, in November 1918, a revolution in Germany brought about the armistice, the Dutch ruling class—including Queen Wilhelmina of the House of Orange—felt there was a real possibility of social upheaval. While reforms such as the eight-hour day and the vote for women successfully prevented full-scale unrest, the period became known as the time of "the trembling bourgeoisie" (*Bibberbourgeoisie*) and was not quickly forgotten by the government or elite.

The labour movement suffered from a structural weakness as it was divided into so-called "pillars" (*zuilen*). Catholics, Protestants, humanists, social democrats and others organised their own schools, youth clubs, unions and a host of other social and cultural organisations.[5] The problems these divisions created would persist throughout the inter-war period.

The most significant workers' party was the social democratic SDAP (*Sociaal-Democratische Arbeiders Partij*) whose first alderman was elected in 1907. It grew consistently going from 83 aldermen in 1919 to 179 in 1939.[6] On the far left the Communist Party (CPN) remained small, being marginalised by the social divisions within the labour movement. However, it expanded in the inter-war crisis years from 1,089 members in 1918 to around 11,000 in October 1937. The print run of its paper *De Tribune* increased from 5,000 in 1931 to 20,000 in 1933.[7] Despite stifling political consensus, the CPN's principled combination of anti-racism and anti-imperialism in relation to Indonesian struggles inspired protests throughout the Dutch empire—enough even to frighten the authorities. But the rise of Stalinism in its ranks led to a breakaway in 1927 led by Henk Sneevliet, who, siding with Trotsky on many issues, founded the sizeable Revolutionary Socialist Party (RSP).

Despite these divisions and its failure to take the revolutionary road that had been seen in Russia, Austria and Germany, the Netherlands experienced growing unrest:

> In the years just after the First World War, the war between employers and workers flamed up in all fierceness. While the number of strike days in the period 1914-1918 did not amount to much more than 400,000 a year, this increased quickly afterwards and between 1919 and 1925 amounted to 1-1.5 million a year. The high water mark was 1920 with 2,334,000 strike days.[8]

However, in 1920 the employers' attitude hardened and they began attacking wages and extending working hours, provoking a defensive metal workers' strike in 1921 that involved 18,000 workers. The dispute became a drawn out conflict involving unions that could not agree on common demands. The divisions within the workers' movement plagued the dispute. A referendum taken at one point on continuing the strike showed two thirds of the secular metal workers' union (the ANMB) in favour of continuation, Catholics less than a third and Protestants just 8.3 percent. When the metal bosses threatened a lockout, the united front crumbled. On 9 January 1922 work was finally resumed—empty-handed.[9] The balance of class forces had shifted.

1929 saw the biggest land labourers' strike in Dutch history. The strike started on 1 May and involved 5,000 men and women demanding a 10 percent wage rise. Farmers hired strike breakers on an unprecedented scale, and they were assisted by the Christian press and their land labourers' unions. A "mini state of emergency" arose in which one bystander was shot.[10]

Then the 1930s world crisis hit. In 1931 the value of sterling fell, adding severely to the crisis in Dutch shipping and trade. A wave of bankruptcies took place. "In the course of 1931 more than one-third of the Dutch merchant fleet tonnage was laid up. In all branches of industry unemployment grew, from 18,000 in the middle of 1929 to over 100,000 at the end of 1930 and 480,000 in 1936".[11] Stability was history.

Five months after the accession of Hitler as German chancellor on 26 May 1933 Hendrikus Colijn, leader of the Anti-Revolutionary Party (ARP), became prime minister, a post he remained in under varying cabinets until 10 August 1939. Colijn served as an officer in Indonesia until 1909, working directly under the notorious General Van Heutsz. On returning to the Netherlands in 1914 he became director of the petroleum company *Bataafse Petroleummaatschappij*, and a multimillionaire. If any single politician ever did, he personified the Dutch military-industrial complex. Little surprise, therefore, that he had a "blind spot on his retina for the social question".[12] Colijn slashed public spending.

When he cut unemployment support by 16 percent in the summer of 1934, a national revolt swept through the country, starting in Amsterdam's Jordaan neighbourhood. On 3 July unemployed port workers collecting their lowered payments protested. The communist *De Tribune* agitated: "Onto the streets! For the struggle against support theft! Make clear to the possessing classes that the workers won't have themselves starved!"[13]

In Amsterdam 500 dockers walked out, and riots occurred in Enschede, Groningen, Haarlem, IJmuiden, Rotterdam, Utrecht and in smaller towns

(Alphen aan de Rijn, Hilversum). Police and army repression saw at least six citizens killed and 200 wounded in Amsterdam. The Communist *De Tribune* was outlawed and demonstrations and meetings were forbidden. Communists and those arguing after the repression that "the struggle has not ended" were arrested.[14]

Possibilities for struggle were shown in the aftermath of the 1934 revolt when women took the initiative and organised a large-scale rent strike in Rotterdam, which made small gains. *De Tribune* wrote: "Women are fighting on many fronts, but do not get the respect that they deserve".[15]

Fascism

It was into this charged atmosphere that Dutch fascism now stepped. Later it was suggested this was "alien to Dutch nature". But the reactionary ideology and organisation composing Dutch fascism were overwhelmingly home-grown. The right prepared the ground, blaming the current malaise on parliamentary democracy. The liberal *Haagse Post* wrote for example: "The best elements of the people are waiting for a Man that will liberate the Netherlands from the tyranny of party politics".[16]

The National Socialist Movement (*Nationaal Socialistische Beweging*, NSB) was founded in November 1932. Its lack of overt anti-Semitism has led some to doubt the NSB's initial fascism, suggesting it used the "Italian model". This not only underplays the violence of Mussolini's movement but crucially the omnipresence of anti-Semitism in Dutch society.

Jews were always a tiny minority—65,000 in Amsterdam around 1930. When Jewish refugees arrived from Germany, however,

> the image of the Jew as other was re-polished until it shone with a glare more striking and venomous than before... In the Protestant and Catholic press ambivalent feelings towards the anti-Semitism in the Third Reich predominated. On the one hand systematic banishment of the Jews from German society and anti-Jewish violence and persecution were severely denounced. But on the other hand those newspapers stressed more than once that the Jews had brought their misfortune upon themselves because of their unbelief and assimilation, their disproportional presence in the press and in the economic and financial world.[17]

Although some Jews were NSB members, they were generally seen as second-rate citizens. Hence anti-Semitism was not a "selling point" at the start. The NSB embraced corporatism. Mussert created a veritable leadership cult and paraded in a black military outfit. What made it fascist from the start were the NSB's organised gangs of thugs, the WA (*Weerbaarheids Afdelingen*), modelled on Hitler's paramilitary SA. The NSB's message was mainly directed at a petty bourgeois and peasant audience.[18] While efforts to recruit workers led to nothing—many unions expelled NSB members—no organised counter-movement developed.

The monarchy did not distance itself from the Nazi movement. An important though symbolical gesture was when Queen Wilhelmina appeared on the balcony when on Budget Day (*Prinsjesdag*) 1932 Nazis from various organisations marched in front of the palace with their arms raised.[19]

However, the establishment did not embrace fascism either. Rather they were content to keep it in reserve. For example, in the 1933 election Colijn rejected a formal alliance with the NSB, and only included them in a list of bodies civil servants were prohibited to be members of under pressure—the others on the list were left organisations. Colijn stated that if his government failed, "the terrain is free for National Socialism, in our country too", adding: "Under the condition of good leadership, it would be possible to work with them".[20] The ban on fascists being members of the Civil Guard (*Burgerwacht*) was not upheld, and NSB mass rallies, so-called "Land Days", took place under police protection.

The pre-war high water mark of the NSB was the 1935 provincial elections, when high unemployment and political crisis helped the NSB gain 8 percent[21] and grow to 50,000 members. However, the NSB then went into decline, attracting a mere 4 percent of the vote in the 1937 parliamentary elections. Membership plummeted and prominent members left. This was partly because of German events. Hitler's suppression of churches led Dutch bishops in February 1934 to issue a Permanent Mandement formally forbidding Catholics Nazi membership. The Night of the Long Knives in June 1934, in which Hitler murdered almost the entire SA cadre, showed the violent face of fascism, while in 1936 Mussolini brutally attacked Abyssinia.

The NSB, once propelled by the "successes" of Hitler and Mussolini, now found them to be a liability. Everyone from left to right accused the NSB of "betraying their country". Furthermore, the worst part of the economic crisis was over by 1936. The need for radical change seemed less urgent for the petty bourgeoisie and fears of revolution were subsiding. Anti-communism consolidated the social divisions and swept all behind the elite and the monarchy. Mussert was put aside by all forms of Dutch nationalism—but neither completely nor for good.

1940: war and occupation

When Hitler invaded on 10 May 1940, the country was militarily weak. The German army took just five days to conquer the country, the bombing of Rotterdam hastening an already certain surrender. The invasion cost the lives of 2,200 soldiers and sailors and 2,159 civilians.[22] The whole Dutch army were made prisoners of war. Most officers were released on their "word of honour" that they would not take part, "directly or indirectly", against German rule. While the army was dismissed, 60,000 remained—they were unemployed. Of those, 500 were allocated to Germany's *Organisation Todt* and 3,000 soldiers plus 500 officers went to the "*Waffen SS* and such".[23]

The response of different sections of the population depended on wealth and politics. Queen Wilhelmina fled to London to save her possessions and the colonial empire from Nazi control. She became the central figurehead for Dutch nationalism. General Winkelman remained in place as deputy head of state. He was previously a military adviser to Philips, a central Dutch industrial enterprise. Winkelman introduced martial law in April 1940, arresting NSB members but also people on the left.[24]

Before the invasion all state civil servants received a secret directive:

> The authorities would strive, in the interest of the population, to continue performing as good a job as possible under the changed circumstances. The government-issued directive assumed that the tenure of office was in the interests of the population. The associated disadvantage that "partly... they serve the interests of the occupier" was in general "considered less than the greater disadvantage that could arise for the population from the non-operation of its own administration". If, however, the official remaining in function would prove such services to the enemy, that this may be considered greater than the benefit connected for the population to his staying, then he will have to leave his post.[25]

The latter caveat proved a dead letter. In June 1940, when the general secretaries of the departments worried about "incorrect behaviour towards German citizens", they instructed the police to act forcefully. "Endangering cooperation between German authorities and Dutch authorities, that was also, as much as possible, pursued from the German side, was at odds with Dutch interests".[26]

Hitler's reasons for occupying the Netherlands were mainly military, but there were economic benefits too, both for the Nazi regime and a minority of Dutch. The German war economy had a growing demand for food and it was hoped that Dutch agricultural surpluses would go to Germany, though due to the Allied blockade and labour shortages production declined.[27] Already in 1940, 99,600 Dutch workers were working in Germany. On 1 April 1942 Duty to Work (*Arbeidsdienstplicht*) was introduced, the same year 162,800 workers were deported for work. On 25 August a 72-hour working week was introduced.[28] "The country was ransacked: factories were dismantled and shipped to Germany. Metals, clothing, textiles, bicycles, food and produce, cattle and livestock, all were sucked into the German war machine".[29] The 1942 large-scale defence works against possible British invasion pushed labour conditions back to semi-slavery. In March a regulation was introduced that any Dutch inhabitant could be demanded to work outside the country. In 1943 young men had to report for *Arbeitseinsatz*.

Not all wealth was exported. The German empire needed the Dutch economy, mainly for agriculture but also for industrial products (including military products). This demanded at least some economic return. "The value of exports to Germany grew from 159.2 million guilder in 1938 to 313.1 million in 1940...497.1 in 1941...peaking at 523.3 million in 1943. At the same time the value of German exports to Holland rose from 308 million in 1938 to a peak of 500 million in 1941, whereafter it declined again to pre-war levels".[30] The mid-war change in export balance and worsening labour conditions would bring the Nazis into increasing conflict with social groups. But before occupation ended, alas, blood had to flow. In the Netherlands the years 1940-1945 would cost an estimated 209,648 lives.[31]

The Jews

The Jewish population was targeted early on. From October 1940 all employees in government and local administrations and public institutions such as schools and universities were required to complete an "Aryan declaration" (*Ariërverklaring*) indicating whether they or their spouses had "Jewish blood". Refusal to sign was one of the first acts of disobedience, but few refusals occurred.[32] Most alarmingly, 12 out of 17 members of the Supreme Court signed and its Jewish president was removed without one voice being raised. From June 1942 onwards "the Germans began a systematic deportation of Dutch Jews." They succeeded in murdering 105,000 out of 140,000, "a higher percentage than any other western European country".[33]

However, some Jews were too useful to deport such as Hirschfeld, general secretary of the Department of Trade and Industry. In 1939 the Dutch authorities wondered about keeping a Jew in such an elevated position, but Germany's Nazi minister Funk had already honoured him:

Once Winkelman was removed and interned, the path was cleared for the *Rüstungsinspektion* Niederlande, an institution that brought harmonious cooperation between Dutch business and the Wehrmacht. In four months, the summer of 1940, the Wehrmacht signed contracts worth *f* 740,000,000 for arms supplies with Dutch businesses. And that was just the beginning. The Dutch business community has, led by Hirschfeld, performed armament orders for Germany throughout the war... Didn't aircraft manufacturer Fokker in Amsterdam also repair the wings of German Junkers-52 bombers and, after all, didn't that pride of the nation— the famous Philips Company of Eindhoven—supply transmitters and radio receivers to the Luftwaffe of Nazi Germany long before the war?[34]

As Jan Rogier wrote, Hirschfeld:

could cover up all economic collaboration, knew how to break illegal sabotage and trade and—being a great admirer of Saint-Simon, moved by the "needs of the great masses"—strove for close collaboration with the occupier. And the man that called protesting against the Jews "a waste of time", though he was one of the first in the Netherlands to know about the mass executions in Eastern Europe, dares tell Lou De Jong in 1961 that he thought the board of the Jewish Council were "naïve people". No, Hirschfeld was not naïve, he was criminal.[35]

Hirschfeld was not an isolated case. Leaders of the Jewish Council such as Abraham Asscher and David Cohen administrated the persecution and deportation. They had their own class interests. Asscher, who owned a diamond factory, said: "Let's be honest, in the vicinity of Waterloo Square there are plenty of little men that are no jewel to the Jewish people and many youngsters idle where strict labour duty would do good".[36] Asscher and Cohen, however, would still be deported themselves, but survived the camps to stand trial later.

The right-wing media, even underground, went along in the anti-Semitic current. "In practice, *Trouw* voiced the views of the 'illegal' ARP".[37] *Trouw* was originally orthodox Protestant, but with a "Christian national" profile. It wrote that among Jews in hiding there was "a large percentage of weaklings and nervous, egoistic, dishonest and inferior individuals".[38] Aiding them despite that was top-down "charity", not solidarity. *Vrij Nederland* took a more liberal view—"The poison of propaganda has affected us unknowingly"—adding "of course there are evil elements amongst Jews, just as non-Jews [but] given the shocking number of Dutch staying aside and waiting, there is no single reason to position ourselves above the Jews".[39]

Although they had largely ignored the Jewish question, Communist papers paid more attention to the pogroms and deportations than all other media combined. On 24 June 1942 *De Tribune* called upon Jews to participate in the national struggle. The editorial of the first *De Waarheid* ("The Truth") declared: "No fascism in the Netherlands! No racial hatred or anti-Semitism with which the Nazis want to poison our people!"[40]

Underground

The structure of the Dutch underground partly mirrored the pre-war social divisions. Communists, religious activists and others formed cells, distributing their own literature and collaborating where there was mutual trust. Groups operated on a provincial scale, rather than locally. Originally the number of resistance fighters amounted to a couple of hundred. After the turn of the war in 1943 the resistance grew reaching 25,000 in September 1944.[41]

The underground consisted of three main groups: the communists (CPN), later part of the Resistance Council (RVV), Fighting squads (*Knokploegen*, LO-LKP) and Order Service (*Ordedienst*, OD).

With around 9,000 members in 1940 the Communist Party had already developed illegal structures and took to operating in their preferred five-strong cells.[42] The core of the organisation was formed by the unemployed and industrial workers. After Hitler attacked the USSR, communist cells carried out attacks on buildings killing Nazi chiefs and collaborators and distributed *De Waarheid*, which had a print run of 12,000.[43]

The LO (*Landelijke Organisatie voor Hulp aan Onderduikers*) was founded in mid-1942. It helped people to flee, providing food, IDs and other documents. In Haarlem the LO had an intelligence service spying on the police and established a clandestine telephone network. The LO became linked to the LKP (*Landelijke Knok Ploegen*) which arose in August 1943 from pre-existing local fighting squads. The LO in West and North Netherlands was dominated by Anti Revolutionary Party members, and in the south by Catholics.[44] Together with the *Trouw* newspaper, this formed the "right wing" of the resistance.

The OD, though underground, was not a resistance group as such. Van Randwijk describes it:

> Order Service. (Telling name! ORDER!), an organisation led by officers, who regarded themselves as the rightful continuers of the military authority proclaimed with the pronunciation of the State of Emergency, in the days before May 1940, when we still feared everything, hoped for everything and were wrongly or badly prepared for almost everything. The OD prepared military rule during occupation, devised laws and lawlets, appointed mayors in advance, etc etc, regarded itself as the lawful extension of the London government, threatening to arrest any politician and civilian [contesting power].[45]

One function of the OD is illustrated by the "Englandspiel", in which German counter-espionage was able to capture British secret agents and a good number of OD members: they were involved in espionage (mapping German units, military infrastructure).[46] Though this is a form of competition rather than "resistance", the Nazi's still were ruthless.

Vrij Nederland (VN), edited by Henk van Randwijk, should also be mentioned. It became the voice of an educated, reformed youth who wanted "modernisation" of the pre-war setup, and were disaffected by the Catholic church and ARP. It grew to 80,000-100,000 copies weekly by the end of the war. The 1 December 1944 issue, with Colijn's death on its front page, remembered him as a "great and honest patriot",[47] though unlike the ARP it would criticise intervention in Indonesia after the war.

In January 1941 the Catholic bishops repeated their prohibition on believers being members of the NSB—and socialist, communist and liberal parties. But whereas communists were refused the sacraments, reading Nazi papers and even membership of ultra-right organisations was allowed. The archbishop wrote to the priests on 15 September 1943 discussing membership of the Waffen-SS: "The Reverend Bishops have not deemed it necessary to speak out in public on this issue, because the number of Catholics that would want to join will of course remain small, and on the other hand because a certain idealism [ie struggle against Bolshevism] does not have to be a priori excluded".[48]

1941: Strikes and the Vichy scenario

On 28 October 1940 communists organised a protest of forced labourers from Amsterdam in Het Gooi. When a lengthening of the working day by half an hour or more was announced, workers took strike action that lasted for weeks. On 1 November, 1,800 were locked out. "In the first half of November the streetscape was dominated by the struggle of forced labourers (*werkverschaffingsarbeiders*). The leadership and delegations of women were in touch with all sorts of institutions... Women had an active part in the actions of forced labourers, and certainly did not have the least dangerous tasks." In January 1941 thousands of forced labourers protested again. The struggle paid off. In February an extra month of unemployment benefit was announced.[49]

On 12 February it seemed the creation of a Jewish ghetto in Amsterdam had begun, while the Jewish Council called on the Jews to surrender their arms. Three days later a protest march raised the slogans "Against the WA rascals!", "Down with the NSB!" "For wage rises and state support!"[50] On 17 February Amsterdam metal workers struck in protest against forced transfer to Germany. The same evening the CPN leadership met, and Lou Jansen argued that "partial action under German occupation irrevocably leads to defeat". The Amsterdam leadership agreed on a general strike against repression and the prospect of a Mussert government. However, the success of the strike meant these plans were withdrawn and no arrests were made.[51]

The dam broke when WA member Koot died after a fight in Waterloo Square. German leaders Rauter (SS) and Seyss-Inquart (Reichskommissar) ordered the arrest of 427 Jewish men. The following day the famous CPN strike manifesto was distributed: "Protest against the awful persecutions of the Jews—Strike! Strike! Strike!" The strike call fed into much wider resentment over freedom of speech, increasing fascist terror and plans to deport workers to Germany.[52] On 25 and 26 February workers in public transport and a host of other sectors walked out, an estimated 60,000 workers altogether. It was one of the few political strikes in the Third Reich and a clear act of solidarity with the Jews.

Women played a pivotal role:

> On the strike day they had an important role in turning out the smaller companies...[such as] the metal company Jonker... It was difficult to get the strike going Tuesday morning... [The women said,] well, then we will take care of that. And those women stormed inside and started to yell at those guys. Tools flew around, and then the whole bunch started running. And that was it.[53]

The Nazi reply was a wave of repression. Four communists were executed, along with 15 members of the Geuzen resistance group. "In the months after the strike, about 500 communist resistance fighters were arrested. A quarter of the original number! The Noorderlicht groups in Groningen and Friesland were almost entirely wiped out." A fascist regime would not tolerate open mass resistance. After the strike the leadership grappled with the experience, as was made clear in *De Waarheid*: "The tone has become more sombre. Again and again there are calls for solidarity with the prisoners of the strike and the razzias. There is virtually no information about industrial action, not even small strikes like those regularly occurring at the start of 1941".[54]

The Nazis considered the Dutch "Aryans" and planned to integrate them into the Reich. Though this foundered due to increasing exploitation and resistance, it is worthwhile examining the role of the Dutch administration early in the occupation. In early May Dutch provincial authorities heavily armed the civil guards to "retain order" and the state wanted to expand the police force with army military police. Though this largely failed, in July and August 1940, 456 state patrolmen (*Korps Rijksveldwachters*) and 1,170 police became available.[55]

Some policemen quit their positions during the war, and a few dozen joined the resistance or used their position to provide intelligence. Of 1,671 members of LO-LKP killed in 1940, 123 were police. It should be noted, however, that most of these only went underground later, during the call for *Arbeitseinsatz* (1943) and liberation of the south (in the autumn of 1944), when they risked being found on the losing side. But the apparatus as a whole and most of its personnel were loyal to right wing ideas and very willing to cooperate. "Serving the public cause" they lent assistance to the German security police (*Sicherheitsdienst*, SD) in political arrests. A minority of NSB members increasingly determined the agenda so that "the Dutch police hunted on a large scale for communists, Jews in hiding and resistance groups".[56]

From September 1941 onwards the city councils were disbanded and the mayors became solely responsible for order in towns and cities. The margins for cooperation without openly embracing fascism became near zero, even for convinced nationalists.

In this situation two groups competed for state positions: the old bosses' representatives and the NSB. On 3 July 1940 ARP leader Colijn published a pamphlet, *On the Border of Two Worlds* (*Op de grens van twee werelden*), saying Dutch democracy was obsolete and that we had to "reckon with a German teacher politically, economically and socially" and "work along in that direction".[57] He criticised the queen for fleeing to London. Colijn called all parties together on 24 July 1940 "for resolute work for the preservation and strengthening of the fatherland and the community", founding the Netherlands Union (*Nederlandse Unie*), that promised "to work in a loyal relationship" with the German Reichskommisar.

The Union, which advocated abolishing political parties, grew from 250,000 to 800,000 in February 1941, pulling in members from across the right wing and social democratic spectrum. It instructed members that "a loyal attitude to occupation authorities is a precondition and that members must keep to this".[58] Formally it was corporatist without anti-Semitism. The Union approved of Nazi state schemes like *Winterhulp* and *Arbeidsdienst*, and eventually purged itself of Jewish members. Colijn's attitude drew venomous criticism from within his own ARP prime minister Gerbrandy calling him "the Dutch Pétain".[59]

The Germans, however, were "not interested in allowing any independent expression of Netherlands' patriotism... The Netherlands Union failed to become a new Vichy, not for want of trying, but because the occupation authorities did not think they needed it".[60] This caused a U-turn. The ARP published a pamphlet, *We Build On, But On What Basis? (Wij bouwen verder, maar op welken grondslag?)* which was forbidden by the authorities.[61]

For his part NSB leader Mussert went out of his way to please Hitler, in an attempt to gain a higher position. While "the NSB was not regarded as their party by the German occupier", it hurried to throw itself into their arms. Individual NSB members acting as Hitler's loyal servants gained rapid promotion. Another NSB official, Rost van Tonningen, was appointed to high office: he became the president of the Nederlandsche Bank and was ordered to establish an SS-Standarte "Westland". In his diary Mussert noted: "talk about the relation between Netherlands and Germany as two brothers of the German race. It turned out the highest SS leadership sees the Dutch people as a German people. This is disastrous... If the NSB adopted this stance propaganda for Dutch National Socialism would be pointless and we would certainly be accused of treachery." However, Mussert's doubts did not last long. Soon he was praising Hitler as a "prophet", "struggling for the construction of a new Europe". Now his own dream was "Netherlands from the Dollart to Calais, with India, with the Congo, a friend of South Africa, closely collaborating with the German brother".[62] This was precisely what "non-Nazi" general secretary Hirschfeld was actually working for in his ministry.[63]

An increasing number of appointed mayors were NSB members or pro-German.[64] Street gangs were given free rein. The uniform ban was lifted in 1940, and after December 1941 the NSB was the only legal party. The WA and Youth Storm were allowed to march without a permit.

Though the police had formal instructions to tolerate no violence, even by NSB members, they were above the law. During riots they would simply call for the help of German soldiers.[65]

The NSB grew to 100,000 strong, about 1 percent of the population. When persecution of the Jews became a branch of industry, NSB members ran seized enterprises and worked at "robbing banks" (*roofbanken*). The active collaboration of the Dutch state machine, including homegrown and German Nazis, combined legal and illegal repression in the most arbitrary and brutal regime the Netherlands had ever known.

One of the most important Dutch enterprises, Philips, had prepared itself for the occupation. It split into three entities based in New York, London and Eindhoven. "That way...nowhere was Philips hostile to capital and everywhere one could earn from the war".[66] Philips and the Germans did not always see eye to eye, however. For example, when Philips himself held his 50-year jubilee on 23 May 1941, he gave a day off to the workforce that turned into a pro-royal manifestation in the company town of Eindhoven. When NSB and WA thugs intervened, a violent confrontation developed. A battalion of Grüne Polizei placed machine guns around the market, threatening a massacre. At the last minute the company convinced the Nazis there was no "revolt", and nobody was shot. But 400 people were arrested and Philips himself was forced into hiding.

But the business continued to thrive. Thus Philips solved its labour shortage by using forced labour in the thousands, many of them Jews and women from the concentration camps. "Industry paid through contributions to the public treasury for the exploitation of the camps, and kept a neat profit for itself", Ad Teulings wrote. Philips took this step on condition that: "The Philips' command had to be under supervision of Philips; the supervisors needed to have unlimited access to the camp; the supervisors decided which prisoners would be added to the Philips command; the prisoners got an extra hot meal—'Philiprak'—and wages are paid to relatives." Yet a former prisoner remembered: "in the end, the SS was the boss and not Philips".[67] Incidentally, Philips's forced labourers were never compensated for their suffering.

The situation changed with Hitler's invasion of Russia on 22 June 1941. Two days later "400 prominent communists were arrested of all people by Dutch police, and on the basis of Dutch data. By the end of August 175 communists would be added to that. Besides some dozens of people from circles left of the CPN were arrested".[68]

De Jong wrote:

The names and addresses of the persons to be arrested were derived by the *Sicherheitspolizei* from data collected in the '20s and '30s by the Dutch secret service, the Central Intelligence Service. In many cases, these were supplemented by information from the municipal police forces. The arrests mainly took place on the night of 24 and 25 June. In Amsterdam, where 75 persons were arrested, *"100 Mann Holländische Polizei"* were involved, some of whom, however, helped some of those who sought to escape. In Friesland the people to arrest were *"ausgesucht in Verbindung und Zusammenarbeit mit den Bürgermeistern und dem Generalstaatsanwalt"* (selected in contact and cooperation with the mayors and attorney-general).[69]

This turn of events spurred the CPN into new action. A communist pamphlet of July 1941 entitled *Comrades!* argued that "there have been two wars raging since 22 June 1941: an imperialist one between Germany and Britain, and a class war between Germany and the Soviet Union". *De Waarheid* called upon all "Dutch, without distinction respecting faith or political revenue, for the decisive battle!" for a national war of liberation. Resistance activities intensified. The CPN established a Military Commission, forming sabotage cells in summer 1941. Workers with the experience of the February strike were part of their backbone.

Queen Wilhelmina expressed her solidarity with the fighting Russians by radio while "remaining loyal to our standpoint vis à vis bolshevism". Despite the latter qualification, *De Waarheid* called for a public celebration of on the queen's birthday on 31 August 1941, stating they were not sympathisers of the monarchy, but "had no special reason for animosity towards the queen either".[70] In November a communist group set a construction site in Fokker on fire, and launched a host of other attacks on transformers (shutting down the Hoogovens steel plant for a while), rail tracks and bridges, wagons and emplacements, German military equipment and NSB and Wehrmacht buildings.

1942: like the war would never end

In spring 1942 the Russian army was approaching exhaustion and foreign minister Molotov visited Britain and the US, asking for the opening of a second front. In March Seyss-Inquart introduced forced labour deportation to Germany. Henceforth the struggle against *Arbeitseinsatz* was central to the CPN. A brief regional metal strike took place against the planned deportations but was unsuccessful: in autumn 38,000 workers were shipped off.[71]

The cadre of the CPN was depleted by arrests, leaving control in the hands of a triumvirate. Cells were run top-down out of necessity, but at the cost of democratic discussion, and Stalin's voice was the main beacon. Communist calls for mass protests, demonstrations and sabotage went unheeded, and rows with the rightward moving SDAP embittered relations still further. *De Waarheid* stated that: "almost all social democrat council members and MPs work for the Nazis..." The SDAP hit back denouncing "Bolshevik totalitarianism".[72]

A secret report of the *Sicherheitsdienst* in 1943 said: "Out of 140,000 Jews presently 102,000 are gone... The raid in Amsterdam was a big success. The Dutch population does not agree, but does not obstruct".[73] Jews were not the only scapegoats. An estimated 2,000 to 2,5000 travellers were deported to concentration camps, according to lawyer Lau Mazirel, who represented persecuted people in Nazi courts.[74] On 19 May 245 travellers were deported to Auschwitz. Only 30 returned alive.[75]

Another though lesser target were gays. The police inspected (invaded) gay cafés, checking for licences and the presence of minors. In November 1943, 48 people were arrested during a raid in The Hague. Most were deported to Germany. General repression, however, was variable, ranging from acquittal to one-year probation. Of the more than 160 Dutch men who were convicted by the Nazis for homosexual acts, relatively few ended up in concentration camps. Koenders has estimated that "some dozen" homosexuals were persecuted and concluded that the occupier "only acted when one way or the other a German interest was involved".[76]

Oppression was part of the ideological glue holding the occupier and its Dutch counterpart together. Even more important to both was dealing with the class enemy. This made the communists a particular target. Aided by lists from the Dutch CID "the Germans again arrested 120 pre-war communist officials who were locked up in Camp Amersfoort. On 15 October 1942, 10 of them were executed as a reprisal for resistance acts in Twente".[77] For the purpose of intimidation, news of executions was reported in all media.

Yet acts of popular disobedience continued. In May, Mussert visited Eindhoven prompting the NSB mayor to hoist the NSB flag over all public buildings. However, City Lyceum pupils refused to enter as long it was waving above their heads. But 1942 ended with the crowning of Mussert as "Leader of the Dutch people".[78] This nomination was qualified: "as long as the war lasted, corresponding competences could not yet be transferred to the NSB leader..."[79] Mussert hoped that recruiting 25,000 volunteers for the Eastern Front would soften this stance.

1943: turning point

1943 began as depressingly as the previous year had ended. The Final Solution for the Dutch Jews was one ghastly feature. Police Summary Justice (Politiestandrecht) was another. Then Hitler announced "*Totalkrieg*" (total war). However, Stalingrad (February 1943) proved a turning point. Realisation that Nazi rule was ultimately doomed inspired increasing attacks on state authority. Another resistance group, CS-6, began to operate. It was composed of Amsterdam students and intellectuals, many with communist sympathies. Its "actions were about liquidation of political opponents, a kind of public execution".[80]

The Nazis responded with raids on the universities and streets, arresting thousands of youth and deporting them to the Vught concentration camp or to Germany. From London Radio Orange denounced "vigilantism", and *Trouw* criticised "political murder".[81]

In April and May the Germans asked businesses to hand over personnel lists. While the majority refused, according to Van Randwijk it was actually a "cunning little German plan". "The employers could ask for dispensation! It could hardly be better, since now all men of 18 to 35 years were effectively driven to become slaves for their employer..."[82] The upper age soon became 45.

The ambiguity in the situation was shown, however, by a railway strike that, in effect, was staged by the Dutch government-in-exile and bosses after the Nazis took more soldiers into war captivity in April. The strike spread beyond the Limburg mining district, and Philips' production was disrupted for ten days.[83] But when the local resistance threatened to take the movement out of management hands, the latter produced leaflets calling for a return to work as the action was "the work of communists". The aftermath was disastrous. The Nazis murdered 200 people in reprisals.[84] Nevertheless, new layers were drawn into struggle as Germany's insatiable thirst for labour continued and labour service was extended to the countryside.

Despite continuing repression, in the spring of 1943 an important new group was founded, the Resistance Council (RVV), by former army officer Jan Thijssen, an ex-OD member who had broken with their strategy taking with him the illegal radio and intelligence service. This group, which the communists joined, forged close links with the Dutch London Information Bureau, the secret service of the government. The RVV demanded from the exiled government the right to retaliate against Nazi attacks, but this was refused.[85] Yet more forces joined, including the LO and Combat Forces (*Knokploegen*, LKP). From then onwards the RVV grew to about 1,000 members. Other than the LO-LKP it was the biggest resistance organisation.[86]

The resistance professionalised creating an Identity Card Central (*Persoonsbewijzencentrale*) and the National Support Fund (*Nationaal Steunfonds*, NSF). The NSF, which became the "resistance bank", initially questioned whether the communists were "good Dutchmen" but relented, offering the CPN support from January 1945.[87] Fake IDs had a mass circulation, causing their value to rise. Warnings against registering with the authorities now gained momentum, with *Trouw* and *Het Parool* calling on people to refuse registration or destroy the registration systems.[88]

The authorities counter-attacked. From May onwards the political information service (PID) was extended to many cities. It was led by a new layer of Nazis and supported by an increasing group of NSB policemen. In The Hague, Rotterdam, Amsterdam and elsewhere the police played a crucial role in the persecution of communists.[89] All resistance was persecuted relentlessly throughout the year, by either the Germans or the Dutch police on their own initiative. Initially being tried according to German military law, partisans were sentenced to long sentences or even death.

From 1943 onwards repression was "on the cheap". Following acts of sabotage and liquidations, partisans and random individuals were taken hostage or executed in public. Between September 1943 and September 1944 the murder gang code named *Silbertanne* committed 54 extrajudicial murders and attacks.[90] A civil war raged in the streets, fought by all available means; a war the Nazis. Mussert publicly denounced the resistance, saying: "assassination, under all circumstances, is cowardly and mean... These crimes are therefore committed by a small gang of dislocated elements that by and large do not understand they are at the service of Moscow".[91] With his own castle crumbling, Mussert played his trump card—anti-communism. It would not help him.

1944: hunger winter

Years of war took their toll and by early 1944 conditions were "near intolerable. The Dutch economy had been stripped bare and the only available foods were potatoes, mealy bread and beets. Children were beginning to show signs of malnutrition while diseases like diphtheria and typhus had begun to break out".[92] Liberation of the southern Netherlands in September 1944 actually exacerbated problems elsewhere.

On 17 September the government-in-exile called for another national rail strike to support the failed Operation Market Garden. As traffic had already been disrupted, the ensuing strike of 30,000 rail workers stopped transport almost completely.[93] It took the struggle up yet another gear. As it exposed thousands to possible vengeance, all 30,000 train staff had to go into hiding. Resistance groups took increasing risks to fulfil their growing tasks.

On 15 November 1944 the KP Almelo carried out what is probably the biggest robbery in bank history. Days later, however, they were caught by accident and had to reveal the location of the loot to protect other activities. They died in Neuengamme:[94]

> Thinking liberation was at hand, the Dutch railway workers had gone on strike, and in retaliation the Germans cut the gas, electricity, water and food supplies into these parts of Holland. Throughout the cold winter of 1944-45 the situation of the Dutch trapped in this pocket became desperate... The Red Cross lobbied to transport food into the area, but Churchill remained as unwilling as ever to feed European civilians trapped behind German lines. He argued that the food would just be eaten by the Germans. The American government was also concerned that the Soviets may be antagonised if any food transported into the area by the allies fell into the hands of the Wehrmacht. The Soviets were in no mood to countenance feeding German soldiers while still spilling blood trying to defeat the Wehrmacht in the east. Reports began reaching Britain that the Dutch were dying in the streets of Amsterdam. In the end the death toll reached 22,000 people. The Dutch prime minister in exile informed Churchill that his people would hold him responsible for the deaths, and General Eisenhower, supreme commander of the Allied forces, pointed out that he did not want to send Allied troops into an area where people were already starving.[95]

Food was but one element of the general crisis:

> According to the Dutch government's assessment, stocks of bread grains would run out by the end of October; the occupied territories had but three weeks of potatoes left; there was no milk; and most calamitous of all, military operations had disrupted coal shipments into the cities so that the gas and electric works, as well as bakeries and factories, could not function. Coal stocks would be gone by mid-October, Dutch sources reported. The country was on the verge of total collapse.[96]

On 2 November the British Chiefs of Staff finally allowed Swedish ships to deliver to Amsterdam, but far too little to avert a mass famine. There had been another option: using the Kiel Canal. This, however, was blocked by the British Chiefs of Staff on 14 February 1945. As one writer put it:

> The ugly truth is that the liberation of north-western Holland was simply not a strategic priority for the Allies. The Anglo-American armies hit the Germans along the Siegfried Line in Belgium and France, and in spring 1945 pushed eastward into Germany proper. This left a large contingent of German soldiers effectively cut off in Holland, though still in command of much of the country. A gruesome sideshow ensued: the doomed German occupiers pursued a policy of vengeance against the citizens of the Netherlands, and deliberately allowed them to starve.[97]

While the Nazi machine was gearing up for a final confrontation, the Allied powers were of very little help. Because Dutch industry and labour were fully integrated into the *Reich*, both increasingly drew Allied bombing. Caught in the crossfire for half a year, popular anger with the Nazis grew—and with the Allied powers and exiled government and queen. This would be one element in the crisis of authority in 1945. A secret service report in June 1944 said that people "were becoming increasingly anti-American and anti-British because of the reckless bombardment".[98]

The masses were not passive, particularly in the struggle for more food. CPN members gave an excellent lead here, despite doubts expressed by the CPN's own leadership that mass protest was "too risky". In the autumn of 1944 women in Rotterdam organised a petition and demonstration against hunger. In Amsterdam, in February 1945, they petitioned the mayor. Mien de Vries recounted: "When I think if it now I don't understand how we dared do that, with all the responsibility you had for your kids. But it was precisely that responsibility that made you do it".[99]

Mad Tuesday: the beginning of the end game

When Radio Orange incorrectly reported the liberation of Breda, the result was *Dolle Dinsdag* (Mad Tuesday), 5 September 1944. Rumours of German capitulation sparked spontaneous mass resistance. Crowds collected in city centres, decorating the streets with orange and the national tricolour flag. A wave of panic engulfed the NSB, with members destroying documents, insignia and uniforms. Scores started fleeing the country, leaving luggage, writing desks, typewriters and livestock behind on station platforms. NSB membership halved.[100]

The question of what would replace the Nazi regime now arose in an acute form. One answer to this had been developed by prominent individuals who, refusing to cooperate with the occupiers, were seized in successive waves and held in a camp at Sint Michielsgestel.[101] Unwittingly, the Nazis provided the elite with an unelected shadow government plus think tank. Here businessmen and politicians elaborated plans for postwar economic and political organisation. The discussion did not exclude collaborators, either political or economic, and Philips took part, setting up a radio link to the camp. All the plans they devised were to be imposed from above.

Due to crisis and unemployment, the question of social and economic organisation had already been debated before the war. Now the argument raged between the idea of a planned economy and liberal and corporatist models. Crucially, the planned economy lost the final "debate", as did possible forms of mass democracy. For these people the end of the war would not bring a new society but restore the old. Critics of these discussions spoke of anti-parliamentarian and anti-democratic manoeuvring, a point illustrated by the composition of the second Gerbrandy cabinet in exile (February 1945), the dictatorial approach of Supreme Headquarters Allied Expeditionary Force (SHAEF) that took over as the Allies "liberated" the country, the postponement of elections and the prominent influence of Netherlands Union members.[102] These suspicions were not without reason.

Ideologically the Catholics saw society as an organic whole. In this view class cooperation would replace class struggle. For the SDAP the reorientation was led by Christian socialist priest Dr Willem Banning. He argued that the "democratic corporative organisation sketched by us means *saying goodbye to class struggle*", thus explicitly rejecting forms of direct democracy that could have limited arbitrary power from above. Van der Goes, chair of the SDAP, also rejected economic democracy, arguing that "social-economic interests would become too much a world of its own, the body elected would be too cumbersome, in which representation would be regulated only at random".[103] Banning saw himself moved by a religious socialism, defining his own task as "enlightening" the workers with knowledge. Banning campaigned against the idolaters of "temporary earthly powers like people, class, race, but also possession and science..."[104] His solution was to unify all society in a corporatist style (inspired before the war by the Belgian De Man), campaigning for a united Protestant church and a united labour party with a Christian character.

The authoritarian plans of the Sint Michielgestel group were never fully implemented because of the pressure coming from below. Resistance groups had, in fact, created a shadow state, mirroring state administration with forgery, housing and food "departments" and the police with armed guerrillas. Most of all they controlled the only legitimate press, which had a mass circulation. The workers and intellectuals running these "enterprises" themselves would not accept more state censorship, or a continued fear of repression.

Thus the SDAP leaders' plans clashed with those of *Vrij Nederland* and *Parool*. The two papers published a manifesto in April 1944 stating that "the old groups and parties, that already were out of touch with reality in 1940, are in no better a position regarding the reality which will confront us after liberation". They therefore called for "radical renewal of our popular life in political, social, economic and cultural sense".[105] The Sint Michielgestel group and ex-Union members refused to sign this, and their attempts to launch their own Dutch People's Movement (NVB) after the war failed to take off.

The CPN was wary of speculating on post-war arrangements as "now it first came down to expel the German occupier". Indeed it had its hands full as one leadership after another fell to the Gestapo. Eventually a post-war strategy was elaborated in the People's Programme (*Volksprogram*). This, sounding radical, argued: "Only when power gets into the hands of the working people, ie when democracy is actually realised in a practical sense...the communists deem a radical change of the social relations possible. This certainly gives the socialist workers' movement the power to fight for democratic demands, of which the fulfilment must lead to the vanquishing of all resistance and the construction of socialism".[106]

In reality this amounted to supporting the reconstruction of parliamentary democracy, with one party representing workers: "We are of the opinion that the dissolution of the Third International has greatly improved the prospect of restoring the unity of the workers' movement on a socialist basis. For this unity we fight and for this unity we *gladly relinquish our party*".[107]

However, the Dutch communist Koejemans sounded a note of alarm in *The Dutch Rebirth, Reaction or Progress?*:

> Dutch big capital strives for concentration, it strives for national organisation, that is, limitation of internal competition to spread its wings all the wider in the area of international competition [with a] single purpose:

restoration of Holland as a colonial power and society led by strong men, undisturbed by unnecessary interference by parliament, an utter restriction of social policies at the behest of the "renewed national spirit", suppression of class struggle.[108]

Discussions of a theoretical character were soon interrupted by practical issues. Two days before Mad Tuesday the government in exile appointed Prince Bernhard as commander of the Internal Combat Forces (*Binnenlandse Strijdkrachten*, BS). Bernhard, engaged to Princess Juliana in 1936, was the son of an impoverished German nobleman who had served as an army commander under the kaiser. In his youth Bernhard himself had: "served the SS and SA, worked for one of the most criminal companies of the Third Reich, IG Farben, and acted as liaison between the Nazis and the Falange in Spain".[109] Those right wing sympathies meant Bernhard was not credible as a liberator.

Bernhard instructed the RVV, LKP and OD to collaborate together by forming regional "triangles". Both the RVV and LKP refused. When Jan Thijssen protested too much against this "order", he was brushed aside. One day later he was arrested by the SD and executed. Such was the fate of more than one RVV leader.

Running alongside the BS was the College of Trust (*College van Vertrouwensmannen*, CvV). This was an unelected interim government designed to prevent a power vacuum. It was chaired by Willem Drees and included representatives from the pre-war government, opposition parties and the newly reorganised resistance.[110] However, when Queen Wilhelmina asked for a delegation from the resistance to visit her, Communists and Social Democrats failed to agree to the composition of the delegation. They also found it difficult to reach a deal with *Trouw*, which rejected communism in particular.

Although the left clearly had varying views on post-war society there was, at least, some common ground. It shared a belief in "such an organisation and control of economic life by the organs of a democratic state, and the abolition of mass unemployment and disparity in wealth between groups in society", as well as a new union with Indonesia on the basis of equality. Moreover, the left resistance as a whole refused to hand in the few arms they had as required by the CvV, "to avoid situations such as in Belgium and Greece". The left was indignant that its loyalty should be questioned in this way.[111]

These early political skirmishes were but the prelude to larger conflicts. Soon the resistance would be faced with an establishment backed by Allied armies moving in from the south. On 20 September these forces had reached Nijmegen. Rather than restore democracy immediately, the SHAEF, a military authority, ran the liberated zone. It freed the 270 remaining prisoners in Sint Michielsgestel in September 1944 and immediately helped catapult them into high positions. This supplemented the activities of the circle around the queen. After the Gerbrandy cabinet dissolved in January 1945 "new, fresh" figures were selected for government.[112] This move has been characterised as follows:

> The most important reasons for the authoritarian pattern of Bernard, and of Drees, Schermerhorn, Romme, De Quay, Kruls, Schouten, and of course the liberals, must be sought in the fact that they, at any rate, wanted to eliminate the influence of the resistance movement and its leaders. You can say that has completely succeeded. After having the Resistance Council RVV seemingly play a role in conversations regarding the liberation of our country, the ties between old powers and parties were forged again, with no other intention than to liquidate the RVV and return to the order of the day".[113]

The strategy was clear in the way the left press was treated. *De Waarheid* was critical of the SHAEF, nepotism and the labour situation in Philips, the mines and other industries. The authorities restricted allocation of paper to *De Waarheid* and banned the Brunssum edition for a period.[114] Although secret police reports of communist meetings expressed fear of an armed rising, "*De Waarheid*...accepted the role of being part of the Western armies." It wrote: "Mistrust every rumour and trust...the broadcasts of the BBC and Radio Orange".[115] Despite such statements the communists in the "liberated" south were excluded from all influence.

1945: the Reich collapses

In January 1945 Dutch press criticism of the Allies increased when they managed, at last, to move sufficient food—to their soldiers. Famine was not restricted to the north; the "liberated" south also suffered. Though it was known that people were on the verge of dying, the "SHAEF refused to delegate the job to the Dutch government itself while the region was still part of an unstable military front".[116] Only in February, when General Montgomery intervened, did stocks in Britain scheduled for the emergency relief of the *north western* Netherlands get shipped to feed the liberated south.

Then the CvV started negotiations with Seyss-Inquart, which left *De Waarheid* outraged: "Food and freedom. Dutch resurrection cannot be the result of haggling." On 29 April, just a week before official liberation, the first bomber convoys started to drop food supplies.[117] Malnutrition in the Netherlands persisted for months. In May in Utrecht there were 50,000 cases of "extreme starvation" and possibly 50,000 in Amsterdam. Hospitals were overcrowded with patients with hunger oedema (15,000 in Amsterdam, 10,000 in Haarlem). Some people were hardly able to walk. *The Times* of 7 May 1945 reported that "horrors comparable to those of Bergen-Belsen and Buchenwald appear to have been enacted".[118] One commentator has even argued:

> If this course of action is taken in conjunction with the earlier request of the CvV for the underground to hand in arms immediately after liberation, it strongly suggests the College was striving to evoke as much passivity as possible in the Dutch population regarding its liberation.[119]

This impression is confirmed by William Hitchcock, who quotes a police intelligence report to SHAEF: "There is a strong element of communism among them because now they have nothing and communism offers them at least a share-out of what remains." The report concludes: "should a man with a really strong personality arise in the western Netherlands and go over to the Communists or present a radical program, the bulk of the people would be with him".[120]

The Allied command's fears were reinforced by contemporary events in Greece, and even closer, in Belgium. Allied troops took Brussels on 3 September. On 11 September the Pierlot government arrived from London but the resistance, dominated by communists, publicly refused to hand in their arms. On 25 November a demonstration was called, which was suppressed by the Belgian police. Gabriel Kolko writes: "The revolution now seemed imminent, for the FI (*Front de Indépendence*) then called a strike for the 29th."

If this strike had not failed because "the leaders were able to re-establish control", the alternative according to Churchill would have been "bloody revolution".[121] He did not hesitate from bloodily suppressing two other revolts: Greece and Indonesia. Thus on 4 December British troops fired on a mass demonstration in Athens, behaving—in Churchill's own words—as if "in a conquered city where a local rebellion is in progress".[122]

The spirit of revolt even infected the German *Wehrmacht*. Five battalions of "East troops" (*Osttruppen*) had been despatched to the

Netherlands in the summer of 1943. Their choice had been between concentration camps or serving in the Nazi army. In North Holland they met the Communists and discussed the possibility of handing over arms and joining the resistance. After the Georgians were relocated to Texel in September 1944, the Nazis demanded that they fight. Their uprising, on the night of 5-6 April 1945, was crushed. With liberation just around the corner, 570 Georgians were bloodily murdered along with 89 inhabitants of Texel. The leadership of the BS refused to support the rebels, a decision that was defended by the CPN leader, Wagenaar.[123]

On 29 April 1945 Amsterdam inhabitants were celebrating on the streets because of the rumours of negotiations on capitulation. On 4 May, after capitulation, the same happened, and both times the Nazis opened fire. On 6 May BS troops went out onto the streets in uniform, but unarmed. They proceeded to arrest 12,000 people, NSB members and others chosen partly based on lists held by their own administration.[124]

By the end of the war there was a real vacuum in the Netherlands. It was, however, much less a physical power vacuum than an ideological one. The bearer of traditional ideology and authority, the Dutch state was in the eyes of many wholly discredited. This was why the Allied forces had to proceed cautiously but also rapidly. And in their role as "benefactors" they were to some degree forced to act after moving in. Finding the Northern Netherlands looking like one large concentration camp fanned the anti-war mood of Canadian, British and American soldiers. Any plans there might have been to alter the initial post-war division of Europe and pursue war against Stalin's Russia thus became impossible. Workers, the oppressed and ordinary soldiers in Europe were fed up.

Legacies of war

If liberation meant an end to Nazi rule for ordinary people, for the Allied governments it was an opportunity to re-establish former glories—in the Dutch case this meant Indonesia. On 7 December 1941 after the attack on Pearl Harbor, prime minister Gerbrandy declared war on Japan. The Japanese army conquered Indonesia in the following three months. One writer summarised the process: "As Germany stormed across Western Europe in the spring and summer of 1940, the weakness of the European colonial powers encouraged the Japanese Chiefs of Staff to think that they could take over the entire south east Asian treasure house of resources".[125]

In a radio speech in December 1942 Queen Wilhelmina had already mentioned plans to create a Commonwealth of the Netherlands, Indonesia, Surinam and the Antillean Islands after the war.[126] A year later she signed two Royal Decrees sanctioning the restoration of Dutch authority in Indonesia. On 28 September 1945 war minister Meijnen announced the despatch of 27,000 troops to suppress "extremists". As volunteers quickly ran out conscripts were sent. One hundred and thirty thousand soldiers were eventually despatched to Indonesia.[127]

Opposition to this came from the Union Netherlands Indonesia (VNI) founded at the end of 1945 by communists and non-communists. Despite its formal policy on Indonesia being equivocal, the communist movement was pushed into this position by the spirit of the resistance, while the SDAP supported intervention. The number of people avoiding call-up swelled into the thousands, in response to which the military police conducted raids. At the end of 1946 anarchists and communists in Friesland revived the wartime underground organisation for hiding people to assist avoiding call-up. The police uncovered the organisation in 1947 and its members were imprisoned.[128]

In September 1946, 30 percent of one contingent of conscripts failed to turn up, causing panic in the war ministry. Lieutenant General Kruls then addressed the nation: "There are irresponsible groups that try to mislead our conscripts, using propaganda and untrue slogans".[129] When, three days later, a conscript was denounced to the military police in Amsterdam, riots ensued. One demonstrator was killed, another wounded.

In response the CPN called a strike which "was heeded on a massive scale. City tram workers took the lead. The strike soon spread to other companies",[130] Fokker, Schiphol, Verkade, Bruynzeel, and cities, Delft, Enschede, Groningen, Rotterdam, The Hague, Velsen and Zaandam. In Amsterdam people started to erect barricades and 20,000 strikers joined the protest on Waterloo Square which was attacked by the police. A national poll in July 1946 showed the majority of the population was against the intervention. In November the VNI presented a petition to parliament signed by 200,000 arguing for a peaceful solution.

That month a military court opened a special chamber in Rotterdam for the trials of those who refused the call-up to fight in Indonesia. A significant group had highly politicised views, comparing occupation of Indonesia to the occupied Netherlands. They were punished almost as harshly as the war criminals of the 1940-1945 period.[131] In 1949 the Netherlands received 430 million dollars in Marshall Aid, 68 million of which was for intervention in Indonesia. Yet despite this and the combined efforts of Dutch, British and Japanese troops, in that same year Indonesia gained its independence after nine years of intense war and occupation.

Racism was not regarded as an issue immediately after the war, it being claimed to be a "non-Dutch" question. But anti-Semitism had never left: "After the liberation in 1945, there were polemical articles in the press and in letters to editors, with questions such as 'How many Jews didn't betray their hosts?' and comments about Jews digging up their money, driving big cars and securing the best jobs".[132] Post-war anti-Semitism, according to De Gans, performed two functions: "First, a psychological one, blaming the victim because Jewish survivors, purely by coming back, reminded Gentiles of their own failure. But above all, anti-Semitism performed a social-economic function in a post-war society of scarcity and upheaval".[133]

It was also of use to business and authorities who had profited from the Holocaust as this denied the Jews their original possessions. This psychology amounted, *de facto*, to a *reversal of responsibility*. An excellent and painful example was the removal of the two communist aldermen L Seegers and B Polak from their functions by the Dutch Labour Party in 1948. When Polak returned from hiding to reoccupy his pre-war position, *Het Parool* commented: "Mr Polak left his post during the German invasion without any particularly pressing reasons." When *Het Vrije Volk* suggested it might be because he was a Jew, *Het Parool* considered that a "side matter" and pointed to his supposed "lazy life in South America".[134]

Official prejudice against Roma, Sinti and other travellers also continued after the war. At a meeting of the Commissaries of the Queen on 10 February 1946 the various mayors argued to reimplement the Nazi law of 22 June 1944, concentrating travellers in camps once again.[135]

On the parliamentary front there had been a political shift. In November 1945 the Dutch parliament reassembled in a lame rump institution; 40 out of 150 seats in the First and Second Chamber together were unoccupied due to death, purges or resignations. After a long delay elections were finally called. On the right the ARP once again posed as the party of "law and order", calling for the "maintenance of authority" and extending this to Indonesia. The voters rewarded them with defeat. The party declined from its 16.4 percent in 1937 to 12.9 (17 to 13 seats).[136]

On the left the CPN vote rose due to its role in the resistance and, in particular, the February 1941 strike. The first post-war commemoration of this event, on Monday 25 February 1946, was huge: "Large companies and firms in the city shut down and tram traffic was halted. Long queues of working men and ex-strikers journeyed to Waterloo Square...50,000 people, the papers said".[137] While the social democrats claimed the strike had been "spontaneous", the CPN could legitimately lay claim to having called it. It commanded so much respect they got three extra seats in the Amsterdam city council, plus, for the first time, an alderman. CPN leader Wagenaar was offered a ministerial post, albeit without a budget (*zonder portefeuille*). In the May 1946 elections the CPN proudly raised the slogan "Forward with the party of the February strike", and gained ten seats (up from three in 1937). However, it was excluded from the cabinet that was formed. In the summer of 1946 the CPN became the biggest party in Amsterdam, gaining 15 of the 45 council seats and getting two aldermen.

In terms of purges, the number of "political criminals" jailed for collaboration with the enemy in August 1945 was about 90,000, of whom 23,000 were women. Mr Nagel, a member of three purge committees, wrote in retrospect:

> The result of our work is rather laughable. As the chairman of a purge committee for building I got a big entrepreneur in front of me who, amongst many other things, had constructed air plane hangars for the enemy and defended himself now with the assertion he had constructed them so badly they could neither open nor shut the doors when they had finished. An excursion to the airport took place; one could open and close the hangar doors with one mere finger. The defence was therefore not accepted and the verdict was corresponding. Not long after, this industrious entrepreneur again was the biggest builder of his region and far beyond.[138]

Capital punishment was pronounced in 140 cases. The main blame was shifted to a minority of NSB members and collaborators. Mussert was executed, and his right hand Van Geelkerken got a life sentence. That the persecution of Jewish Council leaders Asscher and Cohen was eventually stopped was solely due to "the interests of the Dutch elites; too much incriminating material on Dutch non-Jewish individuals and institutions would be macerated with it, so those would be questioned".[139]

Thus "the members of the Supreme Court, after 'purging' of some councillors, were left off freely. The same applies to the Secretaries-General, while for example Hirschfeld was directly involved in the 'legalisation' of the authority of Seyss-Inquart and economic extradition of the Netherlands to Germany. With the top of the Nederlandse Unie it was no different. They could all 'wash themselves clean' because almost everyone had dirty hands in the higher echelons".[140] Hirschfeld became post-war general director for Marshall Aid and later left for Indonesia as economic adviser to Lieutenant Governor-General Van Mook.[141]

After the war 25 percent of the Dutch police force was sacked and disciplinary punishment meted out against another 22.4 percent.[142] Because of the inefficiency and hypocrisy of the purges, scandals erupted. On the request of post-war prime minister Schermerhorn, a commission was established to "investigate" the Union. Strong evidence suggests that the commission was actually intended to clear the names of prominent Union members. Indeed, two former Union members were on the commission itself.

During the war the priorities of the Nazi economy meant street terror and insane mass murder—for ordinary people. But the elite were treated more carefully because of Nazi respect for their wealth and authoritarianism. Although the spirit of the resistance imposed limits, in their barbed-wired backroom at Sint Michielsgestel big business and politicians successfully concocted institutions, parties and union structures for post-war Netherlands. It was a fundamentally undemocratic process which allowed most of the authoritarian oriented figures to join the "underground" (though, it must be stressed, they had not been part of the resistance).

Furthermore, post-war "justice" whitewashed the crimes of war criminals and collaborators. The top industrialists, monarchy, police, politicians, scientific elite and judiciary were too intertwined with the far-right and enmeshed in economic collaboration for a more thorough purging. Post-war society was founded on a sort of corporatism based on class collaboration that had been developing before and during the war. It is true that, for a time, the Nazis had modulated this with another more extreme type, stretching the concept to the extreme to increase exploitation. Yet, to quote Jan Rogier, ultimately: "there is no break between past and present. There is no significant difference in the system of rule of past and present authorities".[143] For the establishment, then, fascism had just been an intellectual phenomenon. But in the February strike, and beyond, the working class fought fascism *physically*.

NOTES

1   In 1939, under the increasing threat of war, a new regiment was created. In May 1940, shortly before war broke out, the brigade was increased to a "Light Division" ("Lichte Divisie"), totalling 5,190 soldiers. www.benvanhelden.nl/Condorclub/Fiets/Holland/Army%20 Bikes%20Holland.html

2   "It would appear that only in the 1880s was the demand for labour balanced by the supply, a situation that had already occurred in Belgium in the 1850s." While in Belgium 46 percent of the population worked in industry in 1910, in the Netherlands this was only 33.4 percent (E H Kossmann, "The Low Countries 1780-1940", in *Oxford History of Modern Europe* [Oxford University Press, 1978], p216).

3   River transport increased from 4.7 million tons in 1880 to 9.9 in 1895, and about 30 in 1910. Rhine vessels carried ores and wheat upstream, and coal downstream—J C Boogman et al (eds), *Geschiedenis van het moderne Nederland. Politieke, economische en sociale ontwikkelingen* (De Haan, 1988), p259.

4   Kossmann, p553.

5   Kossmann, p620.

6   Ton Geurtsen, *Sociaaldemocratie in Nederland—Een geschiedenis van verloren illusies* (De Papieren tijger), pp72-74.

7   Wolf Kielich, *Jordaners op de barricaden. Het Oproer van 1934* (De Walburg Pers, 1984), p61.

8   Igor Cornelissen, Ger Harmsen and Rudolf de Jong (eds), *De taaie rooie rakkers. Een documentaire over het socialism tussen de wereldoorlogen* (AMBO, 1965), p41.

9   On 5 October 1920 the bosses' Metal Union decided to actually impose a wage cut of 10 percent for adults and 20 percent for youth—Ger Harmsen and Bob Reinalda, *Voor de bevrijding van de arbeid—Beknopte geschiedenis van de Nederlandse vakbeweging* (SUN, 1975), pp140-141.

10   Cornelissen, Harmsen and De Jong (eds), pp59-63.

11   Boogman (et al, eds), p390.

12   Boogman (et al, eds), p421.

13   Kielich, p93; Harmsen and Reinalda 1975, p180.

14   Cornelissen, Harmsen and De Jong (eds), pp88-90.

15   Els Blok, *Uit de Schaduw van de mannen. Vrouwenverzet 1930-1940* (Sara, 1985), p169.

16   Robin te Slaa and Edwin Klijn, *De NSB—Ontstaan en opkomst van de Nationaal-Socialistische beweging 1931-1935* (Boom, 2009), p61.

17   Evelien De Gans, 'They have forgotten to gas you: Post-1945 anti-Semitism in the Netherlands', in Philomena Essed and Isabel Hoving (eds), *Dutch Racism* (Rodopi, 2014), p76.

18   The figure the NSB provided (32 percent workers among the last 5,000 members) is probably highly inflated for propaganda reasons. Te Slaa and Klein, p663.

19   Jan Rogier, *De geschiedschrijver des rijks en andere socialisten. Politieke portretten 1* (SUN, 1977), p24.

20   Te Slaa and Klijn, p21.

21   Josje Damsma and Erik Schumacher, *Hier woont een NSB'er—Nationaalsocialisten in bezet Amsterdam* (Boom, 2010), p15.

22   Lou De Jong, *Het Koninkrijk der Nederlanden in de Tweede Wereldoorlog*, vol 3 (Nijhoff, 1969-1991), p499.

23   Hendrik Mattheüs Van Randwijk, In de schaduw van gisteren. Kroniek van het verzet in de Jaren 1940-1945 (Bert Bakker, 1970), pp150-151.

24   Bas von Benda Beckman, *De Velser Affaire: een omstreden oorlogsgeschiedenis* (Boom, 2013), pp42-43, mentions the arrest in Velsen of 300 Germans and 25 Nazis. In Eindhoven 266 "male strangers of the German nationality over 16 years" were arrested, and NSB members— Desiderius Marinus Dejaeger, *De houding van de Nederlandse politie tijdens de Tweede Wereldoorlog in de grote steden in Noord-Brabant* (Thesis Tilburg University, 1999), p19. Susan Galesloot and Hansje Legêne, *Partij in het verzet. De CPN in de Tweede Wereldoorlog* (Pegasus,

1986), p22, incompletely list arrested communists of 10 May: David Wijnkoop, Gerrit Roorda, Louis de Visser, Frans Olfers, Wiep van Apeldoorn, Gerrit Sterringa and others.
25 Dejaeger, p31.
26 Dejaeger p39.
27 "The Dutch responded to this problem by quickly converting from livestock to arable farming and although they were able to send large quantities of meat and fat to the Reich in the first two years of the war, by the end they were only able to supply potatoes, feed grain, sugar and large quantities of fruit and vegetables"—Lizzie Collingham, *The Taste of War. World War II and the Battle for Food* (The Penguin Press, 2012), p175.
28 Van Randwijk, p166.
29 William I Hitchcock, *The Bitter Road to Freedom: The Human Cost of Allied Victory in World War II Europe* (Free Press, 2009), p100.
30 James Heartfield, *An Unpatriotic History of the Second World War* (Zero Books, 2012), p169.
31 Alan S Milward, *War Ecomomy and Society 1939-1945* (Pelican, 1987), p211.
32 Von Benda-Beckmann, p45.
33 Hitchcock, p100.
34 Nanda van der Zee, *Om erger te voorkomen. De voorbereiding en uitvoering van de vernietiging van het Nederlandse Jodendom tijdens de tweede wereldoorlog* (Meulenhoff, 1997), p172.
35 Rogier, 1979, p65.
36 Rogier, 1979, p103. It must be noted that post-war criticism of the Jewish Council was partly popular due to anti-Semitism, as this "You did it yourselves" could function as a lightning rod for the labour employment agencies (Arbeidsbureaus), city administrations and ministries.
37 Doeko Bosscher, *Om de erfenis van Colijn. De ARP op de grans vat twee werelden* (1939-1952) (Sijthoff, 1980), pp80-81.
38 Von Benda-Beckmann, p130.
39 Mr Abel J Herzberg, "De Joden", in Bert Bakker, D H Couveé and Jan Kassies (eds), *Visioen en werkelijkheid. De illegale pers over de toekomst van de samenleving* (Semper Avanti, undated), pp253-258, p254.
40 Galesloot and Legêne, p65.
41 The NIOD estimated resistance "industries" as: illegal press, pilot aid and forgery 25,000; finance 4,000; espionage 5,000; armed resistance 2,000 and aid for hiders 40,000. This included "September Knights" and "May Beetles" (Evert Werkman (ed), *Ik néém het niet! Hoogtepunten uit het verzet 1940-1945* (Sijthoff, 1965), p348).
42 Galesloot and Legêne, p43.
43 Galesloot and Legêne, p59.
44 Von Benda-Beckmann, p132.
45 Van Randwijk, p218.
46 Von Benda-Beckmann, pp180-183.
47 Werkman (ed.), p71.
48 Rogier, 1979, p75.
49 Galesloot and Legêne, pp54-56.
50 Galesloot and Legêne, p67.
51 Galesloot and Legêne, pp73-74.
52 De Jaeger p42.
53 Galesloot and Legêne, p80.
54 Galesloot and Legêne, pp87-88.
55 De Jaeger, pp34-35.
56 Von Benda-Beckmann, pp80-81.
57 I Schöffer, *Het national-socialistische beeld van de geschiednis der Nederlanden. Een historiografische en bibliografische studie* (HES, 1978), p73.
58 Heartfield, pp168-169.
59 Bosscher, p58.

60 Heartfield, p169.
61 Madelon de Keizer, *De gijzelaars van Sint Michielsgestel. Een elite-beraad in oorlogstijd* (Sijthoff, 1979), p113.
62 Schöffer, p76.
63 Rogier, 1979, pp103-104.
64 Amounting to 130 mayors, "ruling" circa 40 percent of the population in 1943 (Von Benda-Beckmann, p77).
65 Damsma and Schumacher, p30.
66 Frans Dekkers, *Eindhoven 1933-45. Kroniek van Nederlands lichtstad in de schaduw van het Derde Rijk* (Onze Tijd/In de Knipscheer, 1982), p182.
67 Dekkers, pp214-216.
68 Galesloot and Legêne, p99.
69 Lou De Jong, *Het Koninkrijk der Nederlanden in de Tweede Wereldoorlog*, vol 5 (Nijhoff, 1969-1991), p100.
70 Galesloot and Legêne, p93-95. The RSAP (ao) criticised the CPN for this move.
71 Galesloot and Legêne, p124.
72 Galesloot and Legêne, pp131-133.
73 Van Randwijk, p165.
74 Rogier, 1979, p280.
75 Erica Moens and Piet Eken, *Vervolging van wagenbewoners in Nederland, 1900-1945* (Doctoral thesis Cultural Anthropology Utrecht University, 1988), p104
76 Pieter Koenders, "Isolement. Homoseksualiteit in de jaren dertig en veertig", in *Fascisme en Homoseksualiteit* (SUA/De Woelrat, 1985), p150.
77 Galesloot and Legêne, p101.
78 This was the notorious "Flag incident" (Werkman [ed], p146).
79 Ruud Koole, *Politiek partijen in Nederland. Ontstaan en ontwikkeling van partijen en partijstelsel* (Spectrum, 1995), p329.
80 Galesloot and Legêne, p114.
81 Galesloot and Legêne, p119.
82 Van Randwijk, p165.
83 Heartfield, p241.
84 Van Randwijk, p166.
85 Joost Divendal, *Arnold Koper, Max van Wezel* (eds), *De moeizame destalinisatie van de CPN* (Van Gennep, 1982), p51.
86 Von Benda-Beckmann, p144.
87 Galesloot and Legêne, p169.
88 Moens and Eken, p61.
89 Von Benda-Beckmann, p90.
90 Von Benda-Beckmann, pp127-129.
91 Van Randwijk, p224.
92 Hitchcock, p101.
93 Galesloot and Legêne, p194.
94 Werkman (ed), pp314-322.
95 Collingham, pp176-177.
96 Hitchcock, p103.
97 Hitchcock, p98.
98 Hitchcock, p101.
99 Galesloot and Legêne, p216.
100 Damsma and Schumacher, pp136-141.
101 Elaborately documented by Madelon De Keizer.
102 De Keizer, pp41-42.
103 De Keizer, p72.
104 De Keizer, p87.

105 De Keizer, p163-165.
106 Arnold Koper, *Onder de banier van het stalinisme. Een onderzoek naar de geblokkeerde destalinisatie van de CPN* (Van Gennep, 1984), pp41-43.
107 Divendal, Koper and Van Weezel (eds.), p47.
108 Galesloot and Legêne, p171.
109 Rogier, p29
110 Galesloot and Legêne, p184.
111 Galesloot and Legêne, p201.
112 De Keizer, p165.
113 Dirk Schilp, *Dromen van de revolutie* (Wereldbibliotheek, 1967), 156.
114 Galesloot and Legêne, p226.
115 Divendal, Koper and Van Weezel (eds), p51-52.
116 Hitchcock, p106.
117 Hitchcock, p110.
118 Hitchcock, p119.
119 Galesloot and Legêne, p205.
120 Hitchcock, p110.
121 Gabriel Kolko, *The Politics of War: The World and United States Foreign Policy 1943-1945* (Pantheon, 1990), p97.
122 John Newsinger, *British Intervention and the Greek Revolution* (Socialist History Society Occasional Papers Series no 16, 2002), p21.
123 Divendal, Koper and Van Weezel (eds), p53.
124 Damsma and Schumacher, p143.
125 Collingham, p63.
126 Bosscher, p211.
127 Kees Bals and Martin Gerritsen, *De Indonesië-weigeraars* (Materiaalfonds Vereniging Dienstweigeraars, 1989), p11. There were also Dutch soldiers in Indonesia, so the total forces were about 200,000.
128 Bals and Gerritsen, p27.
129 Bals and Gerritsen, p16.
130 Bals and Gerritsen, p17.
131 Bals and Gerritsen (p42) explain: "The usual pretext was that a mother could not do without her son. If you stood up for your political motivation, then you would be singled out and got the heaviest punishment...everybody understood it was very stupid to stand up openly for your political motivation."
132 De Gans, p77.
133 De Gans, p80.
134 Dienke Hondius, 'Thans dienen de Joden hun dankbaarheid te tonen', in Hansje Galesloot and Margreet Schrevel, In Fatsoen hersteld. Zedelijkheid en wederopbouw na de oorlog (SUA, undated), p138.
135 Rogier, p92.
136 Bosscher, p246.
137 Annet Mooij, *De strijd om de Februaristaking* (Balans, 2006), p20.
138 Prof M. W H Nagel, 'Berechting en zuivering', in Bakker, Couveé and Kassies (eds), pp112-146, p119.
139 Van der Zee, p139.
140 Van der Zee, p180.
141 Rogier, p65.
142 Von Benda-Beckmann, p95.
143 Rogier, p88.

5

Russia: Stalin and the People's War

Donny Gluckstein

The battle between Germany and the Soviet Union formed the largest and most important theatre of operations during the Second World War. Hitler's Wehrmacht deployed 674 divisions there compared to the 56 to 75 opposing the D-Day landings in Western Europe.[1] Yet the Soviet Union sits uneasily within the history of a war that officially began when Germany attacked Poland in September 1939.

Just a week before, Stalin and Hitler had jointly signed up to a pact partitioning Poland. Indeed, the Soviet Union only fought Germany in 1941 after it was itself attacked. Due to this belated entry Russians refer to the "Great Fatherland War" rather than the Second World War.[2] The Soviet Union seems so very different, politically and socially, to all other protagonists that it is legitimate to ask whether it fits into the pattern of war from above and below seen elsewhere.

The roots of Soviet imperialism

The Tsarist Empire was 5,000 miles across and 2,500 miles from top to bottom. It employed a powerful, centralised state to intensively exploit the people to both staff and pay for a large army. This was imperialism on a grand scale but of the traditional kind rather than the modern version described by Lenin as "the highest stage of capitalism". Indeed, the heavy burden of the state depressed economic development, perpetuating a backward semi-feudal society composed of a vast amalgam of Russian and non-Russian groups.

The "Russian steamroller" could prevail as long as the sheer number of soldiers deployed brought success. But advances abroad in military technology threatened this strategy. Fear of falling behind motivated Tsar Peter the Great to open a window on the west by moving his capital from Moscow to St Petersburg in 1712. Thus industrial development was consciously championed by the state in order to provide the military basis for its survival.

In 1914 the Russian economy was still largely dominated by agriculture and the challenge of war proved too much for it. Mass strikes, army mutinies and peasant seizures of the land swept Tsarism aside in February 1917 and carried the Bolsheviks to power in October. The peasantry gained the land while the working class established a new form of democracy through soviets. The Bolshevik rejection of imperialism was expressed by Lenin's Decree on Peace: "The government considers it the greatest of crimes against humanity to continue this war over the issue of how to divide among the strong and rich nations the weak nationalities they have conquered, and solemnly announces its determination immediately to sign terms of peace to stop this war".[3] The principle of opposing the dominance of "the strong and rich nations" over "weak nationalities" was also applied at home when oppressed non-Russian nationalities were offered the chance to secede.

The October Revolution represented the antithesis of the past. If the state had formerly been shaped by the needs of imperialism, now there was a chance of escaping these imperatives in favour of internationalism and socialism. A new society, however, could not survive as an isolated socialist island in a sea of capitalism. Successful international socialist revolution was vital for two reasons.

Firstly, only this could provide the resources needed to improve the lives of the masses rather than merely sharing out poverty equally. Secondly, unless capitalism was undermined the state would again face pressure to defend its vast, economically backward territory from attack. That threat was evident in the foreign intervention and civil war of 1917-1921.

By 1923 hopes of international revolution had passed, ending hopes that isolation would soon be broken. The working class was decimated, leaving a society dominated by the state/party bureaucracy. Once collective control from below had disintegrated a factional struggle developed within the Bolshevik Party itself. Trotsky, who was loyal to the original aim of internationalism, clashed with others who, like the Romanovs, saw their state as jostling for position in a world interplay of states. In the latter camp were Stalin and Bukharin who saw the national state's interest as paramount.

Though they claimed to be building "socialism in one country", that phrase was merely a staging post towards imperialism because if survival was not secured by international revolution, it would have to be sustained through military competition. As Stalin put it: "We are 50 or a hundred years behind the advanced countries. We must close this gap in ten years. Either we shall do it, or they will crush us".[4] Everything was now "subordinated to the supreme question of the defence of the USSR [Union of Soviet Socialist Republics]".[5] Therefore, in conscious emulation of Tsar "Peter the Great [who] built mills and factories to supply the army and strengthen the defences of the country",[6] Stalin launched a policy of intensive industrialisation in 1929. As before, the method employed was massive exploitation of both the workers and the peasants. From now on the state did not exist to defend the population; the population existed to defend the state.

Military power required the expansion of heavy industry (coal, iron and steel) and that could not wait for light industry (making consumer goods) to develop in parallel. The five-year plan involved spectacular growth in heavy industry. By 1932 output was almost double the pre-war level with particular areas, such as electric power and machine tools, seven and 13 times greater respectively.[7] While all forms of capitalism are exploitative, Soviet industrialisation, which put huge demands on labour while offering few consumer goods in return, was particularly brutal.

That was obvious in agriculture. The October Revolution legitimised the peasant seizure of the land and its division into family plots. But Stalin wanted forced collectivisation so as to release labour and food for burgeoning towns, along with earnings from grain exports to buy foreign technology. In the four years to 1933 state procurement of grain doubled while grain exports increased 56 times over.[8] But the process was deeply contradictory. Seizure of peasant farms led to resistance and a cut in output. By 1933 the country was in the grip of an appalling famine which cost millions of lives in the Ukraine and elsewhere.

In the towns there were few consumer goods, housing was totally inadequate and from 1929 to 1933 workers' wages fell by half.[9] Disgruntled workers kept labour productivity low and, deprived of the right to strike or protest collectively, discontent was expressed individually through changing jobs. This was economically disruptive. In 1930 the average worker moved workplace every eight months. In 1939 it was every 13 months.[10] At one Moscow factory half the workforce quit during the first half of 1936 due to a drop in earnings.[11]

Forced labour was another feature. At this time there were between 3 and 5 million people in slave labour camps—the notorious *gulag*. Filtzer writes that: "By the time war broke out in June 41 the Soviet working class was in a worse position politically and socially than it had been at any time since the Bolshevik Revolution".[12]

To enforce such draconian policies Stalin not only had to repress society in general but also parts of the state itself, starting with the

Bolshevik Party. By 1927 Trotsky's Left Opposition was destroyed. Then Stalin turned on his erstwhile ally Bukharin and his Right Opposition. The scale of repression was revealed in President Khrushchev's "secret speech" of 1956: "Of the 139 members and candidates of the party's Central Committee (elected in 1934) 70 percent were arrested and shot... Of 1,966 delegates...1,108 were arrested".[13]

Stalinist terror is often portrayed as the arbitrary, irrational result of one man's obsession. However, it had a double purpose. The gains of October 1917 had to be nullified in order to meet the requirements of imperialist competition. Therefore, as Reiman has pointed out, repression had a horrible logic:

> While political terror played an important role, the real core of Stalinism...was social terror, the most brutal and violent treatment of very wide sections of the population, the subjection of millions to exploitation and oppression of an absolutely exceptional magnitude and intensity. The social function of terror and repression explains the apparent irrationality, senselessness, and obscure motivation of Stalin's penal system. As a social instrument, terror could not be aimed narrowly, at particular persons. It was an instrument of violent change, affecting the living and working conditions of millions, imposing the very worst forms of social oppression, up to and including the slave labour of millions of prisoners.[14]

The results of this programme were impressive at one level. The first Russian tank model appeared in 1929 and by 1933, 3,000 were produced annually. The Soviet Union developed the equivalent of the Panzer Division two years before Germany. By the mid-1930s "the Soviet Union led the world in production, planning, and fielding of mechanised forces. Perhaps most important, the Red Army was well ahead of its German counterparts".[15] On the eve of war, while Germany marginally outnumbered the Soviet Union in divisions and soldiers, the ratio of Soviet to German tanks was 3.8:1, planes 2.2:1 and artillery 1.4:1.[16]

And yet Stalinism risked its own core purpose—the defence of the state. Suspicion of virtually every segment of the population, including its own high officials, became a self-destructive process. The repression designed to ultimately strengthen the military spilled over into repression of these very forces. Between May 1937 and September 1938:

> 36,761 men were purged in the army and more than 3,000 in the navy...
> All military district commanders were removed, 90 percent of the district chiefs of staff and deputies, 80 percent of corps and divisional

commanders, 90 percent of staff officers and chiefs of staff. A sharp fall in the intellectual quality of officers resulted. By the beginning of 1941 only 7.1 percent of commanding officers had a higher military education...and 12 percent of officers and political personnel had had no military education at all. By the summer of 1941, about 75 percent of officers and 70 percent of political officers had been in their posts for less than a year.[17]

This not only removed valuable experience. US historians conclude that those who survived realised that "in contrast to the German belief in subordinate initiative...any show of independent judgment was hazardous to their personal health".[18] Thus: "The bloodletting...tore the brain from the Red Army, smashed its morale, stifled any spark of original thought, and left a magnificent hollow military establishment, ripe for catastrophic defeat".[19]

Stalin's domestic policies had both prepared the Soviet Union for an inter-imperialist conflict and damaged its chances of success. It possessed mountains of military equipment but had destroyed the skilled people who could deploy it. This did not go unnoticed. Hitler commented: "This guy is a lunatic! He is destroying his own army!"[20]

Foreign policy

The same contradictions obtained in the sphere of foreign policy. The millions of foreign Communists who made up the Communist International (Comintern) identified the Soviet Union as the embodiment of socialism and Stalin was perfectly prepared to subordinate their energy and enthusiasm to his imperialist goals.

In 1929 he needed left cover to carry through counter-revolution at home and so adopted an insane policy called "the Third Period line". This led the powerful German Communist Party to categorise the German Socialist Party as "social fascist". To divide the working class at a time when the real fascists, the Nazis, were making a bid for power was an awful mistake. The error became clear after Hitler became German chancellor in 1933 and wiped out the Communists. Stalin had helped an aggressive imperialist committed to *Lebensraum* ("living space" in the east) gain command of Europe's strongest economy.

Now that the Soviet Union was under increased threat the question was, who were its real allies? Although the prospects of international revolution had receded for the time being, grassroots opposition to imperialist policies was still the best means of avoiding a war for repartition of the world. Stalin did not see it that way. He was now a player in the imperialist game and saw his future as playing one state off against the other. This was the genesis of the Popular Front, a policy diametrically opposite to the Third Period. Launched in 1934, it consisted of seeking an alliance with Britain and France against Germany. To achieve this Stalin was prepared to sacrifice the revolutionary potential of the mass uprising in Spain against Franco and his Nazi/fascist backers. A workers' victory in the Spanish Civil War (1936-1939) would have boosted the confidence of anti-imperialism everywhere. The Popular Front policy prevented that. During the Second World War the interests of the resistance movements led by Communists would also be sacrificed.

Despite the switch to a popular front policy Soviet appeals for friendship were ignored by the British and French governments. This was epitomised by the fate of Czechoslovakia, the last surviving parliamentary democratic state in Central or Eastern Europe. When Hitler threatened invasion an alliance of the Soviet Union and the West would have confronted Germany with war on two fronts. But the British prime minister, Neville Chamberlain, signed a non-aggression pact with Hitler at the Munich Conference of September/October 1938, handing over the key defensive region of the Sudetenland. In March 1939 the rest of Czechoslovakia was dismembered.

If one imperialist camp was uncooperative, Stalin concluded, why not collaborate with another? The result was the Hitler-Stalin pact, signed on 23 August 1939. It is true this mirrored the Chamberlain-Hitler pact of Munich,[21] but that is not a justification. Making Poland the victim after Czechoslovakia was no improvement. Yet Volkogonov argues: "Looking back, the Non-Aggression Pact appears extremely tarnished, and morally an alliance with the Western democracies would have been immeasurably more preferable. But neither Britain nor France were ready for such an alliance. From the point of view of state interest the Soviet Union had no other acceptable choice".[22] And that is precisely the point. Once the force that could oppose imperialism, the international working class, was abandoned for "state interest" in the imperialist game, the outcome could only be a self-serving admixture of fear, cynical greed and shared imperialist interests.

Alongside public phraseology of non-aggression secret protocols made it a pact for war of conquest.[23] As Stalin said, the non-aggression pact was "cemented by blood".[24] While Germany seized western Poland, the Soviet Union would be authorised to occupy what remained as well as the Baltic states and Romanian territory. This added 23 million people to the Soviet Union's population of 170 million.[25] It also meant that during the Second World War the Nazis found numerous collaborators in the (formerly Polish) Western Ukraine, the Baltic states, Romania and Finland.[26]

On the first anniversary of the signing of the Hitler-Stalin pact the official Soviet newspaper, *Pravda*, admitted it assisted Hitler's war strategy: "this pact has made things easier for us; it has also been of great advantage to Germany, since she can be completely confident of peace on her Eastern borders".[27] Exploiting this confidence for his own ends, Stalin used Germany's preoccupation with the Second World War to launch an ill-fated war with Finland. Not for nothing did Molotov, the Soviet foreign minister, tell the Supreme Soviet on 31 October 1939 that: "the new Soviet-German relations are built on a strong basis of mutual interests".[28]

It is easy to imagine the demoralising effect on anti-fascists everywhere of Molotov welcoming the subjugation of Poland, "that monster child of the Versailles treaty".[29] And later on as the Wehrmacht stormed across Western Europe *Pravda* put forward an extraordinary explanation for who was at fault: "the German armies have achieved considerable successes. They have occupied the greater part of Holland... We can see how great is the responsibility of the Anglo-French imperialists who, by rejecting Germany's peace offers, set off the Second Imperialist War in Europe".[30]

When Germany came to invade the Soviet Union, it descended upon an imperialist competitor which had partly wasted its advantage at home and damaged potential for resistance to Nazi war plans abroad.

From imperialist rivalry to people's war

Despite Stalin's manoeuvring, war was virtually inevitable, and his approach to it combined avarice and cowardice. On 5 May 1941 he told his generals they were entering an "era during which the Soviet state would develop and expand".[31] At that time he expected to make the first move,[32] believing Hitler would not start a war on two fronts and would first defeat Britain before acting.[33] In June, however, Stalin was warned no less than 80 times that Germany was about to invade:[34]

> Communist railway workers in Sweden, resistance fighters in Poland, and numerous other agents reported the massive buildup of forces in the east. German high-altitude reconnaissance aircraft flew over Soviet territory on more than 300 occasions...[35]

Unfortunately, Stalin's fear of displeasing Hitler had become "maniacal", according to General Zhukov, the most important Soviet military figure of the war.[36] So while senior commanders called for a general alert, Stalin responded by saying that "it would be premature to issue that order...border units must not allow themselves to be provoked".[37]

This mistake came very close indeed to losing the entire war[38] because it gave Operation Barbarossa (the German codename for the invasion of the Soviet Union) the overwhelming element of surprise. The experience of Oleg Ozerov shows the consequences:

> I was a participant in the fighting from the very start, 4am on the morning of 22 June 1941... The terrible pressure of the fascists compelled us to withdraw from prepared positions. The route was difficult and long. Enemy aircraft commanded the sky, German tanks bypassed our positions and threatened to surround us... It was totally unlike what we were told to expect; that we would be fighting "on the enemy's territory, and at little cost in blood".[39]

On the first morning 1,200 aircraft were destroyed, mostly on the ground.[40] After the first day the Germans had penetrated some 60 km.[41] By the end of the first week "virtually all of the Soviet mechanised corps lost 90 percent of their strength".[42] In the period June to December 1941 the Germans took some 3 million prisoners of war (POWs). Their fate was tragic. The total number of Soviet POWs who died from hunger, cold and torture was 5 million.[43]

The impact on civilians was similar. Grossman was a witness:

> I've never seen anything like what I am seeing now... Exodus! Biblical exodus! Vehicles are moving in eight lanes... This isn't a flood, this isn't a river, it's the slow movement of a flowing ocean, this flow is hundreds of metres wide. Children's heads, fair and dark, are looking out from under the improvised tents covering the carts, as well as the biblical beards of Jewish elders, shawls of peasant women, hats of Ukrainian uncles, and the black-haired heads of Jewish girls and women. What silence is in their eyes, what wise sorrow, what sensation of fate, of a universal catastrophe.[44]

With Stalin close to a nervous breakdown it fell to Molotov to inform a stunned population by radio that yesterday's friend had committed an aggression "unprecedented in the history of civilisation".[45] By 3 July Stalin's courage had returned but he gave no hint of apology. "The war of fascist Germany against the USSR began under favourable conditions for their army, and unfavourable ones for the Soviet army." His speech combined two key elements. The first was an appeal for "a great war of all the Soviet peoples against the German-fascist army...a fatherland war". Yet even as the general secretary called for war by the people, it was not a war for the people but for his repressive regime.

> Stalin would not be Stalin if he did not call for the extermination of the internal enemy. With no sense of self-reflection Stalin declared: "We must organise merciless struggle against all disorganising forces, deserters, panic-mongers... All those whose cowardly panic interferes with defence must be immediately judged by military Tribunal, regardless of who they are".[46]

It was ironic that the people's war that Stalin now invoked was hampered by his own past policies. It is difficult to ascertain popular opinion under a totalitarian state but a study of NKVD (secret police) files in Volodosk, Eastern Ukraine, gets over this obstacle. Lack of enthusiasm for war showed itself in 1940 when the government sought to raise three battalions from the area: 500 invitations to recruitment offices were issued, 40 individuals attended but only three actually joined the Red Army.[47] Significantly, the imperialist seizure of Eastern Poland was disapproved of: "The Bolsheviks said that we didn't need any foreign land. So why are they crossing the Polish frontier and seizing foreign land".[48]

On the eve of Barbarossa comments like this were recorded: "Advance towards socialism? We are miles behind the bourgeois countries," and "Communism is supposed to be less about worrying about work, and more about yourself." Thus the latest extension of working hours felt like "the imposition of martial law" and just "a way of replenishing the prisons". The most negative views were expressed by women whose husbands had been purged. Even after 22 June one woman said: "We are happy if the Germans cross the Soviet Union's frontier as our men will be released from prison. Hitler will replace the current leaders. That would make them cry, but we are crying too." Another opined: "Thank goodness the war has begun...without the Communists life will be better".[49]

The mood in the Soviet Union changed very quickly once the imperialist character of the invaders was revealed. German soldiers were told: "For your personal glory you must kill 100 Russians. Have no heart and no nerves—in war they are unnecessary. Extinguish pity and compassion, kill all Russians; none should remain—old, women, girls or boys. Kill. That will save you from defeat and guarantee your land forever".[50] The general guideline for German rule was: "Under no circumstances should the status quo be maintained... This will necessarily lead to the extinction of both the [native agriculture] industry and larger segments of the population... Tens of millions of people in these areas will become superfluous and either die or have to move to Siberia".[51] Along with this came the Holocaust and involved directly targeted murder, such as the mass shooting of 34,000 Jews at Babi Yar, Kiev.

Other horrors were recorded by Grossman. He described conditions for miners under the Germans: "One day of absence from work meant a concentration camp... They were beaten with lashes while working".[52] He interviewed a young teenage boy:

> "Where is your father?"
> "Killed," he answered.
> "And mother?"
> "She died."
> "Have you got brothers and sisters?"
> "A sister. They took her to Germany."
> "Have you got any relatives?"
> "No, they were all burned in a partisan village".[53]

Werth, another eyewitness, summed up the general reaction to the carnage:

> They were robbing, and looting and killing; when they were retreating they would burn down every house, and in the depth of winter civilians were left without house and home... The anger and resentment against the Germans, mixed with a feeling of infinite pity for the Russian people, for the Russian land, defiled by the invader, produced an emotional reaction of national pride and national injury.[54]

Volodosk's NKVD registered the impact of Nazi aggression on popular consciousness. During the first half of 1941 there were 2,304 army deserters and 1,684 draft dodgers; but between 22 June and 1 September 1941 the figure for deserters was 59.[55] In workplaces large-scale collections were held to support the army. The 2,270 workers of a locomotive factory set out to "double and then triple production" norms. This may have been management propaganda but it was the case that at the end of 1941 output had exceeded the annual norm by 123 percent. Thousands of local people also became blood donors.[56]

The peculiarities of the Soviet Union's war from below

War from below, a people's war, was a common phenomenon in the Second World War and the Soviet Union was no exception. Many commentators have argued that it was this which rescued the country. Volkogonov, historian and former head of the Soviet military's psychological warfare department, writes: "In those dark days, the enemy struck blow after blow and Stalin felt that only a miracle would save him. But it was the people who saved him, the people who found the strength to stand firm".[57]

It was this readiness of ordinary people to risk their lives in fighting fascism that turned the situation around. And, as one veteran puts it: "We were not defending Stalin, but our homes and families... At the front, in our battery were Armenians, Kazakhs, Russians and representatives of other nationalities. There were many nationalities in my unit. There were those who didn't want to fight, but we were an example of heroism".[58] Another explains that: "For me Stalin appears to have been the embodiment of an evil genius—cunning, but absolutely amoral and ruthless. We did not win the war thanks to Stalin, but despite him!"[59]

The people's war saved the Soviet Union in spite of Stalin. It does not follow that it was an independent alternative to Stalin.

In the rest of Europe the rapid advance of Axis forces either drove governments into exile (as in Greece or Yugoslavia) or induced them to collaborate (like Vichy France). In these circumstances resistance movements were relatively free of Allied imperialism and reflected the needs of the ordinary people who participated. That was not the case in the Soviet Union. The social atomisation wrought by Stalinism, fear of repression and the destruction of viable alternatives such as Trotskyism, made it virtually impossible to generate a collective response that stood apart from the regime.

This did not mean that the state could do without the people's war. One difficulty Stalin faced was that official "Communist" ideology was tarnished by association with repression and exploitation, so it was sidelined. On the anniversary of the Bolshevik Revolution in 1941 Stalin talked of a war inspired by "our great ancestors", victorious in battles in 1242, 1380, over Poland in the 1600s, and against Napoleon.[60] Relations with the Russian Orthodox Church were also carefully cultivated.[61] Instead of combating extreme German nationalism with internationalism, he invoked Russian chauvinism.

The dissolution of the Comintern in May 1943 was emblematic of the new direction in internal propaganda as well as a move to placate Britain and the US. To the extent that such reactionary appeals were felt to be effective, this unfortunately proved the lack of a meaningful alternative on offer. But such chauvinism came with a price—the alienation of numerous non-Russian victims of "Russification" under the tsars.

The presence of people's war but its lack of independent self-expression was evident in four arenas: the Red Army, partisan struggles, among Soviet citizens in the unoccupied areas and non-Soviet movements under Nazi occupation.

At the front

It was in the Red Army that the mettle of the people's war was tested to the greatest degree. According to one fairly conservative estimate, the Soviet Union suffered 10 million military deaths. Britain and the US lost 300,000 and 274,000 respectively.[62] This disparity cannot be attributed to inferior fighting abilities on the part of the Red Army. Although 3.2 Red Army soldiers died for every one German,[63] this ratio was partly due to the disastrous way Stalin allowed millions of his soldiers to be captured and killed early on. The ratio of Allied to Axis deaths on the eastern front was 1.3 to 1 compared to 2.2 to 1 in the west.[64]

The shattering assault of the Wehrmacht did lead to disarray and a loss of nerve. In July 1942 Stalin's Order 227, "Not one step backwards" introduced draconian penalties for "cowards and deserters". Anyone who surrendered would be "be shot on the spot" and their family arrested.[65] This undoubtedly helped restore order and stem the rout. But soon afterwards the war from below against fascism became a self-generating phenomenon and so, as one veteran puts it, "The impact of Order 227 was not prolonged. Already after a few months...it was more or less 'forgotten' as more punishment measures were not needed".[66]

The Battle of Stalingrad, fought during the winter of 1942-1943, is generally recognised as the key turning point in the fortunes of war. Before this event the Axis powers were in the ascendant. Afterwards their doom was generally predicted, even though many years of fighting lay ahead. Chuikov, a key commander at Stalingrad, told Grossman: "A soldier who'd spent three days here considered himself an old-timer. Here, people only lived for one day".[67] Viktor Karelin lost both hands in fighting and describes the circumstances:

> We had to fight the enemy step-by-step, one room after the other, floor after floor, structure after structure... I made it to the middle of the street in two or three leaps. And suddenly a burst of fire flashed in front of my eyes...my left forearm began to burn with pain. A round had passed through it... Then I looked at my right hand. The fingers on my gloves had been mangled into unrecognisable shreds, like the frayed ends of a

rope... A mine detonated several metres behind me... Twice my comrades had tried to drag me out from under fire, each time unsuccessfully. One Soviet soldier was killed, the other seriously wounded.[68]

While civilians, partisans and soldiers centred their fight on the Nazi enemy, the state focused on maintaining its grip. It fought the imperialist rival but continued to suppress its own population. Order 227 had established penal battalions to which those who had been imprisoned by the enemy were sent. Almost half a million Red Army POWs ended up in these units. Alexander Revich, who escaped from the Germans twice, was one:

> Punishment battalions meant death. 90 percent of the time they were used for surprise attacks, usually without artillery support. While army advances were backed by tanks, a soldier in a punishment battalion fought with bare hands and virtually all of them died. They could go to hell, because to have been captured, was an absolute crime.[69]

Oleg Ozerov was taken as a POW to France but managed to join the Resistance there. He was bitter about his return home in 1945. Interrogated by SMERSH, the counter-terrorist department, he felt:

> Stalin simply betrayed us. He considered anyone who became a POW to be a traitor. We were not even recognised as having stoically resisted fascist conquest before or after capture. Yet we had created secret cells and organised escapes. According to German figures, 500,000 Soviet prisoners successfully broke out in the war years. Many were recaptured or shot, but those who made it to freedom, joined partisan units and continued the fight against occupation.[70]

Nevertheless: "The majority of my comrades, former prisoners of the Germans, ended up in the Gulag after the war despite their fighting for the Resistance! Many were shot without a trial or died in Soviet camps".[71] Stalin's assault on his own people was less intense than against his imperialist rival but the scale was still enormous. When the occupied territories were recovered the NKVD arrested 931,549 people for "checking" of whom two thirds were in the armed services.[72]

The partisans

Partisans in occupied Soviet territory, like their counterparts elsewhere in Axis-occupied Europe, acquired a powerful reputation for anti-fascist activity. Yet their path to struggle was fraught. In the 1920s and 1930s the Soviet Union, marshalling the skills and experience of veterans from the civil war period, made considerable preparations for partisan warfare. However, as P K Ponomarenko, who led the Second World War partisan movement from Moscow later wrote, "Due to Stalin's wrong and mistaken position, that we would only be fighting beyond our own frontiers...all that work was cast aside".[73] Many experts in partisan warfare were killed in the purges of 1937-1938. The movement developed in spite of these obstacles.

It is important not to idealise the red partisan movement. Sokolov suggests that it was often sheer survival under conditions of occupation that drove some to join. Some 60 percent were escaped POWs or Red Army soldiers overtaken by the swift enemy advance.[74] The rest were local inhabitants. There were examples of partisans pillaging local villages, massacring the families of those believed to be collaborators, fighting each other or lapsing into passivity rather than confronting the enemy.[75] Although the Nazi view that Slavs were "Untermenschen" (sub-human) was a drive towards resistance, defections in both directions indicate that ideological principle was not always the main motivation, with some choosing the path of working for the Germans as an alternative survival strategy.[76]

Nonetheless, between November 1942 and March 1943 some 125,000 fighters[77] undertook 2,500 attacks on the enemy railway system, wrecking 750 locomotives and 4,000 wagons. In the summer of 1943 there were 142,000 partisans with 215,000 reserves.[78] A German officer described the impact:

> The struggle with the partisans is different to the fighting at the front. They are everywhere and nowhere...blowing up railways, communication routes, acts of sabotage at all existing enterprises, robbery etc. They become ever more brazen and unfortunately we don't have enough security forces to act decisively against them. We only have the strength, with the Hungarians, to guarantee the main roads, railways and centres of population. Over broad swathes the partisans rule, with their own government and administration.[79]

Some partisan operations were on a grand scale. The destruction of the Savkino Bridge in March 1943 was the work of a 3,000-strong assault force.[80]

Such feats were often accomplished without external assistance, arms coming from supplies left behind by the retreating Red Army. In 1942 a commander in Belorussia sent this radio message: "Young men and women, the old, beg with tears in their eyes to be taken into the partisans, but the numbers we can take are limited by the supply of guns... We need armaments if we are going to put more people on the front line." This plea was echoed by many others.[81] And yet the risks of joining up were enormous. In the autumn of 1943 partisan brigades attempting to force the Dnieper lost 70 percent of their number in a few days.[82] Captured partisans were tortured and killed. The Germans reported that:

> In the overwhelming majority of cases the interrogation of partisans is very difficult. Despite the brutal methods employed, due to their fanatically-held convictions, members of partisan groups refuse to give testimony. It is only at the moment of their being shot that they confess their devotion to Stalin and membership of the partisans.[83]

Though red partisans fought heroically like their counterparts elsewhere, they never developed an independent trajectory. Foreign partisans clashed with the Axis and pursued a path different to that of Allied governments. In their situation admiration for the Soviet Union, mistakenly identified as the embodiment of "actually existing socialism", was no immediate hindrance to this dual struggle (problems arising mainly after the war). But under occupation the proximity of the Stalinist regime across porous front lines tied the red partisans to the Soviet government.

Furthermore, that institution left nothing to chance. Top-down control of the partisans was ever-present. A Central Partisan Headquarters was established in Moscow in May 1942. Stalin's instructions were that "alongside their fighting activities, the leading organs of the partisan movement, commanders and commissars of partisan units must always disseminate among the population the rightness of the Soviet Union's cause".[84] Another source of control was through the supply of weaponry. One directive required that apart from arms seized from the enemy, "all arms and equipment for the partisan movement...must go through the appropriate application process".[85]

The unoccupied areas

The incredible speed of the German advance, which overtook so many Red Army formations, meant that basic defence tasks often fell to civilians. Veterans describe the role of the people's militias that formed spontaneously in the defence of Leningrad: "Volunteers showed exceptional heroism, though it was fairly absurd that they were fighting at the front at all. They had insufficient military training and lacked arms. We had one gun between three! Still, I am quite certain that it was the volunteers who saved Leningrad".[86] The whole population was involved.

Another Leningrad veteran was then a 13-year-old girl. Elena Rzhevskaia watched the militia march off from her window: "There were workers, students, white-collar employees, musicians and professors... They all went to fight the enemy inspired by an enormous wave of patriotism. I didn't feel like a hero. I simply had to share the fate of my people, of my country".[87] So she joined the partisans in the woods.

The evacuation of industry to the east, well beyond the reach of the advancing Germans, was one of the most extraordinary non-military feats of the Second World War. It could not have been achieved without a titanic physical effort. The figures are staggering. By October 1941, 65 percent of the Economic Ministry's military-industrial enterprises had been relocated. Between July and November 1941, 1,523 factories, 1,360 related to armaments, were transferred using 1.5 million railroad wagons.[88] These plants were dismantled, loaded, and reconstructed "non-stop for 24 hours a day, often under enemy bombing".[89] Writing in 1942 a US eyewitness wrote: "Even if Moscow is lost, the Red armies will be able to go on fighting for months, even years, basing themselves on the stronghold of the Urals... All this sums up one basic reason why the Soviet Union has not suffered decisively as a result of Hitler's attack. The second basic reason is the Soviet people".[90]

Non-Soviet movements under Nazi occupation

If in the occupied lands Soviet partisans were unable to develop any real independence from the Stalinist state, were there alternative currents ideologically free from both Moscow and Berlin? We have seen that Stalinist repression in the pre-war period minimised the chances of organised opposition developing in the Soviet Union. Now in the parts under German control there was a new, equally vicious power at work. How would the population react?

We have seen the core of German policy was racism and imperialist exploitation which planned the deaths of millions. But there were countercurrents to this blanket approach. Klaus von Shtraffenberg of the SS wrote in 1942: "The SS, despite its Untermenschen theory, uses people without scruple. And if Himmler organises a Russian liberation movement, he will win for the SS hundreds of thousands of Russians".[91] This more flexible approach opened the way for Germany to encourage collaboration.

Caught in a vice between the two power blocs, some chose the German side, though the number of Soviet citizens who did this is disputed.[92] Zhukov and Kovtin think the number between 700,000 and a million, Medinskii suggests 200,000,[93] while Burovskii says "millions".[94] Given that there were over 5 million Soviet POWs and the population under German occupation reached 80 million, even the higher estimates show collaboration was limited.

In May 1943 Germany's "Eastern troops" were formed of 170 battalions, of which 30 came from Turkestan, 21 were Cossack, 12 Azeri, 12 Georgian, ten Ukrainian, nine Armenian and so on.[95] Interpreting such data is difficult, and there is no agreement among contemporary Soviet historians about whether the Germans were using the collaborators as their tools or whether these people were leaning on Nazi support as a necessary resource to defend themselves from the Stalinist system. Undoubtedly the motives were varied. Some joined the Axis to escape life as Soviet POWs, whose death rate at the hands of the Germans was 58 percent, compared to 4 percent for British and US POWs.[96] Others were reacting to Russian chauvinism stretching back to tsarist times. No doubt some wholeheartedly agreed with fascism and became its willing perpetrators.

The complexity of the issue at the level of whole ethnic groups can be illustrated by reference to the Crimean Tatars and Chechens. During the Second World War Germany hoped to bring Turkey on to its side and so wooed the ethnically related Tatars. "Racial specialists" from Berlin were tasked with reclassifying them from "lower race" to "Eastern Goths". Between 8,000 and 20,000 volunteered for active military service under the Germans.[97] Traffic was not all in one direction, however. At Soviet Partisan HQ the person responsible for the area reported: "The atrocities, pillaging and violence of the Germans embitters and enrages the population of the occupied territories... In the last six weeks 14,060 have joined partisan units, of which there are now 138".[98] Tatars played a part in the Red Army too. While they formed 2.5 percent of the Soviet population, they made up 1.4 percent of those given the military honour of Hero of the Soviet Union. This ratio compares favourably with other ethnic groups such as Uzbeks, Kazakhs, Georgians and so on.[99]

Chechnya illustrates the link between pre-war Soviet imperialism and the unfolding of events later on. The "Autonomous" Republic of Chechnya had a population of 380,000 in 1939, of whom 57,000 were Chechen and 258,000 Russian, the rest coming from a variety of backgrounds. There were very few city dwellers among the largely Muslim

Chechens whose occupation was overwhelmingly farming. Therefore, they were disproportionately hurt by forced collectivisation in the 1930s. A key element of Chechen personal property was livestock, including horses. In the process of concentration into 490 giant collective farms incorporating 69,400 villages, most livestock was removed. The 1938 purges hit Chechen Communists hard and the party halved in size.[100]

Despite this background, in August 1942 the region produced 18,500 volunteers for the Red Army and eventually 36 Heroes of the Soviet Union.[101] Under occupation it is true that the number of red partisans was limited and collaboration occurred but overall Burovskii concludes: "If you compare those fighting for the Third Reich and the USSR, it seems that the Chechens were 'less guilty' than the Crimean Tatars... A lower percentage of Chechens fought for the Third Reich than did Crimean Tatars, while they performed well as soldiers in the Red Army".[102]

The Soviet state had no time for subtle analysis and showed no awareness of class differentiation or the legacy of Russian chauvinism and religious intolerance. All Crimean Tatars and Chechens were victimised for the actions of some, because, as one writer puts it, the state adopted a "final solution for these undesirable peoples".[103]

In early 1944 Moscow issued a decree to: "Evict all Tatars from the Crimea and place them permanently as special settlers in areas of Uzbekistan".[104] The action took place on 18 May, affected some 200,000 and included Tatars fighting in the Red Army who were sent into forced labour camps. Many people died as a result of this deportation. In February 1944 the entire population of Chechens, young and old, women and men, was declared a collaborationist enemy people and deported. It took 40,200 railway wagons to transport them to their destination.[105] In addition hundreds of thousands from other ethnic groups—Balkars, Ingushes, Kalmyks, Karachays and Meskhetian Turks—were forcibly removed from their homes in collective punishment for collaboration.[106]

Writers hostile to the repressive role of the Soviet regime have searched for popular movements that escaped the confines of Stalinist ideology. The Lokot Republic has been held up as evidence of "an independent Russian state flourishing deep in the German rear", a third way between Nazism and Stalinism.[107] From the German point of view this small Russian administered enclave was an experiment in collaborationism. Its leader, Bronislav Kaminskii, drew on resentment of Stalin, and the Republic's newspaper, *Voice of the People*, reminded readers of mass exploitation and falling living standards in the Soviet Union.[108] One article contrasted "Their way and ours": "Our way—the peasants get the land. Their way—forced collectivisation".[109] However, this did not lead to independence from imperialism in general, simply an alliance with the imperialist rival:

> It is the bloodthirsty Stalin and his Communist and Commissar henchmen who need war, but they are not the ones fighting in the regular army, they are hiding in the rear... They brought poverty and hunger, sending tens of millions of Russians to labour camps, martyrdom and death... The people, our people, do not want a war that will only benefit a handful of scoundrels and active traitors of the population. The German army is the liberator of the Russian people, the friend of the Russian people, and together with them, is the enemy of the entire Stalinist structure and its lackeys.[110]

In practice this meant that the Lokot Republic became an arm of the Nazi war machine. From the first day the "Russian National Liberation Army" of some 8,000 undertook anti-partisan operations, thus relieving the Wehrmacht of that task in the area. In July 1942, 42 clashes between the Lokot militia and red partisans were recorded. In December 1943 there were 573.[111] The administration declared that for every one of its fighters killed, 20 partisan hostages would be executed, the tariff being 50 if a commander died.[112] The Republic finally fell to the Red Army after two years. It had killed some 10,000 civilians including all the Jews in its reach.[113]

If the Lokot Republic failed to achieve an independent stance between the rival imperialisms, the same applied to the purely military experiment that was led by Andrei Vlasov. He was captured by the Germans in July 1942 and like many POWs given the choice of continued captivity or freedom through collaboration.[114] But being a decorated Red Army general he was allotted a special role as leader of an alternative Russian force to the Red Army. Did Vlasov offer a genuine anti-Stalinist alternative or was he simply a pawn in the Nazi propaganda machine?

His manifesto accused Stalin of military failings and ruling through "the terror system". It claimed broad sections of the army and population realised further war could only bring "the destruction of millions". The question was: "What road can lead to the overthrow of Stalin's government and the creation of a new Russia?... And who can best assist that—Germany, England or the US?" Vlasov concluded it was the Germans since they were already at war with Stalin. However, he made a gesture towards an independent stance by suggesting that the millions of Russians in the occupied territories were the basis for "implementing a new Europe in parallel with the Germans".[115]

The hollowness of this pose was exposed when Vlasov called on the Germans to help him establish a Russian army with legal authority in occupied areas. The answer from the German leadership was a flat "No". Goering stated that Germany "never included Vlassov and his army in its calculations".[116] Himmler too was dismissive: "I guarantee we can make almost any Russian general into a Vlasov! And their price is incredibly cheap...schnapps, cigarettes and women".[117]

Although Vlasov's Russian Liberation Army was much vaunted in leaflets dropped behind Soviet lines, it was entirely a fiction. Only in September 1944, when the Germans were in full retreat, was a Russian force of ten divisions agreed to.[118] It fought one unsuccessful battle against the Red Army and soon afterwards, in true opportunist fashion, Vlasov declared: "only if we become a real power alongside the Czechs, Poles, Yugoslavs and prudent Germans will the Anglo-Saxons eventually recognise us." So in May 1945 Vlasov switched sides and backed the Czech resistance to Germany in Prague.

The Stalin phenomenon

In 1945 Stalin triumphed against his imperialist rival but, as Volkogonov writes: "Utterly insensitive to the countless tragedies caused by the war, Stalin was guided by the desire to inflict the greatest possible damage on the enemy without regard to the human cost for the Soviet people".[119] Pursuing a scorched earth policy the general secretary thought nothing of laying waste to vast tracts or destroying entire towns.[120] His guiding star was this: "The law of war is such that whoever seizes booty, keeps it".[121] Whatever country the Red Army marched into was counted as booty and that amounted to most of Eastern Europe.

Hitler and Stalin were both imperialists, though there were differences between them. The former, for historical reasons (related to defeat in the First World War and the Treaty of Versailles), was expansionist. Stalin's initial stance was rather more defensive (though this changed when the opportunity presented itself in 1945). Hitler was the unashamed representative of violent counter-revolution, racism and untrammelled capitalist exploitation. Stalin's regime was the product of counter-revolution but clung to the socialist rhetoric of October 1917. If within the Soviet Union this merely covered up the horrors of forced collectivisation, industrialisation and the gulag, internationally the struggles at places like Stalingrad were a potent source of inspiration for resistance movements and anti-fascism generally.

Soviet victory over Germany ultimately relied on war from below. It cost the lives of some 27 million Soviet citizens, most of them civilians,[122] and was motivated by a hatred of occupation and hope for a better life. As one war veteran puts it: "I didn't think about the Gulag or other sad things. I believed that after the war, as an ally of Britain and the US, Stalin would see the sense of introducing democratic reforms".[123] Another affirms that: "many hoped that after the war the country would be more democratic, [but, alas] after the victory arrests gained a new intensity".[124]

It was out of the disjuncture between imperialist and people's war that one of the most extraordinary phenomena of the era was to emerge. Despite the famine and pre-war repression, despite the disaster of Barbarossa, despite the deportations of entire populations and the interrogations of SMERSH, Stalin acquired the status of demigod.

As we have seen, the returning POW, Ozerov, felt betrayed by Stalin but writes: "He was often right, and in a big country like the USSR you can only maintain order through iron discipline. Stalin was the man who united the whole people... Without him victory was impossible".[125] Another veteran says: "I was thrown in jail at the age of 13, my mother-in-law was arrested, my father-in-law shot, yet I still believed in Stalin!"[126] Finally, this soldier, after noting the killing of millions of innocent people, including his own father, concludes that: "Stalin united the whole Soviet Union in the struggle for victory".[127]

These are classic examples of what Marx calls the "enchanted, perverted, topsy-turvy world" of reification.[128] In a similar vein Wilhelm Reich wrote how repression makes a person hide "behind illusions of strength and greatness, someone else's strength and greatness. He's proud of his great generals but not of himself".[129] The masses suffered enormously in their successful war against fascism but were unable to claim victory for themselves. So they projected their achievements onto Stalin. His cult was inverted proof of their strength and greatness.

NOTES

1   V Medinskii, *Voina, Mify SSSR, 1939-1945* (Olma, Moscow, 2012), p394.
2   Medinskii, 2012, p39.
3   Vladimir Lenin, Second All-Russia Congress of Soviets of Workers' and Soldiers' Deputies, *Report on Peace*, October 26 (November 8) 1917, at www.marxists.org/archive/lenin/works/1917/oct/25-26/26b.htm.
4   Quoted in D Hallas, *The Comintern* (Bookmarks, London, 1985), p123.
5   M Beloff, *The Foreign Policy of Soviet Russia 1929-1941*, vol 2 (Oxford University Press, Oxford, 1949), p20.
6   Quoted in A Applebaum, *Gulag: A History* (Penguin, London, 2004), pp68-69.
7   Details from T Cliff, *Trotsky: The Darker the Night, the Brighter the Stars*, vol 4, ch 2, at www.marxists.org/archive/cliff/works/1993/trotsky4/02-industrial.html.
8   Cliff, *Trotsky*, vol 4, ch 1, at marxists.org/archive/cliff/works/1993/trotsky4/01-collect.html.
9   Cliff, *Trotsky*, ch 2, at marxists.org/archive/cliff/works/1993/trotsky4/02-industrial.html.
10 D Filtzer, *Soviet Workers and Stalinist Industrialization* (Pluto Press, London, 1986), p135.
11 Filtzer, 1986, p138.
12 Filtzer, 1986, p150.
13 N Khrushchev, *The Secret Speech* (Spokesman Books, Nottingham, 1976), p33.
14 M Reiman, *The Birth of Stalinism* (Bloomington, Indiana University Press, 1987), p49.
15 D M Glantz and J House, *When Titans Clashed* (Birlinn, Kansas, 2000), pp9-10.
16 A Burovskii, *Velikaia Grazhdanskaia Voina* (Iauza Eksmo, Moscow, 2011), p211.
17 D Volkogonov, *Stalin: Triumph and Tragedy* (Grove Weidenfeld, New York, 1991), pp368-369.
18 Glantz, 2000, p33.
19 Glantz, 2000, p44. This judgement is confirmed by Stepan Mikoyan in E Joli, *Pobeda liuboi tsenoi* (Iausa:Eksmo, Moscow, 2010), p116.
20 Elena Rzhevskaia, in E Joli, 2010, p215.
21 Medinskii, 2012, p54.
22 Volkogonov, 1991, p395.
23 Danilov in V Suvorov and M Solonin (eds), *Pro... li Voinu! Kak Stalin Ugrobil Krasnuiu Armiu i Pogubil SSSR* (Iauza-Press, Moscow, 2012), p193.
24 Quoted in A Werth, *Russia at War* (Dutton & Co, New York, 1964), p71.
25 Quoted in Werth, 1964, p111.
26 Werth, 1964, p111.
27 Quoted in Werth, 1964, p96; Pronin in Suvorov, 2012, p191.
28 Aleksandr Pronin, "Sovetsko-Pol'skie Sobytia 1939 g", in Suvorov, 2012, p104.
29 Quoted in Werth, 1964, p62.
30 *Pravda*, 16 May 1940, quoted in Werth, 1964, p86.
31 Danilov in Suvorov, 2012, p221.
32 V Suvorov, "Vdrug oni Voz'mut i Pomiriatsia", in Suvorov, 2012, p17.
33 Danilov, 89 and Kirill Aleksandrov, "Planirovalsia Udar po Rumynii v napravlenii neftianykh mestorozhenii", pp219-233, in Suvorov, 2012. Also Georgii Kumanev 238, why did we lose at first? Stalin was convinced Hitler would not fight on two fronts and so would have to defeat the UK first. 393 A month before the G attack, S, speaking to a close circle, said: "The conflict is inevitable, perhaps in May next year." By the early summer of 1941, acknowledging the explosiveness of the situation, he approved the premature release of military cadets, and young officers and political workers were posted, mostly without leave, straight to units which were below full strength. On 19 June begin camouflaging aerodromes, transport depots, bases and fuel dumps, dispersing aircraft. The order came hopelessly late, and even then Stalin was reluctant in case "all these measure provoke the German forces."
34 Vasily Grossman (author), A Beevor and L Vinogradova (translators), *A Writer at War: Vasily Grossman with the Red Army 1941-1945* (Pimlico, London, 2006), p3.
35 Glantz, 2000, p41.

36 Volkogonov, 1991, p400.
37 Volkogonov, 1991, p401.
38 Stepan Mikoyan, in Joli, 2010, p117.
39 Oleg Ozerov, in Joli, 2010, p87. Confirmed by another veteran—30 we didn't think there would be fighting in Russia but in Germany; Dannil Granin in Joli, 2010.
40 Glantz, 2000, p49.
41 Volkogonov, 1991, p406.
42 Glantz, 2000, p51.
43 Joli, 2010, p23.
44 Grossman p48.
45 Burovskii, 2011, p234.
46 Burovskii, 2011, p236.
47 Aleksandr Kuz'minykh, "Navernoe, budet voina..." in Suvorov, 2012, p278.
48 Aleksandr Kuz'minykh, "Navernoe, budet voina..." in Suvorov, 2012, pp273-275.
49 Aleksandr Kuz'minykh, "Navernoe, budet voina..." in Suvorov, 2012, p280.
50 Quoted in Mediniskii, 2012, pp127-128.
51 Quoted in G Aly, *Hitler's Beneficiaries* (Verso, London, 2006), p171.
52 Grossman, p222.
53 Grossman, p249.
54 Werth, 1964, p271.
55 Aleksandr Kuz'minykh, "Navernoe, budet voina..." in Suvorov, 2012, p286.
56 Aleksandr Kuz'minykh, "Navernoe, budet voina..." in Suvorov, 2012, p288.
57 Volkogonov, 1991, p434.
58 Y Grigorian in Joli, 2010, p313.
59 S Mikoyan in Joli, 2010, p262.
60 Werth, 1964, p249.
61 Volkogonov, 1991, p486.
62 I C B Dear and M R D Foot, *The Oxford Companion to the Second World War* (OUP, Oxford, 1995), p290.
63 Volkogonov, 1991, p505.
64 Medinskii, 2012, pp394-395.
65 Quoted in Volkogonov, 1991, p427.
66 G Ter-Gazariants in Joli, 2010, p129.
67 Grossman, p155.
68 Quoted in D Loza, F*ighting for the Soviet Motherland* (Nebraska Press, Nebraska, 1998), pp129-130.
69 Alexander Revich in Joli, 2010, p167.
70 Oleg Ozerov in Joli, 2010, pp87-88.
71 Ozerov in Joli, 2010, p96.
72 Volkogonov, 1991, p445.
73 B V Sokolov, *Okkupatsiia, Pravda i Mify*, 2002 in militera.lib.ru/research/sokolov3/index.html.
74 Sokolov, 2002.
75 Sokolov, 2002.
76 Sokolov, 2002.
77 A S Sawin et al (eds), *Der zweite Weltkrieg* (Dietz Verlag, Berlin, 1988), p366.
78 Sokolov, 2002.
79 I Ermolov, *Russkoe Gosudarstvo v Nemetskom Tylu. Istoria Lokotskogo Samoupravleniia*, militera.lib.ru/research/ermolov_igo2/index.html.
80 Sawin et al, 1988, pp366-367.
81 Sokolov, 2002.
82 Sokolov, 2002.
83 Sokolov, 2002.
84 Sokolov, 2002.

85 Sokolov, 2002.
86 D Granin in Joli, 2010, p30.
87 E Rzhevskaia in Joli, 2010, p218.
88 Glantz, 2000, p72.
89 Werth, 1964, p215.
90 J Scott, *Behind the Urals* (Riverside Press, Cambridge, Mass, 1942), p263.
91 D A Zhukov, I I Kovtin. *RNNA. Vrag v Sovetskoi Forme* (Veche, Moscow, 2012), p18.
92 Zhukov, 2012, p27.
93 Medinskii, 2012, p302.
94 Burovskii, 2011, p343.
95 Burovskii, 2011, p344.
96 Medinskii, 2012, p391.
97 Burovskii, 2011, p353.
98 T Selesnev, quoted in Sokolov, 2002.
99 Medinskii, 2012, p265.
100 Burovskii, 2011, pp359-361.
101 This latter figure is for both Chechens and Ingushes—Volkogonov, 1991, p444.
102 Burovskii, 2011, p363.
103 As Burovskii puts it, Burovskii, 2011, p363.
104 GKO decree no. 5859. www.memorial.krsk.ru/DOKUMENT/USSR/440511.htm.
105 Burovskii, 2011, p363.
106 Volkogonov, 1991, p444.
107 See Medinskii's critique, 2012, p331. Ermolov writes, for example: "An important role was played
     by individuals who against the background of the collapse of soviet power in the remaining Red
     Army regions attempted to create a political movement, which, in its conceptions, could in future
     develop beyond the limits of the Lokot district and achieve an all-Russian dimension."(I,
     Ermolov, *Russkoe Gosudarstvo v Nemetskom Tylu. Istoria Lokotskogo Samoupravleniia*, p32.)
108 D I Cherniakov, *Lokotskaia gazeta, 'Golos naroda', na sluzhbe u Natsistkoi propagandy*, www.
     august-1914.ru/occupation2.pdf, p68.
109 Quoted in Cherniakov, p69.
110 Quoted in I Ermolov, p31.
111 Ermolov, p21.
112 Ermolov, pp16-17.
113 Medinskii, 2012, p332.
114 Zhukov, 2012, p67.
115 Oleg Smyslov, *Predateli i Padachi* (Veche, Moscow, 2013), pp76-77.
116 Goering, quoted in Smyslov, 2013, p95.
117 Quoted in Smylsov, 2013, pp94-95.
118 Smyslov, 2013, p147.
119 Volkogonov, 1991, p456.
120 Volkogonov, 1991, p456.
121 Volkogonov, 1991, p491.
122 Volkogonov, 1991, p505.
123 L Rabichev in Joli, 2010, p202.
124 S Mikoyan in Joli, 2010, pp121-122.
125 Ozerov in Joli, 2010, p97.
126 S Mikoyan in Joli, 2010, p262.
127 V Etoosh in Joli, 2010, p150.
128 www.marxists.org/archive/petrovic/1965/reification.htm.
129 W Reich, *Listen, Little Man!* (Farrar, Straus and Giroux, New York, 1974), p7 at www.
     wilhelmreichtrust.org/listen_little_man.pdf

6

The Slovak National Uprising of 1944

Tomáš Tengely-Evans

Introduction

The Slovak National Uprising of 1944 was one of the largest—and shortest—instances of armed insurrection against Nazi occupation during World War Two. It didn't just involve the Slovak partisans, underground guerrilla fighters, but also international volunteers and regular troops. During the height of the Slovak National Uprising (henceforth referred to as the "SNP") 18,000 partisans fought alongside 60,000 standing and reservist troops from the Slovak army, who had answered the call by rebel commanders to fight against father Jozef Tiso's fascist puppet regime, the "Slovak State". This insurgent force was pitted against military units and paramilitary forces loyal to the Tiso regime and 48,000 Waffen SS and Wehrmacht troops who had just occupied the territory on 28 August 1944.

Within two weeks of the start of the SNP on 29 August the insurgent army was in control of central and parts of eastern Slovakia. But this wasn't a purely military operation. The insurgent command directed a basic war economy from its capital in Banska Bystrica in central Slovakia; and small attempts at building a "civil society" were also made, such as a free press and radio station and moves towards reforming public education. However, by the end of October 1944 Nazi forces had successfully recaptured the liberated territory in bitter fighting that saw 10,000 resistance fighters killed and a further 5,000 suffer capture and execution. While a small partisan force continued to fight the Nazi occupation, Slovakia would be liberated not by the partisans but by Marshal Ivan Konev's Russian tank columns.

The insurgent army faced a difficult situation, but the uprising and the way it went down to defeat were both shaped by its own leadership, the broader inter-imperialist rivalry and the relationship between the two. It's not a mere detail that Konev's tanks began rolling through the Dukla Pass into eastern Slovakia just as the Nazis were recapturing Banska Bystrica—and less than a month after the fall of the Warsaw Uprising.

Yet very little is written about the SNP in English or Slovak histories of the Second World War, and Slovak historiography is mired in a right wing revisionist debate. When the Communist Party ruled Czechoslovakia, the SNP was a cornerstone of its propaganda and portrayed as an example of heroic communist resistance to fascism with the party playing the leading role. Now, unsurprisingly, this interpretation is unfashionable, but it has been replaced by a dangerous revisionist trend that paints the SNP as a "Bolshevik putsch" and the fascist "Slovak State" as a progressive, albeit flawed, episode in history (and this is something that reaches far beyond fascist pseudo historians, who can easily be disregarded). Meanwhile, trying to straddle somewhere in the middle is today's official history of a "democratic coalition" against German occupation with the emphasis on social "history from below"—on "what did I do"—without the broader political picture. Neither grasps the reality and full complexity of the SNP, which can only be understood by using our analysis of an *imperialist war from above* and a *people's war from below*.

The "Munich Betrayal" and Czechoslovakia's old ruling class

The SNP was directly triggered by the Nazi occupation of the "Slovak State" on 28 August 1944, but it had been in the making for the previous five years since the British and French governments struck a deal with Hitler that dismembered the Czechoslovak state in 1938. The "Munich Betrayal" illustrates that the Second World War was not a war of the "democratic powers" against fascism; but it was also important in shaping how the uprising played out in a number of ways from both above and below. While the SNP weakened the old ruling class and opened up the possibility for fightback against the Nazis from below, it left the old rulers strong enough to make the running for leadership of any resistance movement.

The representatives of the dominant wing of Western Europe's ruling classes—that favoured "appeasement"—made clear the position of imperialist powers throughout the 1930s. Anthony Eden, the British foreign secretary, had said in 1936 that: "Nations cannot be expected to incur automatic obligations *save for areas where their vital interests are concerned*".[1] The strategic interests of British imperialism did not extend into Eastern Europe, and certainly didn't include safeguarding "plucky little" Czechoslovakia's independence.

France had signed a treaty in 1925 that guaranteed Czechoslovakia's borders and there had been a long-standing relationship between both ruling classes. During the First World War a group of middle class nationalists set up the Czechoslovak National Council with the aim of gaining independence from the Hapsburg Empire. This group represented an aspirant Czechoslovak ruling class, and it would indeed become the ruling class that tried to cling onto power right up until the Communist Party took control in 1948. It included the likes of Edvard Benes who was the president in the run up to the Munich Betrayal and led the "Czechoslovak government-in-exile" during the war. Its strategy was to win the ruling classes of Europe to supporting Czechoslovak independence through fighting alongside the Entente. The council organised Czechoslovak Legions in France and Italy, and the infamous one that fought against the Bolsheviks during the Russian Civil War.

However, it wasn't in France's imperialist interests to face an all-out confrontation with Nazi imperialism in 1938 either; its government privately hoped that Britain would itself "suggest that pressure should be put on Prague...to acquiesce without seeming to have taken the initiative in the matter".[2] Trotsky aptly summed up the situation at the time: "England and France threw Czechoslovakia into Hitler's maw to give him something to digest for a time and thus postpone the question of the colonies".[3 4] Russia also signed a similar treaty in 1935; however, it could afford to posture much more than the West European powers as it was only obliged to act alongside France and did not actually share a common border with Czechoslovakia.

When the Czechoslovak ruling class had resigned itself to the Munich agreement, President Benes protested that: "We have been disgracefully betrayed" and the new prime minister General Jan Syrovy tried to explain that: "We had no other choice because we had been left alone".[5] But Syrovy had previously promised, "I guarantee that the army stands and will stand on our frontiers to defend our liberty to the last".[6] The dismemberment and subsequent occupation of the inter-war Czechoslovak republic discredited the bourgeois politicians who been hung out to dry by the same West European powers that they had looked to (in particular for Czechoslovakia's rulers, the French state). "I think that the bourgeoisie was discredited...first of all by the defeat of the First Republic in 1938 and secondly by collaboration of part of it with the German", rightly summed up by Jiri Pelikan, a Communist Party member who participated in the resistance in Moravia but fled after the Russian invasion in 1968.[7]

This discrediting meant that the Communist Party in both the Czech and Slovak lands was able to play an important part in the underground resistance, which helped it to attain its relatively strong political position following the war's end in May 1945.[8] But while the party's members on the ground were important resistance fighters, its own leadership sitting in Moscow was under the direction of Russian foreign policy. In the first phase of the occupation the Comintern argued that the main enemy was the Czechoslovak bourgeoisie headed by Benes and backed by the US and British imperialists. While working with the old ruling class would have been wrong and would weaken the resistance movement, the Communist Party wasn't fighting for a revolutionary alternative but was following the sharp changes in Russian foreign policy. The Comintern's line included: "Even messages signed by [the party leader] Gottwald himself stated that the German soldiers who had invaded Czechoslovakia were, in fact, proletarians in soldiers' uniforms and therefore in no way class enemies".[9]

The Molotov-Ribbentrop Pact that made an alliance between Russia and Nazi Germany further disorientated Communist Party members.[10] This was similar to the experience of other Communist Parties in France, Italy and Greece, which also played an important role in resistance movements. Pelikan argues that: "In fact, the party throughout the country modified these instructions, saying firstly that the comrades in Moscow were not well informed about the situation and secondly that the instructions were completely out of touch with reality".[11] Nonetheless, the party's positions did severely compromise working class resistance to fascism and damaged resistance during the SNP itself.

While the old ruling class's alliance with the West European imperialist powers had discredited them, the Munich Betrayal also meant that a number of them around the old president Edvard Benes could form a "government in exile" that was able to present itself as leading resistance to Nazi occupation. When the Czechoslovak government admitted capitulation on 21 September 1938, there was a public backlash where many of the contradictions in the future resistance first came out. In the capital, Prague, there was a general strike, and then an estimated 100,000 people gathered in Wenceslas Square. The dissident Czechoslovak communist Joseph Guttman wrote:

> On the following day there was a spontaneous outburst of popular wrath. Without any call, without any leadership the workers, in spite of martial law and the prohibition of meetings, went on a complete general strike

and marched in tremendous masses into the heart of Prague. The police disappeared, the soldiers were kept in their barracks to prevent their fraternising with the demonstrators.[12][13]

But this movement wasn't a straightforward expression of workers' anger. While workers did partake in a backlash against the Benes government, the outcome wasn't necessarily progressive. It is true the "state was powerless and the government had to resign", and the crowd was also placing demands on the government for national resistance. However, in response Benes unilaterally appointed General Syrovy head of a "government of national defence". Benes "the democrat" then took what seemed to be his final bow and exited the stage on 5 October 1938.[14] This didn't necessarily counter what the protesters had been demanding and looked like a concession. Trotsky argued, "This summons at first had some semblance of a concession to the people, who were aroused, and who were protesting, demonstrating and demanding resistance to Hitler, arms in hand".[15]

Following Munich different sections of the ruling class looked to shore up their position, and this would have its own particular dynamic in Slovakia. This new military government banned the Communist Party in the Czech lands and Moravia and brought in anti-Semitic legislation in schools to try and appease Nazi imperialism. Nonetheless, Benes's successor Emil Hacha was almost immediately forced to surrender to Hitler but managed to hang on as the nominal head of the Nazi "Protectorate of Bohemia and Moravia". Hacha and co represented a wing of the ruling class that tried to adapt to the occupation, but the other more significant wing sought to regain its old position.

The search for an imperialist sponsor—and the pivot towards Russia

Benes had no intention of going down with the sinking First Republic and now said that his resignation was null as he had given it up under Nazi pressure and betrayal. He appointed himself head of the Czechoslovak National Liberation Committee (CNLC) in Paris in October 1939, which sought diplomatic recognition from the allies as an official "government in exile". To get official recognition and restore the inter-war republic, Benes's committee initially pursued the same strategy that the old Czechoslovak National Council had done during the First World War and set about trying to find new imperialist sponsors.

It sought, in effect, to resurrect the Czechoslovak Legions and began organising military units to fight alongside any ally that it could find—and this went beyond probably the most well known example of Czechoslovakian pilots fighting in the British RAF. Poland used the Munich agreement to annex a part of Czechoslovakia that it had laid claim to, but this didn't stop the formation of the Czechoslovak Legion in Poland. The legion was led by General Ludvik Svoboda, who would later command Czechoslovak troops attached to the Russian army on the Eastern Front and become an important Communist Party ally. Units fought under British command in North Africa against the German North Africa Corps, in the Middle East to regain French imperial possessions and later on on the Western Front following the Normandy landing in 1944.

The Francophile Czechoslovak bourgeoisie first concentrated its efforts on Daladier's French government. Yet while Daladier had not been as enthusiastic as Chamberlain during the Munich negotiations, he proved to be much less open to Benes than Britain's new prime minister Winston Churchill. Despite both France and Britain having declared war on Germany in September 1939, the possibility of face to face confrontation with Nazi imperialism made recognising the CNLC an unsafe and unnecessary option. But as the prospect neared, Benes's strategy of forming military units to fight alongside the Allies began to bear fruit. His promise of Czechoslovak troops meant that France was the first imperialist power to sign a treaty with the CNLC—under the agreement that was signed on 2 October 1939, the Czechoslovak army was formally allowed to reform in France and would fight in the "Battle of France" in 1940.

Following France's defeat in the summer of 1940, Benes now swung his efforts onto the British, having already moved the CNLC's headquarters to Buckinghamshire. Britain's ruling class now found itself in a confrontation with Hitler and so was willing to support Czechoslovakia's dispossessed rulers; and while Benes had complained of "betrayal", the strategy of the Czechoslovak ruling class had always been to find an imperialist sponsor so it found no contradiction with aligning itself with the Western Allies. Trotsky explained that: "The experience revealed in a chemically pure form that Czechoslovakian democracy was not an expression of the "people's will" but simply an apparatus *whereby Czech monopoly capitalism adapted itself to its patron states*".[16]

The impact of Munich on this "apparatus" also meant that this absentee Czechoslovak government recognised the need to find more than one imperialist sponsor. In doing so, it would realise which way the wind was blowing in Eastern Europe and sought to gain Russia as a new sponsor, while still maintaining a balancing act with the Western Allies. The important Treaty of Alliance was signed in December 1943 and another Treaty of Military Cooperation was signed the following spring. The push for recognition by France and Britain initially tied the CNLC's fate to that of the Allies. But moving closer towards Russian imperialism would also have a significant impact on the resistance, and particularly during the SNP in 1944.

Czech resistance in the "Protectorate of Bohemia and Moravia"

The CNLC's strategy to restore the inter-war republic also involved trying to direct actual resistance to the Nazis in both the Czech and Slovak lands. Nazi repression was relatively successful at holding down mass acts of resistance in Czechoslovakia, but it broke out from the beginning of the occupation. Not long after Wehrmacht troops marched into Prague, students took against the Nazi occupation on Czechoslovakia's Independence Day on 28 October 1939. The demonstration attracted an estimated 100,000 people onto the streets, who waved the banned Czechoslovak red, blue and white tricolour and chanted "Germans, get out", "We want freedom" and "Hitler, go away". Nazi forces brutally suppressed the demonstration, during which they shot Vaclav Selacek and medical student Jan Opletal, who was hit in the stomach and would die of his injuries on 11 November. But his funeral procession in Prague on 15 November became the focal point for another demonstration against the occupation in Prague. There were also protests in Ostrava, Pilsen, Hradec Kralove, and Pribram, among a few others. In response the Reich Protector Konstantin von Neurath's forces stormed student halls and beat up and rounded up students who were taken to Prague's Pankrac prison and the Ruzyne barracks on night of 17 November. More than 1,200 students were sent to Sachsenhausen concentration camp near Berlin, the Czech universities in the protectorate were shut down and nine student leaders were executed without trial.[17]

The student demonstrations surrounding the Nazi occupation and Jan Opletal's death showed the potential for mass resistance from below, but this would be the last mass acton in the Czech lands until the Prague Uprising of May 1945. However, following the Nazi occupation a number of resistance organisations with varying political perspectives were formed, which included the Political Centre (PU), Nation's Defence (ON), the Petition Committee, "We Remain Faithful" (PVVZ) and the Communist Party of Czechoslovakia (KSC).[18] These different groups' political outlook and relationship to the Benes government would be crucial to shaping the resistance.

The PU was led by Premysl Samal, one of the middle class nationalists who had agitated for an independent Czechoslovakia before 1919. Its main task was to gather intelligence and maintain contact about the situation with the Benes group in London—but also to make sure that London did not lose contact with the Protectorate prime minister Alois Elias. Here we can see how there was some overlap between ruling class figures who tried to adapt to the occupation and those who fought from the outside to get back their old position. The group was wiped out through a slew of Gestapo arrests in 1940, leaving only a few individuals, and Elias was put on trial and executed in September 1942.

Meanwhile, the ON had a similar political outlook but was a military organisation led by high ranking generals of the First Republic and drew its ranks mainly from the Czechoslovak army's intelligence department. Initially it argued for a national uprising but in reality it would concentrate on intelligence gathering and acts of terrorism and sabotage. The Nazis smashed up its organisation numerous times and by the beginning of 1942 all but a handful of individuals were captured; it managed to successfully renew its leadership and carried on until 1945 but with reduced strength. The fact that the ON still had representatives on both the PU and PVVZ leaderships was also a sign of the influence that the old ruling class had on the movement.

The PVVZ was a broadly social democratic organisation, which included left wing intellectuals and social democratic trade unionists from transport and the postal service. It formulated a programme, "For Freedom: Into a New Czechoslovak Republic", which combined both national and socialist aspirations as a blueprint for post-liberation. These contradictions were reflected in its programme and its membership, which included members of Benes's petty bourgeois Czechoslovak National Social Party.[19] While the programme called for the restoration of the First Republic, it also argued for "socialist" reforms such as national planning, nationalisation and land reform to take place afterwards.

The contradiction in its politics and membership meant that it would gravitate towards Benes's leadership. Many of its members had begun "for the defence of the republic against Hitler", which basically called for the government to put up a proper fight in 1938. Its slogan would later evolve into "We are faithful to Masaryk's ideals"—the founder of the Czechoslovak bourgeois republic. In this way, it propagated real socialist rhetoric and aspirations, but still bound itself to an overriding principle of restoring the inter-war republic and its dislodged ruling class that had coalesced around Benes. The smashing up of the PU and ON meant that the PVVZ sought to take a lead in the resistance movement; it established a "coordination centre" that was supposed to be representative of different civic organisations and workplaces. But by 1942 the Gestapo had managed to smash it up, too.

This Nazi success in smashing up the different resistance organisations meant that there was growing pressure for them to merge, which culminated in 1941 when the three main ones joined forces to become the Central Leadership of the Home Resistance (UVOD). The new UVOD organisation was loyal to the Benes government in London, notwithstanding some friction, but the most dominant group was the left wing PVVZ and the new organisation signed up to its "For Freedom" programme.

Meanwhile, the Communist Party acted as a separate resistance organisation throughout the war, which was partly a result of its political summersaults before Russia was attacked in 1941. However, Benes's pivot towards Russia and the consolidation of the resistance into the UVOD began to change the situation. Russia encouraged the Communist Party to cooperate with the UVOD, including having people on its leadership, in order to gain influence in the resistance. Benes would also use the party leadership to make contact with Moscow as part of the pivot towards Russia. The Communist Party leadership was able to become a go between of a sort with the Czechoslovak bourgeoisie but still remained outside a mass resistance organisation.

Benes, the resistance and "Operation Anthropoid": a clash of interests?

The aim of the Benes group was to regain its old position as Czechoslovakia's ruling class through finding an imperialist sponsor, and it would also try to use the resistance to that end. Hitler appointed SS General Reinhardt Heydrich as Reich Protector of Bohemia and Moravia, instead of the "lenient" Neurath, with the task of stamping out the resistance movement. In Czechoslovakia this would be known as the "Heydrichiada", the period of brutal repression when the different resistance groups would have their organisation smashed.

The CNLC in London and the resistance in the Czech lands planned to assassinate Heydrich alongside the British Secret Operation Executive (SOE), which was tasked with carrying out terrorist operations. Jozef Gabcik and Jan Kubis, two officers from the 3,000 strong Czechoslovak army based in Britain, were parachuted into the Czech lands in 1942 where they made contact with local resistance fighters and made plans of when to carry out the assassination. Gabcik and Kubis deemed the safest option was to kill Heydrich on his way to work in Prague—one of them jumped out in front of his car, but the gun jammed so the other one shot him instead.

Heydrich was wounded in the attack and died in hospital a few days later. What followed was a more brutal wave of repression that is sometimes referred to as the "second Heydrichiada". The Nazis alleged that people from the village of Lidice had helped Gabcik and Kubis and that they found a radio near the village of Lezaky. In response the SS destroyed both the villages, murdered the men, sent the women and older children to the concentration camps and "spared" a few babies to be "re-educated" in German families. The Gestapo cracked down on the resistance organisation and murdered around 2,000 people, including General Elias. Meanwhile, Gabcik and Kubis were holed up in Prague's cathedral. The Nazis found out and stormed it, fighting Kubis first who shot himself to avoid capture. Gabcik and a few other resistance fighters bravely held off the 800 SS troops outside from inside the catacombs. But they all shot themselves to avoid capture, too, when the fire department was brought in to drown them out.

There was nothing wrong in itself with planning to assassinate Heydrich, but what the CNLC aimed to get out of it is indicative of its strategy. It hoped that assassinating Heydrich would prove to the Western allies that the Czech resistance was a serious part of the fight against Nazi imperialism, and that this would lead the Allies to officially repudiate the Munich Agreement and sign up to restoring the First Republic. The CNLC achieved this when the Western Allies formally repudiated the Agreement after the assassination. The resistance, including the UVOD and the Communist Party, would not begin to recover until 1944.

The partial discrediting of Czechoslovakia's old ruling class opened up the possibility of working class resistance from below and discussion about what society after liberation should look like. But the fact that a group around Benes was able to form a "government in exile" still allowed it to play a role in the resistance in both the Czech and Slovak lands and had a significant impact on its outcome. It meant that there was struggle from below but it was still partly led by the dead hand of the old order. This was particularly true in the SNP and this general context is crucial to understanding it, but the uprising also has to be understood against the backdrop of Tiso's fascist puppet regime.

The "Slovak State"

In Slovakia, as in the Czech lands, the ruling class split in different directions under the pressure of Nazi imperialism and the disintegration of the inter-war republic. But Slovak nationalism and the lack of direct occupation meant the local ruling class bending towards different imperialisms took on a particular dynamic. Following the Munich Agreement the nationalist movements and local ruling classes inside the inter-war republic made bids for autonomy or independence.[20] Father Joseph Tiso's Hlinka's Slovak People's Party (HSLS) led the charge in Slovakia and achieved its long fought for aim of Slovak autonomy with the "Zilina Declaration" on 6 October 1938, though the party's ultranationalist wing still pushed for full independence. However, the HSLS and the new Slovak regime would be totally dependent on their Nazi imperialist sponsor.

The HSLS—"Ludaks"—was formed as a nationalist party in 1906 during the Hapsburg Empire and appealed to a Slovak "national identity" constructed around agrarianism and a reactionary brand of Catholicism. But following the First World War it began cooperating with political forces further to its right. Vojtech Tuka, who would become the prime minister of the "Slovak State", had also been a member in 1919 of the Provincial Christian Socialist Party (OKSZP), which was led by an alliance of local landowners, the clerical hierarchy and the middle class. It based itself among the Hungarian minority and agitated for Slovak autonomy and against the threat of socialist revolution—a threat that had been made all too real by the Hungarian Soviet Republic and the short lived Slovak Soviet Republic of 1919.

These sorts of developments led the HSLS to develop two wings: its traditional conservative wing and Tuka's openly fascist wing that would come to politically dominate it. Tuka founded the party's first paramilitary unit, the Home Defence, in 1927, which would develop into the notorious Hlinka Guard and was the main figure behind the murder and deportation of Slovak Jews.

Following the declaration of Slovak autonomy, Tiso moved to cement the Ludaks political hegemony as the ruling party. All the old political parties, except the Communists and the Social Democrats, merged under pressure with Tiso's Hlinka's Slovak People's Party, which now suffixed its name with "The Party of Slovak National Unity". Then on 9 October 1938 the ministry of the interior of the autonomous Slovak government officially banned activity by the Communist Party of Czechoslovakia in Slovakia. Not long afterwards, its affiliated organisations, such as the "red trade unions", the "Unity" gyms and sectional groups, were also stopped from organising openly. While the Communists were one of the new regime's main targets,[21] it also moved against other mass organisations and left wing and Jewish groups. The Czechoslovak Social Democratic Workers' Party (CSDSD), the German Social Democratic Workers' Party in Czechoslovakia (DSAP), the Jewish Party (ZS) and the United Socialist Zionist Party were all dissolved.[22]

During the dismemberment of the Czechoslovak state its territories were divided between Nazi Germany, Hungary and Poland under the "Vienna Arbitration" that followed the Munich Agreement. It was a free for all for the ruling classes of Czechoslovakia's neighbouring states, who felt that they had been done out or sold short of territory after the First World War. Slovakia had to abandon substantial territory along its southern border to Hungary and two smaller areas near its capital Bratislava to Germany.[23]

This political situation opened up more possibilities for a war from below, and meant that the Communists and Social Democrats could play an important role in the underground resistance. But the old ruling class was still able to assert itself in the resistance, albeit initially to a lesser extent than in the Czech lands. While a chunk of the old order willingly supported the "Slovak State" throughout the war on the Eastern Front and the Holocaust, the Nazis' greatest crime, another part of the old ruling class remained committed to the idea of the old Czechoslovak republic. This included the bourgeois democratic politicians and Protestant religious leaders, but also dissident military commanders who now served in Tiso's army—this specifically allowed the old order to play a decisive role in the SNP itself.

The generals and the new ruling class: protest and adaptation

The Czechoslovak army had always been an important group during the inter-war republic, because of its officer corps' links to the Legions that helped Masaryk's nationalist movement find imperialist backing for independence during the First Word War. Its material and ideological basis was firmly tied to the old ruling class and the idea of a unitary Czechoslovak state. This meant that during the last days of the inter-war republic the significant bulk of the army high command tried to resist the momentum of further disintegration. When Tiso's parliament declared Slovak independence on 14 March 1939, a group of prominent former legionnaires, including one of the SNP's generals Rudolf Viest, published a protest:

Honourable Diet of Slovakia

Gentlemen,

If you are to decide today whether Slovakia is to be a part of the Czecho-Slovak Republic or an independent state by the side of some neighbouring country, bear in mind that:

Brave Slovak patriots fought and died together with the Czechs for the liberty of the Slovak Nation; that it was the Czechs who helped the Slovaks in the worst moments of their history and that all that we have from the spiritual and material point of view today we have acquired with Czech help during the last twenty years.

We implore you not to tarnish the national honour of the Slovaks and the memory of our fallen comrades, foremost among whom was General M R Stefánik.

For lack of time it is not possible for all Slovak Legionaries and volunteers still living to join us in reminding you, but we are certainly voicing the feeling of them all and of the great majority of the Slovak people.

Bratislava, March 14, 1939

General Rudolf Viest

Lieutenant Colonel Augustine Malár

Anton Granatier

Arch Juro Tvarožek

Staff Captain J. M. Kristin

Josef Kustra

M Miškóci

Dr Ján Jesenský

Jozef Gregor-Tajovský

Ing Kalamen Králiček[24]

However, the unity of the Czechoslovak officer corps' old guard would not hold, with some emigrating to serve in Benes's reconstituted "free army" and others loyally taking part in the Nazi invasion of Poland and then Russia. General Viest hung on as the inspector general of the Slovak Army as a member of the ON group and maintained contact with the CNLC in London, but fled to join the "free forces" in France in 1939 as the prospect of invading Poland neared. In seeming contrast, Malar remained a loyal officer in Tiso's army and commanded Slovak troops during the Nazi invasions of both Poland and Russia. But the apparent differences between the signatories belie the fact that they were part of a general preocess whereby the various sections of the old ruling class tried to either *adapt to* or *resist* the new situation.

The turning point that would fracture the Legionaries was the war with Hungary, which invaded southern Slovakia in March 1939. Admiral Miklos Horthy's Hungary now sought to expand the territorial acquisitions it had made in southern Slovakia during the "Vienna Arbitration". Hungary had began occupying Ruthenia on 16 March 1939 as agreed in Vienna, but it sought to take advantage of the official limbo before the Nazi foreign minister Joachim Ribbentrop counter-signed the "Treaty of Protection". Its troops attacked the eastern border of the "Slovak State" on 23 March. The war lasted only three days and was a military and political defeat for Tiso, but the Slovak Army had been commanded by the old legionnaire Malar. For many of the generals, protecting what was left of the old order by *adapting* to the new reality became the order of the day.

The "Slovak State" was a ramshackle mix of competing interests temporarily glued together by the political situation, and led by Tiso's HSLS under the tutelage of Nazi imperialism. When the tide began to turn against Nazi imperialism on the Eastern Front, parts of the Tiso apparatus and military began to plot against the regime as the different groups' unified purpose began to fracture. The machinations among the officer corps that resulted weakened the SNP both military and politically. Furthermore, many now hoped to do a deal with Russian imperialism that wasn't interested in the uprising's success either.

Resistance in the "Slovak State" before the uprising

There is little evidence that the majority of the population supported the new fascist regime, while people might have still preferred Slovak independence as an alternative to direct Nazi occupation and becoming a "protectorate" of Hitler's Reich.[25] There was resistance, albeit predominately passive at first, to the Tiso regime from the beginning, which included left wing groups and groups of organised workers. That it did not translate into a mass resistance movement is down to repression but also the dead hand of the old order still playing a part. The military nature of organisations such as the National Defence (NO), made up of officers loyal to Benes, partially limited mass participation and their focus was on intelligence gathering and maintaining contact with the London government.

There was resistance from within the old ruling class that reached outside of the old officer corps. Many Protestants were sympathetic to the resistance because of the Tiso regime's reactionary Catholic chauvinism. This was driven home with its regular denouncements of Protestants as disloyal to the Slovak nation. Indeed, when the Slovak National Uprising began it was denounced as a "Czecho-Lutheran-Jewish-Bolshevik putsch". This general trend among Protestants was evident in the high rate of abstention in mainly Protestant wards during the rigged elections of 1938 and later in participation in the SNP.

Resistance from the Lutheran church hierarchy continued throughout the Tiso regime. The Lutheran bishops' group also officially denounced the actions of the Hlinka Guard and the persecution and deportation of Slovak Jews. The official Lutheran newspaper, *Church Letters*, frequently published articles denouncing the Ludaks until it was shut down on 15 January 1940. The Tranoscius Evangelical group and printing press in Liptovsky St Mikulas were then shut down for publishing propaganda leaflets on the 25th anniversary of the birth of the Czechoslovak state. Members of the Union of Evangelical Youth (SEM), the main Protestant youth organisation, refused to step into the Hlinka Guard and Protestants were part of all the main resistance organisations.[26]

However, it would be wrong to look at this superficially through a religious lens. The history behind Tiso's repression and Protestant allegiances to the resistance had a definite class character. Many of the industrial and middle class interests in Slovakia were Protestant, meaning it was in their interests to oppose autonomy and subscribe to "Czechoslovakism", the official ideology of the inter-war republic that espoused a single "national identity".

Protestants also willingly joined the HSLS and prominent figures, such as the defence minister General Ferdinand Catlos, were also Protestant. Meanwhile, the Democratic Party was predominantly Catholic, but was set up in 1944 as the non-communist wing within the Slovak National Council (SNC) that became the umbrella resistance organisation. Underlying all of this were the contradictory directions the ruling class was pulled in after the Munich Agreement. When it comes to the official "Protestant resistance" from the church, it should be firmly placed in among resistance from the old order.

Resistance from below

Broadly speaking, there were three streams in the Slovak resistance before the SNP: the Communist Party, the Social Democratic Party and the bourgeois democratic politicians and "civic resistance" organisations such as Vavro Srobar's group and "Flora".

Debates about what position the resistance should take towards the "Slovak question" were dominant—primarily because the aim of the old ruling class resistance was to restore the inter-war republic—but this didn't stop the development of a national liberation programme that contained both national and socialist aspirations. The Communists and Social Democrats both agitated around social issues. There were, for example, KSS leaflets entitled "Give us work" and "Lower Taxes". However, until the tide began to turn against Nazi imperialism, the focus would be on building tight knit illegal political organisations.[27]

The Communist Party of Slovakia and Soviet imperialism

The Communist Party in Slovakia (KSS), now independent from its mother party, was set up illegally in 1939 but remained unrecognised by Moscow and the Comintern. The Communists' own claims that the KSS was *the* leading resistance organisation are false. However, it was one of the largest groups alongside the Social Democrats and the strongest organisationally.[28] The KSS was the Tiso regime's main political target. The fact that the Centre of State Security (USB), the Tiso regime's secret police force, had a dedicated department for suppressing Communist activity is testament to this.

There was a sense of impending hard times when the Slovak leadership of the Communist Party of Czechoslovakia met in Zilina on 6 October 1938, as the Ludaks, their old opponent, consolidated their power. Nonetheless, it was seemingly unprepared for how quickly the autonomous Slovak organs would move against it. Within a few days KSC *activity* in Slovakia was officially banned, while the party itself technically remained legal.[29]

The Communists already had experience of working under attack from the state. The Czechoslovak police had a special team dedicated to monitoring the KSC from 1933 because of its working class agitation and allegations of Russian espionage. The party also had some experience of effective illegality between 1934 and 35. Despite this experience, although illegality was discussed at the Zilina meeting, no actual steps, such as establishing an underground leadership, were taken.[30] Steps were only taken after it could no longer work openly. It was paralysed during the initial period of illegality, which forced it to focus on holding the organisation together rather than on anti-fascist resistance.

Tiso's police raided and shut down its party offices, documents that had not been hidden or destroyed were confiscated and party functionaries' and activists' houses were also searched. In this context, leading Slovak Communists met in Vilian Siroky's house in Prague in late October 1938 to discuss the transition to illegality. It was necessary to establish a new leadership with cadres who would not attract so much attention from the police. So the first illegal Slovak leadership was set up with the lesser known Koloman Mosko as its political head, Karol Bacilek in charge of organisational matters, and Julius Duris responsible for ideological work. The leadership moved to Brno in Moravia to escape the reach of the Slovak authorities. Duris, who still resided in Prague, was also charged with maintaining contact with the national party through Emanuel Klima, a member of the KSC's first illegal central committee.[31]

However, it faced insurmountable problems and wasn't active politically apart from propaganda work. During the rigged Slovak autonomous elections it put out a flyer urging people to boycott or "vote negatively" against the single HSLS candidate. The leaflet was addressed "To Slovak voters and the Slovak People" and presented its readers with a simple choice: "Those who want war, vote Yes. Those who want order and peace, vote No!" Following KSC's seizure of power in 1948 it was claimed that this leaflet was responsible for the low turnout, although while it contributed to it, its impact was most likely wildly exaggerated. The Communists didn't actually claim responsibility for the leaflet, which was signed off "From Friends of the People", so as not to alert the police to it organising illegally.[32] Nonetheless, the police found out that it was written by Mosko and Duris and began an unsuccessful hunt for the culprits, which led to the official banning of the Communist Party and the losing of all its elected representatives. The actual production and distribution of the flyer point to the difficulties the illegal party faced. The flyer itself was written in Prague. Jozef Valo, Karol Smidke, Stefan Kosik and Ferdinand Zupka then transported copies to Slovakia, while others were taken to Hodin in Moravia to a contact and then picked up by Slovak Communists.[33]

Duris explains what the party's situation meant for its anti-fascist activity:

During the first sitting, district heads were already referring to great difficulties in Slovakia. Above all that the organisation had collapsed, the membership disintegrated, many full time workers had gone abroad, and many, mainly older ones, didn't want to work any more. They [the district heads] reported that they had difficulties making contact, finding flats, taking subscriptions, and holding the old membership together. Similarly all the district heads reported that it's not possible to count in the longer term on more substantial activity, when the old membership is demoralised, waiting to see how developments unfold, and is sometimes surprised by international events. We [the Slovak party] had great difficulty with collecting subscriptions, which severely held back the district heads, meaning we were reliant on a contribution from Prague. In this state, we met around twice in the run up to 14 March 1939 [the independence declaration]. *In this period of uncertainty, we didn't intervene, because we were only concentrating on securing our membership* [my emphasis].[34]

Its focus was on building an illegal organisation capable of surviving Tiso's repression, so it turned its energies to building "cell structures" of three to five loyal cadre capable of carrying out clandestine party work. However, it did still try to capitalise when there was discontent with the regime, for instance when the Tiso regime made it compulsory to join the Hlinka Guard, it was able to tap into discontent among workers.

The KSS was also politically disorientated as it somersaulted in sync with Moscow's shifting foreign policy line. The party published material giving the party line on all major domestic and international developments.[35] However, in the initial stages of the break-up of the Czechoslovak state Moscow's foreign policy was shifting to an accommodation with Nazi imperialism, and on 23 August 1939 the Soviet Union and Nazi Germany formally signed the Molotov-Ribbentrop "non-aggression pact". This led the Soviet Union to formally recognise the fascist "Slovak State" the following month—and to also break off diplomatic contact with the leadership of the Czechoslovak resistance abroad. While the Soviet Union recognised Slovakia as part of the Nazi "sphere of influence", it went further than just formal recognition and included promises of economic cooperation with the Tiso regime.[36] In an attempt to respond to these "shocking" international developments, the KSS raised the slogan "For free and independent Slovakia" but later changed it to "For a Soviet Slovakia". It would not officially change the "Soviet Slovakia" slogan until 1943, and some local organisations continued to use it until 1944 because of political differences and organisational disconnect with the leadership. Following the Nazi invasion of the USSR in June 1941, which the "Slovak State" participated in, Communist agitation swung towards agitating against the war.[37] Its propaganda included appeals to "Slavic unity" as well as anti-fascism and its leaflets were signed off with "Long Live the USSR".[38]

Working class resistance

The KSS, like the party in the Czech lands, remained a resistance organisation in its own right, However, there is still evidence that it tried to relate to instances of mass resistance, including workers' struggle, while on the whole it did not initiate them. There is further evidence that the majority of the population in Slovakia didn't accept the Tiso lies in instances of social unrest, including workers' struggles, that took place during the years of the "Slovak State".

The Soviet delegation in the "Slovak State" reported a "worsening economic situation in Slovakia, which has caused many strikes of an economic character". Many historians report that strikes were a "regular occurrence" from the beginning of 1940 in the "Slovak State".[39] For instance, the police detail of the USB reported that during the construction of the Bratislava to Leopoldov railway 300 workers downed tools. Among their main demands were higher wages. In a meeting between the ministry of transport officials and workers' representatives the government was forced to concede to their wage demands.[40] This was typical of one of the responses of the Tiso regime, which tried to both suppress and contain working class resistance. If strikes were around "economic demands" it would make some concessions but take precautions to stop them happening again. However, if there was a potential that these could spill over to become political, or if there were political elements involved from the beginning, then it would begin the "legal process" and put the strike leaders into the notorious Ilava prison as "communist provocateurs".

There is substantial controversy about the biggest instance of workers' struggle during the years of the "Slovak State". In the Handlova district in western Slovakia a militant miners' strike involving some 3,000 workers, both Slovak and ethnic German, broke out on 30 October 1940 around wage demands. It would only end on 4 November after being brutally suppressed. During the period of Communist Party rule the party claimed that its cadres were at the heart of initiating and running the dispute. The dominant narrative today is that it was primarily a strike by ethnic German workers for pay parity with workers in the Greater Reich—and certainly without any Communist input.

The USB arrested the ringleaders and following the strike tried to find out what caused it, in line with the Tiso regime's twin strategy of suppressing and containing workers' struggle. USB agent Jozef Glinda was sent into Ilava prison, posing as a prisoner, to get to the root cause.

According to his testimony to the National Court, "The origin of the strike lies in the fact that workers were convinced to strike. Members of the German minority in Handlova did it...they wanted the whole mine complex to be put under the control of the Herman Goring Works".[41] This argument, then, rests on the fascist interior minister Alexander Mach and Koloman Skacani, the USB agent who led the operation, both "confirming" it in their testimonies.[42]

However, this strike did involve both Slovak and ethnic German workers, showing the possibility for working class unity, and was a sign of the social discontent brewing at the base of society. It is clear that the Handlova miners' strike posed a serious threat to the Tiso regime, and caused serious embarrassment to the minority German Party (DP) that claimed to have ethnic German workers under control. To suppress the unrest, the interior minister Mach and the Ministry of National Defence were forced to dispatch 250 police officers, 50 regular troops, four tanks, four armoured cars and 22 secret USB agents to hunt down the main militants.[43] News of the unrest spread throughout the local area and farther afield despite tight press regulation. "The whole mine is on strike, there are 400 gendarmes here, and the army and two tanks as well. Well, there's talk that there's going to be revolution—all won't be well," wrote one local resident to their relative.[44] There were also signs that it was developing into more than just an "economic" dispute and spilled into a demonstration against the Ludaks regime.

Jan Osoha, one of the leaders of the illegal KSS, said in custody that the strike had come as a complete surprise to the party leadership.[45] This would not be surprising considering the fragmented nature of the party; nonetheless, around 100 illegal party workers were arrested after the strike and the party did put out agitational material during the walkout.[46] The KSS published a leaflet entitled "The Truth about Handlova" in Slovak and "In Handlova: the Strike and the State of Emergency" in German to inform wider layers about what had taken place. These flyers got to almost every district in Slovakia.[47] The Handlova revolt was no doubt contradictory in its content and was typical of workers' struggles during the period. The social situation meant that workers did fight back after Handlova, but were brutally suppressed by the regime. Three years later textile workers in Zilina and Rajec walked out over the payment of living allowances on 13 June, but security forces successfully suppressed it the following day.[48] The strikes began on "economic" demands, but were suppressed before they could generalise and spill into full-on protests against the regime.[49]

The shift towards unity and a social programme

Following the Nazi invasion of the Soviet Union in June 1941 the Communist Party of Slovakia was politically able to step up its efforts. It carried on with its work of building its clandestine organisation—and rebuilding it after repeatedly getting smashed—and putting out propaganda. Its main organ was the national *People's Voice* (*Hlas Ludu*) newspaper, but it also published regional newspapers, such as *Spark* (*Iskra*), *The Hammer* (*Kladivo*) and a German language version (*Der Hammer*).[50] However, it also undertook acts of sabotage to disrupt the regime's transport and communications infrastructure and began trying to set up actual partisan groups. Partisan groups were set up across Slovakia—in western Slovakia the J Kral group, in central Slovakia the Sitno and Vtacnik groups and in eastern Slovakia the P Borosa group, and later in Turec under Viliam Zingor and in Slanske Vrychy under Kukorelli.[51]

However, there was also a battle taking place inside the Communist Party about the direction the resistance ought to take. Repression meant that, as in the Czech lands, there was pressure for the different resistance organisations to forge some kind of unity. Yet while there had already been cooperation between different organisations, the movement was split on whether or not to work with the Communists.

The turning point began in 1941 and came to a head in 1942, and this would cause friction with the Benes leadership and its allies inside Slovakia. With the KSS's initiative, the Central Revolutionary National Committee (URNV) was formed in March 1942. Its political leadership was made up of P Stahl and M Hrusovsky representing the KSS, M Polak who had been a member of the Agrarian Party and the writer F Kral. The USB secret police swiftly arrested all of them and shut it down. However, it was renewed in the autumn of 1942, with the Communists M Faltn and J Pall, the Social Democrat F Komzal and I Doxner representing the "civic resistance". It released two new declarations, namely "Response to the Slovak Nation" (*Ohlas Slovenskemu Nardu*) and the Directive for the Organisation of National Revolutionary Committees (*Smernice pre organizaciu narodno-revolucnich vyborou*). This second publication was met with some success, with the setting up of the first local Revolutionary National Committee, including in larger cities such as the capital Bratislava, and in Zilina and Zvolen.[52] Their main role was to unify and coordinate the resistance groups that already existed. But the Communist Party still had a sectarian attitude, which reinforced its focus on conspiratorial activity seen in opposition to building mass resistance. It also insisted, much like the other resistance organisations, that unity would be on the basis of the party's "leading role".

The momentum was lost again in 1943, when in April the RNV's leading members were arrested. However, this move coincided with a change of leadership within the Communist Party, also because of arrests. The KSS's fifth illegal leadership, formed in August 1943 with Karol Smidke, Gustav Husak and Laco Novomestky, made a sharp break with the party's strategy up until then. It actively discouraged open party activity: it shut down the party newspapers, halted its agitational and propaganda activity, and forbade large gatherings. This was in response to its organisation continually being smashed by the Tiso regime, but also marked a shift in political direction. Yet, most significantly, the new Communist Party leadership definitively broke with its calls for a "Soviet Slovakia". Its orientation was towards forging "national unity" with the different resistance currents, with the primary aim of restoring the Czechoslovak republic with equal status for Slovakia. This move was positive, in one respect, as it represented a move that would lead to a real grassroots resistance organisation with a social programme.

However, the major factor behind it was the shifting dynamic of imperialist rivalry and the old Czechoslovak ruling classes' relationship with the Allied powers and the Soviet Union. During this period Benes's "pivot" towards the Soviet Union was becoming more definitive as it signed the "cooperation" treaty with the Soviet Union on 12 December 1943.

This put pressure on the Communist Party to push for unity in the resistance movement, but it meant that there was also pressure on the "civic resistance" groups to work with the Communists. This would not be a straightforward process and it would lead to a clash *within* the resistance elements in the old ruling class—both in the Benes group, those working within the "Slovak State", and in the "civic resistance"—and *with* the Communists. This process would ultimately allow both the old ruling class and Soviet imperialism to assert their interests on the resistance and the uprising. What's more, the competing interests within the "Slovak State" had begun to fracture, with some looking to do deals.

The tide began to turn against Nazi imperialism during 1943-1944 as the Western Allies and the Soviet Union began to score decisive military victories, namely in Stalingrad and Kursk on the Eastern Front and El Alamein in North Africa in 1943. The majority of the Italian ruling class had switched sides in the war, Romania and Finland jumped ship from the Axis, and there was a ramping up of resistance across occupied Europe, namely in Yugoslavia, against Nazism. In direct relation to

Czechoslovakia, the Soviet Union's army was also gaining ground in its former territory of Ruthenia and nearing the Slovak border.

This fed into a general feeling against the Tiso regime and the Nazis—but this played out in a highly contradictory way. So on the one hand it meant that the resistance groups would get more of a hearing, as many ordinary people had begun to realise that the tide had turned against Nazi imperialism and that the fate of Tiso's Slovakia was inextricably tied to it. However, elements *within* the "Slovak State" had also come to this conclusion. It included all manner of state officials but also high up members of the legislature, the judiciary and the police.

But by far the most significant group was the Slovak Army's officer corps, which included officers who had remained loyal to Benes and those who had loyally served in Tiso's army in the service of Nazi imperialism. Indeed, it is safe to say that by 1943 the majority of the Slovak officer corps saw its allegiance with the Benes group.

It was in this context that part of the "civic resistance" began making moves towards a unity that included the Communist Party and approached the illegal party leadership. The "civic resistance" had also been trying to negotiate with the minor Ludaks minister Karol Sidor, who was considered a "moderate".[53] In reality, he was no "moderate". He had been part of the Tuka wing of the HSLS, a Hlinka Guard commander and an ardent anti-Semite, but had fallen out with Tiso over the degree of control Nazi imperialism would have. The London government argued against working with him; not on the basis of any principle, but because he firmly clashed with its aim of restoring the inter-war Czechoslovak republic. Jan Masaryk said in a broadcast from London, "I am strongly warning against any proposals and ideas, which you've come to or have come from Karol Sidor. I'm warning against Sidor. He's a traitor".[54] With this avenue shut, the former Agrarian Party member Jan Ursiny made contact during the latter part of 1943 with the old Communist leaders V Siroky and J Duris who were imprisoned. They recommended that he contact Laco Novomestky, one of the members of the fifth illegal KSS leadership, which kickstarted negotiations.[55]

This initial meeting was followed by months of negotiations between Ursiny and co and the Communist Party. It culminated in the signing of the "Christmas Agreement" as the founding document of the Slovak National Council (SNC) in December 1943.[56]

It was a broad based organisation and this was reflected in its leadership and its general programme combined both national and "socialist" aspirations:

On achieving political liberation, our aim will be to ensure a better and happier life for the socially weak strata of the nation, that is for the Slovak worker and peasant. In order to secure a higher standard of living for the nation we are in favour of equitable distribution of national wealth, and a new land reform for the benefit of the small peasant. The worker shall have wages corresponding to a higher standard of living and share in the results of his labour.[57]

Karol Smidke, Gustav Husak and Laco Novomestky represented the KSS alongside Jan Ursiny and Jozef Letternich from the former Agrarian Party and the National Socialist M Mosk. Then as the momentum behind the SNC built in the run up to the uprising, it was further broadened, first in January 1944 with the inclusion of J Horvath for the Social Democrats and the economist P Zatko, and then in July 1944 with another Social Democrat and old Agrarian, J Sotesza and J Styk. However, it is significant that the Social Democrats, one of the largest and best organised groups, were not party to the negotiations or on the SNC leadership when it was founded.

The SNC drove a wedge into the non-communist resistance and would trigger a battle for hegemony within the resistance movement. The non-communist resistance was effectively split down the middle on whether to unite with the KSS. Those who argued for unity with the Communists included left wing social democrats and sections of the "civic resistance". The SNC also did not include V Srobar's group in its plans for the uprising. He was a direct link to the old order and remained loyal to Benes and the idea of "Czechoslovakism", and likewise Benes and its military representative J Kratky were supportive, but it was a battle that Srobar's group ultimately lost.

This led to clashes with the London leadership and more significantly impeded the process of building Revolutionary National Committees in localities. Srobar's group and "Flora" continued to act as independent organisations and also tried to bring the resistance under their leadership. They had both issued calls for unity, including the "Flora" in August 1943, and despite the formation of the SNC and local RNVs, Srobar continued in his efforts to set up "national committees" and central leadership.[58] However, Jan Golian, the old legionnaire who would be the uprising's military commander, tilted towards support for the SNC.

The Revolutionary National Committees (RNV) were crucial to the armed uprising, both as symbols of a united resistance and in terms of organising. The highest density of RNV networks was in central Slovakia, which would become the epicentre of the uprising, but this movement still had to compete with Srobar's "national committees". Their organisation was further strengthened in October 1943 when the SNC set up a committee to try and organise district RNVs, The first was set up in Zvolen with the Communist R Blazovsky, the Social Democrat D Ert, and V Wittman for the "civic resistance".[59]

Through setting up the SNC and the network of RNVs the resistance movement was making an impressive attempt to build an alternative government structure to the Tiso regime. However, the RNVs' main task would become making plans for the armed uprising and aiding Soviet partisan groups that would infiltrate Slovak territory.

The "Long Hot Summer"

It was during this period that the idea of an armed insurrection was formulated, and it came from both the Benes government and the Slovak resistance groups themselves. For the Slovak "civic resistance" groups it was to give the resistance leverage in the post-war political situation. The bourgeois democrat Fedor Thurz wrote in his memoirs, "We made the Uprising so the Slovaks would liberate themselves, so they could decide politically after the war... The Uprising had a political reason, so the Slovaks wouldn't be a defeated state".[60] The Benes government had been making its pivot towards Russia, but it still wanted to strengthen its position with the different Allies by encouraging resistance.

Yet for Benes this crucially meant trying to get Soviet sponsorship for the uprising, which would tie its fate to Stalin's imperialist interests. Stalin received repeated appeals from both the London government and the Slovak resistance groups to support their plans. Benes made the first appeal directly, when he personally met with Stalin while signing the "cooperation" treaty in December 1943. Then the Czechoslovak mission in Moscow, headed by general Heliodor Pika, appealed for support. Most significantly the SNC leadership itself made a direct appeal just before the uprising broke out in August 1944, which included both Lieutenant Colonel Mikulas Ferjencik *and* the Communist Karol Smidke.[61]

However, Stalin had no intention of supporting a "Slovak National Uprising" just as he was letting the Warsaw Uprising go down to defeat. The Stavka, the Soviet high command, had said from the beginning that such an uprising was unrealistic, but the Soviet Union's imperialist considerations are of greater importance here. It is not coincidental that, only 12 days before signing the Czechoslovak "cooperation" treaty, Stalin had won important concessions regarding the "Soviet sphere of influence" at the Tehran conference.

Nonetheless, Stalin still wanted to have a degree of control over what was about to unfold, while doing nothing to help the Slovak resistance. So not long after Benes's appeal for support, the Soviet Union set up partisan training camps in Ukraine with their command headquarters in Kiev. They began training partisan units in February 1944 and by the summer of 1944 the Soviet partisan units were infiltrating eastern and the north of central Slovakia. Following the war much was made of the fact that "volunteers" from 30 countries fought in the uprising, but they were in fact sent from the Ukrainian training camps.

The Slovak resistance, whether the SNC or the generals, had no control over these units. They were under the direct command of the Stavka in Moscow.[62] This would have two significant impacts on the resistance both in the run up to and during the uprising, and was where the resistance would visibly clash with Soviet Union imperialism. The units were tasked with disrupting Nazi supply lines, transport links and sometimes targeting Wehrmacht officers, This sort of activity would help the Soviet war effort but leave the Slovak resistance without support for liberating itself.

The uprising's planners were immediately concerned that the Soviet partisan activity would lead to a brutal crackdown directly from the Nazis before the Slovak military was ready. The Benes government sent several communiqués to Moscow asking them to make the partisan units stop their activities until the SNP had begun. General Jan Golian held meetings with partisan commanders and sent a delegation to Moscow, protesting against "premature actions" and the Slovak leadership's lack of control.[63]

These concerns were raised again and again throughout August 1944, but again and again were ignored. The Slovak resistance and the fate of the uprising were becoming caught between the Soviet Union's interests and being tied to the old order. Not long before the uprising the Soviet senior lieutenant and partisan commander Peter Aleksejevic Velicko agreed to dampen partisan actions on 13 August, but within a week it had restarted with its previous intensity.[64]

The tensions between the uprising's planners and the Soviet Union's imperialist interests only intensified. Lieutenant Colonel Mikulas Ferjencik, General Golian's chief of staff, departed to Moscow with details for the uprising. But when Ferjencik's party arrived in Moscow they were placed under arrest. Soviet authorities refused to acknowledge they had ever arrived and only let them go back to Slovakia on 5 September once the uprising had already started.[65]

These clashes were not because of some tension between Czechoslovakia's "democratic" leadership in London and the "civic resistance" groups on the one hand and "Soviet totalitarianism" on the other. There was a real clash of interests between imperialism and the SNC's programme that combined national and social aspirations—and the former did stamp on genuine potential for a *people's war from below* being waged. But the tensions that damaged the uprising were the logical conclusion of the old Czechoslovak ruling class's strategy of finding an imperialist sponsor—from 1943 increasingly the Soviet Union—and using the resistance movement to do so.

Imperialism, the "Slovak State" and the uprising: the clash comes to a head

In the summer of 1944 the Tiso regime was rotting from the inside. The unity forged under the tutelage of Nazi imperialism had cracked as the different competing interests splintered and this combined with the splits among the generals. General Ferdinand Catlos was the minister of national defence of the "Slovak State", but was one of those officials who realised the tide was turning against Nazi imperialism and the Tiso regime. He sought to make a deal with the new imperialist power or preferably broker a rapprochement with the Benes government.

He issued a memorandum to Moscow in July, which made an offer to carry out a coup against the Tiso regime and join with the Soviet army in exchange for Slovak independence after the war. It perfectly spells out the general's rationale for supporting the Tiso regime and then trying to break with it. It explains that Slovakia, "as a state dependent upon Germany" and "whose foreign policy is contradictory and is conditioned to act according to Germany's", had to "declare war against the USSR and her allies". But now that "German strength is breaking and in Slovakia the bond of dependence is loosening...*a small nation in the position of being so dependent must accommodate to powerful neighbours* [my emphasis]." Catlos's aim was to ensure that Slovakia's ruling class could hang onto its position, and to get rid of the Tiso regime if that was the price that had to be paid. "We want to wait out in the interests of our nation so that Slovakia does not become another unfortunate Italy," the memorandum warned.[66] To do this he wanted to draw Soviet fire on German divisions in Hungary and—eventually—allow the Slovak Army to depose Tiso.

While the plan to focus on Hungary was not out of sync with Soviet strategy, it still risked an independent ruling class emerging and so was not taken up. However, it was all part of broader machinations among the generals, which would actually impact on and weaken the uprising.

The plans for the Slovak National Uprising were tied to the fate of Soviet Union imperialism from the beginning. There were two plans for the uprising, one "defensive" and the other "offensive". The latter involved an insurgent Slovak Army moving towards Eastern Slovakia and helping the Russian army capture the Dukla pass on its way into the country; the former was for rebel forces to take control of central Slovakia, liberate as much territory as possible and hold out for the Russians to arrive. While seemingly different scenarios from a military point of view, both involved relying on helping the Soviet Union to "liberate" the country.

The two heavily armed infantry Slovak divisions and their airforce group in the East were crucial to both plans. But neither of these divisions would ever see action against the Tiso or Nazi forces. Both were disarmed by the 24th Panzer Division without a shot being fired on 31 August 1944 and the airforce group left to Soviet held territory.

Yet the uprising would not break out at its planners' own choosing. Not long after Romania had switched sides, Soviet army lieutenant Peter Aleksejevic Velicko's partisan group captured and killed a Nazi military detail on 27 August 1944 that was making its way from Romania. The Nazis were aware that the Tiso regime was fracturing and was unable to suppress Soviet partisan activity on its territory. To deal with the situation Wehrmacht and Waffen SS troops moved into Slovakia on 29 August 1944.[67]

The generals split among themselves again, and weakened the possibilities for the SNP succeeding. So while Catlos announced on the airwaves that Nazi forces had occupied Slovakia and called on the army to stand down, the SNP's commander General Golian issued orders to begin the uprising. During this critical moment General Malar, the corps commander in Eastern Slovakia, left his post in Eastern Slovakia and headed to Bratislava. He then also made a plea on national radio for Slovak troops to stand down and not to take part in a "premature" uprising.[68]

The uprising's planners had tried hard to get Malar's backing despite him being an ally of "Catlos's man" since both had fought together against the Red Army in the Russian Civil War, and now this reliance on the officer corps showed its real weaknesses. With Malar having sided with the regime against the uprising, the SNP leadership now looked to Colonel Talky who headed the airforce group. General Golian's call for a mobilisation had relied on the "defensive" plan for the uprising, but instead of carrying out this plan Talsky flew the group to Kalinuv and

Lvov, which were held by Soviet forces, to try and convince Marshal Konev to mount an offensive.

Eventually, Konev launched the Dukla Pass operation on 8 September, but Soviet forces only reached Bratislava on 4 April.[69] *The USSR's primary aim was to push south and decisively defeat Nazi forces in Romania and Hungary, where there were important supplies of oil.* The remaining forces in Eastern Slovakia, namely General Ludvik Svoboda's 1st Czechoslovak Army Corps, fought on but did not liberate Kosice and Presov until 19 January 1945 and Banska Bystrica, the epicentre of the SNP, until 26 March 1945.

During the uprising the Soviet Union managed 682 successful flights into rebel held territory with 610 tons of supplies and 2,000 soldiers, namely Czechoslovak parachutists. But these flights often came with strings attached—and sometimes political commissars on board—and were primarily meant for the Soviet partisan units rather than Slovak forces.[70]

The dominant narrative is that the Slovak National Uprising was "premature" and puts the blame on different military commanders. But the reason it broke out when it did and its failure were because of the reliance on the generals and how it was tied to Soviet imperialism. Malar's "treachery" and Talsky's leaving gutted the Slovak army in the East and the military strength of the uprising, but both were in keeping with trying to maintain or regain the ruling class's position.

The Slovak National Uprising

Nonetheless, the insurgent forces were initially successful in capturing large swathes of territory in central and eastern Slovakia. While the SNP's plans were hampered from the beginning by imperialism and the generals, it would be wrong to dismiss the Slovak resistance and the uprising as just playthings of imperialism and the generals.

There were serious clashes between the old order and the SNC, as soon as the latter declared on 1 September 1944 that it was the ruling body in the liberated territory. Benes did not want some "Slovak National Council" ruling Slovakia, which could then have its own base, but rather for it to be subordinate to the London government when its time came to restore the inter-war republic. But the SNC's leaders, including many Communists, were serious about liberating Slovakia from Tiso and Nazism as part of a revolt from below. During the uprising itself a delegation flew to London to carry out negotiations with

Benes but remained committed to the idea of the SNP and an "equal Slovakia" in a post-war republic.[71]

That was also evident with some of the political developments that took place. In liberated territory the network of RNVs began organising political administration and basic economic life. New RNVs, which had not been part of the set up before the SNP also sprang up, were part of the local overthrow and then local administration. The individual committees had some autonomy from the SNC and the insurgent military command and took their own initiatives, whether that was recruiting into the rebel forces or providing social support for soldiers and fleeing civilians.

The Communists and the Social Democrats also held a "unity conference" on 17 September 1944, which was attended by around 700 delegates from 46 districts, tens of workplaces and 12 partisan groups. The two parties merged their local party organisation and the mass organisations that they had set up before the war.[72]

Most importantly, the Social Democratic and "Red Union" were merged and set up in the liberated territory. The unity conference of the trade unions, held on 15 October, was attended by around 200 delegates from 130 plants, which was not insignificant given the political and military situation. The final resolutions called for workplace union committees to be placed in charge of running factories.[73]

These were genuine demands, but Moscow had no intention of allowing them to be fulfilled. Gustav Husak from the KSS was joined by Jan Sverma, who had been dispatched from Moscow to let the KSC influence the political direction. Following the war there were indeed factory committees and original calls for nationalisation were fulfilled, but these bodies would be controlled by the new trade union bureaucracy and would only be used as a passive stage army during 1946-1948.

Meanwhile, the RNVs would lose their grassroots elements and were succeeded by official governing structures. When Eastern Slovakia was finally "liberated" by Soviet and Czechoslovak troops in 1945, the "Kosice Governing Programme" was set up. While it had some roots in the uprising, it was not a genuine grassroots organisation. Integral to it was the new "National Front" that was the basis for the post-war government, which was used by Stalin to increase influence in Eastern Europe.

The old ruling class managed to temporarily regain some control of both the Czech lands and Slovakia under the sponsorship of Soviet imperialism, but it would not be a lasting triumph. Firstly, with the onset of the Cold War trying to balance "neutrally" between the West and the Soviet Union, while relying increasingly on the latter, was not possible in the long run. Either one of the imperialisms would have to win out—and Moscow's tool for doing so was the reconstituted KSC.

The old ruling class was dislodged in the KSC's palace coup in 1948. The Communist Party was not leading the resistance any more and was not a revolutionary organisation willing to agitate among workers after the war. Instead in line with Moscow's policy it took over and would rule a "state capitalist" regime where workers had no power. The Communists would also play a key role as talk of "autonomy" was quickly abandoned in favour of a centralised state apparatus.

Secondly, the contradictions within the ruling class did not disappear under the new path of state capitalist development. It merely found expression in conflicts between the different parts of the new ruling bureaucracy in the industrialised Czech lands and the less developed Slovakia. This is what partly lay behind the differences between the "conservative" and "reforming" wings of the KSC during the 1968 Prague Spring (although now the largely "conservative" Slovak bureaucracy favoured centralised development instead of autonomy). It would again resurface during the dissolution of Czechoslovakia, with Czech capital wanting to cut itself loose from "dead weight" and the new Slovak ruling class wanting to pursue development autonomously.

The uprising had genuine potential, but was limited from birth by the ability of the old Czechoslovak ruling class to assert a degree of control and its relationship to the Allied and Russian imperialist powers. It was this twin pressure that ultimately allowed the Nazis to crush the uprising.

NOTES

1   D Faber, *Munich: The 1938 Appeasement Crisis* (London, 2008), p157.
2   Faber, 2008, p161.
3   While Trotsky's writings on the Czechoslovakian crisis are dated in parts, they are still valuable to look at today.
4   L Trotsky, *A Fresh Lesson: On the Character of the Coming War* (October 1938), www.marxists.org/archive/trotsky/1938/10/imperial.htm
5   Faber, 2008, p323.
6   Faber, 2008, p324.
7   J Pelikan "The Struggle for Socialism in Czechoslovakia", *New Left Review*, 1/71, January-February 1972.
8   The role of the Communist Party in the resistance movement and popular perception of the "Soviet Union" as the liberator undoubtedly helped the party win the 1946 general election. However, the fact that it had already existed as a "legal party" throughout the 1930s and had built up a base within the industrial working class was also an important factor.
9   Pelikan, 1972.
10 Pelikan writes, "What we did not understand at all were all the positive articles which we started to read in the German newspapers and the broadcasts we heard on Radio Moscow at the time. Instead of working to build up the resistance, they began toning down all anti-fascist propaganda and just putting out items about how many pigs there were on some kolkhoz or other and how many tons of such and such a product the Soviet Union had produced". See Pelikan, 1972.
11 Pelikan, 1972.
12 This was written under the pseudonym Jan Buchar.
13 J Buchar, *The National Question in Central Europe*, July 1939 www.marxists.org/history/etol/newspape/ni/vol05/n007/buchar.htm
14 General Syrovy had made his name as part of the Czechoslovakian Legion, which had fought against the Bolsheviks during the Russian Civil War.
15 Trotsky, 1938.
16 Trotsky, 1938.
17 17 November was officially designated as International Students' Day and would be the springboard for the student demonstrations and "Velvet Revolution" in 1989.
18 This does not include the Communist Party of Slovakia, which had separated during the Munich crisis and had a degree of autonomy during the war.
19 The party's name frequently changed throughout the period from "National Social" to "Socialist" to "National Socialist", reflecting the changing pressure of different social forces. In 1926 Jiri Stribrny and his supporters were expelled from the party for the being supporters of Italian fascism, not long after the high ranking general Radola Gajda was forced to stand down for the same reason. The former went on to found the fascist "Slavic Socialist Party" and later participated in the "National League". Here, however, I have used the translation National Social Party to avoid confusion with Hitler's National Socialist German Workers Party.
20 This was in Slovakia and Ruthenia, but nationalists among its Hungarian and German populations also raised demands for autonomy and independence
21 Xenia Suchova (ed), "Ludáci a komunisti: Súperi? Spojenci? Protivníci?" Fremal, Karol, *Ilegálna KSS vo vztahu k Hlinkovej slovenskej ludovej strane, Hlinkovej garde a Hlinkovej mládeži v rokoch 1939-1943* (Presov, 2006), pp118-126 www.forumhistoriae.sk/documents/10180/115761/suchova.pdf
22 Syrny, Marek, K problematike represii voci slovenskym komunistom v rokoch 1939-1943, *Perzekucie na Slovensku v rokoch 1938-1945, Slovenska republika 1939-1945 ocami mladych historikov* VII, (Bratislava, 2008), p57.
23 Poland also took two further villages in northern Slovakia as well as territory from the Czech lands.

24 Vlcko B Peter and Vlcko P Ryan, *The Soviet Union's Role in the Slovak National Uprising* (2005), pp68-69. sitemaker.umich.edu/ryanvlcko/files/soviet_role_in_the_slovak_national_uprising__snp_.pdf

25 This is despite the claims of the right wing revisionist historians; see, for example, Martin Lacko, *Slovenske narodne povstanie 1944* (Bratislava, 2008).

26 Micek, Stanislav a kol, *Slovenkse narodne povstanie 1944* (Banksa Bystrica, 2009), pp68-70.

27 Fedorova, Iveta Protifašistické letáky, ich úloha a význam na Slovensku v rokoch 1938-1945, *Slovenska republika 1939-1945 ocami mladych historikov* IV (Bratislava, 2005), pp258-270.

28 Even right wing revisionist historians do not deny this. Martin Lacko writes, "The Communist movement was one of the firmest in terms of organisation." (Lacko, Martin, *Slovenske narodne povstanie* [Bratislava, 2008]).

29 Syrny, 2008.

30 Syrny, 2008.

31 Syrny, Marek, *Slovenski komunisti v rokoch 1939-1944, nacrt dejin komunistickej strany slovenska v odvoji a v povstani* (Banksa Bystrica, 2013), pp10-11.

32 Fedorova, 2005.

33 Syrny, 2013, pp11-12.

34 Syrny, 2013, p14.

35 Federova, 2005.

36 Micek, 2009, pp. 25-32.

37 The Slovak army had also participated in the invasion of Poland, but the party couldn't officially agitate against it because of the Soviet Union's participation.

38 Fedorova, 2005.

39 Rogovyj, Jevgen, Sociálno-ekonomické aspekty procesu slovakizácie v rokoch 1938-1941, *Život v Slovenskej republike Slovenská republika 1939-1945 očami mladých historikov* IX (Bratislava, 2010), pp36-44.

40 Rogovyj et al, 2010, p44.

41 Medvecky, Matej, *Spravodajske eso Slovenskeho Statu: Kauza Imrich Sucky* (Bratislava, 2007), p84.

42 Medvecky, 2007, p84.

43 Medvecky, 2007, p84.

44 *Príspevok k dejinám obcí v handlovskej kotline* [available online at www.chrenovec-brusno.sk]

45 Medvecky, 2007, p84.

46 In Communist Party of Czechoslovakia documents, released in the 1980s for *internal* use, under an entry from 4 November 1940 mentions: "Flyer I of the illegal central leadership of the KSS on the Handlova miners' strike with a call for unity and solidarity with the strikers, for meeting their demands and lifting the state of emergency and recalling the army from Handlova". watson.sk/index.php?option=com_content&view=article&id=2317:malozn amy-zbornik-dokumentov-egy-kevesse-ismert-dokumentum-gyuejtemeny&catid =37:default)

47 Federova, 2005.

48 Micek, 2009, p193.

49 Micek, 2009, p74.

50 Micek, 2009, p74.

51 Micek, 2009, pp74-75.

52 Micek, 2009, p74.

53 Syrny, Marek, *Slovensky demokrati 44-48, Kapitoly z dejin Demokratickej strany na Slovensku v rokoch 1944-1948* (Banska Bystrica, 2010), p11.

54 Syrny, 2010, p11.

55 Micek, 2009, p75.

56 The "Christmas Agreement" talked of "learning the lessons of the past" and states, "The democratic ideals have to be carried over into the economic and social spheres". For a scan of the original see Syrny, 2010, p13.

57 Declaration of the Slovak National Council in Banska Bystrica, 1 September, 1944. See Vlcko B Peter and Vlcko P Ryan (2005), pp66-67.

58 Micek, 2009, pp74-76.

59 Micek, 2009, p76.

60 Syrny, 2010, p11.

61 Peter and Ryan, 2005, p12.

62 Peter and Ryan, 2005, p14-15.

63 Peter and Ryan, 2005, p15-16.

64 Peter and Ryan, 2005, p15-16.

65 Peter and Ryan, 2005, p16.

66 For the text of the Catlos memorandum see Peter and Ryan, 2005, pp70-72.

67 Peter and Ryan, 2005, pp18-19.

68 Peter and Ryan, 2005, p19

69 Peter and Ryan, 2005, p22-25.

70 Peter and Ryan, 2005, p51-53.

71 Micek, 2009, pp132.

72 Micek, 2009, pp132-134.

73 Micek, 2009, pp132-134.

Part Two

WAR IN THE EAST

7

Australia: A war of racism imperialism and resistance

Tom O'Lincoln

After Pearl Harbor, Australian prime minister John Curtin declared: "We are at war with Japan...because our vital interests are imperilled and because the rights of free people in the whole Pacific are assailed".[1] But how many Asian nations were free? Many were in fact colonies including, in the region of Australia, Indonesia, the neighbouring Indo-Malay Archipelago, Pacific Islands such as Fiji, and the great island of New Guinea. Australia, the great white bastion in Asia, was a parliamentary democracy but denied democratic rights to many of its indigenous people. Having seized their colonies by force, the Australian authorities determined to hold on to them the same way.

Australia's mini-empire, racism and world war

In the earliest days of colonisation Australia had been simply a spearhead for the British Empire. In the 1850s, however, gold rushes led to economic boom, making Melbourne and Sydney centres of capital accumulation in their own right. The accumulated wealth began to seek outlets in the surrounding region, giving rise to an expansion drive. In gold-rich Victoria a wide range of business figures backed the Polynesia Company in Fiji, and that led to other ventures—most famously the Melbourne-based Colonial Sugar Refining, which by 1901 held investments in Fiji worth over £2 million.

Well before Japan launched its first war of aggression against China in 1894, Australian expansionism in the Pacific had escalated. Queensland Premier Thomas McIlwraith sent a party led by a police magistrate to raise the flag in Port Moresby in April 1883, hoping to force Britain to annex New Guinea. While this effort failed, it was followed by a campaign to seize the New Hebrides.[2] And by 1914 the Melbourne *Age* newspaper had decided it was time to take New Guinea from the Germans:

We have long since realised that we have a Pacific Ocean destiny... By virtue of the European war an unexpected path has been opened to the furtherance of our ambition [to lay down] the foundations of a solid Australian sub-empire in the Pacific Ocean...[3]

The logic of a white colonial empire fed Australian racism, which in turn meshed readily with anti-Japanese sentiment. Initially racial hostility focused on the Aborigines, but once they were no longer able to resist the white conquest, racism was focused on the "yellow peril" from the north—first the Chinese and later Japan. By the time of the First World War Japan was the main bogey. Racial prejudice was the ideological cement that held the post-1901 federation together. Australia's right wing prime minister William Morris Hughes exploited these fears to the hilt.

One set of race issues were specific to the Second World War. When black American GIs arrived in 1942, Canberra was taken aback. Many local people got on with them just fine, but the authorities did everything they could to implement segregation, resulting in clashes as the GIs stood up for themselves.[4]

The carnage of the First World War is generally recognised as a tragic waste. Hughes, however, made the toll of fallen soldiers into bargaining chips he could cash in at the Paris peace conference. Concerned that the Japanese battlecruiser *HIJMS Ibuki*'s role escorting Australian ships indicated a growing British reliance on Japanese military assistance, he sent as many troops as possible to the European fronts. Reducing British dependence on Tokyo would make Britain less likely to make concessions to Japan in the Pacific. Having invested so many Australian lives, he used them to great effect at the Paris conference, demanding control of all the South Pacific islands taken from Germany. This was about both territory and race. Hughes fought for the creation of a special "C-class" League of Nations mandate to cover what is now Namibia and, more importantly for Australia, certain Pacific islands. Under this mandate the occupying power would be able to impose its own laws, including "White Australia" style immigration controls.[5]

When Japan raised an anti-racist motion at the peace conference, Hughes opposed it more belligerently than any other delegate. The Japanese delegation resented this so bitterly that US President Woodrow Wilson feared the tensions might damage his League of Nations project. To mollify the Japanese and prevent a row over racism at the plenary session, Wilson made concessions to Tokyo over territories in China, allowing Japanese control of German concessions at places such as the Shantung Peninsula. Thus Australian racism helped open the door for Japan's expansion. Hughes's belligerence at the peace conference also helped Japan's militarist faction build popular support for war. Australian intelligence analyst Edmund Piesse complained after the conference: "I withdraw all my optimism about our future relations with Japan...we have been perhaps the chief factor in consolidating the whole Japanese nation behind the imperialists." Academic James Murdoch, visiting Japan around the same time, expressed similar sentiments, adding: "If we are out for a scrap this is just the way to get into one."

In the course of the Second World War Canberra sought to project power throughout the Asia-Pacific. Critics have asked whether Australian commander-in-chief Thomas Blamey's final offensives in the islands were necessary since they cost lives without hastening Japan's surrender. This is to mistake much of their purpose. In addition to restoring colonial rule, they were important for Canberra's strategic position. Blamey told the government:

> Were we to wait until Japan was finally crushed, it would be said that the Americans, who had previously liberated the Philippines, were responsible for the final liberation of the natives in Australian territories, with the inevitable result that our prestige both abroad and in the eyes of the natives would suffer much harm.[6]

The "natives" had already seen what white rule was like. Under the Native Regulations and Ordinances in Papua, according to former district commissioner David Marsh:

> A native wasn't allowed to drink [alcohol]. He couldn't go into a picture show with Europeans. When walking along the footpath the native was expected to move aside. We had the White Women's Protection Ordinance which more or less said that if you smiled at a white woman it was rape... They also had a Native Women's Protection Ordinance which seemed to say something quite different, and didn't mean much anyway.[7]

In 1929, only 12 years before the war for "freedom" began, black workers in Rabaul struck for higher pay. Astonished to find themselves without breakfast, white *mastas* were outraged. "My coon's not here," complained one. Another grumbled that there was "no response from the slave...the government...is disgustingly lenient with the natives...why, the only thing a native understands is a beating." White police put the strike leaders on trial and a white magistrate jailed them.[8]

There was resistance during the war too. Historian Ian Powell quotes a man called Emboge, near Popondetta in New Guinea, who tried collaborating with the Japanese but then moved to attempting to build an independent struggle:

> The *kiawa* [whites] treated us badly before the war and they deserted the people when the Japanese landed at Buna. We tried the Japanese but we did not like them at all. So all we could do was organise ourselves and settle our own differences before we could hope to fight the external enemies.[9]

In other cases local people simply lined up with whoever seemed to be winning in their area or whoever conscripted them. As an inhabitant of the Huon Peninsula told Australians: "We thought the Japanese could beat you when you left these places, so we went their way. Afterwards when you bombed and bombed we were doubtful so we made up our mind to sit in the middle, but when you hunt them from these places we will know you are the stronger".[10]

The patchwork of regional allegiances was very complex. Not only did New Guineans sometimes fight New Guineans, but Fijians fought Bougainvilleans and Pohnpei people fought New Guineans serving with the Australians. Ninety six men and one woman suspected of collaboration with the Australians were massacred at the village of Timbunke by people from other Sepik villages acting under Japanese orders.[11] In return if they believed local Papua New Guinea (PNG) people had helped the Japanese, the Australians served out rough justice. A veteran recalled that Australian troops who had been ordered to massacre entire villages shot the people one by one for collaborating, not aiming to kill immediately, but shooting in the legs so that they could return later and bayonet them to death.[12]

Papuan carriers, later dubbed "Fuzzy Wuzzy Angels", were virtually conscripted by Australians as forced labour to carry the wounded over high mountain trails (Kokoda). No one told them what the war was really about, but they soon learned how cruel it was. Many were paid nothing. According to writer Peter Ryan, recruitment in some villages was 100 percent of fit adult males. The villages suffered without men to clear gardens, hunt and maintain houses and canoes. Diet was poor so diseases increased, with some places facing near-starvation and very high infant mortality.[13] Doctor Geoffrey Vernon recalled that during fighting on the trail, many carriers had no blankets, rice was almost the only food much of the time, meat was not available for two or three weeks at a stretch and tobacco was scarce. Rules mandating reduction of loads to

40 lbs were frequently ignored, and excessive loads and distances inflicted on the carriers.[14]

In the late 1960s former carriers told PNG University's Ulli Beier that about two thirds of them had tried to escape. Reasons for wanting to abscond included bad food, sore shoulders from carrying, beatings, cold and bombs. But whenever some did escape, the Australians conscripted their sons so that fathers were forced back to face ghastly penalties. "The most terrifying punishments were the so-called drum beatings in Kerema... A fire was lit in a 44-gallon drum and when it was hot the unlucky carriers were put cross the drum and beaten".[15] A song still current among villagers in the 1970s ended:

> The white man has brought his war to be fought on this land
> His King and Queen have said so
> We are forced against our wishes to help him.[16]

Tom Hungerford's novel *The Ridge and the River* portrays an Australian musing about local villagers who watched plantation owners, the "little tin gods", driven out by the Japanese and lucky to escape with their lives. He suspects the planters might get a shock after the war when they attempt to get local labour at the old rates, "and there might be something more ugly".[17] At the time the government identified Papua and New Guinea as Australian territory, but Curtin himself was quite cynical about this in private, telling journalists that New Guinea was not Australia and that calling it so was just "military strategy".[18]

At the end of the conflict a man from Wewak in New Guinea told an Australian:

> Yes, we have helped you in this war, now we are like cousins, like brothers. We too have won the war. Now whatever knowledge, whatever ideas you have, you can give them to us. Before all the things we did, you gaoled us, and you fined us, all the time. But now. What now?[19]

Some people in PNG expected whites to compensate them for past plunder, and that was the starting point for many of the social movements known as cargo cults in the post-war period. Instead colonial plunder resumed. People throughout the islands had the bitter experience of whites confiscating gifts from soldiers or money received for carvings on the grounds that it must be stolen. For this Major-General Basil Morris came up with a curious rationalisation. The native mind, he argued, responded most readily to visible marks of distinction, so that money or goods possessed much less value in the eyes of local people than if one gave them a medal.[20] This was consistent with government policy. The pamphlet *You and the Native*, distributed to troops in New Guinea, advised white readers: "Always therefore maintain your position or pose of superiority...always, without overdoing it, be the master".[21]

Invading East Timor

During the campaigns for East Timor's independence from Indonesia from the 1970s to the 1990s, much was made of the warm relations enjoyed by Australian "Sparrow Force" guerrilla fighters in that country during the Second World War. But there is another much darker account: a story of contention by outside aggressors. It began before the war as Australians and Japanese jockeyed for oil concessions in the late 1930s. Qantas even initiated regular flights to the capital, Dili, which would hardly have been profitable, to increase Australian leverage with the local administrators. The seeds were sown for armed conflict.

Despite endless condemnation of the Axis powers for invading neutral countries, until recently few people knew that Australian and Dutch troops had invaded East Timor in violation of Portuguese neutrality. The Portuguese governor called it unlawful aggression.[22] One invading soldier, Archie Campbell, later wrote that it seemed "our single claim to fame and glory is that we shall go down in history as the first troops of Great Britain or Australia to violate another country's neutrality in the war". The aggression is clear from Lionel Wigmore's official war history. Once the invading forces had mobilised, he says, their commanders went to the Portuguese governor and demanded he invite them in. The outraged governor said his orders were to ask for help only after an attack by Japan. He was told that Dutch and Australian troops were already on their way.

Not that we need concern ourselves unduly with the diplomatic rights of the Portuguese colonialists, given they themselves held the colony by force. What matters is that the Japanese, for reasons mainly to do with keeping Portugal out of the war in Europe, were keen to keep East Timor out of the war as well. Neither Macao nor East Timor were on the list of war objectives in the first stage of Japan's war plans because the general staff feared that taking Portuguese Timor would drive Portugal into the arms of the Allies. So it was the Allies who brought the horrors of war to this colony. Ex-diplomat James Dunn would later write that as a consequence of the Allied invasion of December 1941, East Timor became one of the great catastrophes of the Second World War in terms of relative fatalities.

Did the Timorese support Australia? Only sometimes, and then often cynically. Christopher Wray's book on the subject quotes an account saying locals were initially suspicious of Sparrow Force, and only when antagonised by Japanese behaviour did they start helping them. In August 1942 the Australians were attacked by a group of people apparently from Dutch Timor and allied with the Japanese. At one point these Timorese indicated they wanted to use captured Australian Corporal Hodgson for "spear practice".

In August 1942 the Japanese took the offensive. Once that happened the Australians faced increasing hostility from the Timorese. Those in frontier areas were pro-Japanese, or more accurately anti-European. Elsewhere the locals were "no longer as ready to support the Australians as they had been before when the 2/2 Independent Company had the run of Portuguese Timor". Moreover "screens of pro-Japanese natives made it hard to strike at vital parts of enemy columns" and by 23 August, despite a Japanese retreat, unrest among the Timorese was beginning to seriously concern Sparrow Force.

Sparrow Force led raids on villages that did not support Australian troops. "During the raids a number of villages were burned out, about 150 huts being destroyed", says Wray, whose book contains a photograph of Australians burning the village of Mindelo. He tells us that some of the local people who helped the Australians did so in the mistaken belief that the Australian forces would eventually help them overthrow the Portuguese.[23] But for all the wartime talk of liberation, there was no chance of this. On the contrary, the Australians wanted Portuguese officials to stay in their posts to maintain order. And an unedifying order it was. In late August local people at Maubisse rebelled and killed a Portuguese official. A Portuguese-led reprisal force then attacked Maubisse, "burning villages and crops, carrying off women, children and animals and killing everyone else in their wake". A diary kept by Australian troops recorded their relaxed attitude to such events:

> The private local war, Portuguese versus native, still goes on in its bloodthirsty way, and provides some humour for sub units. One of our patrols near Mape, out hunting the Jap, encountered a Portuguese patrol out hunting some natives, they exchanged compliments and went their various ways.[24]

Ultimately the position of Sparrow Force became untenable as the Japanese offensive escalated and villagers became unfriendly and even hostile.[25] As in so many places around the Asia-Pacific, it appears most villagers were friendly when the Australians had the upper hand in fighting, but became unfriendly when the Japanese looked like winning. Which makes sense. They would be less likely to make a serious commitment to the Australians when some of them acted like this:

> Many times a native would pull into an Aussie camp, proudly produce a surat [letter of IOU used to secure provisions] on which someone had written: "Give the bastard a kick in the arse and send the useless bugger on his way." It added to the general enjoyment of the hard dull work of the day's patrolling.

Some had very sobering memories of the East Timor campaign. Australian soldier Jim Landman remembers that Sparrow Force, like so many military interlopers in history, killed recalcitrant local people and treated women as commodities. Alfredo Pires, son of a Portuguese official and a Timorese mother, remembered a common saying that when it came to punishment the Japanese were very cruel, but in matters of justice the Australians were worse. The Japanese might torture to extract information, but they might let you live. But if the Australians suspected you, you were dead.[26] Another sort of cruelty was to follow. Archie Campbell and his comrades were haunted by the likely fate awaiting their remaining Timorese allies when the Australians pulled out:

> we are now their only source of protection. If only we could take them with us when we go, but Australian HQ has vetoed the idea... Our poor Timor *criados* look so bewildered...our hearts are weighed down by a persistent and terrible ache.[27]

Indonesia

Further east, Australian troops restored Dutch control. Not all of the soldiers liked doing this. George Bliss of the 7th Division recalled:

> About six weeks after the war ended we were told we were going into the Celebes [Sulawesi] "to supervise the rounding up of the Japanese". We realised later that it was to prevent the locals organising against the return of the Dutch. We went by ship to Makassar. The feeling among the troops was mostly against the Dutch. On arrival we were lined up on the wharf, fully equipped in battle order, and marched through the town out to the Dutch barracks about three miles out. That was the first act of intimidation.

Later in Pare Pare, Bliss found the independence movement was stronger. "All along the road the Indonesian flag was flying and people wore the red and white colours of the flag. The top brass gave orders forbidding fraternisation. Most ignored that order".[28] Gavin Long's official history reports that in Balikpapan on 14 November up to 8,000 Indonesians gathered and raised banners, and ten to 15 Australian soldiers were present "inciting" the Indonesians.[29] Such public appearances weren't the norm, but anti-colonial sentiment was widespread in the ranks, which is why on Tarakan Brigadier David Whitehead organised special lectures to combat pro-Indonesian sentiment.[30] Much of the impetus for this came from the Communist Party of Australia (CPA), which had mobilised in support of the Indonesian Communists (PKI). PKI leaders, transferred to Australia as prisoners from the Dutch prison camp at Tanah Merah, built an Australia-wide movement with CPA support, culminating in rebellions by Indonesian seafarers and Australian union bans on Dutch ships. They managed this despite repression by Dutch representatives, who the Labor government allowed to arrest and even deport activists.[31] The Indonesian people, who often displayed hostility to the Australian military, were enthusiastic about solidarity from Australian trade unionists. News bulletins posted in some cities referred to Australian waterside workers' support for Indonesian strikers, the key passages prominently outlined in red.

But Australian leaders were determined to complete their colonial mission. In Sumbawa after clashes between Indonesian nationalists and Japanese forces, the latter were told to instruct the Sultan that attacks must stop and that the Australian army had ordered the Japanese to shoot to kill.[32] And so whatever their personal sentiments, the Australian troops helped entrench Dutch power with terrible consequences. Their intervention in Sulawesi paved the way for Dutch captain Paul Westerling, who developed ferocious new tactics in counter-insurgency. He punished whole villages for Republican actions in their areas, lining people up and executing them one by one until an informant spoke out. Westerling's reign of terror is reliably estimated to have cost as many lives as the battle of Surabaya. Emboldened by the success these methods brought, the Dutch increased the use of such repressive tactics in Java.[33]

Meanwhile preparations were under way to assemble Australian troops on the island of Morotai (Moluccas). The Australian force responsible for the occupation and military administration of eastern Indonesia was headquartered at Morotai until April 1946, when the Dutch colonial government was re-established. This was one place where rank and file troops proved able to shrug off wartime hostilities, which to a degree alarmed the brass. Officers told the rank and file that they had seen too many cases of fraternisation, extending as far as gifts of food and cigarettes. This would not be tolerated. In response to Japanese prisoners' salutes, Australians were to stare them "fiercely and fixedly in the eye".[34]

On the home front

The Second World War broke out at the conjuncture of two periods of working class unrest. The mood in the working class was savage at the start of the 1940s, reflecting bitter experiences of the Depression and the First World War. Anti-war agitation during the first war had been colossal, culminating in two working class campaigns which defeated attempts to introduce conscription. Later in 1940 coal miners and dock workers— traditionally militant groups of unionists—moved aggressively to restore their pre-Depression bargaining position. But the mood extended far wider. The director-general of health, reporting on a survey of 1,400 women, highlighted this response:

> I believe you desire the reasons of mothers for only having a limited family. Well, one of them is this: What do we owe to Australia? It starved us and our children after the last war and it will do the same after this, *If We Let It*. Therefore, we have decided that there won't be so many of us to starve this time... If we find out any birth control hint, we pass it on. I myself know of an easy, safe method of abortion. I know of hundreds of ideas that have been passed on to me by desperate and despairing mothers of hungry children. Things will have to be mightily attractive in the New World before we consider the inconvenience of big families.[35]

The government soon realised that in a tight labour market it could not keep too severe a clamp on women's wages given their importance for the war effort. It therefore created the Women's Employment Board (WEB) in 1942 to determine pay for new jobs or those previously done by men. As a rule the Board granted female employees in these jobs 85 to 90 percent of the male rate. But the WEB pay rate was not easy to get. Unlike some other wartime regulations which they patiently accepted, bosses hated the board. They challenged it in the courts, used delaying tactics in hearings or simply refused to implement WEB decisions.

Employers claimed women needed more supervision or were physically unable to do certain tasks, or they altered job descriptions.[36] Women had to stage strikes just to get the WEB rate. Like the government, employers referred to conventional beliefs that a woman's place was in the home, yet in practice they did not oppose women working in low paid jobs. Their real opposition was to women's entry into new sectors at higher rates of pay. Even this was not just about money. In fact employer representatives said some firms were prepared to face prosecution for refusing to pay WEB rates—even though under a cost-plus system compliance with the WEB would increase profits. What they most feared was female labour becoming rebellious.[37]

And it did, as a second wave of unrest opened up in the working class. Ironically women's lack of union traditions meant they listened less to union leaders' calls for war restraint than did men. At the Small Arms Ammunition Factory in Footscray, Melbourne several thousand workers held a stop work meeting in early 1943 demanding a 90 percent pay rise. Union leaders urged them to return to work for the sake of "the boys in the trenches", which provoked angry shouts of, "We know all about the boys in the trenches—they're our husbands and sons".[38] Another centre of militancy was textiles. In September 1941 mass meetings in Victoria culminated in a 20,000-strong stoppage over pay:

> After the strike decision, about fifty men and women rushed the stage and tried to take over the meeting. They were quickly dispersed by the police. Speakers were howled down and counted out... Women screamed at one another, and when the division...was carried by a large majority, calls of "what about the boys overseas fighting for 5/- a day", "scab" and "Fascist" were heard above the din.[39]

The pattern continued at Alexandria Spinning Mills in Sydney in 1943. A thousand women picketed and sent delegations to other factories, where they climbed wire grilles to reach those working inside. Within a week rank and file committees were leading 10,000 workers on strike.[40] Union membership rose from 33 percent of the female workforce in 1939 to 52 percent in 1945, and the number of disputes rose from 416 to 945.[41] Attempts to control female labour were far from successful and this was true of labour generally.

At Dunlop management faced strike action because it had withdrawn employees' right to showers. No sooner had it settled that dispute than women began industrial action over equal pay, which in turn was followed by a strike over piece rates. Arbitration judge Edmund Drake-Brockman called a compulsory conference and ordered the tyre men back to work. They refused, also ignoring orders from the executive of the Rubber Workers' Union that they should go back on the old basis.

Week after week the stop-work continued, with more and more government agencies trying to intervene. Only threats of conscription into the army ended the unrest.[42]

No such fate awaited printers at the Sydney *Sun*, who in September 1944 demanded a 40-hour week along with four weeks annual leave. Management's rejection of the claim led to a historic strike. The employers sent articles to the other dailies for incorporation in a "composite" paper, but the other papers' printers refused to typeset them. The stoppage spread to journalists as well. The strikers produced their own paper, which had a virtual monopoly of sales because transport unions refused to handle the bosses' composite effort. Each day the union paper sold its print run, and the profits reached £3,000. The strike's success created something of a vogue for industrial unrest, and within a few months the commercial section of the industry was organising a campaign for a 40-hour week based on direct action.[43]

A general industrial mobilisation was under way well before the war ended. Indeed as early as 1944:

> New South Wales, during the 20 months ending August 31, had 1,432 industrial disputes [depriving] the neutral citizen of meat, bread, laundry, newspapers, tyres, theatrical entertainment, hospital attention, buses and trams, coke for stoves, potatoes, restaurants, hot baths, country and interstate travel and other amenities.[44]

A remarkable strike took place in 1945 in Sydney's Balmain dockyards. At Mort's Dock leftist followers of Leon Trotsky used their influence to resist the more oppressive aspects of the war effort. For this, and for his challenge to the union leadership controlled by the enthusiastically pro-war Communist Party, the Ironworkers' executive took action against the Trotskyist shop steward Nick Origlass. In February 1945 the federal leadership found a pretext on which to charge Origlass with breaching union rules, and on this basis banned him from serving as a delegate. Union members demanded his reinstatement. By late April nearly 3,000 were on strike over the issue, a stoppage lasting several weeks. The outcome was a new, independent union branch in Balmain and a triumph for the rank and file.

Strike days passed the 2 million mark in 1945 and the unions made plans to campaign for a 40-hour week. The stage was set for a stormy industrial scene after the war. 1946-7 would see a six-month dispute in the Victorian metal trades, followed by major rail and coal strikes towards the end of the decade. So intense was the general ferment that in

September 1946 the Communist paper *Tribune* reported that the Leichhardt Boy Scouts Band in Sydney was on strike and had placed bans on its scout hall.

A democratic army?

When the Aid Russia Committee circulated a booklet called *Democratic Army of a Democratic People*, they expressed a common aspiration. To this day many believe the Australian military at the time of the Second World War did have particularly democratic qualities. And indeed it was reasonable to hope that with Labor in government and claiming to be the party of the workers and in a war presented as a crusade for democracy, Australia might have expected some sort of democratisation of the military. But in *At the Front Line* Mark Johnston puts all such notions in perspective. The casual Australian style may have found some expression in the services, Johnston writes, but the army was still modelled on its British equivalent, a structure which had an inescapable logic: "the structure of the Australian army provided plenty of evidence for those who regarded everyone as either a privileged leader or an underprivileged follower".[45]

Joan Beaumont's analysis of the battalion group known as Gull Force, which documents members' previous jobs, shows almost 30 percent of officers came from professional, managerial or executive-type careers, compared to 3.6 percent of privates. A further 59.3 percent of officers came from supervisory and other non-manual jobs, compared with 8.6 percent of privates. Close to half of privates had been unskilled manual workers.[46] John Barrett's survey of veterans likewise shows that nearly two thirds of the commissioned officers came from among the higher-educated.[47] This might have been a tolerable starting point in a meritocracy, but the fact was that if you were working class you were often stuck at the bottom no matter how well you performed. Even demonstrated leadership under fire often did not bring promotion. It was so hard for the lower ranks to move up that in the final year of the war situations arose where seasoned soldiers were led into action by officers with no previous experience of battle.[48] Yet rank brought privileges; for example, each officer had a batman (a servant).

Elite status also bred contemptuous attitudes. Officers spoke about their batmen in language that was "condescending and even redolent of the British upper class".[49] Private Les Clothier reported on life aboard a ship in Cairns Harbour: "We had a sloppy stew for breakfast and sat on a dirty floor to eat it. As usual, the officers are in cabins and eat like civilised beings".[50] Soldiers returning to South Australia on leave were delighted when billeted with civilians who "gave us beds with sheets, *even though the army officers told them to leave all the furniture out and leave the room bare* for us. We felt like human beings".[51] (Emphasis added.) It would be wrong, however, to think the oppressive side of military life stemmed primarily from the arrogance of individual officers. It was systemic. According to one private, a sergeant informed a group of recruits that "we were leaving behind our civilian life and name to become just a number in the army".[52] Some thought the army's plan seemed to be to make soldiers live like animals so they would fight like animals.

Where oppression is systemic rebellion is on the cards. It began early in the navy. There was a minor strike on HMAS Perth in New York in August 1939 and a sit-down strike the following July on HMAS *Voyager*. In late 1941 the captain of the *Westralia* ordered machine guns trained on rebellious seamen, and a further upheaval occurred on HMAS *Pirie* in June 1943. Grievances commonly concerned the behaviour of officers and the quality of food. On the *Westralia* seamen received rice and prunes to eat for three weeks, and finally rebelled when given the same for Christmas dinner.

Everyday military life was full of implicit conflict, with contempt bubbling from below as well as trickling from above. A diary from the Middle East relates how "the officers give us the usual baloney and give orders and immediately contradict them... The more one sees of the officers in charge of us, the more readily comes the explanation of the Malayan and Singapore disasters".[53] The troops cheered when Soviet leader Joseph Stalin's image appeared at film screenings, as much from ideology as from cheeky rebellion. Not everyone cared that much about Uncle Joe but they knew it annoyed the officers.[54] There were also other ways to annoy them. A soldier reported his experience on an AIF parade ground:

> today we sure have been fighting for our rights... They started giving us drill this morning. We were not in a very good mood. So we went as slow as possible... The Lieut tried to march us about but we only moved at a crawl...so he gave the about turn to head us back from camp again. But this time we had him in a good place to make a fool of him... Instead of turning round and going where he wanted us to go, we broke off and headed in all directions.[55]

Unrest continued in the Pacific War even during the 1942 invasion scare. A rebellion took place in the Northern Territory among military transport companies. Crackdowns on a two-up school and on minor misuse of official property were the immediate causes, though denial of leave was apparently the underlying issue. Dissatisfaction led to a march, which in turn led to a riot. The crowd toppled a petrol bowser, overturned vehicles and ransacked the mess.[56] Dissatisfaction was also rife on the Atherton Tablelands near Cairns, where the army brought large numbers of troops together for training exercises. One company on the Tablelands refused to carry out its duties—an event veterans later variously described as "a rebellion, strike, riot or incident"—when ordered to parade less than fully dressed, as part of an investigation into a clash with an officer.[57] At another time, according to Bob "Hooker" Holt's reminiscences, some of the men:

> reckoned they were being treated like dogs, so at Retreat they began to bark like dogs. The idea took on like wildfire... Faintly at first, you could hear the yapping and barking from far away units and then louder, until it reached our camp. We would take up the call and then it could be heard fading away into the distance.[58]

In Western Australia in early 1942 there were strikes against "brass-hatted stupidity" and curtailment of leave. At one army camp soldiers held a sit-down strike for a day and a half, at another up to 3,000 troops held mass meetings and boycotted parades, and a strike took place at a third camp. After the war ended troops held mass protests on Morotai and elsewhere at the lack of ships to bring them home. Anecdotally there was even talk of attempting armed seizures of ships.[59]

Some of the well known conflicts between Australian and American servicemen turn out, on closer examination, to have originated in a common discontent with the authorities. A report to General Blamey about the notorious clashes in Brisbane referred to "brawls between groups of American and Australian troops or less frequently between Americans and Australians together against the Military Police, whether American or Australian". The report cited one upheaval involving hundreds of men after Australian soldiers objected to the arrest of an American enlisted man.[60]

Despite the history of conflict, Johnston plays down the scale of insubordination. The soldier's most common state, he reminds us, was fatalistic submission rather than enthusiasm or insubordination. This was partly because repression was so harsh in a military setting that "the basic foundation was fear of punishment".[61] Soldiers described the typical commander, only half in jest, as "held in respect by majors, awe by

captains, fear by lieutenants, and fear and trembling by other ranks...
After the war they usually become members of exclusive clubs and are
attacked by gout".[62] Even keeping a diary was mildly subversive, since the
brass preferred to forbid them for security reasons.

How significant we consider the recorded instances of individual
rebellion is a matter of perspective. The provost marshal reported in
November 1942 that only 89 assaults had been made on MPs in the
course of 33,000 arrests between April and September. These are not
large numbers in the great scheme of things.[63] Still, the figures do show
that military authorities made many thousands of arrests, and MPs experienced more than a few assaults. Had the war gone badly the number
and impact of such incidents could have been much greater.

Two veterans have intimated more radical conclusions than Johnston
about the significance of rebellion inside the military. Bob Holt, reflecting on the unrest on the Atherton Tablelands, thought it was all in fun;
yet he suggested the authorities did their best to stamp it out because
they had apprehensive memories of a similar agitation among French
troops in the trenches during the First World War. That unrest was part
of a European wave of discontent that culminated in social revolutions
and the fall of governments. Admittedly much of the unrest Holt
describes was spontaneous and anarchic, including an episode in which
rank and file soldiers chased military police—"these louts", as he calls
them—back to their barracks in Cairns.[64] There was also a force leading
soldiers' revolts that was better organised and more focused in its
approach. This was the Communist Party, which had 3,000 to 3,400
members in the military. Ted Bacon, one of the wartime communists,
reflected later on the impact of more carefully considered, better organised actions:

> Successful strikes without victimisation of leaders were far more common
> than might be imagined by those who may believe a military bureaucracy
> is practically unbeatable. Refusals to parade until food or conditions were
> improved occurred in almost all training camps [and] even the most
> anti-democratic commanders were compelled to move cautiously in their
> dealings with the rank and file.[65]

The Communists were also leaders of the solidarity actions with the
Indonesian independence movement, but again they were constrained
by instructions from the Soviet regime, which did not want the war
effort jeopardised. By the 1940s the Communist Party was no longer a
force for revolution so that its agitation never exceeded certain limits.[66]

Tragically, fatalistic submission remained the norm. As a result the Australian military command escaped lightly from the consequences of unrest in the ranks. In a more radical political environment, revolts against brass-hatted stupidity could have grown into struggles against the stupidity and the obscenity of imperialist war itself.

Despite all the arguments in this chapter, the great majority of Australians would endorse the war effort on the simple grounds that a Japanese invasion must be avoided. Most scholarship today, however, accepts the fact that Japan had no plans to invade Australia. In fact, Japan intended PNG and Indonesia as the southern boundary of its empire rather than as a springboard to launch troops at Darwin. In any case, the Japanese forces were too devastated by fighting on the Kokoda Trail to even capture Port Moresby. Veteran war correspondent Osmar White recalled they were "exhausted, diseased and starving"—hardly in a condition to conquer the huge Australian continent.[67]

And with this recognition, the last argument for the war effort falls.

NOTES

1   Quoted in Kristin Williamson, *The Last Bastion* (Lansdowne, Sydney, 1984), p125.
2   On Australia's 19th century Pacific imperialism see Tom O'Lincoln, *The Neighbour from Hell: Two Centuries of Australian Imperialism* (Interventions, Melbourne, 2014), ch 1.
3   Editorial, *The Age* (Melbourne, 12 August 1914), p8.
4   Peter Thompson and Robert Macklin, *The Battle of Brisbane: Australians and the Yanks at War* (ABC Books, 2001), p102ff.
5   These events are well summarised in Humphrey McQueen, *Japan to the Rescue: Australian Security Around the Indonesian Archipelago* (Heinneman, Port Melbourne, 1991), p282.
6   David Horner, "Strategic Policy Making 1943-45", in Michael McKernan and M Browne, *Two Centuries of War and Peace* (Australian War Memorial, 1988), p293.
7   Quoted in John Waiko, *A Short History of Papua New Guinea* (Oxford University Press, Melbourne, 1993), p77.
8   Waiko, 1993, p93, p100, p101.
9   Alan Powell, *The Third Force: Angau's New Guinea War 1942-46*, (Oxford University Press, Melbourne, 2003), p208.
10   Powell, 2003, p216.
11   Geoffrey White and Lamont Lindstrom, *The Pacific Theatre: Island Representations of World War II* (Melbourne University Press, 1990), p23. John Robertson says New Guinea tribes "tended to support whichever army was in control of their area" (1981), p139.
12   Timothy Hall, *New Guinea 1942-44* (Methuen, Australia, Sydney, 1981), p134.
13   Quoted in Waiko, 1993, p114.
14   Quoted in Peter Brune, *Those Ragged Bloody Heroes: From the Kokoda Trail to Gona Beach* (Allen and Unwin, Sydney, 1991), p52.
15   Humphrey McQueen, *Social Sketches of Australia 1988-2001* (University of Queensland, St Lucia, 2004), p176.
16   McQueen, 2004, p176.
17   TAG Hungerford, *The Ridge and the River* (Penguin, Melbourne, 2003), p152. The book also mentions locals collaborating with the Japanese. Likewise Osmar White, *Green Armour* (Penquin, 1992), p165, describes villagers guiding Japanese patrols.
18   Clem Loyd and Richard Hall, *Background Briefings: John Curtin's War* (National Library of Australia, 1997), p98.
19   Waiko, 1993, p124.
20   Grey, *The Australian Army: A History* (Oxford University Press, Melbourne, 2001), p148.
21   Geoffrey White and Lindstrom Lamond, *Pacific Representations of World War* (Melbourne University Press, 1990), p9.
22   Christopher Wray, *Timor 1942: Australian Commandos at War With the Japanese* (Hutchinson, Melbourne, 1987), p29. My account of the Australian incursion mostly follows Wray.
23   Wray, 1987, p131.
24   Wray, 1987, p132.
25   B J Callinan, "The August Show on Timor", in Norman Bartlett (ed), *Australia at Arms* (Australian War Memorial, 1955), p209.
26   Landman and Pires interviewed in Michelle Turner, *Telling: East Timor* (UNSW Press, Sydney, 1992), p36, p38.
27   Archie Campbell, *The Double Reds of Timor* (John Burridge Military Antiques, Swanbourne, 1995), p132, p134.
28   George Bliss, "Australian Army Coms in Indonesia", *Tribune* (30 July 1980), p11.
29   Gavin Long, *The Final Campaigns* (Australian War Memorial, Canberra, 1963), p569.
30   Peter Stanley, *Tarakan: An Australian Tragedy* (Allen and Unwin, Sydney, 1997), p191. Forty five Australian servicemen on Balikpapan wrote to Chifley supporting the proclamation of an Indonesian republic and deploring the use of Japanese forces to put

down the independence movement, according to David Day, *Chifley* (HarperCollins, Sydney, 2001), p423.

31 Rupert Lockwood, *Black Armada* (Australasian Book Society, Sydney, 1975).

32 Gavin Long, 1963, p572.

33 John Keay, *Last Post: The End of Empire in the Far East* (John Murray, London, 1997), p266.

34 Alan Clifton, *Time of Fallen Blossoms* (Cassell, Sydney, 1950), pviii.

35 Bettina Cass, "Population and Families: State Conscription of Domestic Life", in Cora Baldock and Bettina Cass, *Women, Social Welfare and the State* (Allen and Unwin, Sydney, 1988), pp176-177.

36 Janey Stone, "Class Struggle on the Home Front", in *Rebel Women in Australian Working Class History* (Red Rag, Melbourne, 2005), p70.

37 See Lynne Beaton, "The Importance of Women's Paid Labour", in Margaret Bevege et al, *Worth Her Salt* (Hale and Iremonger, 1982), p95 and throughout.

38 Quoted in *Jesse Street: A Revised Autobiography* (The Federation Press, 2004), p160.

39 "Victorian Textile Strike Vote Affects 20,000", *Melbourne Sun* (9 September 1941), p3.

40 Stone, 2005, p82.

41 Stone, 2005, p81.

42 Geoffrey Blainey, *Jumping Over the Wheel* (Allen and Unwin, Sydney, 1993), p178. From the context Blainey provides, these events mainly occurred in 1942.

43 Jin Hagan, *Printers and Politics: A History of the Australian Printing Unions 1850-90* (Australian National University Press, 1966), p275.

44 Quoted in Tom Sheridan, *Mindful Militants: The Amalgamated Engineering Union* (Cambridge University Press, Melbourne, 1975), p168.

45 Mark Johnston, *At the Front Line: Experiences of Australian Soldiers during World War I* (Cambridge University Press, Melbourne, 1996), p140.

46 My compilation from Jean Beaumont, *Gull Force: Survival and Leadership in Captivity* (Allen and Unwin, Sydney, 1988), p29, Table 2.6.

47 John Barrett, *We Were There: Australian Soldiers of World War II Tell their Stories* (Penguin, Melbourne, 1987), p85.

48 Johnston, 1996, p141.

49 Johnston, 1996, p140.

50 Les Clothier, "Diary of a Soldier", in Hugh Gillan (ed), *We Had Some Bother: Tales From the Infantry* (Hale and Iremonger for the 2/3 batallion association, 1985), p105.

51 Johnston, emphasis added, 1996, p98.

52 Johnston, 1996, p92, p93.

53 Johnston, 1996, p120.

54 Peter Medcalf, *War in the Shadows: Bougainville 1944-45* (Australian War Memorial, 1986), p36.

55 Quoted in Johnston, 1996, p147.

56 Alex Tanner, *The Long Road North* (Alex Tanner, Adelaide, 1995), pp178-181.

57 Margaret Barter, *Far Above Battle: The Experience and Memory of Australian Soldiers in War* (Allen and Unwin, Sydney, 1994), p217.

58 Bob Holt, *From Ingleburn to Aitappe: The Trials and Tribulations of a Four Figure Man* (R Holt, Lakemba, NSW, 1981), p173.

59 Beverly Symons, "All Out for the People's War: Communists in the Australian Army in the Second World War", *Historical Studies* 26 (105) (October 1995), p61.2. David Horner, "Standing Up for Ourselves", *Week-End Australian* (7-8 October 1995), p24.

60 Peter Thompson and Robin Macklin 2001, p158, p230. Barry Ralph, *They Passed this Way: The United States of America, The States of Australia, and World War II* (Kangaroo Press, Sydney, 2000), p175, says US and Australian troops had a "resentment, indeed hatred" towards authority, especially armed and aggressive military police.

61 Johnston, 1996, pp157, 158.

62 An unnamed soldier, "About Officers", in *Australian Military Forces, Jungle Warfare: With*

the *Australian Army in the South-West Pacific* (Australian War Memorial, Canberra, 1944).

63 Johnston, 1996, p154.

64 Holt, 1981, pp173-174.

65 Symons, 1995, p612.

66 On the Communists in the Second World War see Tom O'Lincoln, "Fatal Compromises: The Australian Communists in World War", redsites.info/cpaww2.htm, 2011.

67 Osmar White, *Green Armour* (Penguin, Melbourne, 1992), p208. For a lively yet academic discussion see Peter Stanley writing under the ironic title *Invading Australia* (Viking, Melbourne, 2008).

8

Burma: Through two imperialisms to independence

William Crane

Introduction

Like all of South East Asia, Burma was subject to two occupations during the Second World War, firstly of British colonialism followed by a brief occupation by Japan, and then return to an even briefer interregnum of British rule before independence was gained in 1948. The fact that Burmese nationalists, anti-imperialists and leftists could be found on different sides of the struggle for Burma at any one time poses a thorny problem for the historian trying to reconstruct the war from below in this backward country.

Part of the forgotten history of the war in Asia, which for European historians is only of note once the bombs were dropped on Hiroshima and Nagasaki, the war in Burma is rarely treated as anything other than a conquest by the barbaric Japanese, followed by a heroic reconquest by the British. The classic movie *The Bridge on the River Kwai* is one such tale of subversion and heroism by Allied forces against the Japanese.

This point of view developed from British war memoirs and finds its reverse in the post-colonial memoirs and official histories of the Burmese military regime, for which the glorious national war of liberation surged forever forward, barely stopping to consider the complicated politics of its leaders' manoeuvres between British colonialism and Japanese imperialism.

What both these trends of history have in common is that they deny the agency of the Burmese themselves in making the history of the war as they resisted both British and Japanese occupation and fought for self-determination. This chapter is a brief but necessary overview of their struggles.

Burma from the Ancien Regime to the Age of Colonialism

Entering the 19th century as the rulers of the territory now known as Burma, much of contemporary Thailand and north eastern India, the Third

Burmese Empire ruled by the Konbaung Dynasty was ill-placed in the age of emerging western imperialism. Located right on the border between British ruled India and expanding French colonialism in Southeast Asia, the millennium-old Burmese kingdom was bound to become a component in the classic age of imperialism in one way or another.

Three wars were fought between dynastic Burma and British India during the 19th century. By the time of the second war, which ended in the 1850s, Burma was already *de facto* subjected to British rule, while the third Anglo-Burmese War in 1885 merely accomplished the formality of annexing the remnants of the Burmese kingdom. The pronouncements of the last king, Thibaw, who mobilised his army promising to defeat the British, conquer their country and convert them to the true religion of Theravada Buddhism, only served as pathetic bluster at the beginning of the road that would lead to the end of his kingdom. Promises of French aid never materialised, and Thibaw and his family ended up in exile in India while the British took over administration of their new province.[1]

Like India, Burma was a territory that was deeply divided by ethnicity and territory. If the Russian Empire had been "the prison house of nations", pre-conquest Burma could perhaps be called at least a "garden shed of nations". While the plurality of people at the centre of the country were from the dominant Bamar group,[2] the majority of the eastern half of the country come from the Karen and Shan groups. In the north and north east Burmese territory becomes a bewildering patchwork of tribes and ethnicities with their own customs and long-established ways of life.[3] Burma had always had strong trading links with China that had left a significant Chinese community in the eventual colonial centre of Rangoon/Yangon, and British rule brought with it significant numbers of Indians as administrators and coolies.

The British were prepared to use both existing divisions and those they established in order to rule Burma, which from its conquest until the 1930s was administered as a province of the Raj. Unlike India, however, Burma had a long and recent history of union, and the dominant Bamar had a recent memory of ruling over the area as a united kingdom.[4] Both the existing divisions in Burmese society and the proto-national consciousness of the Bamar are factors that must be taken into consideration as we review Burma's wartime history.

The British had gobbled Burma up in no small part because it helped to secure the Indian crown jewel against the nearby French possessions of Indochina. Just as it became politically dependent on colonised India in the form of a joint colonial administration, Burma also became economically subordinate to India as the main provider of rice to feed the subcontinent. Hence its economy entered the modern era as a periphery to a periphery.[5] Intensive capitalist development did not take place in Burma even to the limited extent that it had started to in India. The place of the "rice bowl of India" in the global economy was decidedly marginal, and although rice production suffered a profound crisis with the Depression of the 1930s, the effects of this on countryside producers were highly varied and mitigated through a variety of strategies.[6]

The pacification of rural Burma was for the British authorities a never-ending job. Even where they would have preferred not to go, for example into the northern territory of the Wa people, known for their practice of head-hunting, their legendary filthiness and copious consumption of alcohol and opium, British forces felt they had to establish their authority to seal off the area from the influence of the French and Chinese, and because any future problems with their rule had to be dealt with pre-emptively.[7] Meanwhile, they also had to deal with the occasionally rebellious mood of the Shan states, which had been divided between Britain, France and Thailand and whose leaders constantly attempted to play one off against the other.[8]

British colonial policemen in Burma, the Indian soldiers they commanded and the eventual recruits to the British army from the Karen and other native groups constantly felt themselves on the precipice of rebellion even in the most peaceful of times. George Orwell, who served for several years as a colonial official in towns on the river deltas of lower Burma, expressed this feeling when he complained of being hated by the vast majority of the people:

> As a police officer I was an obvious target and was baited whenever it seemed safe to do so... In the end the sneering yellow faces of young men that met me everywhere, the insults hooted after me when I was at a safe distance, got badly on my nerves. The young Buddhist priests were the worst of all. There were several thousands of them in the town and none of them seemed to have anything to do except stand on street corners and jeer at Europeans.[9]

We should not have too much sympathy for the policeman Orwell who, as a British representative trapped by the expectations of the subject Burmese, felt himself an "absurd puppet pushed to and fro by the will of those yellow faces behind" him. Nevertheless, his viewpoint turned out to be prescient when the river districts he had policed rose in rebellion under a religious leader three years after he resigned his commission and returned to England. The Saya San rebellion was only the climax of a series of rural rebellions that had taken place since the British conquest. Saya San, a traditional Buddhist healer, roused the countryside of Insein and Tharawaddy in revolt as pretender to the vacant Konbuang throne. The rebellion was commanded by a man who proclaimed himself "Glorious King of the Winged Creatures" and urged his followers into massacres armed with spears, crossbows and swords.[10] Nevertheless, it was a rebellion that took two years and thousands of Indian troops to subdue.

In the first decades of the 20th century Burma had only made halting steps in the direction of modernity. Still ruled as a province of India, it was among the most backward of British possessions. However, it was not guarded against the winds of change from the outside world, especially those of anti-colonial resistance. British rule would bring together explosive ingredients that would catapult Burma to the forefront of anti-colonial struggles, and, within the native educated elite it sought to help rule the country, it would help create the men who could lead this process.

Early nationalism: From Buddhism to the Dobama Asiayone

The earliest expression of nationalist consciousness in British-ruled Burma took the form of associations of elite Bamars aiming to protect their culture, especially Buddhism, which they saw as being under attack by American and British missionaries who were engaged in proselytising, especially among Burma's ethnic minorities. The Young Men's Buddhist Association (YMBA) was founded in 1906 by English-educated barrister U May Oung, who with other moderates set himself the aim of promoting and defending Buddhism and the glories of classical Bamar civilisation. Though inspiration is frequently cited in the British YMCA, this organisation was just as much the outgrowth of the monastic culture of Burma as foreign influence.[11] Like the men who had founded the Indian National Congress in 1885, the members of the YMBA had aims that were mostly non-political, and hoped merely to increase Bamar influence within the colonial administration.

But also like the Congress, the moderate, gentlemanly and pro-colonial stance of the YMBA would be challenged in ways that forced the organisation to reinvent itself in order to express its people's aspirations. It transformed itself into the General Council of Burmese Associations (GCBA) in 1919, the year its members began to lead protests demanding that the British respect the Buddhist temples by removing their shoes and demanding due reverence to holy images.[12] Though the GCBA was displaced in the 1930s, it would be the crucible for many cadres of the later nationalist movement.

Developments under British rule and in the rest of the world were bringing to fruition the conditions that could foster a more militant nationalism that would take its cue from the anti-colonial present rather than Burma's illustrious monarchic past. Central among these was the developing antagonism between the Bamar and Indians who had been brought to Burma by British rule. The colonial capital of Rangoon, though in the centre of the Bamar homeland, was dominated by foreigners among whom the Indians were the most conspicuous at the top as administrators, in the middle as soldiers, and at the bottom as labourers. The British relied on these Indians to run the most important functions in colonial Burma, a responsibility which was increasingly taken amiss and served to radicalise young men of the emerging middle class.

In 1930, on cue with the Saya San rebellion, race riots between Indians and Bamar rocked the capital city. The immediate cause was a labour dispute over jobs being given preferentially to Indians, a source of strife that continued throughout the 1930s. Out of this strife emerged the Dobama Asiayone (We Burmans Association). Dobama quickly grew into the vanguard of militant Bamar nationalism. Its members were largely students at Rangoon University who had sworn loyalty to the cause of the Burmese race and were known as "Thakin" (master). This was a calculated provocation to the British, who were addressed as "thakin" in Burma just as they were addressed as "sahib" in India. Two young Thakins, U Nu and Aung San, led the nationalist cause. In 1936, when they were both expelled from university for printing anti-British tracts, their supporters went on strike and won their reinstatement in addition to the firing of the chauvinist rector.[13]

Thakins led all the major disturbances against British rule during the 1930s, from boycotting the colonial elections to organising unions of Bamar workers. A number of these campaigns came together in the "1300 Revolution," in 1938, named after the year in the Burmese calendar. The Thakins were supremely confident in their ability to lead their people forward to freedom, especially after disturbances in the mid-1930s led the British to give Burma its own administration separate from that of India.

The prominent nationalists of this decade were Bamar almost to a man, and saw their own patriotism as being consonant with that of the whole territory of Burma that the old monarchy had once ruled. Their ideology developed, as with all nationalisms, in the form of a highly eclectic mix of influences from home and abroad. Arguably the most important among these was Bamar racial pride. A Dobama song, a version of which would later become the national anthem of Burma, went:

...Be brave, be brave, like a true Burman,
Burma, Burma for us Burmans.
Act and behave like Masters,
For Burmans are a race of Masters...

For so long as the world will last,
Burma is ours, Burma is ours.
This is our country, this our land,
This our country till the end.[14]

Along with racial pride, the Bamar people were influenced by a bewildering mixture of foreign ideologies. The activists who had joined the GCBA in the 1920s hoping for militant action against British rule had been fascinated with Ireland's Easter Rising in 1916, and many continued to look to Sinn Féin as a successful example of anti-colonial resistance.[15] Others found in the new government of Mustafa Kemal in Turkey an exemplar of the national strength and unity they desired. The racial pride that had been bred into early Bamar nationalism also accorded well with the fascism of Hitler and Mussolini, who seemed to some to show that nationalist revival was best accomplished through strong leadership rather than attention to the welfare of democracy.[16]

Right wing and left wing trends within Thakin thought were not so much in competition as collaboration, as both were part of the mélange of foreign ideologies that Bamar intellectuals reached out to for inspiration for the economic and political revival they felt their country desperately needed. As with all colonial peoples, the Burmese had heard of and taken inspiration from the October Revolution in Russia. Many Thakins as anti-colonial intellectuals in the 1930s looked to the Soviet Union as a model for economic transformation and revival, as they felt its experiences of being a backward country were similar to their own. Texts such as Lenin's *Imperialism* and the Comintern's documents on the Popular Front began to circulate in Burmese through the agency of the Red Dragon Club, which aimed to distribute popular Marxist pamphlets and the works of Thakins aiming to analyse Burma's conditions through a Marxist lens.[17] In 1939 the Indian communist Narendra Dutt brought together Aung San, Ba Hein, Soe Hla Pe, and others to form the first communist cell in Burma.[18]

Other influences were closer to home. Collaboration between Burmese and Indian nationalists led to Aung San and others attending the 1939 Ramgarh meeting of the Congress Party, when Subhas Chandra Bose was elected to its presidency on a militant platform of wartime resistance to British rule.[19] Ba Maw, who was elected to head the colonial ministry in Burma that year, was so impressed by Bose that he named the new party he formed with Thakin collaboration the Freedom Bloc after Bose's Forward Bloc. Indian nationalism in the forms of Gandhism, Bose's militant anti-colonialism, and Nehru's democratic socialism would be key reference points for Burma's leaders throughout the war. Like Bose and other Indian leaders, many of the Thakins were inspired by Japan's rise in the east following its defeat of Russia in 1905, though they were divided on their views of the Japanese occupation of China. The question of attitudes to Japan would obviously be a key area of contention.

Thus the twilight of British colonialism in Burma in the 1930s produced a generation of nationalist cadre who sought to free their country using militant methods. While drawing inspiration and ideology from a wide and contradictory array of sources, the apprenticeships they served in activism and (for some of them) government and the military would prepare them to play leading roles in the coming conflict when Britain was defeated.

A deep breath: Burma on the edge of world war

Pre-war Rangoon was a cauldron of plots, suspicions and covert activities by the British government, Japanese agents and Bamar nationalists that could provide the stuff of a great spy novel. While labour disturbances and nationalist agitation continued apace, Ba Maw's attempts to gain the promise of Burmese autonomy in any possible war followed by a guarantee of independence ran into typical chauvinist obstruction from the British both in Rangoon and London. The leaders of ethnic minorities such as the Karen and Shan felt British rule teetering on the abyss, and a grim future of Bamar domination ahead of them. Meanwhile the Japanese were already preparing the ground for invasion. Keiji Suzuki, a colonel in the Imperial General Headquarters, had come to Burma disguised as a businessman, and arriving in Rangoon made contact with several Thakins hoping to lure them to the side of Japan, promising an independent Burma as part of the "East Asia Co-Prosperity Sphere".[20] Suzuki entered the realm of a Bamar nationalism that was beginning to fracture under the pressure of the coming war. Ba Maw, who considered his attempt to win over the British to independence pretty much failed, had resigned his ministry and travelled to London to seek an audience with Churchill in a last-ditch effort. The Thakin movement was deeply confused about the nature of the coming war. By and large the left wing Thakins were not at first inspired by the aims of either Britain's anti-fascist colonialism or Japan's militarist colonialism. Aung San expressed this later when he wrote, "the war in Europe was plainly a war between two sets of imperialists and could have no appeal of any kind. We therefore firmly resolved to conduct an anti-imperialist, anti-war campaign".[21]

But Britain's difficulty was always Ireland's, or Burma's, opportunity. The invasion of the Soviet Union by Japan's ally Germany did not resolve this question, as it did for communists and many left-leaning nationalists in other countries. Aung San, though he was general secretary of Burma's first communist cell, maintained it would be acceptable to seek aid from the "fascist" Japanese as the war in Asia had a substantially different character from that in Europe.[22] Other Thakins looked to democratic Britain as the lesser evil. Than Tun broke with Aung San while in prison in early 1941 when he drafted a document calling for unconditional support to Britain in the anti-fascist war.[23] Others among the left wing Thakins sought to use Britain's distraction as an opportunity to overthrow colonialism and then fight for independence against Britain and Japan alike.

Aung San had probably resolved by mid-1940 that seeking Japan's aid held the best prospects for his cause. Though in August he escaped arrest by slipping on board a ship bound for China claiming to be seeking the aid of the Chinese communists, when *Kempetei* agents discovered him he was perfectly amenable to going to Japan to discuss his options.[24] In Tokyo he and Suzuki hammered out a plan for achieving Burma's freedom in collaboration with Japanese forces. As the Imperial Army prepared to extend its South East Asia campaign into British territory, Aung San and his followers would foment an anti-British uprising and become recognised by the Japanese as the official government of independent Burma as soon as it gained control of the south eastern districts. This would achieve the Imperial Army's aim of cutting off the "Burma road", which was the main supply route for the Chinese resistance, and would also leave the way open to India.[25]

In March 1941 Aung San covertly arrived back in Rangoon to begin recruiting his Thakin comrades to the force of pro-Japanese rebels he aimed to establish. These are the "Thirty Comrades" of nationalist mythology, who became the core of Burma's independent wartime armed forces.[26] They arrived at Hainan Island in China to begin a gruelling boot camp instructed by Japanese officers. To cement their loyalty to each other and Burma, the Thakins made a blood pact and adopted new names: Aung San became Bo Teza (Commander Fire) along with the honorific title *Bogyoke* (General), Tun Shein became Bo Yan Naing (Commander Vanquisher) and Shu Maung became Bo Ne Win (Commander Sun's Brilliance).[27] The Thirty Comrades then gathered their forces across the Burmese border in Siam and waited for the signal to rise.[28]

The signal came at the beginning of 1942. At the turn of the year Japanese troops swept down the Malayan peninsula on bicycles, first laying siege to and then capturing Britain's naval base at Singapore, a catastrophe for the colonial power in the Pacific theatre of the war. The colonial administration was thrown into panic, deserting Rangoon as the Fifteenth Imperial Army marched into the south east, dragging thousands of British, Indian and minority Burmese along with it overland, to eventually re-establish itself in exile at Shimla in the Indian Himalayas. The stage was set for a long Japanese occupation, which Aung San and his comrades hoped would bring the prospect of Burmese freedom for the first time in 70 years.

Japanese occupation: A sort of independence

Like any other country that suffered occupation by the Imperial Army, the Burmese people have plenty of bad memories of the Second World War. The suppression of the native population including ferocious reprisals against members of minority groups could be recounted at some length. The fate of slave labour forced to construct the Siam-Burma railway to supply the army is particularly well known even among the other horrors of the Japanese war effort in Asia and the Pacific.

Any attempt to describe the Japanese occupation has a difficult line to walk. Burma, like any other country in the East Asia Co-Prosperity Sphere, was regarded by the army as territory to be conquered and secured against its enemies. At the same time the Japanese had been favoured early on by native elements in Burma who saw their presence as a stepping-stone towards independence. Behind the scenes of official Japanese conquest there was an intense struggle going on led by Bamar nationalists Aung San and Ba Maw to make Japanese-sponsored faux independence a reality for their people, one that ended in the nationalists finally breaking with Japan.

In 1942 the Japanese Fifteenth Army, in collaboration with Aung San's Burma Independence Army (BIA), successfully moved through and occupied Burma up to the Arakan frontier in the west and the tribal territories of the north. Establishing the occupation was a bloody job accomplished by both the Japanese and the BIA. In the course of establishing their autonomy the BIA often seemed to be matching the Japanese atrocity for atrocity. Immediately after crossing into Burma, Aung San himself took on the job of executing elders in a Shan village who were suspected of being in league with the British. The Shan and Karen, being the main nationalities besides the Bamar and the ones who had filled the ranks of the British forces in Burma, had the most to lose. Ian Morrison described the BIA's treatment of one Karen Catholic village. First 152 men, women and children were massacred in cold blood. When they reached the compound:

> Father Blasius, the Karen priest in charge, was sick in the clergy-house. The Burmans set fire to the house and burned him and the two men who were looking after him. They then burned down the church... The girls took refuge upstairs. The Burmans shot up through the ceiling... Four Karen lay sisters were killed. The great majority of the girls were cut down inside the mission compound, some on the road outside. The youngest victim was a baby of six months... [They] went in a mass to...the other side of the town. Here they killed another 52 people, all Karens, men, women and children... A few days later 47 Karen men were taken out and bayoneted to death.[29]

The atrocities committed early in the occupation by the Bamar are attributable to the lack of concern that the pre-war nationalists had for other Burmese nationalities, the celebratory mood that prevailed once the British had evacuated, and the profound disorder created by the power vacuum they had left. No organised force had emerged to join the 300 or so nationalist cadres of the BIA as they swept into the country on the heels of the Imperial Army, and it is doubtful that the Japanese would have encouraged or accepted one. Thus it was primarily the criminals, the outcasts and the dissatisfied of all shades that initially signed up. Maung Maung, who was Aung San's aide at the time, contemptuously referred to early BIA soldiers as "a rabble without a minimum of military training".[30]

Indeed, so many young Bamar men signed up to the BIA in the first few weeks of the occupation that its numbers skyrocketed from a few thousand when it crossed the frontier to as many as 200,000.[31] This created a problem both for the nationalist cadre in charge of the BIA, who had none of the resources necessary to command or even at times to keep track of them, and for the Imperial Army, whose commanders with a few exceptions were not given to much trust or indulge an independent native initiative in a country they felt they had conquered.

Some scholars, in awe of Bamar nationalism during the period, have termed the BIA "a political movement in military garb".[32] This is to project matters forward to the time when Aung San had regained control of the forces he had been carried along by after allying with the Japanese and was in the process of turning against them.[33] This took several years in which they were bedevilled by Japanese intransigence and bewildered as to their next steps.

Aung San and the Thirty Comrades had expected, in accordance with Aung San's agreement with Suzuki when they first met in Japan, that Burma would be granted its independence immediately after the British had been driven back from the south east of the country. The commanders of the Imperial Army had different ideas. Akiho Ishii, colonel of the Fifteenth Army and the officer responsible for command of civilian matters in Rangoon, denied any knowledge that Burma was to become independent and insisted, with the agreement of his command, that this would have to wait until after the war.[34] A military administration was quickly established in the south east and, despite Suzuki's promises that the BIA could set up a government when Rangoon was occupied, it was extended to Rangoon.[35]

A part of the Japanese military in Burma, as elsewhere, was deeply influenced by pan-Asian ideas and believed that granting Burma its independence was the only sure way to ensure support of the Burmese for Japan. Suzuki, who has since been regarded by Bamar nationalists as their Lawrence of Arabia figure, was among them. He clashed with Ishii, demanding the formation of a nationalist administration. In January the Tojo government in Japan came down on his side.[36] The independent State of Burma was formally granted its independence in August 1943, with Ba Maw, who had returned from England via Portugal, as the *Adipati*[37] and Aung San as the minister of war in command of the BIA, renamed the Burma National Army (BNA). The institution of Burmese independence was accomplished with some fanfare, flags and other symbols of the old monarchy and a few of the fascist and militarist trappings adopted by other governments in league with the Axis powers. A declaration of independence cited Burma's history of empire, the "long bondage" Burmese had endured under the British, and its "unconquered" national spirit as the precursors to Burma before proclaiming Burma a "fully independent nation and sovereign state...as part of a world order which will ensure justice, peace and prosperity to all peoples".[38]

But this was not to be a real independence, and every significant matter of state remained in the hands of Japan. U Nu, a prominent Thakin before the war who served as foreign minister, complained of Japanese condescension from the ambassador, who micromanaged all his ministry's business and forbade Burma from establishing diplomatic relations with other nations, on down to the lowliest Japanese soldiers. He wrote of his daily business as minister:

> From the day when independence was declared there were numerous telegrams to the Axis powers. But this was all trifling business... However, the wires were so numerous that before long the Foreign Office came to be known as the Telegraph Office. We noted down in a calendar the national days of every country and the birthdays of statesmen and that kind of thing, so as to send off our wires punctually. And we had to acknowledge the receipt of similar messages from other countries.[39]

He was not alone in his resentment of the Japanese, who even their highest collaborators began to think of as occupiers rather than liberators. Aung San certainly felt this way in mid-1943 and was confident enough to voice his feelings to Ba Maw, telling him that "the Japanese are insincere and overbearing", and that the Burmese people were needlessly suffering for what was in the end "only the Japanese version of home rule".[40]

How Aung San felt in 1943 must have been just a faint reflection of how the Burmese people in general were suffering. The elimination of Burma's export markets, including its primary one in India, had led to a drastic decline in paddy cultivation. The efforts of the Burmese government to alleviate this by purchasing excess rice ran into problems of bureaucracy and lack of resources, and by the end of the year it was broadcasting radio programmes that encouraged peasants to look to the nutritional value of grass.[41] Burmese auxiliary troops promised by the state to help maintain security were instead sent to Rangoon to labour under the Imperial Army, where most faced harsh and racist treatment.

From 1942 the Japanese had embarked on the project of building a railway from Bangkok to Rangoon in an attempt to shore up their supply lines to defend Burma and in preparation for an eventual invasion of India. This became known as the "Death Railway" and was among the most notorious of the Japanese crimes against humanity during the war.

Allied prisoners of war (POWs) from Britain, Australia and elsewhere are, of course, the best remembered of these victims. But the majority of its victims were Asian labourers from Malaya and Burma.[42] The death toll of the railway accelerated in tandem with military imperatives, as the American victory at Midway opened the Pacific and threatened the survival of all the Japanese armies in South East Asia.

British POW Jeffrey English described how the massive death toll from Japanese violence and disease came to be treated as a matter of course by the labourers:

> We burnt the bodies in the afternoon... Some men would put on some bamboo shoots or wild sweet potatoes to roast in the embers. If, on trying to recover them, you got the odd toe or wrist by mistake, you just threw it back and went on scrabbling for your potato, probably using a charred rib as a rake. Death had long since lost its dignity.[43]

The conditions for the native labourers in Burma were equivalent if not worse as they were unprotected by even the semblance of concern for the welfare of POWs. The railway upon its completion had consumed as many as 100,000 lives. But we need to draw no special conclusions about the Japanese psyche from the "Death Railway" or any of their other horrific crimes. For the Japanese were trying to catch up with the "civilised" empires of Britain and France, and in the course of this ended up competing with the death tolls they had accumulated over a much longer period of time during the few years of the war. The railway, like the Shoah in Eastern Europe, was the outcome of this process, the realisation of a dream that "projected Japanese dreams of industrial fortitude, economic robustness, and Asian domination".[44]

By the time the railway had been completed, however, the purpose for which it had been built was coming into question. The Imperial Army, with aid from the BNA and Subhas Chandra Bose's Indian National Army, had entered north eastern India only to be ignominiously thrown back at the battle of Imphal. As the US Navy swept across the Pacific towards Japan, Britain prepared to retake Burma. The nationalists who had aided Japan would again have tough choices ahead of them.

Colonialists, communists and nationalists in the anti-fascist war

The post-war mythology of the Burman state likes to cast Aung San and his compatriots as semi-clairvoyant political actors who knew precisely when to side with the British or Japanese, and precisely when to abandon them when this would be to the advantage of Burma's freedom.[45] While we can certainly recognise the pragmatism of Aung San, it strains credulity given what we know of him to deny a certain naivety about the role of the Japanese when the war began. Similarly, while he clearly had thoughts of abandoning his Japanese allies as early as 1943, his actions did not match this until somewhat later.

For the Bamar nationalist leadership and the BNA to switch sides required both Japanese setbacks in the war and the growing resistance movement in Burma itself. Though the British had evacuated Burma completely, as they left their native soldiers faded into western jungles rather than surrender and abandon their arms. This was the case for the soldiers of the Burma Rifles battalion, who returned to their villages with their rifles to await the opportunity to aid in the British reconquest.[46] Other hillmen along with Indian troops followed the British to Manipur, where they would fight the Japanese and their countrymen at Imphal. But though the British loyalists were among the fiercest fighters against the Japanese occupation, another component came from the pre-war nationalist cadre, particularly those identified with communism.

In one respect it was fortunate that there had not been a well-established Communist Party in Burma (CPB) before the war, as it would have been subjected to the same pressures all Moscow-oriented parties came under to conform with the waverings of Soviet foreign policy. The Indian CP next door, for example, risked being completely discredited by standing with the British against the Quit India movement.[47] Whether due to their allegiance to the Soviet perspective or their adroitness in guessing the nature of the coming Japanese occupation, the Thakins of the CPB would play a central role in shifting the entire nationalist movement towards the side of the British.

Thein Pe was the major figure in this regard. Having been an early leftist among the Thakins and a supporter of an anti-fascist alliance between Bamar nationalists and Britain since before the war, he set out from Mandalay on foot as the Japanese advanced and reached Calcutta, offering his services to the Communist Party of India (CPI) and eventually the British government-in-exile of Burma.[48] In India and briefly in China, Thein Pe worked as a left propagandist for the Popular Front, publishing a book on the Japanese conquest of his country[49] and writing long features for *People's War*, the newspaper of the CPI. As Japanese fortunes dimmed, the British would see his use as an asset for their eventual reoccupation of Burma, and his place as a link between Britain and the Burmese communists would become particularly important.

Meanwhile in Burma other leftist Thakins operating as the CPB were laying the ground for rebellion against the Japanese within the BIA. Thakin Soe in 1943 began meeting with some of the lower-ranking BIA officers to instruct them in Marxism and recruit handfuls of guerrillas here and there to communism, relying on his and his party's reputation as a nationalist but anti-Japanese force.[50] His delicate and untiring work under conditions of hostile occupation were soon rewarded; Aung San and others in the BNA finally reached the conclusion that the time had come to sever links with the Japanese. In August 1944, at a clandestine meeting, the leaders of the CPB, the BNA and Ba Maw's People's Revolutionary Party agreed to form the Anti-Fascist Organisation that would rise against the Japanese at the opportune hour.[51] Renamed the Anti-Fascist People's Freedom League (AFPFL), this was the united nationalist coalition that would become the ruling party of independent Burma.

When the Japanese asked for the BNA to assist them in defending the crumbling frontier, it was decided that the time was right.[52] Maung Maung records that Aung San gave a rousing speech in Rangoon on 17 March in which he declared that "the time had come to go out and fight; he himself would lead; danger, hardship and perhaps death lay ahead, but they would all go forward together".[53] But he forgot to mention the name of the enemy.

Post-war Burma: Burmese victory and colonial defeat

To expand too much into the fate of the Burmese after the end of the war would run quickly beyond the scope of this book. Nevertheless, a few brief outlines on the unstable post-war colonial settlement, as a prelude to independence and the simultaneous break-up of the nationalist communist coalition can be written in order to see the effects of the war.

The BIA, after marching from Rangoon under Japanese command, wheeled around and began attacking isolated Japanese units. The Imperial Army, under intense pressure from the British and betrayed by their only local allies, fled from Rangoon, leaving the 26th Indian Division to occupy the city unopposed just as the Imperial Army itself had done three years earlier.[54] When the war ended on 16 August, all effective resistance from this quarter ceased. For the price of one ticket's entry to the war, Burma was twice devastated by occupying armies. Before evacuating, the British set fire to all operating oil refineries near Rangoon, in addition to disabling the city's rail services and scuttling almost all ships in the merchant fleet.[55] In turn, the Japanese before evacuating "destroyed everything from the Irish girls' school on Prome Road to the Yacht Club on Inya Lake", surely a bitter welcome for the returning Raj.[56] The devastated city was soon filled by thousands of squatters from the countryside, which had if anything received much worse treatment from both sides.

The policy of the returning British for Burma and its population was as contradictory as the Japanese policy had been. One section of the military and colonial bureaucracy saw the nationalists as traitors to be punished harshly as part of the process of turning the clock back to the 1930s. It was this sentiment that British general William Smith, the first to meet with Aung San, had expressed when he refused to recognise any authority of the AFPFL and demanded that the soldiers of the BIA be disbanded or placed under British command, a demand which Aung San acceded to in any case.[57] But to Lord Louis Mountbatten, newly created Earl of Burma and overall commander of the British forces' south eastern divisions, it was imperative to show collaboration with native forces in the climate of post-war peace and security. A cautious policy of encouraging Burmese collaboration with economic reconstruction of the country and in exchange having their political voices heard within a Governor's Council (similar to the 1935 set up) to be followed by Home Rule and eventually independence within the Commonwealth was set as British policy in the government White Paper of 1945.[58]

It was certain from the conclusion of hostilities, however, that this set up could not count on any kind of stability. The British were incapable of peacefully returning a twice-occupied country to its rule. Burma's people suffered under lingering wartime economic devastation, which the British exacerbated by declaring all Japanese currency invalid and wiping out millions of people's resources overnight.[59] The promise of new elections and expanded freedom for their country did little to appease the Thakin party led by Aung San, who had tasted independence, however briefly, and were determined to renew the struggle at the earliest opportunity.

The communist/nationalist alliance that formed the core of the AFPFL began to fracture, with Aung San's nationalists increasing in prominence and claiming political leadership of the country. In one respect this was because they could claim, with some credibility, to be more left wing and militant fighters for freedom than the CPB. The Communists, who had led the way in forming a wartime alliance with the British, had drunk deeply from the well of Popular Frontism that erased the differences between rulers and ruled in the anti-fascist war.

Thein Pe had written early on that the natural development of the war internationally would naturally eliminate "the use of violence, bloodshed, and armed uprising in a people's fight for freedom",[60] an opinion that was seconded by Than Tun as late as 1945:

> If we have to arm or rebel it will mean that our second revolution is against the masses of the world and the countries of the allied nations. Even though we say we are fighting for freedom we will in fact become the first army of the Japanese... If such a thing comes to pass the English... will ignore the world and continue to rule us cruelly.[61]

This policy was transmuted to the CPB through their close links to the CPI, especially its general secretary P C Joshi, who, in calling Churchill "more or less progressive" and foreseeing Indian independence coming about peacefully through the agency of British-Soviet collaboration, was primarily responsible for the articulation of what would be called "Browderism" in India and Burma.[62]

The CPB was expelled from the AFPFL under the personal authority of Aung San, who had been its first general secretary and briefly returned to membership at the end of the war.[63] A split in the CPI between Joshi and the hardliners led by B T Ranadive, culminating in Joshi's expulsion for Browderism, would precipitate a similar crisis in its Burmese sister party; Soe, who went to India and met with Ranadive and other CPI hardliners in September 1945, returned convinced of the errors of Browderism and determined to launch an underground struggle.[64] The CPB split into the CPB (Red Flags) led by Soe and the uncharitably named CPB (White Flags) led by Than Tun. The former would lead the uprising several years later leading to a long period of Communist insurgency.

Following the split in the AFPFL, Aung San seemed to go from success to success. A general strike maintained with AFPFL leadership allowed him to first scrap the White Paper by demanding representation for his party that equalled its popular support in the governing council, then staring the British down when he was set to be prosecuted for the execution of Karen villagers, as mentioned above. In January 1947 he sat down in London to sign an agreement with Clement Attlee that guaranteed Burma's independence within a year. He was 32 years old.

Barely six months later, soldiers armed with rifles burst into a meeting of the Executive Council, which Aung San headed as the last head of state prior to independence. They fired indiscriminately, killing the *Bogyoke* and six of his ministers. U Saw, the chief minister of Burma before the Japanese occupation, was implicated in a plot involving some British officers and was quickly arrested, tried, convicted and executed.[65]

At the time of his death Aung San was to all appearances earnestly trying to settle the problem of the national minorities, breaking away from some of the chauvinist legacies of Thakin nationalism and actively soliciting Shan and Karen participation in Burma's independence set up. To them he promised a united federation "with properly regulated provisions as should be made to safeguard the rights of National Minorities" including a constitution that would ensure each ethnic unit autonomy within the union of Burma.[66] Some have concluded on this basis that had the *Bogyoke* not died so young, he might have averted independent Burma's exclusive Bamar domination and bloody record of ethnic strife. It is impossible to say, but it is likely that Burma's chronic economic underdevelopment presented such an intractable problem at independence that it would have stymied even a leader as talented as Aung San.

Conclusion

The wartime history of Burma remains controversial. In particular, the Japanese occupation remains a source of bitter contestation. Did the Japanese defeat of the British provide a major impulse towards freedom by undermining the idea of British "invincibility"?[67] Was the occupation and the limited independence it offered a training ground that talented Burmese nationalists proved capable of passing through, with some adversity, on their way to independence?

These questions are perhaps a crude way of forcing the issue, which is that the Japanese or Axis presence in Burma seems to have a better reputation than all of the other occupations that took place under the Axis powers. Caveats about acknowledged war crimes aside, this does seem to hold up, but only because the Bamar nationalists who sided with the Japanese were by and large the same people who later led Burma to freedom against the British, and like other histories, this one, too, has been written by the victors. The occupation did, briefly, provide an interlude during which a Burmese leadership and national institutions could begin to be formed. But its role was largely one of a catalyst for forces that had been at work since before the war.

Aung San towers over these events to the point that it is hard sometimes to separate the story of the country's wartime fortunes from his personal saga.[68] Aung San became, during the course of the war, the undisputed leader of Burma's independence. Nearly seven decades after his death his legacy remains deeply contested. To the British he was alternatively a traitor and a nationalist hero. Since Burma's independence he has been in turn an icon of the bizarre Ne Win dictatorship beginning in the 1960s, and a symbol of the pro-democracy movement led by his daughter, Aung San Suu Kyi, from the 1980s. All of official Burma reveres him, and wonders what things might have been like had he lived a bit longer.

It is not necessary to attribute to Aung San any quasi-supernatural prescience or military ability enabling him to lead Burma to freedom, as some official accounts have it. His career is best understood as that of a pragmatic nationalist whose highest goal was Burma's freedom, and who found himself in a succession of fortunate circumstances in which he was able to prosecute that goal from different angles throughout the war. But even in this more realistic role, his leadership still depended on the social forces that British colonialism had unleashed. It was the hunger of the peasant, the resentment of the monk and the humiliation of the Bamar student that made Aung San who he was, much as any other great leader. He was able to understand these forces to a limited extent and drive them to the necessary, but unfinished, conclusion of independence.

As Peter Ward Fay writes of Bose and the Indian National Army (who collaborated with Aung San during the period he was an ally of the Japanese), their story is less frequently told than that of Gandhi because it demonstrates the possibility of a more radical, militant path to Indian freedom than the one that ended up being taken.[69] Similarly, the independence of India's next-door neighbour, which had once been ruled as part of India by the same colonial power, shows a militarised struggle for freedom which took place in the pressure cooker of the Second World War. Because of it Burma's road to freedom was shorter, though more violent, than India's.

The wartime history of Burma deserves to be fully integrated into the history of the Second World War precisely because it shows the fundamental ambivalence which the nationalists, contradictory yet genuine fighters for Burma's freedom, saw in both the democratic British and militarist Japanese. It shows, too, that patriots in this instance had, in order to be true to their country, to fight "on all fronts", sometimes with the British, sometimes with the Japanese, sometimes against both. That is the kind of complicated history this book exposes.

NOTES

1 For an enchanting fictional account of the end of the Burmese kingdom and Indo-Burmese relations in the years leading up to independence, see Amitav Ghosh's *The Glass Palace* (New York, Random House, 2002).

2 The dominant ethnicity of Burma, often incorrectly called "Burmese" or "Burman", are here referred to as the "Bamar". "Burmese" signifies all the country's inhabitants. The Burmese language is the language of the Bamar, and each ethnic group has its own language, typically written in the Burmese script.

3 A comprehensible but not overly simplified account of these divisions is found in chapter two of S Tucker, *Burma: The Curse of Independence* (London, Pluto, 2001).

4 This is not to give in to the post-independence revisionism of some Burmese historians who assert that Burma has always had a national identity that was simply awakened in the early 20th century—M Charney, *A Modern History of Burma* (Cambridge, University of Cambridge, 2009), p32.

5 M Smith, *Burma: Insurgency and the Politics of Ethnicity* (London, Zed Books, 1991), pp41-44.

6 I Brown, *A Colonial Economy in Crisis: Burma's Rice Cultivators and the World Depression of the 1930s* (London, Routledge, 2005).

7 Tucker, 2001, pp17-19.

8 A Walker, "Seditious State-Making in the Mekong Borderlands: The Shan Rebellion of 1902-1904", *Sojourn: Journal of Social Issues in Southeast Asia* 29: 3, (November 2014), pp554-590.

9 G Orwell, "Shooting an Elephant", available online at orwell.ru (accessed 29 December 2014).

10 Maung Maung, *Burma and Ne Win* (Rangoon, Religious Affairs Department Press, 1969), p18.

11 R Taylor, "Burma in the Anti-Fascist War", in McCoy, ed, *Southeast Asia under Japanese Occupation* (New Haven, Yale University, 1980).

12 F Donnison, *Burma* (London, Ernest Benn, 1970), p105.

13 Smith, 1991, pp54-55.

14 Khin Yi, *The Dobama Movement in Burma, 1930-1938* (Ithaca, Cornell University, 1988), p8.

15 Thant Myint-U, *The River of Lost Footsteps: A Personal History of Burma* (New York, Farrar, Straus and Thiroux, 2008), p203.

16 Tucker, 2001, p76.

17 B Linter, *The Rise and Fall of the Communist Party of Burma* (Ithaca, Cornell University, 1990), p5.

18 R Taylor, 'The Burmese Communist Movement and Its Indian Connection: Formation and Factionalism', in *Journal of Southeast Asian Studies* 14:1 (March 1983), p97.

19 J Bečka, "Subhas Chandra Bose and the Burmese Freedom Movement", in Bose, Sisir K, *Netaji and India's Freedom: Proceedings of the International Netaji Seminar* (Calcutta, Netaji Research Bureau, 1975), p65.

20 R Taylor, 'Introduction: Marxism and Wartime Resistance in Burma,' in Taylor ed and trans, *Marxism and Resistance in Burma 1942-45: Thein Pe Myint's 'Wartime Traveler'* (Athens, Ohio, University of Ohio, 1984), p9.

21 Aung San, *Burma's Challenge* (South Okkalapa, Tathetta Sapai, 1974), p17.

22 Taylor, 1984, p9.

23 B Linter, 1990, p8.

24 Smith, 1991, pp58-59.

25 Maung Maung, *Burmese Nationalist Movements, 1940-1948* (Honolulu, University of Hawaii, 1991), p27.

26 Maung Maung, *Aung San of Burma* (The Hague, Martinus Nijhoff, 1962), pp31-53.

27 H Tinker, *The Union of Burma: A Study of the First Years of Independence* (Oxford, University of Oxford, 1959), p8.

28 J Bečka, *The National Liberation Movement in Burma during the Japanese Occupation Period* (Prague, Oriental Institute, 1983), p76.

29 I Morrison, *Grandfather Longlegs: The Life and Gallant Death of Major H P Seagrim, GC, DSO, MBE* (London, Faber & Faber, 1947), pp186-187.

30 Maung Maung, *A Trial in Burma: The Assassination of Aung San* (The Hague, Martinus Nijhoff, 1962), p59.

31 J Lebra, *Japanese-Trained Armies in Southeast Asia* (Ithaca, Cornell University, 2010), p65.

32 D Guyot, "The Burma Independence Army: A Political Movement in Military Garb", in Silverstein, ed, *Southeast Asia in World War II* (New Haven, Yale University, 1967), pp51-57.

33 Taylor, 1980.

34 W Yoon, 'Military Expediency: A Determining Factor in the Japanese Policy regarding Burmese Independence', in *Journal of Southeast Asian Studies 9:2* (1978), pp248-267.

35 Maung Maung, 1991, p59.

36 Yoon, 1978, p263.

37 Something like a Burmese or Pali equivalent of "Führer" or "Duce".

38 Ba Maw, *Breakthrough in Burma* (New Haven, Yale University, 1968), pp327-328.

39 U Nu, *Burma under the Japanese: Pictures and Portraits* (Oxford, Oxford University, 2012), p85.

40 Ba Maw, 1968, p335.

41 M Charney, *History of Modern Burma* (Cambridge, University of Cambridge, 2009), p56.

42 "It is generally acknowledged that approximately 60,000-64,000 POWs and over 200,000 Asian labourers were used during the construction of the railway. It is estimated that approximately 12,626 POWs and perhaps between 15,000 and 90,000 labourers died"—K Tamayama, *Railwaymen in the War: Tales by Japanese Railway Soldiers in Burma and Thailand, 1941-1947* (Basingstoke, Palgrave Macmillan, 2005), p8. See also generally G McCormack and H Nelson, *The Burma-Thailand Railway: Memory and History* (London, Allen & Unwin, 1993).

43 J English, *One for Every Sleeper: The Japanese Death Railway through Thailand* (London, Robert Hale, 1989).

44 W Huang, "The Death Railway: Semblances of Modernity", in *Discoveries 6* (2005), p10.

45 See Maung Maung, 1969, for a particularly egregious example. The respected historian was here forced to paint Ne Win as the loyal protégé of Aung San when his role in Burma's freedom struggle itself was relatively minor. (This is not unlike subsequent upgrading of the role of Stalin in the Russian Revolution years after the fact.)

46 Tucker, 2001, p47.

47 For a recent account that emphasises the Indian Communist perspective, see D Gupta, *Communism and Nationalism in Colonial India, 1939-1945* (New Delhi, SAGE Publications, 2008).

48 Smith 1991, p61, also Maung Maung, 1991, p93.

49 Thein Pe, *What Happened in Burma* (Allahabad, Kitabasthan, 1943).

50 Maung Maung, 1991, pp119-121. Though communist initiative in the anti-Japanese war cannot be denied, the later claim that the CPB cost the Japanese 60 percent of total casualties (Linter, 1990, pp8-9) is probably highly exaggerated in the light of the CPB Red Flags faction's need to present itself as the most consistent nationalists in its long insurgency against the heirs of Aung San.

51 Tucker, 2001, p51.

52 Tucker declares that "the nationalists always had the option of siding against the Japanese" and criticises Aung San for opportunism in defecting so late in the day. In his haste to blame the nationalists he ignores the fact that the British command, through communications from Thein Pe to the AFPFL, had repeatedly requested them to delay the rising, probably hoping to position themselves better in post-occupation Burma—Taylor, 1984.

53 Maung Maung, *To a Soldier's Son* (Rangoon, Sarpai Beikman Press, 1974), p57.

54 Thant Myint-U, 2008, p240.

55 Charney, 2009, p58.

56 Thant Myint-U, 2008, p242.

57 Viscount William Slim, *Defeat into Victory* (London, Cassell, 1956), pp516-519.

58 "Burma: Statement of Policy by His Majesty's Government", May 1945. Archived at filestore. nationalarchives.gov.uk/pdfs/small/cab-66-65-wp-45-290-40.pdf.

59 Charney, 2009, p59.

60 Taylor, 1984, pp23-25.

61 Ibid, pp62-63.

62 P C Joshi, *The Communist Party of India: Its Policy in the War of Liberation* (Bombay, People's Publishing House, 1941), p33. "Browderism" refers to Earl Browder, the wartime secretary of the American communist party, who, accepting American and Soviet propaganda, believed that their alliance would continue after the war and hence proposed that wartime class collaboration would continue, dissolving the CP into the Democratic Party briefly after the end of the war. While Browder was the one in the international communist movement to be officially identified with this policy, for which he was criticized by French CP leader Jacques Duclos and eventually expelled from his own party, the existence of parallel trends in European and South Asian communism suggests that this was not an isolated deviation, but a general idea flowing from some communists' understanding of the Popular Front policy.

63 Smith, 1991, pp68-69.

64 Taylor, 1983, p107.

65 Controversy surrounds Aung San's death to this day. Thant Myint-U, 2008, accepts the official narrative and states that if British officers were involved, they were certainly acting under their own initiative. Tucker, 2001, pp155-158, concludes that the case against U Saw is highly implausible and casts Ne Win, who was passed over for promotion by Aung San several times, as the most likely culprit. This long after the event and with the mist of so much official and unofficial history attached to Aung San's legacy, we are unlikely to get definitive proof either way.

66 J Silverstein, ed, *The Political Legacy of Aung San* (Ithaca, Cornell University, 1993), pp148, 153.

67 Guyot, 1967. Taylor, 1980, deals well with this and some other legends of the nationalist period that have led some historians to be soft on the Japanese.

68 The best biography of many is probably A Naw, *Aung San and the Struggle for Burma's Freedom* (Seattle, University of Washington, 2001). The judgment of official Burma may be found in Maung Maung, 1962. Most of his important speeches, letters and public statements in English are found in Silverstein, 1993.

69 P Fay, *The Forgotten Army: India's Armed Struggle for Independence, 1942-1945* (Ann Arbor, University of Michigan, 1995).

9

China: Revolution and war

Donny Gluckstein

China's Second World War lasted from 1937 to 1945 in the form of the Sino-Japanese conflict. Millions perished on the battlefield and on the home front, many succumbing to war-related famine and disease. The themes developed in this book regarding the character of the global conflict applied with full force to China. But here, unlike in other countries, they were superimposed upon a pre-existing social revolution.

From the 1839 Opium War onwards this economically backward territory suffered encroachment by states enjoying the military advantages conferred by industrialisation. In the 19th century its vast size and location at the intersection of many different spheres of influence meant no single foreign power could claim sovereignty and so formal colonisation was limited. However, China was subject to "unequal treaties" with Britain, France, Germany, Japan, Portugal, Russia and the USA granting rights to exploit China's people and resources. Thus the country became a field for inter-imperialist rivalry.

The Chinese government's authority was undermined, although the piecemeal character of the damage meant it did not collapse immediately. Nonetheless, long-established internal social structures were disrupted and new forces unleashed. In 1911 what little remained of Chinese imperial authority was overthrown. But the movement that toppled the last dynasty was too weak to break free of imperialism or even to hold the country together. Regional warlords quickly filled the institutional vacuum. Thereafter China was also a field for internal rivalry between those seeking to claim authority within the country.

There was only one way to overcome these twin problems. For the revolution to succeed and for China to regain independence, to defeat warlordism and to progress, the masses had to throw their weight behind the process. The Kuomintang Party (KMT) founded by Sun Yat-sen claimed it could achieve this objective. But rallying the population was by no means straightforward. Sun Yat-sen's brief presidency ended when he was driven out of power, despite the KMT's success in elections. The KMT then retreated to the south where it was tolerated by local warlords.

The peasantry made up the vast majority of the Chinese population. As one writer puts it, most "never moved outside their immediate home patch, and there was no education or media to spread the idea of national government." Any party purporting to represent the entire population confronted a fundamental social and economic reality—the landlord class owned three quarters of the land and took at least half of peasant income as rent, leaving two thirds of the population living below subsistence level.[1]

The KMT was dominated by privileged groups and, as Isaacs points out, "the gulf which separated them from the great mass of the people was far wider and less bridgeable than the antagonism between them and the foreigners. From the foreigners they could and would try to exact concessions, to demand and secure a larger share of the spoils. But they could not hope to satisfy the masses of the people without undermining themselves... This fundamental and inescapable fact predetermined the limits to which the propertied classes of China would go".[2]

These contradictions would later cripple the KMT's resistance to Japan during the Second World War, but they were evident much earlier. The KMT initially turned to Soviet Russia, then a symbol of anti-imperialism, as a counterweight to the colonialists.[3] It followed logically that the KMT and the newly formed Chinese Communist Party (CCP) should cooperate locally.

Sun Yat-sen died in 1925 and was replaced by the KMT's military leader, Generalissimo Chiang Kai-shek. Bolstered by Russian advisers and assistance, he announced a Northern Expedition to "overthrow all warlords and wipe out reactionary power...and complete the National Revolution".[4] This would be the largest military campaign to occur between the two world wars. In 1927, as the Nationalist Army approached Shanghai, a city largely controlled by foreign "Concessions" and home to half of China's industrial workforce,[5] massive strikes erupted around the slogans "Support the Northern Expeditionary Army" and "Hail Chiang Kai-shek".[6]

The authorities responded by beheading strike leaders and parading their heads on bamboo poles. The stoppages then escalated to embrace over half a million people. When, after some deliberate delay, Chiang's army arrived he did not thank his supporters. Instead:

> machine gunners...opened fire without warning. Lead spouted into the
> thick crowd from both sides of the street. Men, women, and children

dropped screaming into the mud. The crowd broke into a mad flight. The soldiers kept firing into the backs of the fleeing demonstrators.[7]

The KMT had made its choice. Overcoming warlords and imperialists was secondary to exploiting and controlling the masses. With very little to offer the population, Chiang's government became elitist and dictatorial. Between January and August 1928 at least 28,000 people were executed.[8] During the Second World War Chiang claimed to support Sun Yat-sen's three principles: national independence, democracy and rising living standards for the masses. But the last two had to wait: "When victory comes at the end of this war, we shall have fully achieved national independence, but will yet have far to go to attain our other two objectives." In the meantime the population must "restrict consumption and intensify production".[9]

The chief obstacle to the native ruling class and its dictatorial ambitions was the organised working class and its most important political party—the CCP. Chiang launched successive "extermination drives" against it. Driven from the cities, the CCP established rural "red bases", but he smashed these too. In 1934-1935 the CCP was compelled to undertake the perilous 7,000-mile "Long March" to Yenan in the remote north west. Despite this retreat, the KMT focus on the CCP did not diminish when Japan began its conquest of China.

Japan established an important foothold in Manchuria (a region north east of the Great Wall) in 1931 and launched a major expansion southwards after 1937. Chiang did not collaborate, unlike Wang Jingwei, his rival for KMT leadership and founder of a puppet state in 1940. But he was thoroughly equivocal about inspiring resistance either by speech or action, declaring: "Japan is not qualified to be our enemy; our present enemy is the red bandits" who represented a "disease of the vital organs".[10] Chiang had a clear order of priority: "first internal pacification, then external resistance".[11] So rather than fight the 1931 incursion into Manchuria, Chiang appealed to the League of Nations, which was impotent.

Such passivity was rejected by the volunteer armies that sprang up to resist but the KMT refused them all assistance.[12] When a local KMT commander fought Japan's attack on Shanghai in 1932, Chiang put on a belated show of opposition but quickly sought a truce. Demands for resistance from a "National Salvation Movement" were ignored[13] and by 1935 Chiang was offering a "fundamental readjustment" of Sino-Japanese relations through direct talks with Tokyo.[14] During the "Xi'an Incident" in December 1936 he was kidnapped by the former warlord of Manchuria.

Chiang was only released after agreeing to a second united front with the Communists to resist Japan.

Chiang's commitment to this should have been reinforced when fighting at the Marco Polo Bridge near Beijing in July 1937 unleashed a full-scale Japanese offensive. But Chiang soon reverted to type, adopting a policy of "trading space for time".[15] While claiming all the while to be fighting for the nation his forces would consistently "fall back into the interior". As a consequence the Nationalist capital was moved successively further south west—from Nanjing to Wuhan and finally Chongqing.[16]

Any lingering doubts about the KMT's attitude to joint action were dispelled in 1941. According to the terms of the united front, the Red Army was integrated into Nationalist forces under the titles of Eighth Route Army and New Fourth Army. In January of that year the latter, comprising some 9,000 troops, was attacked by 80,000 of Chiang's soldiers.

While suppressing the CCP Chiang planned to avoid any single imperialist power dominating China by exploiting their rivalries. In the early 1920s Russia was the favoured partner, until domestic working class discontent made that alliance inconvenient. After Hitler's accession to power in 1933 Germany became "the KMT's major supplier of military hardware and expertise".[17] When Hitler adopted Japan as his key Asian ally Chiang turned once again to Russia. Diplomatic relations, broken off in 1927, were now restored. Ironically, this led to Russian munitions being used against CCP positions.[18]

New avenues for Chiang to enlist foreign support appeared after Japan struck Pearl Harbor in December 1941. The US had merrily armed both China and Japan in the 1930s.[19] But now, like the Russians, President Roosevelt hoped to use China to absorb Japanese aggression, leaving the US free to concentrate on Europe.[20] Chiang happily received supplies and indeed regularly complained that these were insufficient. But observers eventually realised that his "principal aim was to acquire [US] military equipment and weapons for a post-war conflict with the Chinese Communists".[21]

This suspicion was confirmed by Chiang's day-to-day policies. Whenever Stilwell, the US general assigned to the Nationalists, urged the army towards vigorous action against the Japanese he was blocked. A frustrated President Roosevelt wrote to Chiang: "I have urged time and again in recent months that you take drastic action to resist the disaster which has been moving closer to China and to you." He demanded "immediate action" including granting Stilwell "unrestricted command of all your forces".[22] But Chiang was immovable and on his insistence Stilwell was recalled.[23]

In late 1944, when the Japanese were making major advances during Operation Ichigo, Stilwell's replacement told Chiang: "It is considered essential that all available Chinese troops be organised immediately".[24] This would have meant utilising Chinese Communist troops alongside Nationalist ones; the idea was rejected outright. Washington even considered assassinating Chiang more than once but held back as there was no obvious replacement.

Since the army's role was to suppress the Chinese population rather than combat foreign aggressors, it had to be run on strictly authoritarian lines as an obedient tool of the authorities. Officers embezzled soldiers' pay and, as Chiang admitted, indulged in gambling, smuggling and opium trading. Disease, starvation and desertion destroyed entire units and when someone died:

> his death is not reported, he continues to be a source of income, increased by the fact that he has ceased to consume. His rice and his pay become a long lasting token of memory in the pocket of his commanding officer.[25]

While the rich avoided the draft, conscripted soldiers were tied together and force-marched hundreds of miles, many dying in the process. As one US commander wrote, military service "comes to the Chinese peasant like famine and flood, only more regularly".[26]

Even if the will to resist Japan had been strong, not without reason did Chiang conclude that although 3 million Nationalist troops confronted 680,000 Japanese "if we merely compare the military strength of China and Japan, we are certainly inferior".[27] This judgement conveniently provided an alibi for inaction and a pretext for demanding Allied aid against the Axis. The only alternative would have been to turn to the masses, as US journalist Edgar Snow observed at the time:

> It was clear that the Chinese command could not hope to outmatch Japan in any supreme struggle of arms for vital points and lines. Somewhere it had to find a strategic asset to reinforce the main effort of the regular troops. This asset could only lie...among the millions of people...[28]

But after repressing its own people the Nationalist Army could not engender enthusiasm. To ordinary citizens it appeared as a parasitic body feeding off them. This was literally the case. A US journalist described attending sumptuous banquets provided by Nationalist generals:

> while peasants were scraping the fields...for tops and wild grass to stuff into their griping stomachs. But I was more than ashamed—I was overcome with

a feeling of loathing when I learned that these same generals and the KMT officials were buying up land from starving farmers for arrears in taxes...[29]

Summing up the situation in Nationalist China during 1943, Fenby writes: "Corruption and speculation soared... Across the Nationalist areas, a quarter of the inhabitants were estimated to be refugees or homeless. Drought hit the South, killing more than a million people; yet troops sold food to the Japanese as starving people perished around them".[30]

In places like France, Italy and Greece Allied governments harnessed mass resistance movements during the Second World War, even if their motivation was cynical self-interest. Although the former were fighting for imperialist hegemony and the latter for freedom and democracy, each side shared a common enemy in the Axis. It was only at the end of the war that these partnerships of convenience finally fell apart. The KMT did not get that far.

The Nationalist leadership may have been unwilling to mobilise wartime resistance and by 1944 tens of millions were subject to Japan's rule. Its most notorious atrocity was the "rape of Nanjing" in 1937 during which 200,000 men were killed and some 20,000 women were raped.[31] Rape was a policy systematically used by the invader.[32] In Communist-controlled areas Japanese general Okamura Yasuki introduced a policy called the "three alls"—"kill all, burn all, loot all".[33] Tokyo also promoted large-scale colonial settlement policies and enforced labour conscription.[34] By 1945 tens of millions of Chinese soldiers and civilians were dead compared to 400,000 Japanese troops.

This was the context in which the CCP was able to rise from near annihilation to undisputed ruler of all mainland China in 1949 by espousing the people's war. Mao Tse-tung, the CCP leader, explained:

> two lines have co-existed in China for a long time: the Kuomintang government's line of oppressing the Chinese people and carrying on a passive resistance, and the Chinese people's line of becoming awakened and united to wage a people's war.[35]

The Chinese Communists

The CCP's path to that war was convoluted and shaped by its relationship with Russia and its social position within Chinese society.

In the mid-1920s the needs of Russia's rising state capitalist ruling class were displacing the internationalism of the 1917 Bolshevik Revolution. Having suffered defeat by Japan in 1904, Moscow's priority was that

Japanese forces be drawn away southwards.[36] This meant strengthening links with Nationalist China. The CCP and its working class supporters were ordered to submerge themselves into the KMT. This contributed directly to the massacre of workers by Chiang's forces in Shanghai in April 1927. Afterwards Comintern policy was reversed and the CCP was encouraged to achieve "the immediate establishment of soviets of workers, peasants and soldiers".[37]

So in September Mao led the "Autumn Harvest" uprising in Hunan province, in south-central China. Its failure saw CCP membership there plummet from 20,000 to 5,000.[38] A few months later he wrote how in many areas the CCP "is entirely a peasant party".[39] Together the rightward policy of liquidating the CCP into the KMT and its ultra-left opposite seriously damaged the link between the CCP and the Chinese working class. In 1926 two thirds of Communists had been workers. By September 1930 the figure was 1.6 percent.[40]

Having lost their urban base and faced with Chiang's extermination campaigns, the Communists channelled their efforts into a rural civil war. The intention was that the Red Army would create "red bases" free from Nationalist control and these would be sustained by a local peasantry grateful for the land reforms delivered. But the KMT could draw on much larger resources and outnumbered the Red Army by ten to one.[41] After the successive Nationalist offensives the CCP's bases had been reduced to just 2.5 percent of the Chinese population.[42] Survival, for the time being at least, depended on the desperate retreat to Yenan, an area described by the Communist military commander Chu Teh as "the most backward economically in the whole country".[43] It was precisely its remoteness from centres of economic life (and opportunities for exploitation) that meant the Nationalists lacked a local presence and so were too weak to deliver the death blow.

It is important to note that, notwithstanding professions of loyalty to Russia, the CCP did not always slavishly follow Soviet demands. This became apparent in the mid-1930s when the Comintern abandoned its ultra-left position and adopted the "popular front" tactic, which meant renewed collaboration with the KMT. If the CCP had uncritically accepted that it would have meant subordination to Chiang (and his passivity towards Tokyo) at a time when the CCP's very survival depended on fighting him.

Therefore Mao's version of the united front was made dependent on signs of real national resistance coming from the KMT. A frustrated Comintern official assigned to the CCP wrote:

In 1935 the CCP was pursuing two independent and contradictory lines. One of them, favouring continued civil war, was directed by Mao Tse-tung and approved by the Central Committee and Politburo members in the Red Army. The other...strove for a national united front against Japan...[44]

Such relative independence from imperialism (in this case Russian) was an important factor in making the Chinese people's war possible.

The CCP's removal from the cities and direct physical confrontation with the state changed it from being a conventional political organisation. While retaining the ideological features of a party, it acquired the characteristics of a military formation. This inevitably affected the people's war. This term says little about internal dynamics. "People" are a heterogeneous group, yet warfare, even of the populist kind, requires a level of definite, organised leadership. Whether decisions are shaped and controlled from below or determined by those acting "on behalf of" the people is an important consideration. In the case of China, it was very much the latter. There were social and organisational reasons for this.

Workers have the greatest potential for collaborative, democratic, action because production brings them together in comparatively large units. Individual family production is the norm for peasants. Agriculture is geographically dispersed, reinforcing obstacles to sustained collective control and representative decision-making. Mao hinted at this in 1928 when he complained that: "Once the land has been divided up, they have all gone to till it".[45] Although often called a peasant revolutionary, Mao was therefore dismissive of the ability of the peasantry to run affairs, stating that: "given the various kinds of deep-rooted feudal relationships in the countryside...this will definitely require that the Communist Party and the Soviet Government" play the leading role.[46]

With working class presence now minimal and peasants the main source of recruitment, it is clear the rank and file could hardly control the people's war, despite providing the vast bulk of the foot soldiers and it being in their interests.

What of the CCP leadership? Unaccountable to either the working class or the peasants, it consisted of professional revolutionaries and soldiers whom both Johnson and Selden, historians with very different views, call an "elite group".[47] In practice many were drawn from the Chinese intelligentsia and Mao himself used the term "déclassé" to describe them.[48] The character of this section has been described as follows: "as the only non-specialised section of society, the intelligentsia is the obvious source of a 'professional revolutionary elite' which appears to represent the interests of the 'nation' as against conflicting sectional and class interests".[49]

If the social composition of the CCP circumscribed its internal regime, the CCP's Stalinism also left little room for rival organisations. Potential alternatives such as the various Sacrifice Leagues and Anti-Japanese Associations emerged in the 1930s but were caught between the repression of Chiang's regime and intolerance of the Communists. They were either crushed by the former or absorbed by the latter.[50] As a consequence the history of people's war in China came to be dominated by the CCP.

From civil war to people's war

In an influential book Chalmers Johnson points out that the CCP made little headway in the early 1930s because policies like eliminating the landlords and total land redistribution "failed to obtain mass support". But after the Marco Polo Bridge incident:

> war presented the peasantry with a challenge to its security of such immediacy that the peasants could not ignore it. Pre-war pressures on the peasantry—such as economic exploitation, Communist ideology, warlord wars, and natural calamities—had never been sufficiently widespread or sufficiently intense to give rise to a peasant-based mass movement. But after July 7, 1937, the peasants spontaneously created resistance organisations in many areas of China; and they felt a heightened sensitivity to proposals for defensive organisation throughout the entire occupied area. People's war had "a new kind of political appeal—namely, the defence of the fatherland".[51]

Selden, who is more sympathetic to Maoism, argues that while Johnson:

> focuses correctly on relationship between the Communists and peasants as the critical factor in people's war, in attempting to define that bond exclusively in terms of nationalism, however, it ignores central features of the wartime resistance movement... [Patriotic] appeals were effective in securing active peasant support only when linked to a program focused on rural problems... In the resistance war a peasant revolution was transformed into a national revolution, and a people's war was directed simultaneously against Japanese imperialism and the root problems of rural society.[52]

The blend of social radicalism and resistance to imperialism that would make a people's war was summed up by the banner that greeted Edgar Snow on his arrival in Communist territory during 1936:

Down with the landlords who eat our flesh!
Down with the militarists who drink our blood!
Down with the traitors who sell China to Japan!
Welcome to the United Front with all anti-Japanese armies!
Long live the Chinese Revolution!
Long live the Chinese Red Army![53]

The balance between the two factors was not constant, however. For example the CCP modified its initial policy of total land redistribution during the 1930s. There were several reasons for this. One was pressure from the Comintern for compromise with the KMT. Another was that for the slogan of a united front to be credible confiscation of the land of rich or middling peasants was difficult to sustain. Therefore, by the Second World War Mao had altered policy overall:

We see to it that, on the one hand, rent and interest are reduced so that the peasants may have food to eat, and on the other hand, rent and interest at the reduced rate is paid to the landlords...we on the one hand help the workers so that they may get employment and food, and on the other pursue a policy of developing industries so that the capitalists may reap some profit. In all this our aim is to unite the people throughout the country...[54]

A reduction of land rents by 25 percent was a retreat from land redistribution but was still very different from the situation in Nationalist areas. The same was true of taxation. In one Communist district the share of income taken during 1943 was as follows: poor peasants 0.3 percent; middle 26.4 percent, rich 42.2 percent, landlords 222.3 percent.[55] In another, peasants found to have repaid in interest more than twice their original loan had the debt cancelled and land given away as security returned.[56]

Surveys of CCP members showed how attractive such policies were. In one typical sample, of 16 CCP members questioned: "Most of them stated that they joined the party in order to oppose the old rulers of the village. Three or four said that they joined in the hope that the party would help reduce their tax burden... One said that the War of Resistance against Japan motivated him to join".[57] Other progressive Communist policies in the base areas included a ban on arranged marriages, and the buying or selling of women. Marriage and divorce were by consent and free.[58]

For many a CCP-led people's war behind enemy lines meant practical liberation from the occupier. By 1945:

In every one of the provinces occupied by the Japanese, which covered an area three times the size of France, partisans had set up village and country councils... These behind-the-lines regimes performed nearly all the functions of normal administration. They had their own postal system and radio communications. They published their own newspapers, magazines and books. They maintained an extensive system of schools and enforced a reformed legal code recognising sex equality and adult suffrage. They regulated rents, collected taxes, controlled trade and issued currency, operated industries, maintained experimental farms [and] a grain-rationing system.[59]

If such radical social content explains civilian support for the people's war, it also shows why the Red Army survived "against vastly superior military combinations [despite] lacking any industrial base, big cannon, gas, airplanes, money, and the modern techniques".[60] In the late 1930s Snow interviewed a soldier who explained:

Here we are all equals; in the White Army the soldier masses are oppressed. Here we fight for ourselves and the masses. The White [Nationalist] Army fights for the gentry and the landlords. Officers and men live the same in the Red Army. In the White Army the soldiers are treated like slaves.[61]

Snow himself observed that: "From the highest commander down to the rank and file these men ate and dressed alike...there was even an equal sharing of the delicacies available..."[62] This lack of hierarchy translated into battle conditions with officers fighting alongside their men and suffering their fate.[63]

He found that "the Reds had no highly paid and squeezing officials and generals, who in other Chinese armies absorbed most of the military funds".[64] It was frequently the case that neither Red commanders nor ordinary soldiers received conventional salaries. Instead they and their families were given land to farm.[65] This reflected the poverty of the Red bases but had the political advantage of reducing demands on the local population.[66] To the extent that the Red Army did make local demands, the better-off were expected to contribute the greater amount in taxation.[67]

Compare that to the KMT army which drew on assistance from imperialist supporters. Russia, for example, sent US$250 million in 1928,[68] a figure much greater than the paltry US$15,000 per month spent on its Comintern operations across the Orient.[69] The USA subsidised Chiang from 1933.[70] Even before Pearl Harbor it provided the "Flying Tigers" air squadron plus many millions of dollars in additional military aid.[71] Consequently KMT officers lived in luxury though their troops earned very little at a time when inflation stood at 243 percent.[72] Yet, notwithstanding the generosity of its foreign backers, Chiang's army still took 60 percent of the Nationalist budget.

Mao claimed that "there are two totally different states in the territory of China. One is the so-called Republic of China, which is a tool of imperialism... The other is the Chinese Soviet republic, the state of the broad masses of exploited and oppressed workers, peasants, soldiers and toilers".[73]

It would be a mistake to idealise the role of the CCP, however. The Communists were ideologically tied to Stalinism (if strategically wary of Russian foreign policy demands) and were ready to accept aid from imperialism if it was on offer. In late 1944 and early 1945 there were serious negotiations between the CCP and the USA.[74] A recent account suggests that "the picture of the 'revolutionary holy land'" given by Snow and others was "too rosy...the view from the archives reveals a greater importance for local military superiority, a far greater role for coercion, and a smaller role for popular participation".[75]

There are, for example, serious question marks about how genuine the 1940 "New Democracy" policy[76] really was as there was only one party inside the Red bases. The so-called "three thirds" system of that year assigned just one third of official positions to CCP members but was largely a sham.[77] Although the CCP provided a channel for a popular movement against foreign occupation and domestic exploitation, the broad masses did not and could not control it.

The move to united front propaganda and moderation of land policy also led to the CCP taking a more conservative attitude towards women than previously. By 1942 "the CCP abandoned any attempt to mobilise women behind appeals to emancipation and gender equality".[78] Women's economic participation was encouraged but political involvement was discouraged. Nevertheless, the people's war had a dynamic of its own so that over the course of the conflict:

> women [were] mobilised by the climate of social change in which they lived. This was a climate for which the CCP was partly—particularly

through its call for gender equality and women's emancipation at the start of the war—but only partly, responsible.[79]

Criticisms need to be seen in the context of the situation of the KMT and Japanese occupation and, while recognising the limitations, the achievements of the people's war under CCP leadership should not be underestimated. Stalinism in Russia reflected a new exploiting class but in Yenan there was little surplus available and survival depended on Spartan equality and strong ideological commitment.

Two types of warfare against Japan

People's war and inter-imperialist war employed contrasting strategies. Chiang prioritised defeating the Red Army over fighting the invader but after 1937 he had no choice but to mount resistance. Tokyo's highly efficient conventional army had limited numbers of personnel so it directed its chief blows against the Nationalist government, hoping to rapidly annihilate it. There were therefore some major set-piece battles such as the struggle over Wuhan (June to October 1938) during which a million Chinese soldiers were wounded or died.[80]

Chiang's troops were successful on occasion. Victory in 1938 in the Battle of Taierzhuang, "the Chinese Stalingrad",[81] destroyed the myth of Tokyo's invincibility. To the extent that the Nationalist government survived, "trading space for time" did not fail entirely. But it was costly and inefficient and did not take into consideration the consequences for civilians. For example, in 1938 dykes on the Yellow River were breached to create a temporary watery barrier to Japanese troops of up to 20 miles wide. But 6 million people were displaced and an estimated 800,000 died.[82]

The alternative was to employ guerrilla tactics. A commentator wrote in 1940 that "the question on the Chinese side can be reduced to this: How effectively can all of China's military forces employ the method of fighting used by the Chinese Communists between 1930 and 1936?"[83] Such methods required popular backing, to feed and hide partisans after hit and run operations and provide enthusiastic fighters capable of local initiative rather than depending on orders from a hierarchy, as well as belief in a cause rather than obedience under the whip. Such attributes were entirely lacking on the Nationalist side and cursory attempts at partisan warfare were abandoned.[84]

For the CCP such methods came naturally[85] and were indeed a necessity. Firstly, they lacked the arms to fight prolonged conventional battles.

Their own weapons production was minimal so arms had to be seized from the enemy. During the civil war period, for example, 80 percent of guns and 70 percent of ammunition were taken from the KMT[86] and Japanese supplies played the same role later.[87] It was not sheer bravado for Mao to ask: "Should we fear...the fact that [the enemy] has weapons? We can find a way to seize his weapons".[88] Secondly, the CCP's Red bases were behind Japanese lines. Once again the Red Army was surrounded by an enemy that was far superior in firepower and guerrilla tactics were again applicable. The situation was summed up by this slogan: "The enemy advances, we retreat. The enemy camps, we harass. The enemy tires, we attack. The enemy retreats, we pursue".[89]

Even so, conditions were difficult. In addition to the "three alls", the Japanese adopted the KMT tactic of installing troops into a string of blockhouses at regular intervals across the countryside. This was designed to intimidate the population and smash resistance. At the lowest point the population of the Red bases fell from 44 to 25 million and troop numbers declined by a quarter.[90] Yet the people's war proved resilient. A study of one CCP-controlled area shows how hatred of occupation and privileged Chinese elements was a factor:

> Villages during the war were like small boats drifting on a vast ocean, tossed about and threatened with being swallowed by mounting waves. The villages in Licheng county during the war suffered tremendously from the repeated mopping-up operations of the Japanese army. Villagers had their houses burned, were deprived of their domestic animals, and lost family members. In order to resist the Japanese forces, the leaders of the villages organised guerrilla corps. Villagers were held responsible for providing guerrilla soldiers with food. Given the Communist Party of China's policy of making the "distribution of burdens more reasonable and equitable", better-off families must have been forced to take on heavier burdens in providing food for the guerrillas. Some of the well-off families who were displeased with such an arrangement sometimes opted to defend the village by collaborating with the Japanese Army but ended up being executed as "collaborators".[91]

Partisan warfare effaces the division between soldiers and civilians. In Red areas large numbers were involved in bodies such as the "Youth National Salvation Association", "Women's Association" and "Peasants' Association".[92] Snow estimates that in 1943 the Red Army was backed by a militia of 7 million with another 12 million in anti-Japanese associations.[93] Liu Shao-ch'i, an army political commissar during the war, wrote:

"Who will fight Japan? Too many think it should be done by specialists, summed up as 'Let the Eighth Army do it.' Wrong. The army must indeed fight the enemy, but the people—every single Chinese citizen— also ought to be armed and ought to fight the enemy".[94]

Mao's partisan strategy generally involved avoidance of frontal attacks. This has led some to suggest he was no more committed to fighting Japan than Chiang, both leaders being intent on marshalling resources to fight each other after the war. A Comintern representative within Red territory itself made this criticism,[95] and the Nationalist press claimed the Red Army devoted twice as much effort to the civil war as Japan: "the 'move and hit' style of Communist guerrillas, much lauded by Mao, was in fact mostly moving, and very little hitting".[96] Perhaps such accusations spurred the Eighth Route Army to launch the "Hundred Regiments" anti-Japanese offensive in 1940. It proved costly and led directly to Okamura's "three alls" policy.

However, a simplistic comparison of Communist and Nationalist contributions in the fight against Japan is unfounded. Chiang had Allied backing, a large-scale state and over 4 million troops. The Communists began with around 50,000 soldiers, though this had grown to 500,000 by the end.[97] Another way of considering the issue is to observe that, excluding Manchuria, half of the Japanese army was involved in fighting the Chongqing government while the other half (with puppet troops) spent their time confronting the Communist threat behind its lines.[98]

Ultimately neither the Nationalist nor Communist war strategies succeeded. By 1944 Japan was close to victory in China. It was the combined pressure of US bombing (including the nuclear bombs dropped on Hiroshima and Nagasaki on 6 and 9 August 1945) and the Russian invasion of Japanese-occupied Manchuria (on 9 August 1945) that led to the formal ending of war on "Victory over Japan" Day (V-J Day) on 14 August 1945.

Manchuria after 1945

In 1937 China prefigured the Second World War in the way it interwove massive domestic social struggles and inter-imperialist war. It continued to reflect these characteristics even after peace was concluded. It was at that moment that the question of what the fighting had been for arose. Would the end of occupation bring improvements for ordinary people or just the victory of one imperialist gang over another? The answer to that question would have far-reaching consequences. Fenby describes what the return of Nationalist government meant: "Peasants who had taken part in [Communist] land reform were publicly executed. Farmers who had campaigned for rent reductions were buried alive, sometimes together with their families".[99]

The key post-war events took place in the north east province of Manchuria: "Nearly one sixth the size of the United States, with a population of about 45,000,000, Manchuria in 1945 was the richest single region of East Asia in natural resources, developed and potential power sources, industry, transport facilities, and agricultural production".[100] For this reason the Nationalist government's slogan was: "China will survive or perish with the Northeast",[101] believing its fate depended on preventing a Communist takeover there.

A simple chronology demonstrates how quickly imperialism showed its hand. Even before V-J Day the former enemies—Russia, the USA and Japan—came together behind Chiang Kai-shek. Having "traded space for time", the KMT government's writ only ran in the south west. So, on 10 August 1945 Washington pledged to help the Nationalists retake the north: in addition to 60,000 US troops already deployed south of the Great Wall, 53,000 Marines and half a million Nationalist soldiers were to be shipped or flown into Manchuria.[102] The same day Stalin warned the Nationalist foreign minister that "the Chinese Communists would get into Manchuria first"[103] unless the Soviet Union also played its part in preventing that eventuality. Moscow therefore approved a treaty granting Chiang "full authority" as soon as military operations were concluded.[104] The following day Chiang incorporated the 1 million or so puppet troops who had been collaborating with Tokyo into his own forces. He asserted they had been an "underground army" for the KMT all along.[105]

Only Japan was missing here. But rumours abounded of a secret agreement between the Nationalists and the Japanese military[106] and three days after Tokyo's surrender General MacArthur's Order Number One ordered Japan to "hold intact and in good condition" all its conquests "pending further instructions".[107] These came from Chiang who openly negotiated with General Okamura, notorious author of Japan's "three alls" policy and forced prostitution. The latter formally agreed to "surrender unconditionally...to the forces specified by Generalissimo Chiang Kai-shek, all arms, ammunition, equipment, supplies, records, information and other assets of any kind belonging to the Japanese forces".[108] Privately he promised to "assist the National Government" and "resolutely chastise" the Communists.[109] As a consequence:

for the better part of a year after the war was over, much of the Japanese Army remained in China, most of it fully armed and frequently still in charge of rail zones, cities, and even many towns in North China...there were in eastern and north western Manchuria eighty thousand Japanese troops as late as 30 January, 1947, completely equipped and operating under the command of Chiang Kai-shek's headquarters. Such troops were being issued rations that were at least twice as generous as those given to Nationalist soldiers...some Japanese comprised a part of Chiang's officer corps. Chiang's efforts to make use of the defeated Japanese were dwarfed, however, by those of his ally, the warlord Yen Hsi-shan. Yen not only employed Japanese officers but also was determined to use the entire Japanese army stationed in his north western province of Shansi against the Communists, which he succeeded in doing for nearly four years after the war's end.[110]

Fighting between Japanese and Reds continued. In Shanghai Japanese bayonets helped smash a strike of 50,000 workers in support of the Communists. When Okamura was at last convicted of being a war criminal, the Nationalist government stepped in not only to protect him from punishment but to employ him as an adviser![111]

There were Japanese soldiers fighting on the side of the Communists but they had defected to join the fight against imperialism, seeing their real enemies as:

Japanese officers and other members of Japan's ruling class... After all, the vast majority of them came from the farming and labouring classes in Japan, with a small admixture of students and merchants. Few had been treated with respect in Japan and, especially, in the Japanese Army, where there existed a rigid hierarchy in which inferiors, meaning those who came from the poor and had little education, were often treated with considerable brutality by their superiors. Inevitably, such men were profoundly impressed by the egalitarianism that was perhaps the most important characteristic of the Chinese Communist armies.[112]

The unholy coalition of imperialist powers was short-lived as hostile brothers are bound to fall out. As long as Stalin believed the invasion of Manchuria by 630,000 of his troops guaranteed Russia strong influence, and aided the prospect of occupying Japan, the Nationalists were courted as allies. He therefore committed Russian forces to leaving Manchuria within three months.[113] But the advantages conferred on the US by the atom bomb and the swift peace Tokyo concluded with the US alone dashed these prospects.

Now that the KMT would be a client state of the US, Russian withdrawal was delayed so that, under the pretext that nine days of conflict with Japan justified seizure of "war booty", Manchuria could be plundered on an astonishing scale. A contemporary report said:

> In addition to taking stockpiles and certain complete industrial installations, the Soviets took by far the larger part of all functioning power generating and transforming equipment, electric motors, experimental plants, laboratories and hospitals. In machine tools, they took only the newest and best, leaving antiquated tools behind... By the end Manchuria's electric power capacity was reduced by 71 percent, its metalworking by 80 percent and textiles by 75 percent.[114]

The new Russian policy was one of malevolent neutrality. Treaty obligations meant they handed Manchuria's cities to Chiang[115] but with the Cold War developing they did not want the Nationalists to be too strong. Therefore Moscow did not oppose the advance of Communist troops in the countryside and left behind captured Japanese stockpiles amounting to 700,000 rifles, 14,000 machine guns and hundreds of vehicles including tanks.[116]

There has been debate about how calculated an act this was. Some see it as a Communist conspiracy hatched by Stalin and Mao. But according to one historian, although the Russians did not prevent CCP infiltration "it is by no means certain that they could have done so even if they had wanted to, for the guerrillas were innumerable, omnipresent and indistinguishable from the peasantry".[117] Whatever the reason, the Manchurian windfall was a godsend to the CCP, which had popular support but always lacked the military hardware to make this effective.

Between 1946 and 1949 Mao's forces went on to defeat Chiang's Nationalist government and his US backers in what Schramm describes as "unquestionably one of the most striking examples in history of the victory of a smaller but dedicated and well-organised force enjoying popular support over a larger but unpopular force with poor morale and incompetent leadership".[118] The Second World War with its combination of inter-imperialist rivalries and struggles against oppression and exploitation made a huge contribution to that outcome.

The place of China in an understanding of the Second World War

The Second World War encompassed two overlapping processes that exist within capitalist society at all times—the competitive struggle between the capitalists themselves and class/social struggles between the capitalists and other sections of society. The usual sequence of events between 1939 and 1945 was that the struggle between capitalists (imperialist war) opened the way for powerful movements from below to develop. China provides an interesting variation to this. A prolonged revolutionary process had begun before the Second World War and the imperialist Sino-Japanese War was overlaid upon it.

A Marxist analysis of the Chinese Revolution needs to take account of Trotsky's theory of permanent revolution. The argument is that the world progression of capitalism generates forces within economically backward countries which drive them to develop this social system domestically. To do so they need to break through limits imposed by archaic social and state structures.

Initially this led to bourgeois revolutions such as occurred in England in the 1640s and in France starting in 1789. Here, as capitalists were a relatively small minority in society, their political representatives (like Cromwell and Robespierre) had to mobilise the masses to overcome the feudal state. The New Model Army and the London mob, Jacobinism and the Parisian *sans-culottes* tore down the old regimes and established capitalist state power.

However, even in these early revolutions reliance on the activity of lower sections was potentially risky as they could begin to impose their own needs. In England egalitarian currents like the Levellers and Diggers emerged. In France the *enragés* stepped forward on numerous occasions to provoke radical changes threatening capitalist interests. Once state power was secured for capitalism, such popular movements were cut down. England's monarchy was restored (though constitutionally hedged in). In France, Robespierre and the Jacobin leadership were executed in the so-called Thermidorian Reaction.

With the passage of time and the development of industry the gulf between rich and poor grew greater and the working class became more organised and conscious of its own interests. During the European revolutions of 1848, Marx already noticed that the developing German bourgeoisie feared those below it more than the feudal state:

> at the moment when it menacingly confronted feudalism and absolutism, it saw...pitted against itself the proletariat and all sections of the middle class whose interests and ideas were related to those of the proletariat... Unlike the French bourgeoisie of 1789...it was inclined to betray the people and to compromise with the crowned representatives of the old society...[119]

Conversely, there could be moments when bourgeois revolutionary demands, such as national independence, were championed by other classes. As Trotsky wrote of the 1871 Paris Commune:

> The Parisian workers took power...because they were compelled to do so by the bourgeoisie's betrayal of national defence... It was only possible to defend Paris and the rest of France by arming the proletariat. But the revolutionary proletariat was a threat to the bourgeoisie, and an armed proletariat was an armed threat.[120]

At the beginning of the 20th century Trotsky related this understanding to the Russian situation to develop a fully rounded theory of permanent revolution whose validity was confirmed in 1917. The Russian bourgeoisie would not initiate or even support a bourgeois revolution and in their absence another section would take the lead. For reasons discussed above the peasantry could not fulfil this role but the working class could. That class, in accomplishing the tasks of the bourgeois revolution, would also impose its own demands and thus the bourgeois revolution would grow into socialist revolution—and so be "permanent". This is what happened in Russia in 1917.

At its start the Chinese Revolution seemed to fit Russia's pattern. Its bourgeoisie faced the obstacle of foreign imperialism and backward internal social relations such as warlordism. Like its Russian equivalent, fear of mobilising the masses outweighed the determination to overcome these barriers. This was graphically demonstrated in the KMT's massacre of Shanghai's workers in 1927. At that point China diverged from Russia's pattern. Such was the scale of repression that the workers' ability to champion the revolution was destroyed in the long term. Its leadership, the CCP, not only lost its link with the proletariat but was ideologically distorted by Stalinism.

The CCP leadership was, in class terms, independent of both workers and peasants. In future this grouping would form the embryo of a new ruling class set on achieving the tasks of the bourgeois revolution –independence, national unity and economic growth—using the tools of state power. For this reason Cliff described the rise of Mao to power as an example of "deflected permanent revolution" because it was not the working class but "the intelligentsia as the leader and unifier of the nation, and above all as manipulator of the masses" who shaped the process.[121]

During the Sino-Japanese War in poverty-stricken Yenan the CCP leadership had little property to protect from those beneath it and therefore lacked the constraints on mass mobilisation experienced by bourgeoisies ever since 1848. However, the result was ambiguous. This was not socialism but it cleared away much of the "muck of ages"[122] and at the same time established a new, state capitalist ruling class.

This experience illuminates the forces at work during the Second World War in an unusual way, because it demonstrates the relevance of the theory of permanemt revolution to the war generally.

1. The theory of permanent revolution is usually applied when Third World countries struggle against imperialist oppression and various social forces are unleashed in the process. The onslaught of Germany in Europe aimed to shackle weaker countries to (Axis) imperialism, though in this case the intended victims were developed capitalist formations. So despite the massive economic contrast between China and France, for example, the issue of what forces might be unleashed at a national level to counter the imperialist threat was posed in a similar way.

2. Each bourgeoisie had to consider the degree to which it was prepared to work with, or indeed encourage, mass mobilisation from below in order to ward off the imperialist threat to its future, or collaborate with the enemy to avoid a domestic threat.

3. Movements from below varied from place to place. They were shaped by the character of the leadership and this determined the degree to which they merely mirrored the bourgeois revolutionary demand of national sovereignty or went beyond this to begin to express their own independent interests (and threaten "permanent revolution"). However, the dominance of Stalinism meant that nowhere did the working class step forward as an independent force capable of completing the process in the direction of socialism.

It would be going too far to suggest that all the people's war and resistance movements of the Second World War were examples of "deflected permanent revolution"; but it is clear that the basic elements operating in China were not unrelated to global currents. There was (excuse the pun), no Chinese wall between events in undeveloped countries and the war as a whole.

NOTES

1 J Fenby, *Generalissimo: Chiang Kai-shek and the China He Lost* (Free Press, New York, 2003), p106.

2 H Isaacs, *The Tragedy of the Chinese Revolution* (Stanford University Press, Stanford, 1961), p32.

3 R C North, *Moscow and Chinese Communists* (Stanford University Press, Stanford, 1953), p51.

4 Quoted in Fenby, 2003, p114.

5 E Snow, *Red Star over China* (Harmondsworth 1972), p456.

6 Isaacs, 1961, p133.

7 Isaacs, 1961, p179.

8 Isaacs, 1961, p295.

9 *The Voice of China. Speeches of Generalissimo and Madame Chiang Kai-shek* (London, 1943), pp 20, 50, 25.

10 Quoted in So Wai Chor, "The Making of the Guomindang's Japan Policy, 1932-1937: The Roles of Chiang Kai-Shek and Wang Jingwei", *Modern China*, vol 28, no 2 (April 2002), p231. See also M Schaller, *The US Crusade in China 1938-1945* (New York, 1979), p42, who quotes Chiang in similar terms: "It is not the Japanese army that we fear, because our army is able to deal with it, but the defiant Communists."

11 So Wai Chor, 2002, p213. See also Hu Pu-yu, *A Brief History of Sino-Japanese War* (Taipei, 1974), p7.

12 A Coogan, "The Volunteer Armies of North East China", *History Today*, vol 43, no 7, 1992, p40.

13 See P M Coble, "Chiang Kai-shek and the Anti-Japanese Movement in China: Zou Tao-fen and the National Salvation Association, 1931-1937", *Journal of Asian Studies*, vol 44, no 2, February 1985, pp293-310.

14 So Wai Chor, 2002, p240.

15 Quoted in Fenby, 2003, p441; Isaacs, 1961, p298.

16 Hu Pu-yu, *A Brief History of Sino-Japanese War* (Taipei, 1974), p7.

17 J W Garver, "Chiang Kai-shek's Quest for Soviet Entry into the Sino-Japanese War", in *Political Science Quarterly*, vol 102, no 2 (summer, 1987), p32, and E Snow, *Scorched Earth* (Gollancz, London 1941), Part 1, p104.

18 E Snow, 1972, p473.

19 E Snow, 1941, Part 1, p105.

20 J R Miller, "The Chiang-Stilwell Conflict, 1942-1944", *Military Affairs*, vol 43, no 2 (April 1979), p59.

21 R Spector, "The Sino-Japanese War in the Context of World History", M Peattie, E Drea and H van de Ven (eds), *The Battle for China* (Stanford 2011), p473.

22 Quoted Fenby, 2003, p425.

23 See Miller, April 1979.

24 Quoted in P Chen-Main Wang, "Revisiting US-China Wartime Relations: A Study of Wedemeyer's China Mission", *Journal of Contemporary China* (2009), 18 (59), p242.

25 M Schaller, *The US Crusade in China 1938-1945* (New York, 1979), p105.

26 Quoted in Schaller, 1979, p105; Spector, 2011, p475.

27 Chang Jui-te, "The Nationalist Army on the Eve of War" in M Peattie, E Drea and H van de Ven (eds), *The Battle for China* (Stanford, 2011), p104.

28 Snow, 1941, Part 1, p48.

29 M Selden, *The Yenan Way in Revolutionary China* (Harvard University Press, Harvard, 1971), p154.

30 Fenby, 2003, pp408-409.

31 See I Chang, *The Rape of Nanking: The Forgotten Holocaust of World War II*, Penguin USA, 1998 (Paper).

32   E Friedman et al, *Chinese Village, Socialist State* (Yale University Press, New Haven, 1991), p36.

33   C A Johnson, *Peasant Nationalism and Communist Power* (Stanford University Press, Stanford, 1962), p56.

34   Chalmers Johnson, for example, notes that in 1944 there were ten times as many Japanese nationals living in China as in 1937 (Johnson, 1962, p44).

35   Mao Tse-tung, *Selected Works*, vol 4 (London, 1956), pp248-249.

36   J W Garver, "Chiang Kai-shek's Quest for Soviet Entry into the Sino-Japanese War", *Political Science Quarterly*, vol 102, no 2 (summer, 1987), p32. For a summary of Sino-Russian relations see Snow, 1972, p407.

37   Mao's letter welcoming the new Comintern policy, quoted in S Schramm, *Mao Tse-tung* (Penguin, London, 1967), p109.

38   Schramm, 1967, p112.

39   Quoted in N Knight, "Mao Zedong and the Peasants: Class and Power in the Formation of a Revolutionary Strategy", in *China Report* 2004, no 40, p63.

40   T Cliff, *Deflected Permanent Revolution*, www.marxists.org/archive/cliff/works/1963/xx/permrev.htm.

41   O Braun, *A Comintern Agent in China 1932-1939* (C Hurst, London, 1982), p40.

42   Braun, 1982, p51.

43   Quoted in Cliff, 1963.

44   Braun, 1982, p134.

45   Quoted in Selden, 1971, p73.

46   N Knight, "Mao Zedong and the Peasants: Class and Power in the Formation of a Revolutionary Strategy," in *China Report* 2004, no 40, p73.

47   Johnson, 1962, p157; Selden, 1971, p142.

48   Selden, 1971, p73. See also Schramm, 1967, p115.

49   T Cliff, 1963.

50   See, for example, D S Goodman, "The Licheng Rebellion of 1941: Class, Gender and Leadership in the Sino-Japanese War, *Modern China*, vol 23, no 2 (April 1997), pp216-245; P M Coble, "Chiang Kai-shek and the Anti-Japanese Movement in China: Zou Tao-fen and the National Salvation Association, 1931-1937", *Journal of Asian Studies*, vol 44, no 2, February 1985, pp293-310; and Donglan Huang, "Revolution, War, and Villages: A Case Study on Villages of Licheng County, Shanxi Province during the War of Resistance Against Japan", *Frontiers of History in China*, 2011, no 6(1), p106.

51   Johnson, 1962, p2.

52   Selden, 1971, pp119-120.

53   Snow, 1972, p77.

54   Mao Tse-tung, *Selected Works*, vol 4 (London, 1956), p25.

55   J Esherick, "Revolution in a "Feudal Fortress", Feng Chongyi, D Goodman (eds), *North China at War* (Lanham, Maryland, 2000), p69.

56   Huang, 2011, p106.

57   Huang, 2011, p109. This is confirmed by another example given by Selden: "Third Township provides unique local data illustrating relationship between land revolution and political participation... The majority of the 134 who had become party members by 39 joined because they believed in the Communists' commitment to redistribute land, improve standards of living, and abolish oppression... On one point the report is unequivocal. As late as 1939, after three years in which the united front was reiterated as a fundamental principle, only one person out of the total of 134 had joined the party primarily to resist Japan, and that was in 1937 long after Communist control and land revolution had been consolidated." Selden, 1971, p110.

58   Snow, 1972, p261.

59   Snow, 1972, p469.

60   See Snow, 1972, p47.

61   Snow, 1972, p330.

62 Snow, 1972, p299.
63 Snow, 1972, p296.
64 Snow, 1972, p300.
65 Snow, 1972, p296.
66 Selden, 1971, p254.
67 Huang, 2011, p115.
68 Fenby, 2003, p322.
69 Snow, 1972, p410.
70 Snow, 1972, p410.
71 See Tai-Chun Kuo, "A Strong Diplomat in a Weak Polity: T V Soong and wartime US-China relations, 1940-1943", *Journal of Contemporary China*, no 18, March 2009, pp219-231.
72 This figure is for 1943 (Fenby, 2003), p408.
73 Quoted in Fenby, 2003, p199.
74 See for example, Schramm, 1967, pp210-214.
75 Esherick, 2000, p79.
76 See for example Mao, *On New Democracy*, in www.marxists.org/reference/archive/mao/selected-works/volume-2/mswv2_26.htm
77 Selden, 1971, p135.
78 D S G Goodman, "Revolutionary Women and Women in the Revolution: The Chinese Communist Party and Women in the War of Resistance to Japan, 1937-1945", *The China Quarterly*, no 164 (December, 2000), p919.
79 Goodman, 2000, p941.
80 S MacKinnon, "The Tragedy of Wuhan, 1938", *Modern Asian Studies*, vol 30, no 4 (October, 1996), p933.
81 According to Fenby, 2003, p318.
82 Fenby, 2003, p320.
83 Quoted in Snow, 1941, Part 1, pp48-49.
84 Selden, 1971, p174.
85 For a discussion of this aspect, see K Gawlikowski, "Traditional Chinese concepts of warfare and CPC theory of People's War (1928-1949)", *26th Conference of Chinese Studies Proceedings: Understanding Modern China, Problems and Methods* (1979), pp143-169.
86 Snow, 1972, p299.
87 Johnson, 1962, p59.
88 Quoted in Schramm, 1967, p196.
89 Quoted in Schramm, 1967, p45. Snow gives a detailed discussion of partisan tactics (see Snow, 1972, p317).
90 Johnson, 1962, p58.
91 Huang, 2011, p115
92 Selden gives the following figures for 1938: Workers Organisation 45,000; Youth National Salvation Association 168,000; Women's Association 173,000; and Peasant Association 421,000 (Selden, 1971, p142).
93 Snow, 1972, p468.
94 Quoted in Johnson, 1962, p147.
95 Braun, 1982, p49. Fenby quotes a Russian commentator who in 1943 wrote that "the Red Armies have long been abstaining from both active and passive action against the aggressors" (Fenby, 2003, p441).
96 See D M Gordon, "The China-Japan War, 1931-1945, Historiographical Essay," *The Journal of Military History*, vol 70, no 1 (January, 2006), pp169-170.
97 Johnson, 1962, p72; Schramm, 1967, pp199-200. Snow quotes a Japanese source that suggested between 500,000 and 600,000 (Snow, 1972, p469).
98 Snow, 1972, p469.
99 Fenby, 2003, p461.

100 O E Clubb, "Manchuria in the Balance, 1945-1946", *Pacific Historical Review*, vol 26, no 4 (November, 1957), p377.

101 Quoted in Clubb, 1957, p381.

102 Clubb, 1957, p379.

103 Schramm, 1967, p218.

104 Note accompanying the Sino-Soviet Treaty of Friendship and Alliance of 14 August 1945, in *American Journal of International Law*, vol 40, no 2, April 1946, p59.

105 Schramm, 1967, p 218; Xiaoyuan Liu, *A Partnership for Disorder: China, the United States, and Their Policies for the Postwar Disposition of the Japanese Empire 1941–1945* (Cambridge University Press, 1996), p279.

106 D G Gillin and C Etter, "Staying On: Japanese Soldiers and Civilians in China 1945-1949", *The Journal of Asian Studies*, vol 42, no 3 (May, 1983), p499.

107 Supreme Commander for the Allied Powers General Order no. One. This was formally accepted by the Japanese on 2 September. www.taiwandocuments.org/surrender05.htm

108 Act of Surrender—China Theatre, 9 September 1945, www.taiwandocuments.org/surrender02.htm

109 Quoted in Gillin and Etter, 1983, p501.

110 Gillin and Etter, 1983, pp499-500.

111 I Buruma, *Year Zero: A History of 1945* (Atlantic Books, London 2013), p193.

112 Gillin and Etter, 1983, p511.

113 *American Journal of International Law*, vol 40, no 2, April 1946, p53.

114 American investigation report quoted in E D Hawkins, "Manchuria's Postwar Economy", in *Far Eastern Survey*, vol 16, no 3 (12 February 1947), p35.

115 C P Fitzgerald, *The Birth of Communist China* (Penguin, Harmondsworth, 1964), p97.

116 Fenby, 1961, p306.

117 Fitzgerald, 1964, p97.

118 Schramm, 1967, p225.

119 K Marx, "The Bourgeoisie and the Counter-Revolution", *Neue Rheinische Zeitung*, no 169, December 1848, www.marxists.org/archive/marx/works/1848/12/15.htm. For a discussion of this see R Day and D Gaido, *Witnesses to Permanent Revolution* (Haymarket Books, Chicago, 2011).

120 L Trotsky, "Foreword to K Marx Parizhskaya Kommuna", in R Day and D Gaido, *Witnesses to Permanent Revolution* (Haymarket Books, Chicago, 2011), p503.

121 T Cliff, 1963.

122 K Marx, "Feuerbach. Opposition of the Materialist and Idealist Outlook D. Proletarians and Communism", *The German Ideology*, part 1, www.marxists.org/archive/marx/works/1845/german-ideology/ch01.htm

10

Japan: Against the regime

Kaye Broadbent and Tom O'Lincoln

"Thousands die for the glory of a single general." This classical Chinese saying was found on a telephone pole in 1945, according to Tokyo secret police reports.[1] That such a thing occurred may seem surprising given the way the Japanese population has been portrayed as of one mind with the ruling elite. For example, in response to military aggression towards China at the time of the Manchurian Incident (1931), it was reported that "the populace was swept away by a nationalistic euphoria".[2] And following the Marco Polo Bridge attack (outside Beijing) in 1937 "public opinion was marked by great patriotic fervor".[3] The army developed a series of pamphlets which Borton notes indicated that: "As the crisis in Asia increased, persons from all classes in society—the political parties, businessmen, labourers and farmers—found...philosophical and religious justification for the national expansionist program".[4]

These and countless other examples portray the Japanese population as totally carried away with the war effort and possessed of a mindless unanimity—what the Japanese state called "100 million hearts beating as one".[5] This perspective is symbolised by the *kamikaze* suicide flights which are used to show how fanatical the Japanese population was—with young men eager to die for the emperor. The individual soldier has also been caricatured in the same way: "He was cruel, and dirty, and bestial...he plundered and raped the natives".[6] In reality, political uniformity was imposed on the Japanese population and it did encounter resistance.

Much of the English language literature on this period in Japan's history focuses on Japan as a monolithic entity with the population united behind the militaristic goals of the state. This chapter documents another aspect of Japan's history, that of resistance to the Japanese state's military expansion. It focuses on both collective and individual acts of resistance. The banning of left wing groups, the forced amalgamation of unions into an industrial association, *Sanpō*, and the gaoling and torturing of political and union activists, did not stop the resistance.

There are numerous examples of individual resistance from the military, including within the ranks of the renowned *kamikaze* pilots, by peasants, Koreans forced into slave labour in the mines, workers and the intelligentsia. The resistance took the form of violent struggle, workplace sabotage and absenteeism and activists continuing their activism in the form of poetry, graffiti, jokes and publications. One union activist Yamashiro Yoshimune was gaoled for leading a miners' strike in 1927; he continued his activities on his release in 1936 and was imprisoned again in 1940. He refused to renounce his Marxist views and convert to "Japanism" despite pressure from the authorities. Representing only the tip of the iceberg, this chapter indicates there is clear evidence that resistance to Japanese militarism occurred within Japan, and from many levels.[7]

The origins of the Pacific war

The blame for the Pacific War is usually laid at Japan's feet. As Peter Edwards says, Japan "had revealed an expansionist and profoundly anti-democratic underside. This had to be eradicated, and it was".[8] But the causes lie deeper; they lie in the rise of global imperialism and industrialism. By the 19th century predominance within the system of empires was going to those who embraced industrial capitalism. But there were some who sought to defy this. Among them was a set of islands in the north west Pacific.

For two centuries Japan had isolated itself and it had threatened no one outside its borders. But the Western powers would not allow it to remain a backwater forever. In 1853 Commodore Perry's US ships arrived to begin forcing Japan open to foreign trade and influence and the British followed. Karl Marx and Friedrich Engels had described how western expansion was breaking down the "Chinese walls" of recalcitrant peoples.[9] They might have been writing about Japan.

The war was sold to the population as a "righteous war".[10] Early in the 20th century nationalist thinker Hibino Yutaka wrote in an influential book that his country faced a world of annihilating competition. Indeed a "discarded scrap of flesh upon the Asiatic continent has the power to assemble the hungry vultures from the whole earth".[11] Japan would need to match the vultures for strength and so it began building an empire. In doing so it adapted and modified Dutch and French colonial practices the brutality of which were to make it notorious.[12] The Japanese ruling groups had entered a period of crisis that was only resolved after a series of struggles consolidated power and led to the return of the emperor as the symbolic head of state in what is referred to as the Meiji Restoration.

By 1905 Japan had defeated Russia in a major war but Russia was weak and it remained difficult to impose militarism on the people of Japan. It was not some historical inevitability; rather there were sharp struggles over what direction society would take. Millions of workers opposed capitalism, expansionism and the military. During the sensational 1930 Toyo Muslin strike young working women singing the Internationale waged street battles with police and company guards.[13]

Japan's brutal aggression against China was partly a response to Western pressure. Joseph Grew, US Ambassador to Tokyo, said that the Japanese, believing that Britain and the US threatened them, "sought to carve out an economic sphere in which to operate should the Western world deny them access to raw materials and markets".[14] Chris Harman has outlined how both Germany and Japan, as late-comers to the global carve-up, were impelled by a sinister logic:

> Once the path of military expansion had been decided upon, it fed upon itself. To challenge the existing empires required the maximum military-industrial potential. Every successful imperialist adventure increased this—for example, the Japanese takeover of Manchuria, the German annexation of Austria and then Czechoslovakia. But at the same time it increased the hostility of the existing empires—leading to the need for a greater arms potential and further military adventures. The breaking points were the German seizure of western Poland and the Japanese onslaught on Pearl Harbor.[15]

The US forced Japan to take the road of conquest, then blocked the road. Washington imposed a savage oil blockade on Japan, apparently to provoke war. It demanded a large-scale Japanese retreat, something Tokyo saw as impossible. However, Japan lacked the material resources to confront the US. Or did it? Was there any way to break out of the circle? The key problem, said a senior Japanese Navy Ministry official, was oil and if its reserves were depleted, Japan would grow weaker: "A grim and humiliating end. However if we could strike boldly and get the oil in the south..."[16] The south meant Indonesia. But a strike to the south would only succeed if Japan could cripple the US Pacific fleet centred on Pearl Harbor.

A British Admiralty intelligence report acknowledged that "had she not gone to war now, Japan would have seen such a deterioration of her economic position as to render her ultimately unable to wage war, and to reduce her to the status of a second-rate power".[17] Joseph Rochefort, Commander of Station HYPO (combat intelligence centre for the Pacific Fleet) was blunter: "We cut off their money, fuel and trade. We were just tightening the screws on the Japanese. They could see no way of getting out except going to war".[18] The Japanese government's "Main Principles of Basic National Policy", formulated in 1940 and adopted after the move to the south began, underpinned the southern strategy and emphasised bringing "the eight corners of the world under one roof".[19]

Historical overview

The 1870s and 1880s had seen the emergence of a democratic broadly popular People's Rights Movement which focused attention on political freedoms and individual rights through demands for a national assembly and a broadening of the political power base.[20] The movement secured the establishment of a parliament and was only halted in the end by tough internal security laws.

The new climate created greater space for the left. A proletarian literature movement arose which "with an explicit class perspective presented anti-war ideas and unflattering descriptions of the military".[21] These had some appeal because in a time of détente and relative prosperity the military lost prestige. Young men sought careers in other fields and "the public began to look down upon the army as a superfluous if not parasitical element of society in a peaceful world".[22] However, the relatively peaceful climate ended in 1891 after which Japan was almost continuously at war.

Japan went through a tense time during the First World War, experiencing food riots and a wave of labour disputes. But the 1920s were a time of relative prosperity as well as international détente, exemplified by the 1921 Washington Conference at which the powers arrived at a set ratio for naval assets. As long as the world capitalist economy grew, allowing Japan a certain affluence and social peace at home and reducing external pressures on the imperial state, elements of liberal government could emerge.

The rule of the Taisho Emperor (1912-1925) is popularly referred to as Taisho Democracy. Universal male suffrage, granted in 1925 following mass protests, expanded the electorate from 3 million to 13 million. There was growing interest in left wing ideas and the General Election Law of 1925 benefitted some left wing candidates. Attempts to pass legislation protecting workers' rights to join unions, however, continued to be blocked by business interests.

Nevertheless, although the period was characterised by a two-party parliamentary system, the repression identified with the 1930s is evident. Laws such as the Police Security Law (1900) were introduced to contain mass protests and the growth of left wing ideas and combined with the Peace Preservation Law (1925) to curb "radical" elements in the labour movement.

The Communist Party was formed in 1922 but due to the increasingly repressive conditions decided to dissolve in 1924. It reformed in 1925 as a broader based party. Continued repression decimated the party and by 1935 it had ceased to operate. The government conducted a series of "red" mass arrests, murders and torture of left wing activists—in 1922, 1928 and again in April 1929. On 15 March 1928, 1,600 people were arrested in a single day.[23] The Great Kanto Earthquake (1923) provided the opportunity to massacre Koreans and Chinese living in Japan and to murder the imprisoned anarchist Osugi Sakae and women's liberationist Ito Naoe. *Burakumin* (ethnically Japanese but considered outcast) activists associated with Marxists were also arrested and tortured in this period.[24]

The state used imperialist adventures to undermine class struggle at home. During 1933 and 1934 cabinet meetings repeatedly complained that domestic unrest was a "great problem, impeding national defence".[25] As early as 1929 Lieutenant-Colonel Ishiwara Kanji had written: "Japan must expand overseas to achieve political stability at home".[26]

The 1931 Manchurian Incident, which opened the way for Japanese invasion to China's north, was the first opportunity to apply this logic. When in September 1931 the Kwangtung Army marched in to set up the puppet state of Manchukuo, it created a surge of patriotism and repression. The labour movement retreated. "In the winter of 1933, an estimated 80,000 union workers and 20,000 non-union employees agreed to work on a Sunday or holiday and donate that day's wages to the army's National Defence Fund Drive".[27] In 1920 *Sōdōmei* (Greater Japan Federation of Labour), the largest trade union federation, had condemned Japan's Siberian intervention in 1918 and called for self-government in Korea. It dropped the word "Greater" from its full name to show its opposition to Japanese imperialism.[28] However, after 1931 *Sōdōmei* union contracts began incorporating a promise of "industrial service to the nation".[29] From this time Japan was effectively at war.

General Ugaki Kazunari wrote that the main objectives of his time as army minister were achieved through the Manchurian offensive: the unity of the military and the people and the "popularisation of national defence".[30] An Army Ministry newspaper remarked: "Since the

Manchurian incident, confrontational attitudes between social classes with differing economic interests appear to have gradually subsided".[31]

Millions of workers opposed capitalism, imperialism and the military. As early as 1903 socialists were working to build an anti-war movement, arguing in their newspaper that "war benefits the bourgeoisie but sacrifices the common people".[32] In Japan as in any other society, there were anti-war and militarist tendencies, liberal and authoritarian impulses, left wing and right wing movements. Tragically, the militarists won.

Resistance to militarism

General society

In the atmosphere of the 1920s left wing culture coalesced, becoming the basis for criticism of the growing militarism. The *Nihon Purōrateria Bunka Renmei* (Japan Proletarian Cultural Association) was formed in 1931 uniting the arts and sciences. It produced numerous journals and magazines. This was the first ever educational and cultural movement in Japan based on workers and peasants and its impact was significant. Films and social criticism also flourished despite heavy censorship. In 1932 over 400 activists associated with the *Nihon Purōrateria Bunka Renmei* were arrested but those who had escaped this fate remained active underground.

Continued repression destroyed the *Nihon Purōrateria Bunka Renmei* in 1934.[33] However, intellectuals and artists still found ways to protest. The *Gakugei Jiyū Yōgo Dōmei* (Federation to Protect Freedom of the Arts), which was formed in July 1933, opposed fascism and the war but was unable to develop because of the repression. Two dissident journals, *Chikaki yori* and *Kashin,* continued to publish monthly even after the beginning of heavy air raids and appeared in mimeographed form until the day the war ended. Even a village theatre performance reflected resistance: "I don't understand the guys that send you off with a cheer (*banzai*). No one comes back alive. Instead of shouting *banzai*, they would be better off saying *Namu Amida Butsu*—the Buddhist death rites".[34]

Cultural circles formed in factories and villages allowing workers and peasants to have their own independent culture. These movements allowed the illegal Japan Communist Party and left wing of the union movement to operate semi-legally and played a major role in the mass dissemination of anti-war ideas and the ideas of scientific socialism and revolution. Education was also affected by the formation of the *Shinkyō Kyōiku Kenkyūjo* (Progressive Education Institute) which opposed imperial and militarist education, instead supporting a democratic education system. The influence of scientific socialism was widespread among primary school teachers. In February 1932 the "Red Teachers' Incident" involved the arrest of numerous teachers in many prefectures and the following February in Nagano prefecture 230 teachers were arrested.[35]

The mood among the public in general, and workers in particular, was hostile to the government and often to the emperor. Police records from as early as 1942 reported growing contempt for existing authority extending even to the emperor. "Ten labourers in the steel industry were apprehended after a conversation in which they reportedly had discussed the emperor at some length and concluded that when the farmers and workers made their own world they should throw the emperor into the Siberian snow, like the Russian revolutionaries did with the tsar and his family".[36]

There was much hostility towards military officers. One report records that when a staff officer inspected an area, he saw burnt-out residents sitting exhausted by the road. "Suddenly they all jumped up and shouted, 'This all happened because of you military men! What's the point of you coming here to look at it?' Without a word, the officer got back into his car and hurriedly drove off".[37]

Anti-war protests

In Nagoya, *Sōhyō* (Nihon Rōdō Kumiai Sōhyō Gikai—union federation) mobilised 300 people at a demonstration commemorating the first anniversary of the Manchurian Incident and distributed leaflets with slogans including "Oppose the Imperialist war!" Students from several of the elite imperial universities formed a movement to protest at the suppression of free speech and government demands for "red" professors to resign. Nationally 1,500 students were arrested.

On 1 August 1931 the Japan Communist Party organised an illegal gathering and demonstration for Anti-War Day in a number of areas demanding the withdrawal of Japanese troops from Manchuria, Korea and Taiwan. Communist Party affiliated unions and the legal left protested against the war in 1932, holding partly illegal demonstrations on International Anti-War Day and International Youth Day as well as a 30-minute strike.

The Japan Communist Party soon attracted the attention of the authorities. While 1932 was the peak of its membership and publication of magazines, in October 1932 nearly 1,500 activists were arrested nationally, including party members, youth activists and *Zenkyō* (Communist

Party dominated union federation) members. By 1935 the last remaining Central Committee member had been arrested and the final issue of the party's newspaper *Akahata* (Red Flag) had been published. Despite the best efforts of activists around the country to rebuild the party, repression stopped it reforming until 1946.[38]

Workers' resistance

In 1933 there were 1.9 million factory workers and of this number women represented 49 percent. This was the first time that men outnumbered women factory workers. As Table 1 indicates, strikes occurred during this period and continued throughout the war. Although unionisation rates were low—about 5 percent—the number of organised workers rose by 25 percent between 1934 and 1936. Strikes reached a high of 2,456 in 1931 and, after a slight decline in 1935, labour began to mobilise and move leftwards once again. There were 1,915 strikes in 1934 and 1,975 strikes in 1936. In 1936 and 1937 the number of workers joining strikes or slowdowns peaked again. In 1937, 231,622 workers participated in strikes, the largest number since 1919.[39]

Table 1: Number of strikes and workers participating

Year	*Number of strikes*	*Number of workers involved*
1931	2,456	154,528
1932	2,217	123,213
1933	1,897	116,733
1934	1,915	120,307
1935	1,872	103,692
1936	1,975	92,724
1937	2,126	231,622
1938	1,050	55,565
1939	1,120	128,294
1940	732	55,003
1941	334	17,285
1942	268	14,373
1943	417	14,791
1944	296	10,026
1945	256	164,585

Sources: Ohara Shakai Mondai Kenkyūjō (Ohara Institute for Social Research), *Annual Report on Japanese Labour 1935*, p217; 1938, p132; 1965, p14; 2011, p1057. A Fujihara, *Nihon Minshu no Rekishi 9: Senso to Minshu* (The History of the Japanese People), vol 9: War and the People), 1975, p180; S Shioda, *Nihon Shakai Undō Shi* (History of Japan's Social Movements), 1982, p62; Y Nishinarita, *Kindai Nihon Rōshi Kankeishi no Kenkyū* (Research on the History of Japan's Modern Labour-Management Relations), 1988, p232.

The main factor causing strikes in the late 1930s was working conditions, which continued to deteriorate with working hours increasing and overtime normalised so that 15-hour days became widespread. Slogans such as "Luxury is the enemy" were fed to the workers to keep them working. Workers, however, were not permitted to celebrate May Day; the 26 February incident (an attempted military coup) was used as the pretext for banning it in 1936 and it was not celebrated again until 1946.[40]

Strikes, including a planned national general strike in March 1932, were suppressed but in the early 1930s the number of actions in the military and military factories increased. In March 1932, under the leadership of *Zenkyō*, the Tokyo subway workers' strike successfully linked the workplace to the war zone and demanded improvements in workers' conditions. The impact of this success was widespread. Strikes were larger and the government classified two thirds of them as "assertive", up from a quarter in 1930 and 1931. It took yet another military adventure to undermine worker resurgence. In July 1937 Japan again went to war, this time invading the Chinese heartland. According to Andrew Gordon, "Had it not been for the war in China, which began in July and led workers to restrain demands in cooperation with the 'holy war', the year 1937 would have been by far the time of greatest labour protest in Japan's history".[41]

For the first time since 1939 the number of strikes increased in 1943 (417), well into the Pacific War, before declining to 296 in 1944. The numbers of workers participating in strike action also decreased between 1940 and 1944. By 1945 although the number of strikes had fallen to 256, the number of workers participating in strikes was 16 times higher than in 1944.[42]

As the war ground on Japanese society and industry descended into a disastrous state. Sabotage was frequent: a general reported that in July 1944 an estimated 10 percent of the aircraft manufactured in Japan were defective. As the old type of strike declined a new kind of "strike" became more frequent: absenteeism. In 1943 a 10 percent absentee rate was reported in war plants, rising to an average of 15 percent by mid-1944. The Kanagawa Prefecture Industry Association newspaper reported on 30 May 1940 that "absenteeism at its peak was 22 percent, and at its lowest 10 percent with the average about 15 percent. This is not just our prefecture but a national trend".[43]

Figures for April 1943 indicate the absentee rate for women workers at the Kawasaki Aeroplane Factory was 44 percent compared with 20 percent for male workers. In general absenteeism was higher among women than men.[44] A doctor reported one third of people claiming illness were not sick, while Dower says that by July 1945 absenteeism had deprived Japan of half of its potential working hours.[45] In the final days of the war Chinese workers forced to labour in a copper mine in the north rose up against the inhumane conditions. Estimates suggest 400 died in the year 1944-1945 and many also died on the day of the uprising.[46]

Dissolution of the union movement

Elements of the union movement had been active in opposing the war and growing militarism but by 1937 many of Japan's representative trade unions had limited their industrial action and virtually stopped functioning as trade unions. Illegal unions, which included groups such as the Japan National Railway Workers Preparatory Committee, were also suppressed at this time. By July 1940 the *Nihon Rōdō Sōdōmei* union federation had dissolved as had most of the remaining non-federation affiliated unions. It became part of *Sanpō* (Sangyō Hōkoku Kai—Patriotic Industrial Association) in which the enterprise was seen as one family (*jigyō ikka*). The police, with the collaboration of right wing labour leaders, organised and supervised *Sanpō* for permanent employees and created *Rōhō* (Rōmu Hōkoku Kai—Patriotic Labour Association) for casual workers in 1938. *Sanpō* organised every workshop with the objective of compelling workers to submit unconditionally to forced labour, overwork and low wages.

With both organisations the police were able to control approximately 80 percent of the workforce. As the war dragged on and managing workers increased in difficulty, big business used *Sanpō* to indoctrinate workers with the ideology that the enterprise was an extension of Japan's unique family system—the head of the enterprise was the head of *Sanpō*.[47] A number of important industrial disputes occurred, however, even after the dissolution of the union movement. Many struggles broke out nationally due to workers' heightened class consciousness and their resistance to the war.[48] In places where unions were weak or where the traditional May Day march could not be held, other forms of celebration were held—union meetings, speeches, forums, mountain-climbing picnics and sumo wrestling.[49]

Strikes did not disappear entirely and not all unions disappeared during the war. Many of the struggles in this period focused on the wages system and from 1939 the labour system.[50] Current research has so far revealed that one of the most active of unions throughout the war was the Printers' Union based in Tokyo which transformed itself into the Printers' Club (*Shuppanko Kurabu*), but there may have been others. The club stated that by continuing to exist they wanted to "show the determination of Japan's entire union movement".[51]

The Director of the Printers' Club, Shibata Keiichiro, stated that "our members thought that no matter how much strain we were put under, we had to ensure the club survived".[52] He observed that: "The right wing trade union officials dissolved the organisations and co-operated with the military. They sold workers out to the enemy and because of that many other organisations were forcibly dissolved. We thought that the club would also be ordered to dissolve. If we continued in the same way and with the same [union] activities we would be looked at as 'red' [communist], which would lead to immediate repression, and we thought we needed to continue the club... If workers stood firm together and fought we would raise our class consciousness... We decided it was important to research becoming an organisation like a consumers co-operative or a study group to improve print workers' skills, organisations that anyone would think was necessary".[53]

In February 1940 the Printers' Club had 1,500 members. When the police demand that it disband in March, members formed a book club and published a *haiku* (Japanese poetry) journal. The Printers' Club held a fake dissolution party in August, but in October they established three travel clubs, initiated a cooking class and organised a hike attended by 50 people. The Printers' Club continued to meet, print materials and conduct political education activities until most of the leading male members were arrested in 1942. The club then continued under the auspices of the women members.[54]

Nothing escaped the eyes of the state. Foreign Ministry files record an official pondering reports of industrial sabotage and rumours of drunken workers cheering Stalin. Even students too young to have learnt Marxism in the 1920s and 1930s who were recruited for factory work "appeared to have imbibed class consciousness almost intuitively".[55]

As the war dragged on the cost of subsidising the conflict increased. Inflation ensured the cost of living rose while wages declined. If wages in 1934 are taken as 100, by 1940 workers' wages had decreased to 81.9 while the cost of living reached 180. Predictably, working conditions deteriorated. Actions occurred because people were angry over the hunger caused by the war, low wages and poor conditions. Workers protested by refusing overtime, were absent or adopted "go slow" measures at work.[56]

In 1942 communists organised and led action in a steel works controlled by the navy, and sabotage by workers at a Hitachi manufacturing works resulted in a 30 percent decline in production. These workers demanded improved working conditions including to the company's pay system. At this factory 13 people demanded improvements to their working conditions. Because of management's negative attitude and under direction from communist members, workers protested by sabotaging the products including by producing "rejects".

At the Nikko Electrics factory 1,500 people signed to register their demand for a wage increase and a reduction in daily working hours. The police concluded that in these last two actions communists had formed a group in the factory and were attempting to convince workers of left politics. The Ministry of Internal Affairs Police Bureau's edited volume, *The State of Social Movements* (*Shakai Undō no Jōkyō*), notes for 1942 that there was an increase in late arrival or early departure from work and an increase in absenteeism, which rose to over 40 percent in some factories. When the bombing of Tokyo started (in 1942 and then again in 1944) absenteeism rose to 49 percent. In 1944 absenteeism levels were running at between 24 and 51 percent in shipbuilding and between 21 and 51 percent in aircraft manufacturing.[57]

In 1943 many of the struggles were around wage increases, improvements to conditions and opposition to management; one was around the unfair distribution of food and other goods and a half-day strike was over the demand for a day off. Women workers from a manufacturer of aircraft parts decided to take a day off; at first they gathered in a nearby shrine and then went swimming. There were also demands for improved working conditions by workers in the Japan Pharmaceutical company.

High school and university students were also forced to work and often did so unwillingly. However, they did resist. The following is an example from Shibaura Manufacturing in Tokyo where several hundred students were confined to their dormitory for stealing some food. They retaliated with two days of sabotage and rotation of work groups so that one group was always absent, ensuring that no finished products could be completed.[58]

The Ministry of Home Affairs Police Bureau reported on the dissatisfactions of workers—including insufficient food, poor wages and conditions—which resulted in increased absconding from factories, absenteeism, sabotage and the production of faulty products right up until the end of the war. In an electrical factory in Nikko in September 1942, 1,500 workers struck to demand higher wages and shorter working hours. However, the workers demands were not realised as they came under increasing repression from the police. In November 1942 in the Hitachi company's Kameido (Tokyo) factory, workers' demanded higher wages and the strike action took the form of a campaign to deliberately produce faulty goods.[59]

Peasant struggles

Even after the outbreak of war and despite increasing government oppression, tenants won 57 percent of their disputes with landlords—more than ever before. In many agricultural villages tenant farmers gathered together and tilled co-operatively on May Day to show their solidarity against the landlords.[60] Table 2 shows resistance by peasants continued until the end of the war.

Table 2: Peasant struggles

Year	Number of disputes	Number of tenants involved
1931	3,419	81,135
1932	3,414	61,499
1933	4,000	48,073
1934	5,828	121,031
1935	6,824	113,164
1936	6,804	77,187
1937	6,170	63,246
1938	4,615	52,817
1939	3,578	25,904
1940	3,165	38,614
1941	3,308	32,289
1942	2,756	38,614
1943	2,424	17,738
1944	2,160	8,213

Sources: A Fujihara, *Nihon Minshu no Rekishi 9: Senso to Minshu* (The History of the Japanese People vol 9: War and the People), 1975, p216; S Shioda, *Nihon Shakai Undō Shi* (History of Japan's Social Movements), 1982, p66.

Resistance inside the military

Unrest among soldiers was more significant than people realised. In Osaka in 1930 a Soldiers' Committee was established under the auspices of the Japan Communist Party and was very active once the Manchurian Incident began. Committees were also established in a number of other facilities. The Communist Party established a section in the party for organising in the military in July 1932 and in September published a magazine for soldiers called *Soldier's Friend (Heishi no Tomo)*, while the *Advanced Military's Bugle (Shingun Rappa)* was established in the Kansai (Osaka/Kyoto) area. These magazines emphasised the freedom and human rights of soldiers and sailors or "workers and farm labourers in uniform".[61] In 1931 the

Soldiers' Committees tried to set up reading groups and while some were stopped using military laws others succeeded. Table 3 shows the number of anti-war actions which took place in the military and in military factories.

Table 3: Anti-war actions by the military and in military factories

Year	Number of anti-war actions
1929	66
1930	158
1931	126
1932	204

Source: A Fujihara (ed), *Nihon Minshu no Rekishi 8: Danatsu no Arashi no naka de* (The History of the Japanese People, vol 8: Amidst the Storm of Repression), 1975, p304.

Soldiers developed tricks to escape fighting—how to get into hospital, how to get a tour at a training camp and how to get the best jobs.[62] Diaries and letters show many *kamikaze* loathed what they were doing and were critical of the war. Diary entries show one pilot, Hayashi Tadao, read Lenin's *State and Revolution* up to the day before he died. He read it secretly in the toilet, swallowing pages as he read and concluding it was an imperialist war. A sailor wrote: "This journey of ours is meaningless from the point of view of military strategy, and will cause no damage to the enemy. Our purpose is to prove the meaninglessness of such an action, and for this we are going to die".[63]

In 1939 soldiers taken prisoner by the Chinese Communist Eighth Route Army formed the *Nihon Heishi Kakusei Dōmei* (League to Raise the Consciousness of Japanese Troops). Other groups also formed including one in May 1940 under the direction of Nozaka Sanzō, who became a Japan Communist Party politician in the 1950s and 1960s, which focused on the Japanese army, and using leaflets, pamphlets and newspapers demanded improvements to the living standards of soldiers and concentrated on notifying Chinese soldiers and peasants of the anti-war activities of Japanese people.

Japanese prisoners of war in China rallied to the Chinese cause. The *Hansen Dōmei* (Anti-war League) formed by captured soldiers engaged in "megaphone propaganda" at the front, appealing to Japanese troops to surrender or refuse to fight. The League was forced to dissolve in August 1941 by the Nationalist government and its members were returned to prison, but even under repression and with limited freedom they continued their activities. With the cooperation of the Chinese Communist Party, Nozaka also established the Japan Workers and Peasants School

(*Nihon Rōnō Gakkō*) in 1940 to educate prisoners about Japan's military and in 1942 established the *Nihonjin Hansen Dōmei* (Japanese People's Anti-war League) and called on Japan's soldiers to participate in the anti-war movement.[64]

After the Armistice, Japanese soldiers also deserted in Indonesia to join the national liberation struggle. According to the *New York Times*, perhaps 1,000 did this. Sergeant Fujiyama heard independence leader Sukarno give a speech and decided to join the liberation struggle. He was twice wounded in combat alongside Indonesians.[65] Others such as Sergeant Ono Shigeru had been sent to Indonesia to train the local nationalist youth. When the war ended, he stayed in Bandung and joined up with the independence fighters. Later he lost his left arm in an attack on a Dutch post office and lived in Batu, Eastern Java.[66]

Resistance took the form of both collective and individual actions including strike action by workers but also collective absenteeism. Graffiti, humour and story telling also expressed resistance. It was resistance such as this that the Japanese elite feared. As navy minister Yonai Mitsumasa commented, "The reason why I have advocated the end of war is not that I was afraid of the enemy's attack, nor was it because of the atomic bombs or the Soviet entry into the war. It was more than anything else because I was afraid of domestic conditions".[67]

In combination the research presented indicates a more nuanced picture which challenges the hegemonic vision of Japan's wartime population as fully supporting the war effort and this may represent just the tip of the iceberg.

Under occupation

Resistance continued during the Western occupation and for good reason.

The occupation was supposed to be humanitarian, foster democracy and work for peace. In practice it was racist, vindictive, favoured the rich and began rearmament. According to Australian cameraman William Carty, the first orders from General MacArthur, commander of US Army Forces in the Far East, to his foreign correspondents' club included no fraternisation or feeding the Japanese although many were starving. The Office of Strategic Services, ancestor of the CIA, said censorship under the occupation continued the "authoritarian tradition" in Japan. Men of influence, said a parliamentary report, wore a mask of democracy but in reality they "swaggered on black markets".[68]

Western attempts to reform Japan were half-hearted. In less than a decade, moreover, the US was pressing Japan to create new fighting forces to be directed against the Communists in Korea and China. The needs of economic reform likewise took a back seat and the purging of elements considered dubious became less of a priority after late 1947. Under the watchword "Reverse course" Japan began to fit into the Western alliance.

The International Military Tribunal for the Far East, also known as the Tokyo War Crimes Trials, judged the chief (so-called Class A) war criminals. Many thought Tribunal president Sir William Webb was biased. The British judge Lord Patrick saw Webb's absences along with those of one other judge as "the gravest blot that had yet stained the honour of the court".[69] After 18 months of prosecution Webb suggested each accused should get only two days rebuttal, prompting outraged protests from the defence.[70]

Webb himself agreed that the crimes of which the German leaders at Nuremberg were accused were far more serious than those of the Japanese defendants. He acknowledged that the Tribunal was flawed because Emperor Hirohito, the leading criminal, had received immunity.[71] The prosecution indicted Japanese leaders for promoting racial superiority in a trial where few of the judges were non-whites. Thus the credibility of the trials was dubious.

The occupation never really finished. Rather a new global political alignment arose with Japan as a crucial strategic base against Russia and China in the Cold War, complemented by a hot war in Korea. As this new global conflict emerged, the US's Japan policy changed dramatically. The new phrase on everybody's lips was "Reverse course". Wartime villains who might once have expected to be purged were now allies against Communism. They were "de-purged" and the occupiers hounded leftists instead.[72] Ambitious plans to break the monopoly power of the *zaibatsu* mega-corporations were quietly abandoned because opening up the Japanese economy to US capital became less important than immediate economic stability and the imperatives of winning the Korean War:

> the changes turned out to be considerably more modest than some had hoped...shifts in American foreign policy towards east Asia...and calls from the Congress to guard against unnecessary overseas spending left the core of Japanese finance unimpaired... The old combines regrouped and returned to something akin to their former status.[73]

In a speech marking the first anniversary of the surrender MacArthur had remarked that Japan's strategic position could make it either a mighty bulwark for peace or a perilous springboard for war. Millions of

Japanese yearned for the former but once Korea blew up US leaders opted for the latter.[74]

The fate of the labour movement expressed wider social patterns. With the end of the war, interest in trade unions had revived quickly. Total union membership was 600,000 in late 1945, rising to 6.7 million or 53 percent of the workforce by June 1948.[75] Conventional accounts attribute this to encouragement by the occupation forces but MacArthur was more interested in a new version of corporatism. Unionisation did not proceed in the normal way, by persuading individuals to join; instead almost the entire company workforce would join *en masse*. According to Japanese expert Kazuo Nimura, most doubt that all these workers joined as a result of freely made individual decisions.[76] Closed shop arrangements can, of course, be a mainstay of genuinely independent trade unionism but that was not the case here. Another writer, Taira Koji, argues that when large enterprises were "unionised" overnight it was really an extension of the corporatist *Sanpō* methods used by the wartime regime to integrate workers.[77]

While these devices sought to restrict unions, large numbers of workers had ideas of their own. In addition to work stoppages they used workers' control strategies (taking control of production) to get around MacArthur's anti-strike restrictions. When employees took control of the *Yomiuri* newspaper and shifted its editorial line to the left, circulation rose sharply. The first peak of struggle was the Food May Day demonstrations of 1946. This attracted some 2 million workers, half a million of them in the capital. Communist leader Tokuda Kyuichi drew prolonged cheers when he shouted "Down with the emperor!" The day was filled, one observer wrote, "with a curious kind of joy—perhaps the kind of luminous joy a war prisoner feels on regaining freedom".[78]

MacArthur's team began looking for ways to get trade unionism back under control. When workers announced a general strike for 1 February 1947, the situation became urgent. US labour adviser Ted Cohen, supposedly a leftist, thought the general strike such a "fearful prospect" that he suggested MacArthur ban it—which he eventually did. Labour leaders who had taken the occupation's pro-union rhetoric at face value were so shattered they wept publicly. From this point labour's position deteriorated steadily. Fourteen months later, in March 1948, the occupation authorities banned regional strikes by postal workers. Then in July MacArthur directed the Japanese government to deprive civil servants and other public sector employees of their right to strike. In December an injunction was issued against a miners' strike. In 1949 the qualifications for legal strikes in the private sector were tightened.[79]

Meanwhile MacArthur's Labor Division encouraged campaigns against the left in the unions, culminating in a "red purge" on the outbreak of the Korean War.[80] They were ably assisted by the Intelligence branch headed by General Charles Willoughby, who had praised Italy's fascist dictator Mussolini in 1939 for re-establishing the traditional military supremacy of the white race and who would later work for Spain's fascist dictator General Franco.[81] In this way the best chance to really democratise Japan was lost. Thomas Bisson, who worked for the occupation authorities, wrote in his diary: "The one really significant challenge to the old guard Japanese establishment has been turned back".[82]

NOTES

1   J Dower, *Japan in War and Peace* (New Press, New York, 1993), p135.
2   E O Reischauer, *Japan: The Story of a Nation*, 4th edition (McGraw-Hill Publishing Company, New York, 1990), p145.
3   M Hane, *Japan: A Short History* (Oneworld Publications, Boston, 2000), p155.
4   H Borton, *Japan's Modern Century: From Perry to 1970* (Ronald Press, New York, 1970), p382.
5   M Hoffman, "Japan's future may be stunted by its past", *The Japan Times*, 15 March 2014, available at www.japantimes.co.jp/news/2014/03/15/national/media-national/japans-future-may-be-stunted-by-its-past/#.VTvk4WRViko.
6   Cited in T O'Lincoln, *Australia's Pacific War: Challenging a National Myth* (Interventions, Melbourne, 2011), p102.
7   Ohara Institute for Social Research *Nihon Rōdō Nenkan* (Annual Report on Japanese Labour), Ohara Shaka Mondai Kenkyūjō, Tokyo 1938), p132; S Ienaga, *Japan's Last War: World War II and the Japanese, 1931-4* (Australian National University Press, Canberra, 1979), pp209,221-222; S Tsurumi, *An Intellectual History of Wartime Japan 1931-45* (Routledge and Kegan Paul, London, 1986); Y Nishinarita, *Kindai Nihon Rōshi Kankeishi no Kenkyū* (Research on the History of Japan's Modern Labour Management Relations), (Tokyo University Press, Tokyo, 1988), p232; D Schauwecker, "Verbal subversion and satire in Japan, 1937-45", as documented by the Special High Police, Japan Review, 15; 127-151, 2003, pp143; M Hane, *Peasants, Rebels, Women and Outcastes: The Underside of Modern Japan*, 2nd edition (Rowman and Littlefield Publishers, New York, 2003), p244; O'Lincoln, 2011, pp82-83.
8   P Edwards, "An honourable war", in Peace, WWII 60th Anniversary Series, *The Australian*, 2005, p6.
9   K Marx and F Engels, *The Communist Manifesto*, www.marxists.org/archive/marx/works/1848/communist-manifesto/ch01.htm).
10 Cited in Hane, 2000, p163.
11 Y Hibino, 1929, p51, cited in O'Lincoln, 2011, p3.
12 O'Lincoln, 2011, p20.
13 A Gordon, *Labor and Imperial Democracy in Prewar Japan* (University of California Press, Berkeley, 1991), p245.
14 J Utley, *Going to War with Japan, 1937-1941* (University of Tennessee Press, Knoxfield, 1985), p32.
15 C Harman, *Explaining the Crisis* (Bookmarks, London, 1984), pp11-12.
16 Ienaga, 1979, p133.
17 Cited in O'Lincoln, 2011, p16.
18 Cited in O'Lincoln, 2011, p16.
19 Hane, 2000, p159.
20 Hane, 2003, p73.
21 Ienaga, 1979, p17.
22 F C Jones, *Japan's New Order in Asia: Its Rise and Fall 1937-45* (Oxford University Press, London, 1954), p5.
23 D Ide, "The prewar Japanese left: A survey and critique", The Hampton Institute, available at www.hamptoninstitution.org/japaneseleft.html#.U8xjS5SSxXF, accessed 21 July 2014.
24 Hane, 2003, pp162, 244.
25 Gordon, 1991, p265.
26 Ienaga, 1979, p11.
27 Gordon, 1991, pp 277, 288.
28 Gordon, 1991, pp 13, 270-271, 277, 288.
29 Gordon 1991, pp 270-271, 277, 288.
30 Gordon, 1991, p290.
31 Gordon, 1991, p291.

32 Ienaga, 1979, pp13-14; J Moore, J Livingstone and F Oldfather (eds), *The Japan Reader*, vol, 1, *Imperial Japan 1800-1945* (Penguin, Harmondsworth, 1974), p301.

33 S Shioda, *Nihon Shakai Undō Shi* (History of Japan's Social Movements) (Iwanami Zenshō, Tokyo, 1982), p132.

34 Schauwecker, 2003, p143.

35 Shioda, 1982, pp131-132.

36 Dower, 1993, pp103, 143.

37 Ienaga, 1979, pp221-222.

38 A Fujihara (ed), *Nihon Minshu no Rekishi 8: Danatsu no Arashi no naka de* (The History of the Japanese People vol 8: Amidst the Storm of Repression) (Sanseido, Tokyo, 1975), pp306, 293-294.

39 Nishinarita, 1988, p232; Ohara Shakai Mondai Kenkyūjō *Taiheiyō Sensōka no Rōdō Undō* (The Labour Movement during the Pacific War) (Rōdō Junpōsha, Tokyo, 1965), p14.

40 Shioda, 1982, pp119, 121, 122.

41 Gordon, 1991 p302; Ohara Shakai Mondai Kenkyūjō, 1935, p217; 1938, p132; 1965, p14; Shioda, 1982, p126.

42 Ohara Shakai Mondai Kenkyūjō, *Shakai Rōdō Dai Jiten (The Encyclopedia of Social Labour)* (Ohara Shakai Mondai Kenkyūjō, Tokyo, 2011), p1057.

43 Fujihara, 1975, p134.

44 Nishinarita, 1988, p412.

45 Dower, 1993, p 115.

46 *The Japan Times*, 30 June 2014

47 J Moore, *Japanese Workers and the Struggle for Power, 1945-47* (The University of Wisconsin Press, Madison, 1983), pp10-12.

48 Ohara Shakai Mondai Kenkyūjō, 1965, p18.

49 A Fujihara, *Nihon Minshu no Rekishi 9: Senso to Minshu* (The History of the Japanese People, vol 9: War and the People) (Tokyo: Sanseido, 1975b), p210; G Totten, *The Social Democratic Movement in Prewar Japan* (Yale University Press, New Haven, 1966), p206.

50 Fujihara, 1975b, p181.

51 Cited in Ohara Shakai Mondai Kenkyūjō, 1965, p13.

52 Cited in Ohara Shakai Mondai Kenkyūjō, 1965, p13.

53 Ohara Shakai Mondai Kenkyūjō 1965, p13; Fujihara 1975b, p81.

54 T Sugiura, *Senjichū insatsu rōdōsha no tatakai no kiroku (A Record of the Struggle of Printers during the War)* (Kōyō Publishing, Tokyo, 1964) (was not printed for sale), pp106-108.

55 Dower, 1993, p117.

56 Fujihara,1975b, p177; Ohara Shakai Mondai Kenkyūjō, 1965, p19.

57 Ohara Shakai Mondai Kenkyūjō, 1965, pp15-20.

58 Ohara Shakai Mondai Kenkyūjō, 1965, pp21, 25, 26.

59 Fujihara 1975b, pp208-210, 293-294.

60 R Smethurst, *Agricultural Development and Tenancy Disputes in Japan 1870-1940* (Princeton University Press, New Jersey, 1986), p354; Totten, 1966, p206.

61 Fujihara, 1975, pp304-306.

62 H Cook and T Cook, *Japan at War: An Oral History* (The New Press, New York, 1992), p129.

63 Tsurumi, 1986, pp82-83; for more on *kamikaze* see O'Lincoln, 2011, pp82-83.

64 Ienaga, 1979, p218; Fujihara, 1975b, pp163-4, 168; Shioda, 1982, p143.

65 D Greenlees, "Occupation Put Indonesia on the Path to Independence", *New York Times*, 15 August 2005; E Hayashi, *Mereka Yang Terlupakan: Rahmat Shigeru Ono: Bekas Tentara Jepang yang Memihak Republik* (Ombak, Yogyakarta, 2012).

66 Hayashi or see surabaya-metropolis.com/serba-kota/gerbangkertasusila/tentara-jepang-bela-indonesia-tak-pernah-tercatat-sejarah.html. Indonesian language website.

67 T Hasegawa, "The Atomic Bombs and the Soviet Invasion: What Drove Japan's Decision to Surrender?", *Japan Focus*, 2007, available at www.japanfocus.org/-Tsuyoshi-Hasegawa/2501, accessed 18 July 2014.

68 Dower, 1999, p119; see also W Carty, *Flickers From History: A Newsreel Cameraman's Story* (HarperCollins, Sydney, 1999), pp155-156; J Dower, *Embracing Defeat: Japan in the Wake of WWII* (W W Norton and Co, New York, 1999), pp11-119; M Harries & S Harries, *Sheathing the Sword: The Demilitarisation of Japan* (Hamish Hamilton, London, 1987), pp72.

69 K Taira, "Economic development, labour markets and industrial relations in Japan", in P Duus (ed), *The Cambridge History of Japan*, vol 6, (Cambridge University Press, New York, 1988).

70 Dower, 1999, p466; Harries & Harries, 1987, pp143, 149.

71 Dower, 1999 pp59, 466.

72 R Harvey, *The Undefeated: The Rise, Fall and Rise of Greater Japan* (Macmillan, London, 1994), p301; Dower 1999, pp525-526.

73 R Buckley, *Japan Today* (Cambridge University Press, Cambridge, 1998), p21.

74 W McMahon Ball, *Japan: Enemy or Ally* (Cassell, Melbourne 1948), p19.

75 K Nimura, "Post Second World War Labour Relations in Japan", in Jim Hagan and Andrew Wells (eds), *Industrial Relations in Australia and Japan* (Allen and Unwin, Sydney, 1994), p67.

76 Nimura, 1994, p69.

77 Taira, 1988, pp648, 652.

78 Moore, 1983, pp52, 178.

79 Taira, 1988, pp648, 652.

80 H Fukui, "Postwar Politics 1945-73", in P Duus (ed), *The Cambridge History of Japan*, vol 6 (Cambridge University Press, New York, 1988), p76.

81 Harries & Harries, 1987, pp xxviii, 222.

82 R Finn, *Winners in Peace: MacArthur, Yoshida and Postwar Japan* (University of California Press, Berkeley, 1992), p141.

11

The Huk rebellion and the Philippine radical tradition: 'A people's war without a people's victory'

Ben Hillier

The Huk rebellion was the most important guerrilla insurgency in Philippine history and one of the most effective resistance operations of the Second World War.[1] Comprising up to 12,000 people under arms with a similar number in reserve, the People's Anti-Japanese Army represented 5 to 10 percent of the total guerrilla forces across the archipelago.[2] Its fighters were drawn primarily from the central provinces of Luzon, the largest and most populous island. Huk commander in chief Luis Taruc later wrote:

> The resistance movement that sprang up in central Luzon was unique among all the groups that fought back, in one way or another, against the Japanese. The decisive element of difference lay in the strong peasant unions and organisations of the people that existed there before the war. It gave the movement a mass base, and made the armed forces indistinguishable from the people.[3]

As the Japanese were swept from the island in late 1944, often by Huk rebels ahead of the advancing US Army, there was relief at the prospect of peace. But soon Huk were being arrested, imprisoned and murdered under US occupation. The example they had set by placing areas under democratic government rattled both foreign occupiers and domestic elite. Returning landlords, who often had been collaborators with the Japanese high command, now sought to exact tribute from the heroes of the conflict. "The war against Japan was a people's war without a people's victory", wrote Taruc.[4]

The guerrilla units were soon reactivated as the People's Liberation Army, drawn from a base of some 50,000 part-time soldiers and half a million sympathisers for whom the question of national liberation was not easily disentangled from class oppression.

A history steeped in rebellion

When Miguel Lopez de Legazpi established a Spanish beachhead in Asia at Manila Bay in 1565, the archipelago was inhabited by fewer than a million people. Social structures were based on a kinship system, the barangay, with a simple class structure.[5] There were no great cities and no central power; the economy was subsistence. The Spanish brought with them an embryo of the society from which they had departed. But the colonists were few in number and concentrated in Manila—the galleon trade with China was the obvious path to wealth. Tribute and forced labour were the conquerors' rewards for securing the territory for King Philip II. Those were enabled by royal land grants to administrators and Catholic religious orders. Jeffry Ocay explains:

> The absence of a centralised government in this society made it extremely difficult for the Spanish colonialists to establish their colonial power and to collect tributes and exact services from the native people. In order to address this problem, the Spaniards systematically reorganised the pre-Hispanic Philippine society...into larger communities called pueblos...[which] became the most effective tool of domination used by the Spaniards during this time because it brought the native people together within close scrutiny and direction of the Spanish colonial officials and friars.[6]

The island provinces by and large were "pacified" by the priests. By one estimate there were more than 1,500 priests throughout the country—more than the Spanish lay population—by the early 18th century.[7] Not until the 19th century was a European garrison stationed in the area.[8] "The fact that the people became Catholics made God the powerful ally of their rulers", explained the radical left nationalist historian Renato Constantino.[9]

Not all co-option was spiritually based. Cooperative local chiefs received tribute and labour amnesties and the lion's share of the official land grants in return for facilitating the exploitation of their barangay.[10] Exploitation often required force, but the paucity of exploitable natural resources throughout the archipelago meant that the occupation was relatively less brutal than had been the case in parts of Latin America.[11]

Still, numerous revolts took place against colonial excesses.[12] In the early years, wrote historian John Phelan, rebellions "usually began as protests against economic exploitation or political injustice, but they invariably terminated on an anti-Catholic denominator".[13] Friars established themselves as landlords and their abuses became systematic.

The Spaniards played one ethnic group against another in the early years. But with integration into the world division of labour, commercial relationships penetrated deeper into the archipelago. A national market was established, the basis of a national consciousness. Revolts also began to take on a class character. Labourers were working on large, often church-controlled estates, breaking their backs to fill sugar, hemp and tobacco quotas. A broader indigenous hierarchy developed. This included the chiefs and other layers of civil authority such as inspectors, deputies and elected officials. They were often more exploitative and corrupt than the friars.[14] A class of wealthy mestizo traders formed (the most important of which were the Philippine born Chinese/indigenous). The mestizos had an interest in the maintenance of the existing economic order. They too began accumulating land and benefitted from the exploitation of the mass of the population. They also received protection from the colonial authorities and culturally became more European than indigenous.

"In the 19th century particularly", wrote US colonialist James Le Roy, "the mestizos (mostly the propertied class) have flocked to [the two Jesuit and Dominican colleges]".[15] Universities in Europe were taking greater mestizo enrolments. Educational and economic advance increased social and political aspirations. These were not welcomed by the Spanish. Peninsulares (Spaniards born in Spain) considered even creoles (those of Spanish descent born outside Europe) socially inferior. Rebellion began to ferment within the ranks of the mestizo and indigenous secular clergy from the 1820s because the Spanish friars often blocked indigenous priests rising to positions of authority and restricted the teaching of Spanish.[16] Colonial policy also limited social advance within the administration and the military. One doctor related the prevailing attitude of the oppressors: "The friar would say [to the indigenous or mestizo who had gained an education], 'You are a very ugly person to try to imitate the Spaniards; you are more like a monkey, and you have no right to try and separate yourself from the carabaos' [water buffaloes]".[17] The social order, however, was butting up against a new reality. As a visiting German observed in the mid-19th century:

The old situation is no longer practicable, with the social change the times have brought. The colony can no longer be excluded from the general concert of peoples. Every facility in communication opens up a breach in the ancient system and gives cause for reforms in a liberal sense. The more that foreign capital and foreign brains penetrate, the more they increase the general welfare, the spread of education, and the stock of self-esteem, the existing ills becoming in consequence the more intolerable.[18]

In late 17th century Spain physician Diego Matheo Zapata had warned that Enlightenment philosophy was a threat not only to the church, but to society.[19] Two hundred years later the radicalism associated with that country's 1868 Glorious Revolution was transmitted to the colony, where an alliance of lawyers, liberal businessmen and clergy began pushing for reform. They were joined by students demanding academic freedom and an end to discrimination against the indigenous population. Enlightenment ideas were permeating through an increasingly literate class of Filipinos. Originally the latter term referred exclusively to the creoles. But with the rise of the mestizo the term broadened in scope. The growing intelligentsia—the ilustrada, the educated sons of the land-owning and trading elite—"infused it with national meaning".[20]

Revolution

The secular concepts of equality, democracy and citizenship contradicted the political and social barriers erected against the Filipinos. Newly appointed governor Carlos María de la Torre wrote to Spain in 1870: "The whole country points its finger at certain individuals of the clergy and certain lawyers, all mestizos and [creoles]… Everything, I repeat, leads one to believe that these lawyers and priests…dream of the independence of the country".[21] His impression wasn't accurate. For many of the Filipino elites, genuine equality meant the political integration of the Philippines with Spain and the granting of citizenship. This was the outlook of the mainstream of the anti-clerical Propaganda Movement, which was organised by Filipino exiles in Europe and in Manila was embodied in the Liga Filipina, founded in 1892 by the European-educated mestizo novelist Rizal and others, including a young self-taught radical named Andres Bonifacio. Its goals were broadly liberal. And while it was anti-clerical, it also attracted priests interested in reforming the church.

The ilustrados were, in Constantino's appraisal "vacillating [and] opportunistic".[22] Rizal and his collaborators were loyal to empire and to the class from which they emerged. He never advocated (at least publicly) Philippine independence and denounced the idea of revolution. Yet de la Torre's intuition captured something of the dynamic in the growing movement: "Liberalism…became a revolutionary force", wrote historian John Schumacher, "when it became evident that the traditionalist, friar-dominated Church, which was the sworn enemy of liberalism, was perceived by Spain as the only prop on which the decadent colonial regime could maintain itself".[23] The Spanish colonial authorities made paltry accommodations to the reformists. But each clear demand for Filipino advancement carried broader implications: to concede one in reality would be to concede another logically.

The logic of belligerence led in the same direction. The Katipunan,[24] a radical separatist wing of the nationalist movement, grew under the leadership of Bonifacio. This wing involved provincial elites but also the labouring classes, who were concerned as much with the appalling social conditions they endured as with social status. By the late 1800s the working class was expanding in Manila. It, and the masses suffering in central and southern Luzon, rallied to the radicals. "The convergence of thousands of workers in a single place necessarily developed in them recognition of their solidarity of interest as Filipinos, though not yet as proletarians", wrote Constantino.[25] Affiliations with the organisation grew to the tens of thousands or more.[26]

National identity as Spaniard or Filipino expressed competing claims. The urban Filipino elite mostly spurned the radical movement—at least at first. Many sought equality with the colonialists, not with the lower classes. Yet the Spanish administration, suspicious of any liberal sentiment, struck out at all—even wealthy Filipinos with a stake in the colonial regime. There could be little distinction when Spanish class privilege rested on notions of racial superiority. As the colonialists lashed out and the ranks of the Katipunan swelled, the latter launched an uprising in August 1896. The Philippine revolution had begun.

Adding to the class and national antagonisms was religion. On one hand, the aspirations of the Filipino clergy were bound up with the anticolonial question. On the other, the agrarian question dominating the minds of the central Luzon labourers also had a religious dimension due to friar control of the large landed estates. The anti-clerical revolutionary movement faced a conundrum—only through alliance with the Filipino clergy could the masses be mobilised. The local clergy played a significant role in bringing their parishes to the revolutionary cause,[27] but often the priests had divided loyalties between the rebellion and the church.[28]

Ultimately the revolutionary forces were not strong enough to rout the Spaniards. Emilio Aguinaldo, one of Bonifacio's lieutenants, took control of Cavite province, just south of Manila. Skilled military leadership and the backing of more conservative rural elites propelled him to prominence. In an ensuing factional struggle Bonifacio was executed.

The revolutionaries eventually retreated to inaccessible areas and engaged in guerrilla warfare before Aguinaldo negotiated an armistice in return for a financial settlement and an agreed exile in late 1897. Popular revolt resumed in several provinces in March the following year.[29]

By the time the US declared war against Spain in April 1898, the rebellion was regrouping. Aguinaldo, in alliance with and funded by the US, returned from exile. As commodore George Dewey's squadron smashed the Spanish fleet in Manila Bay on 1 May, a 30,000-strong insurgency took control of Luzon. A revolutionary government was proclaimed and independence was declared on 12 June. The leaders were keen to demonstrate loyalty to the economic status quo. "We sufficiently guarantee order to protect foreign interests in our country" and "the most holy right of property", wrote Aguinaldo in December.[30] The US allegedly gave assurances that it was the Filipinos' friend despite refusing to recognise the new republic.[31] It was not bringing freedom, but negotiating the transfer of power. "The insurgents and all others", declared President McKinley, "must recognise the...authority of the United States".[32] Aguinaldo capitulated and recognised US authority—at least in Manila and its surrounds. He hoped that international negotiations would nevertheless result in recognition for his independent republic. It wasn't to be. War broke out between the rebels and the US in early 1899.

National and religious questions remained intertwined. Gregorio Aglipay, military vicar general (later excommunicated by Rome for his role in the revolutionary government), attempted to overcome the divided loyalties of the Filipino clergy and pull them decisively into the revolutionary camp. Ultimately he was unsuccessful, but many clergy participated in the war. "Sixty percent of the native priests", advised apostolic delegate Guidi, "are Katipuneros".[33] Some saw the struggle as a religious war—both against what was seen as widespread US desecration and looting of local parishes, and in defence of Catholicism against Protestantism.[34] Arcadio Maxilom of Cebu, for example, was confident:

> that should the starry flag of the Union dominate these islands, our children will not receive the Christian education which is found in the Philippines, through the grace of God, now strongly rooted, and should they be converted to Protestantism and will continue corrupting Christian customs... Let us fight then without hesitation or dismay, because God is in us and his power is great.[35]

The conflict left 200,000 Filipinos dead. The revolutionaries endured defeat after defeat. General Jacob Smith, commander of US forces in Samar, ordered death to every person over the age of ten: "The more you kill and burn", he instructed his commanding officer, Major Littleton Waller, in late 1901, "the better you will please me".[36] Yet in some areas the struggle continued and periodic uprisings occurred for more than a decade. "The diehard resistance", observes historian Jim Richardson, "was sustained almost entirely by less privileged elements who had less to lose from protracted war and less to gain from surrender".[37]

New masters

Under the US colonial regime resistance was brutally put down and the archipelago was unified under the rule of Manila. The Filipino elite flourished. In the provinces surrounding the capital the Spanish friars had accumulated more than half a million acres of land. The new administration confiscated most of this and sold it to the mestizos. So long as the Philippines remained a colony, many of these landowners were protected behind the US tariff. That meant favourable treatment exporting primary products to the largest market in the world. They became the greatest of collaborators. The US substituted education for religion in its pacification attempts. The civil service and government also were opened up to expand the Filipino middle class. This "Filipinisation" helped create a crony political system, by and large controlled by the landowners. The early Spanish rural reorganisation provided the foundation of the modern political unit and the power base of the Nationalist Party, which was originally established by more radical nationalists but in time became the main party of the establishment. Under its domination the Filipino state was built and prepared for eventual US handover. Historian Benedict Anderson explained:

> It was above all the political innovations of the Americans that created a solid, visible "national oligarchy". The key institutional change was the stage-by-stage creation of a Congress-style bicameral legislature... The new representational system proved perfectly adapted to the ambitions and social geography of the mestizo nouveaux riches. Their economic base lay in hacienda agriculture, not in the capital city. And their provincial fiefdoms were also protected by the country's immense linguistic diversity. They might all speak the elite, "national" language (Spanish, later American), but they also spoke variously Tagalog, Ilocano, Pampango, Cebuano, Ilongo, and a dozen other tongues.

In this way competition in any given electoral district was effectively limited, in a pre-television age, to a handful of rival local[s]. But Congress, which thus offered them guaranteed access to national-level political power, also brought them together in the capital on a regular basis. There, more than at any previous time, they got to know one another well in a civilized "ring" sternly refereed by the Americans... They were for the first time forming a self-conscious *ruling* class.[38]

The system created a larger layer of educated Filipinos than could be accommodated within the state and party bureaucracy. This in turn bred resentment, even within the beneficiaries of the US occupation, at the lack of opportunity provided by the colonial system. "New dissident leaders", wrote historian David Sturtevant, "tended to be middle class professionals with grievances against the Nacionalista oligarchy. Disgruntled lawyers, unsuccessful union organisers, disappointed office-seekers and frustrated journalists attempted to assume control of popular movements in both the city and the countryside. While they failed to achieve that objective, their efforts provided organisational models for a handful of attentive contemporaries".[39]

The US regime was politically more liberal than that of the Spanish, but the situation for the majority, particularly those in rural areas, deteriorated with colonial economic dependency. Much discontent was based on the culmination of a belated process of capitalist development opened up by new US markets. New machinery was coming into use. Previously tenant farmers had been able to borrow informally from landlords; they now required moneylenders or were forced to pay interest. One told historian Benedict Kerkvliet: "You know, before the time of the Japanese, the most important thing was that relations between tenants and big landowners went from decent to indecent".[40] The situation proved radicalising. Luis Taruc, who came from an impoverished barrio (village) in San Luis, Pampanga province, and would later become chief Huk commander, explained:

> When I was still crawling the dust of the barrio street, I remember the landlords coming into the barrio, shouting, "Hoy, Puñeta!" and making the peasants run to carry out their demands... If they delayed or perhaps did not do things to the landlord's liking, they were fined, or given extra work. In an extreme case they might be evicted. And where would they go for justice? The landlord owned the barrio. He was the justice, too.
>
> Every year, after harvest, I watched from the dark corner of our nipa hut the frustration and despair of my parents, sadly facing each other

across a rough dulang [table], counting corn grains of palay [unhusked rice]... The debts grew from year to year... By the time I was six years old I had begun to resent the landlords, who made us, children of peasants, go to their houses and clean the floors and chop their wood and be their servants. When I saw them coming I ran to hide in the bamboos. I no longer wished to be their janitor.[41]

Grievances against individual landlords became generalised as it became clearer that the rural masses were all in the same boat. An upsurge in agrarian revolt ensued from the 1920s and grew into the 1930s. In central Luzon the ostentation of the rich was driving the growth of resistance. But the new radicals were often informed by grassroots traditions and took inspiration from the ideas and struggles of previous generations. "Movements led by self-styled messiahs, secret societies with roots in the revolution and revivals of old organisations...burst upon the scene all over the archipelago", wrote Constantino. "Although they were contemptuously dismissed by American officials and Filipino politicians as fanatical movements or plain banditry, they represented the blind groping of the masses for solutions to real and grave socio-economic problems".[42]

Birth of the left

Manila was the centre of the working class, but the majority were dispersed throughout small enterprises; most lacked significant industrial power. In 1928, 80 percent of workers were in "scattered, non-industrial types of employment", and the 59 registered unions claimed a membership of just over 40,000, about 16 percent of the total workforce. Apart from the structural and legal barriers, there were significant ideological weaknesses. Richardson explains:

> The labour movement that developed during the early years of the American occupation reflected the traditions of the revolution in whose embers it was forged... The most striking legacy from the 1880s and 1890s was the obsession with moral regeneration, the conviction that the problems confronting the ordinary Filipino were in large measure internal, springing from weaknesses of his own soul and character... This view of the common masses was still coloured by that amalgam of shame, disgust and fear that had troubled the nineteenth-century ilustrados.[43]

The early years of labour organising were fraught, but powerful workers', peasants' and agricultural labourers' organisations eventually were established under secular leadership. The Workers Party of America (which would become the Communist Party USA in 1929) forged links with Filipino labour movement leaders in the early 1920s, after the Comintern directed affiliates to advance solidarity to revolutionaries in their country's colonies. A number of Filipino leaders also attended a Profintern (Red International of Labour Unions) hosted conference in Canton in 1924.

A left-right split in the main union federation resulted in the majority of unions walking out in 1929 to form the Association of the Sons of Sweat (KAP), which affiliated to the Profintern.[44] The KAP leadership subsequently set up the Philippine Communist Party (PKP) in 1930. The KAP and the National Council of Peasants in the Philippines (KPMP) had communist leadership; the new party therefore considered that the two organisations constituted its mass base. This was despite the fact that, as Richardson says, "the number of KPMP cadres with more than a rudimentary grasp of communist theory can scarcely have reached double figures".[45]

A Socialist Party had also been formed and was organising in central Luzon under the leadership of Pedro Abad Santos. His movement was theoretically inchoate, with an orientation to mass action and self-organisation.[46] The party was relatively small, but led the General Workers' Union (AMT—the largest peasant and tenant farmer organisation in central Luzon) and counted among its ranks Luis Taruc, one of the most talented organisers in the country.

As ripples from the Great Depression lapped the archipelago's shores, labour unrest grew. "Latent discontent among the poor...is developing into a...definite state of unrest", warned an article in *Philippine Magazine* in 1932.[47] The KMPM grew from 15,000 to 35,500 in 1929-31, but the state was now cracking down on the communists. Twenty PKP leaders were jailed, then exiled to different provinces. Along with economic conditions, the fortunes of the revolutionaries now declined. KPMP numbers plummeted to 5,000; KAP affiliations dropped by three-quarters to 7,000; and PKP membership collapsed from up to 2,000 to 230 in late 1933.[48] The lack of funds and organisers greatly inhibited the work of the party. Some of the problems were brought on by the Comintern's ultra-left Third Period orientation, which was uncritically accepted.[49]

As the economy improved and the orientation of the party, along with the world movement, began to shift from mid-1934, the PKP began notching up victories. The leaders were released in 1936, partly because the government was anxious to bring about national unity in the face of what it perceived as Japanese militarism. According to former guerrilla Alfredo Saulo the CPUSA had also dispatched an envoy to lobby President Quezon for the communists' release and, later, for their pardon. The announcement of the United Front Against Fascism (the Popular, or People's, Front) at the Comintern's seventh world congress provided a sweetener. In a letter to President Quezon, the PKP leadership pledged: "We stand ready to drop all difference of the past in the face of the present national emergency in order to make possible the democratic unity of the people".[50]

The party, whose leading members were primarily Manila-based workers, now pushed for unity with the socialists, whose mass rural base had "succeeded in raising hell in Pampanga".[51] Unity was consummated on 7 November 1938 at a convention in Manila. "The discussions had very little to do with ideological and doctrinal differences", Taruc later wrote. "The emphasis was on an urgent program for a united front to fight against fascism and war".[52] The parties merged, retaining the name PKP but maintaining their own organisations for a number of years under the arrangement. Two years after the merger the new PKP had 3,000 members, the KPMP and AMT combined boasted well over 100,000, and KAP affiliations were reportedly 80,000.[53]

The Catholic campaign

The position of the Catholic church had been undermined by US colonialism. Not only had the friars lost their estates in central Luzon and around Manila, but the doctrine of the separation of church and state was introduced, reducing their political power, the education system had been secularised, partly undermining their social role, and the schismatic Independent Church—a nationalist breakaway formed in the wake of the war against the US—brought a degree of formal ecclesiastical competition, particularly in the far north of Luzon and to a lesser degree in the central plains where Catholicism could be associated with the elite.

Yet the vast majority of the population remained true to the faith. The Catholic hierarchy in the 1930s ran a propaganda campaign against the left and abstained from any social movement associated with communists.[54] On one hand the hostility emanated from Rome and the establishment in general. But there was also a deeper reactionary current. Franco's takeover in Spain was backed by the Spanish clergy. Some of their counterparts in the Philippines began writing tracts extolling the virtues of fascism, Franco and Salazar's New State in Portugal,[55] which no doubt pushed them further to the right and possibly made them less able to respond to the needs of the labouring classes.

The PKP, "a significant number" of its leadership being members of the nationalist church,[56] was initially staunchly anti-clerical, but not necessarily anti-religious—although there seems to have been no shortage of "opium of the people"-style denunciations. It was hostile to the Catholic church in particular. The party programme demanded that priests be disenfranchised and barred from public office. After the People's Front reorientation 25,000 copies of "An appeal to our Catholic brothers" were circulated. The pamphlet sought to pry open the divisions between the parishioners and the church elite and gain the sympathies of devout labourers. Some of the passages were politically appalling, such as that "the Communists are staunch upholders of the family and the home. We consider sexual immorality and looseness in family life as the harmful result of bad social conditions." But the broader approach was considered necessary not only to avoid isolation, but to enable the party to gain a mass audience:

> Sections of the Catholic hierarchy, and fascist elements associated with it, are working hard to influence the mass of Catholics against every democratic and progressive tendency or idea... They are trying to create a conflict between Catholics and Communists, a conflict which is not of our choosing at all...a growing number of Party members retain their church affiliations.[57]

Invasion

On 9 December 1941 Japan invaded the Philippines. The impact was immense. People left the provinces for Manila, they left Manila for the provinces and they left the towns and the villages for the mountains. Everywhere they saw looting, burning and people cut off from their families. Abad Santos (by this time frail and sick; he would die before war's end), Evangelista (soon to be executed) and PKP general secretary Guillermo Capadocia were quickly arrested and imprisoned. In Pampang, Pampanga, "the civilians lived in terror", Maria Rosa Henson remembered. "People were afraid to leave their homes, even to plant crops...only the Japanese Army had the fuel to run their trucks and other vehicles. Electricity was only for the Japanese Army... People did as the Japanese ordered because anyone who violated their rules was punished".[58] The people also had grounds for anger because they had to bow to the Japanese in the towns, and especially because of violent raids called "zona" staged against much of the populace.[59]

Not everyone opposed the new invaders. A certain number of the middle class nationalists, many of whom were united under the Ganap Party, hoped that Japan would grant independence. These hopes were not as unreal as they might seem: Japan did take some tangible steps towards Indonesian independence, though not till very late. Also, the Japanese were Asian and claimed that they and the Filipinos were one race; they were going to free the country from the whites.[60] Many of the oligarchy of landowners and local politicians also were pro-Japanese. They were used to collaborating, and Japanese policies were not radically different from those of earlier regimes. Given that much of the Philippine state was run by the Nationalist Party, it was easy to realign power structures to work with the new occupiers.[61] The leader of the ill-fated first republic, Emilio Aguinaldo, also supported the invaders. But broadly speaking there was an interconnection between rural elite, local officials, the Philippine Constabulary and a new puppet government: a loose alignment of everyone hated by the people was supporting the Japanese occupation.

The People's anti-Japanese Army

A combined meeting of the AMT and KPMP in Pampanga immediately after the invasion drew 50,000 to offer their services to the government.[62] Here in central Luzon, where peasant organising was most advanced, the resistance would be most intense. Many were already preparing to fight when the PKP issued a call to prepare for guerrilla warfare. Taruc explained: "Out of [the] call to the peasants and the workers to resist the Japanese, the Hukbalahap was born... Its growth was spontaneous. Whole squadrons came overnight from the towns and barrios".[63]

The most interesting battle took place in Pampanga in March 1942 and led to the formal constitution of the Hukbalahap (Huk). Legendary woman fighter Felipa Culala, known popularly as Dayang-Dayang, led some 130 troops in an ambush of the Japanese. The invaders lost 30 to 40 soldiers, along with almost 70 police officers. It was the first organised encounter against the enemy, and it "electrified the countryside".[64] Dayang-Dayang had been a KPMP member who led squads against strike breakers. Later she was executed for corruption. Such were Huk justice and discipline.

Women such as Sakdalista Salud Algabre had played an active role in earlier resistance movements. The Huk, however, were reportedly the first significant political or resistance organisation to actively recruit them. Jesus Lava, a post-war general secretary of the PKP, estimated that females made up around 10 percent of the guerrillas. In a deeply conservative country—because of the Catholic tradition and the central role of the family in rural life—the participation of women as commanders and comrades in arms, rather than simply as sisters and wives, provoked passionate debate about the role and status of women in Filipino society. It also created conflict within the Huk and the PKP, whose ranks harboured the prejudices of the time.[65] Nevertheless, rebel practice seems far more enlightened than the "civilised" Japanese or US occupiers. Taruc paid particular tribute to two commanders—Remidios Gomez, a former beauty queen and AMT organiser who took the name Liwayway (Dawn), and a former KPMP organiser who took the name Guerrero (Warrior):

> Liwayway...[prior to a battle] would comb her hair, apply lipstick, manicure and polish her nails. "Why shouldn't I?" she said. "One of the things I am fighting for is the right to be myself"... Guerrero...[was] fond of wearing a man's clothes. She became adept at handling an automatic rifle, and would command on the firing line. She was one of the organisers of Apalit Squadron 104, which became one of our best. Guerrero was also a good speaker and an effective rallier of the people's support.[66]

By September 1942 the number of Huk squadrons had grown from five to 35. Gradually, the amateur fighters, who had been trained primarily in labour solidarity, learned through military engagements to become efficient soldiers. The Japanese mounted a show of force against the rebels at this time. But the atrocities and terror tactics of the invaders only drove more locals into Huk ranks. By the end of the year the guerrillas had 5,000 active supporters. US military analyst Lawrence Greenberg later wrote:

> In January 1943, Huk attacks resumed against Police Constabulary garrisons and Japanese supply depots. As their tactical successes grew and the people saw them as more effective fighters, Huk strength grew again—doubling to 10,000 by March 1943. As their strength and popularity mounted, the Huks activated additional squadrons and helped form an all-Chinese force.[67]

In addition to the Huks' main presence in central Luzon and the widespread, but less effective USAFFE (United States Armed Forces in the Far East), there were highly effective fighters in the southern islands of Mindanao and Sulu. Despite their superior resources, a hint of weakness on the side of the US and their protégés in the USAFFE emerges from popular anecdotage. When US forces on Corregidor gave up the fight, General Wainwright ordered all USAFFE fighters to surrender. Their commander, Wenceslao Vinzons, angrily refused. The order was ridiculous, he argued, because local guerrilla fighters had, up to that point, beaten the Japanese. In the following period Huk fighters travelled to the Bataan peninsula to stock up on weapons and munitions dumped by the Americans. Similar procurement exercises occurred in other provinces.[68]

Huk guerrillas were seen as heroes. They killed some 25,000 Japanese, Philippine Constabulary (which worked hand in glove with the Japanese High Command from very early on) and spies. They fought on multiple fronts: against the Japanese, the constabulary, the Ganaps and against potentially thousands of other pro-Japanese collaborators who not only gave up guerrillas to be tortured and murdered, but who sometimes participated in such activities. "There is a point", wrote Taruc, "...where 'turn the other cheek' means to have your head knocked off. Rather than have liberty in our country destroyed, we would destroy the destroyers." In such circumstances mistakes were bound to be made. "Innumerable cases of execution of Filipinos, deemed to have had some kind of rapport with any Japanese, were perpetrated to such an extent that many Filipinos feared the guerrillas more than the Japanese", wrote the historian Teodoro Agoncillo.[69] Yet the guiding principles were clear. Two documents drafted with the assistance of the Chinese guerrillas, "The Fundamental Spirit of the Hukbalahap" and "The Iron Discipline of the Hukbalahap", set protocols for interactions both within the movement and between the guerrillas and the people:

> Everyone shares the same fortune and endures the same hardship... Insults, coercion or deception are forbidden... Neither officers nor soldiers can have any individual privileges... A revolutionary army should not only love and protect the people, but it should represent the people... It should struggle for the benefit of the people. It should regard the people's benefit as its own benefit in all things it does.[70]

A severe defeat in March 1943 at the hands of 5,000 Japanese troops resulted in demoralisation and some strategic rethinking. One result was greater emphasis on broad civilian resistance in the villages and towns. Barrio United Defence Corps (BUDC) were originally developed in 1942 to help supply and provide intelligence to the guerrillas and, importantly, to govern in rebel territory. "After centuries of [appointed administrators] the people were given the opportunity to rule themselves", wrote Taruc.[71] Barrio councils set up schools, carried out anti-Japanese propaganda and administered local non-military justice. Ultimately, self-governing areas under the democratic control of the inhabitants were considered facts on the ground that would shape national politics and lay the basis for independent Philippines at the end of the war. "From the experiences and the pioneering of the BUDC it was only a short step to the establishment of local people's governments, which we began to build in the last stage of the war. The people's horizons had been immeasurably expanded".[72] This was problematic. BUDCs were conceived as cross-class alliances, which would display to those who were not peasants "that the resistance movement was not 'a class organisation.'"

The Hukbalahap was as much a political as a military organisation. "Mass schools" were set up to train organisers who could forge links between various resistance organisations and propagate the ideas of democracy and national independence in order to broaden the base of the rebellion and prepare for victory. Similar study groups were established in the guerrilla units.

The guerrillas regrouped after the March defeat and by the end of the year were better positioned. In Huk strongholds "both the landlords and the Japanese grew reluctant to attempt to seize any of the rice harvest. Freed from the heavy rice payments to their landlords, many of the peasants recalled 1942-1947 as the period in which food was most abundant".[73] They also fought in southern Luzon, particularly Laguna province. Huk growth alarmed the US. USAFFE detachments in Nueva Ecija province fought against the rebels from as early as 1942—sometimes in concert with the Philippine Constabulary and even the Japanese. Captain Alejo Santos, commander of the Bulacan Military Area, in 1943 described the Huk as the enemy.[74] In 1944 General MacArthur, the commanding officer of the US military's Pacific operations, ordered US-controlled guerrilla units to take them on.[75] The broader momentum of the war and USAFFE disorder seem to have made this a distraction rather than a disaster. The US was pushing back into South East Asia and the Japanese were redeploying troops from Luzon. Guerrillas across the archipelago were on the offensive.

Just before the US regular forces landed on the islands in late 1944, the PKP started spreading a leaflet with the slogans "Long live America, defender of democracy! Destroy the puppetry! Establish people's democratic governments everywhere!" PKP leaders Casto Alejandrino, Juan Feleo and Jesus Lava were elected provisional governors in the liberated provinces of Pampanga, Nueva Ecija and Laguna in early 1945 as BUDCs gave way to local government in town after town. However, the party would soon find that the leaflet's first exaltation was misplaced. The US Army took control of the archipelago and was little interested in defending the democratic advances made in its absence.

The left and the resistance

Before the Japanese invasion a small coalition of groups had campaigned against Japanese aggression and atrocities, and against the Axis: these included the League for the Defence of Democracy, the Friends of China and the PKP. These groups organised demonstrations and boycotts of Japanese goods, along with fundraising for China. After Japan invaded they formed the core of the United Front, which sought to bring together all resistance organisations, regardless of political differences, and coordinate the struggle against the occupying army. Other elements operating underground included the organisation Free Philippines with its movable radio broadcasting anti-Japanese and pro-US propaganda, as well as Filipino programmes.

US Army intelligence sought to "decipher the complicated relations" between the PKP and other elements but didn't achieve much clarity. It did register the fact that Huk leaders "preferred legitimate political activity to violence".[76] With a large Communist Party in the field and a broader front embracing the non-communist left and other progressive sectors, we might think that the key initiatives came from those structures. According to Kerkvliet, however, connections with these political currents were weak. "The PKP did not...control the peasant movement in central Luzon during the 1930s and 1940s, the Hukbalahap, or the Huk rebellion itself", he wrote.[77] Untangling the alliances is difficult. The PKP didn't want to go it alone and focused on keeping the United Front together. According to Saulo, the party kept a low profile so as not to alienate the non-communist sections of the resistance movement.[78] Jesus Lava, along with William Pomeroy, a communist who fought in the US Army and the post-war Huk resistance (see below), maintained, "All leaders of significance in the rebellion were party members".[79]

An ex-member of the 1970s party, Francisco Nemenzo, convincingly explained away the contradictions between Kerkvliet's and Lava and Pomeroy's accounts. The Socialist Party, and the unified PKP, he argued:

derived its strength from the fact that it was integrated in the indigenous revolutionary tradition, but its chief weakness lay in the failure to transcend that tradition, to set the movement on a genuine Marxist footing. In the course of armed struggle, the PKP nurtured a millenarian-populist outlook because that was the easiest way to rally the peasants.[80]

The error wasn't simply due to the mitigating circumstances of war, but rooted, Nemenzo argued, in the modus operandi of the SP, which built the largest mass organisation (the AMT) but was hostile to theoretical work. The organisation adapted itself to and even encouraged the prevailing superstitions and prejudices of the peasantry. Part confirmation of this can be found in Taruc's testimony that in the party "all of us... were free to follow our own methods and our own ideas".[81] Of Abad Santos he also wrote: "He knew people better than he knew economics, so there was more psychology than theory in his approach to the movement. He had an immense bag of tricks...which he used to prod the peasants into action".[82] Taruc was a talented protégé, but even after three years in the group—during which time he had risen to the post of national secretary—he clearly found it difficult to communicate in secular socialist language. Of party organising in 1938, he related:

> At demonstrations I got up and spoke to the people... I had not read Marx, or anything about Marxism, so I used quotations from the Bible to defend my arguments. Strip from the ideas and preachings of Christ the cloak of mysticism placed over them by the Church, and you really have many of the ideas of socialism. "We cannot sit back and wait for God to feed the mouths of our hungry children", I said. "We must realise that God is within ourselves, and that when we act to provide for our own welfare and to stop injustice we are doing the work of God".[83]

The approach was born of Taruc's limitations and far removed from that of a theoretically adept agitator. There seems more to the low political level of the PKP than the Socialist Party simply diluting the unified party, however; the socialists numbered just 300 members at the time of the merger. The communists had their own theoretical shortcomings.[84] Jose Lava, an elder brother of Jesus and also for a time PKP general secretary, admitted that, in the early 1930s at least, the party's organisational and propaganda drive in central Luzon was "guided more by determination and enthusiasm rather than solid Marxist knowledge".[85] The 1938 unity convention had passed a resolution on educational work, which proposed weekly classes:

The convention places before the whole party the problem of the education, selection and promotion of the leading personnel in all the party organisations. Great attention should be placed upon the Marxist-Leninist training of the leaders of basic organisations of the party, as well as the training of party members who are carrying on work inside the mass organisations.[86]

Yet there were obvious limitations to carrying out such an undertaking. First, the PKP had only 196 members several months before the merger.[87] James Allen, a CPUSA envoy offering significant guidance to the party during this period, estimated that the core of the organisation numbered "some 40 or 50 comrades"—a minuscule number. Second, the organisation was still developing and was devoid of both the history and the theorists of the European workers' movement. And the Filipino working class was relatively tiny and fragmented; by 1940 still almost half of the labour force was employed in domestic and personal service.[88] That was not the most conducive environment for the development of organic intellectuals. Third, while the PKP grew rapidly in the lead-up to the merger, its base was shifting from Manila and the working class to the countryside, where the land question rather than the labour question was often central and the fundamental principles of Marxism were less relevant. Urban party membership further declined with the advent of war because worker members were instructed to leave and give support to the guerrilla struggle; the membership of the party was almost totally recast by an influx of peasants.[89] Fourth, the tension between leading the mass work, keeping together a variety of anti-Japanese fronts and working through revolutionary theory would have been substantial. Finally, the Japanese occupation again pushed the communists underground.

Most likely is that, while the Huk leadership were in the PKP and the PKP was directing the struggle in a number of ways, the rank and file Huk and even many PKP cadre had not been trained in revolutionary politics. The mass base from the AMT and KPMP were organisationally aligned to the party, but the allegiance seems to have been born primarily from the struggle. Kerkvliet mustered plenty of evidence that backs this interpretation. One tenant farmer told him: "The government said [PKP politburo member and KPMP leader Juan] Feleo was a communist. Maybe he was. But if he was so were I and lots of others here in San Ricardo, because he was telling the landlords and the government the things we wanted".[90] There is also support from other sources. For example San Padreo, a wiry old peasant, told historian Stanley Karnow:

Nobody would give us our rights or hear our demands. They said we were Communists. I didn't know what Communism was, and I still don't. But they called you a Communist, that was that. It made no sense to deny it, because they wouldn't believe you.[91]

Added to this, the structures of one organisation overlapped with the next. One PKP member, a provincial secretary of the large post-war peasant union, complained in 1946, in the words of Kerkvliet, that "only some of those in the party's central committee knew Marxist political theory".[92] Nemenzo mustered an extreme example to force the point:

The group of Teodoro Asedillo [a KPMP organiser] of Laguna, for instance, acquired all the characteristics of a millenarian movement... [involving] the use of amulets and the celebration of rituals. They even linked up with another millenarian leader called Encaldo. It was a rather good version of a primitive rebellion. But it was staged by "communists".[93]

The party's political orientation to the anti-Japanese struggle also had ramifications. "All aspects of the agrarian struggle in central Luzon merged into or were shaped by the needs of the national liberation struggle", wrote Pomeroy. "The KPMP and AMT were dissolved; the attitude towards landlords was determined by the slogan 'Anti-Japanese above all'."[94] As Nemenzo later pointedly said of the slogan, "Nobody becomes a Marxist with that".[95] A united front, in the classic sense, is about joint action to defeat a common enemy; its principal method also involves proving that communist strategy is superior and *politically* winning over the ranks of non-communists to the party. The PKP, by contrast, was searching for allies to wage a patriotic cross-class war. The movement's leaders carried out, through Huk publications, relentless pro-US propaganda and pledged allegiance to the US government.[96]

One can imagine that, in the context of a full-blown invasion, options were dramatically limited to those calculated to ensure survival. Yet while the objective situation surely lowered the horizon of what was possible, making alliances with landlords and a major imperial power, subordinating the class struggle entirely to the military campaign and limiting propaganda to democratic and nationalist slogans (even if various instances could be justified on tactical grounds) could only result in political confusion. The peasant base of the Huk may at times have been clearer than the leadership. "It was difficult during the Japanese occupation", said Peregrino Taruc (brother of Luis), "to convince peasants of the necessity that the United Front could include landlords who were some-times their enemies".[97]

While there were debates and disagreements among the leadership about the strategy that should be followed, particularly as the war drew to a conclusion, the orientation was not simply a result of domestic con-siderations.[98] The party's broader political course was derived from the Comintern via the CPUSA. The Popular (or People's) Front had shifted the international communist movement sharply to the right. Globally the main enemy was now fascism, and alliances were being sought with the "liberal" bourgeoisie. A variant of this reasoning was at work in the Philippines. The party was also for a period strongly influenced by Chinese communist advisers.

The People's Liberation Army

> A people's war differs from most wars because from it the people as a whole have something to gain. That makes it a just war... We fought a just war against Japan; we had an unjust peace forced upon us...[which] sought to rob the people of their victory. The people did not submit... The armed struggle merely became for a time an economic and political one.
> —*Luis Taruc*[99]

People met peace with immense relief. By war's end more than 1 million had been killed throughout the archipelago. The economy was devas-tated. Huk fighters were helping the US take control. But for some there were nagging worries: why had the US begun to exclude Huks from sen-sitive positions while accepting elements who had collaborated with the Japanese? These worries were well founded. The US forces cooperated with the Huks for a month or so after they returned. Then they turned. Said one villager: "At first, the end of the Japanese occupation was like a sunrise on a clear warm morning. It felt good. It promised things would get better. But the sun wasn't coming up after all. It was going down".[100]

In February 1945 the leading Huks were arrested and jailed by the US military. "For 22 days we sat in an imperialist prison in our own country, which we had fought for three years to free", remembered Taruc. "Outside the 'liberation' was in progress".[101] The returning administra-tion, headed by Sergio Osmeña of the Nationalist Party, refused to recognise the provisional governments of central and southern Luzon. Democratically elected officials were removed from office and replaced by anti-Huk elites appointed by the US Army. Nevertheless, with the

Japanese defeated, the Hukbalahap mostly disbanded—although many fighters buried their weapons or fled to the hills. The Huk leadership naively continued to assist the US and the administration, issuing leaflets with the slogans "Long live our American allies!" and "Long live the Osmeña government!" They even went so far as to hand over Huk membership lists to US Army intelligence.[102]

US officers had been welcoming the collaborators back and befriending the landlords. Many of the latter had fled to Manila during the war. Now the landlords were returning and the old antagonisms were back. Some even demanded back rents for the time of their absence. But the peasants were more organised than ever after the experiences of the war. "There is a feeling here more than any other place in the Philippines", noted the US Army's *Daily Pacifican* about one of the regions where fighting had not ceased, "that the Filipinos are not glad to be 'liberated'."[103]

The PKP called for an end to armed struggle to focus on a programme of legal and electoral work in anticipation of the establishment of an independent republic—something that had already been promised by the US prior to the war and would be granted in July the following year. The communists constituted the Committee of Labour Organisations (CLO), which comprised 76 Manila trade unions with a combined affiliation of some 100,000 workers, around 20 percent of the total labour force.[104] PKP members also took leadership positions in the new National Peasants' Union (PKM), which was strongest in the provinces of Pampanga, Bulacan, Nueva Ecija, and Tarlac and claimed up to 500,000 members.

In July the Democratic Alliance (DA) was formed. It aimed to be an electoral bloc that would give due political representation in a new republic to the labouring classes and oust the wartime collaborators from government. Elections took place in April 1946. The DA, against the opinion of the majority of the PKP, allied with the Nationalist Party against the Liberal Party of Manuel Roxas (a breakaway from the Nationalists). In part this was because Roxas, a long-time friend of General MacArthur, had been a senior official in the wartime collaborationist government. It also was because Osmeña's Nacionalistas had promised a new law giving tenants 60 percent of the harvest, rather than the 50 percent or less that had been customary.

The results were a source of pride, but also of bitter disappointment. The left dearly hoped to defeat Roxas. In this it failed. On the other hand, the DA won all the congressional seats in Central Luzon. The mood must have been euphoric, but the DA subsequently was denied the right to take the seats. The new Roxas government unleashed new rounds of violence and pardoned those who had collaborated with the Japanese. All of this rocked the peasantry. Central Luzon already resembled a military occupation; it was about to become a war zone once again. The landlords wanted to crush the mass organisations and impose subservience. Private paramilitary organisations appeared, often drawn out of the ranks of the anti-Huk Philippine Constabulary. These thugs acted in concert with government forces and the US military to intimidate and murder peasant or leftist leaders.

Independence, symbolically granted on 4 July 1946, reinforced these developments. Philippine political sovereignty was predicated on deepening economic subordination. The Bell Trade Act, passed by the US Congress just days prior to independence, gave US citizens and corporations equal rights to Filipinos in exploiting natural resources. Even Osmeña described it as a "virtual nullification of Philippine independence". The wartime devastation of the Philippine economy was just another opportunity to make a buck. As US Army major Andrew Lembke writes:

> [Independence] should have represented empowerment, acknowledging the status quo change in Central Luzon induced by the occupation's effects. Instead it reinforced a return to the status quo ante, and a return to power of the same men the Huks fought during the occupation. Thus, for the Huks and their supporters, independence signalled a continuation of the struggle against a government that looked strikingly similar to the collaborationist government. Independence also provided the elites a mandate to destroy the peasant movement in Central Luzon, ensuring the perpetuation of the old social system.[105]

The widespread, if not majority, view was that there was no alternative to resistance. Although the US press carried stories of looming revolution, official US opinion was somewhat blasé. The Huk movement, according to the new ambassador to Manila, "was essentially socio-economic not political, numbering not more than 2,500".[106] The State Department and the Philippine authorities, who were presumably providing such Pollyanna tones, would soon be taught a lesson in the links between socio-economic and political factors. Taruc recalled:

> Although the Japanese had been driven off the plains long before, central Luzon now echoed with the indiscriminate gunfire of "liberation"... The rumble of American tanks sounded no different than the rumble of Japanese tanks on our streets. Dodging their new persecutors in the

barrios, our comrades looked back on forest life under the Japanese with nostalgia, because there we had at least been able to practise democracy and live as free men.[107]

A symbolic event stirring the mood was the murder of Juan Feleo in late August 1946. This was followed by a huge military campaign by the state, which dwarfed any operation carried out by the Japanese. Taruc wrote to President Roxas to say he was joining the new mobilisation of armed peasants: "I will be more service to our country and to our people and their government if I stay now with the peasants. In spite of every harm and provocation done to them I am still confident I can help guide them in their struggle for democracy".[108]

There was a hardening of attitudes on both sides. Leading some government forces was Carlos Nocum, one-time rebel who had later served as a USAFFE guerrilla. As Huk veteran Robert Aspia described him, Nocum wanted to trample the Huk forces "like you'd stomp on a cockroach".[109] Violence escalated dramatically. The Huk and the PKP were outlawed by Roxas in 1948, but upon his death his successor Elpidio Quirino attempted negotiations. These broke down when it became clear that the Huk leaders' lives were under threat.

The PKP leadership was divided. The majority were in Manila and oriented to rebuilding in the labour movement and focusing on legal work. Those stationed in Central Luzon were closer to the farmers and joined the rebellion, despite the fact that the party officially opposed it. In mid-1948 the party endorsed the armed struggle as its main area of work, after an ideological struggle in the leadership, which resulted in suspensions and later expulsions.[110] It was clear that the structure of Philippine society was a serious barrier to democratic change. Genuine democracy was a direct threat to the economic interests both of the country's rulers and of US interests. This was confirmed in the eyes of many by the 1949 election, which was marred by violence and corruption. Private paramilitaries and local police were mustered for rival candidates. The Nationalist Party launched an uprising in Batangas province following the result. "There is no more democracy in the Philippines", said a senior member of the Philippine Electoral Commission.[111]

The Huk was growing and taking more territory. After 1946 the movement sent units far beyond the Central Luzon area. Taruc explained: "We wanted to be on the offensive politically, but also have a military defence in order to protect ourselves while doing political organising." A further goal of the expansion was to build relationships and a base among a wide range of local groups and ethnicities.[112] Out of the growing spontaneous rebellion, and against persistent attacks from government forces, the Huk was reorganised as the People's Liberation Army (HMB) and further expansion drives were undertaken, now under the leadership of PKP leader Casto Alejandrino.

Its forces grew to perhaps 15,000, drawn from up to 50,000 part-time fighters. "In numbers, organisation and small arms the Huk fighting units were comparable to the government forces", wrote historian Alvin Scaff. "In terms of morale and civilian support in the areas of their operations, they had a decided advantage".[113] The government by this stage seemed in a parlous state, the economy was in ruins and the Chinese revolution had been victorious. The PKP declared a revolutionary situation in 1950. It was an unfortunate miscalculation, both regarding the scale of the revolt, the strongholds of which were confined to Central Luzon, the political development of the mass base of the HMB and the strength of the PKP. However heroic and selfless, PKP cadre were limited both in number and in political education. The masses overwhelmingly were not won to revolutionary conclusions. This was in part the historical legacy of the PKP, now exacerbated again by conditions of war. A party discussion document lamented:

We tried to step up education to the maximum, but after a time we couldn't hold schools because we were continually on the move to evade enemy military operations... We turned out masses of propaganda materials, but very little of this reached the lower organs, let alone the masses.[114]

Yet even if there had been a greater layer of educated cadre, communist forces, numbering perhaps 7,500, were like a drop in a bucket in a country of more than 16 million people. Working class urban insurrection and mass rural revolt might have stood a chance of creating a genuinely independent republic—if the mood had existed, if a general crisis of the Philippine state had come about and if there had been a mass and coherent revolutionary organisation available to lead it. Of those "ifs", only the second seems arguable—but the support of US imperialism for the new government was always a given. Somewhere in an isolated forest HMB camp in August 1950 Pomeroy, cut off from general developments, remained optimistic:

The revolutionary situation is flowing toward a revolutionary crisis, which is the eve of the transfer of power. We are in the period of preparation for the strategic aim of seizing power. Our tactical aims are all those steps that can effectively mobilise the allies and the reserves of the revolution into an increasing assault on the main enemy and their allies.[115]

Decline

By late 1951 there was increasing war weariness among the people. US concern about the depth of the rebellion led President Truman to intervene with financial and military aid. This proved decisive, with 100,000 or more armed soldiers and others now directed against the rebels and the state's integrity strengthened. The PKP Politburo had been captured in Manila in late 1950; many would spend the next two decades behind bars. Prominent Huk leaders were killed and the losses mounted. Those remaining were pursued by the army even into the mountains. Villagers became weary of lending support or just viewed the guerrillas as irrelevant as conditions changed. Fresh national elections turned out to be peaceful and the Nationalist Party victorious. This stoked hope that tangible reforms could be gained through legal means. Police reduced their abuses of the peasants, so the latter were less likely to feel the need for "Huk justice". Pomeroy's enthusiasm by now was sapped. He described the darkening mood in guerrilla ranks:

> Fear is beginning to replace daring in many places. Enemy agents swarm everywhere and have arrested some distributors. Why do they surrender? Because many have joined in the hope of quick victories and they have lost their taste for it. Because...more Huks are dying now than ever before... Because they worry about family back in a barrio without a breadwinner... We had thought that by the leaders setting a high tempo we could set high the tempo of revolution. We have been living in a fool's paradise... It is no longer victory that preoccupies us. It is survival.[116]

By 1955 the HMB was disbanded and the PKP in tatters; almost all surviving leaders were now in prison. Here the party nucleus at least was maintained. Three years later the membership was estimated to be just 700.[117] The coming of the dusk over this remarkable movement, however, would not put the aspirations and grievances of the labouring classes to bed. The defeat of the resistance would prove only an extended interlude to the rising of another rebellious sun.

NOTES

1. The Huk nickname is widely used for both the People's anti-Japanese Army and its post-war successor the People's Liberation Army. The name stems from the Tagalog: Hukbalahap Hukbo ng Bayan Labon sa Hapun (People's Anti-Japanese Army) and Hukbong Mapagpalaya ng Bayan (People's Liberation Army).

2. An estimated 260,000 guerrilla fighters in 277 units were engaged throughout the country. These numbers include US troops, and a range of organisations with various alliances. See L Schmidt, American Involvement in the Filipino Resistance Movement on Mindanao During the Japanese Occupation, 1942-1945, Master of Military Art and Science thesis (US Army Command and General Staff College, 1982), p2; H Crippen, "American imperialism and Philippine independence", Science and Society, vol 11 (2), 1947, pp104-108.

3. L Taruc, Born of the People (International Publishers, New York, 1953), p56.

4. Taruc, 1953, p212.

5. J V Ocay, "Domination and resistance in the Philippines: from the pre-Hispanic to the Spanish and American period", Lumina, vol 21 (1), 2010, pp3-10.

6. Ocay, 2010, pp10-11.

7. W L Schurz, Manila Galleon, p127. Referenced in R Constantino, A History of the Philippines (Monthly Review Press, New York, 1975), p74.

8. D Sturtevant, Popular Uprisings in the Philippines 1840-1940 (Cornell University Press, Ithaca, 1976), fn11, p26.

9. R Constantino, Neocolonial Identity and Counter-Consciousness (Merlin Press, London, 1978), p30.

10. N Cushner and J Larkin, "Royal Land Grants in the Colonial Philippines (1571-1626): implications for the formation of a social elite", Philippine Studies, vol 26 (1/2), 1978, pp102-111.

11. According to Phelan, the peasantry was neither destroyed nor greatly transformed. "In the provinces...no numerous class of wage earners emerged." The indigenous population engaged in agriculture "under a complex system of debt peonage and sharecropping" that lasted through the 20th century. See J L Phelan, The Hispanization of the Philippines (University of Wisconsin Press, Madison, 1959), pp98, 116. According to Ocay, drawing on the more recent scholarship of Corpuz, "the old right of the native people to ownership of land was extinguished. The native people were only assigned a piece of land to cultivate and these were not titled under their names. As a result, the families in the pueblo were reduced to a single class of farmers who were obliged to work their assigned land. In this new system...there were no longer sharecroppers because everybody became a farm worker." See Ocay, 2010, p12.

12. "Some of the most famous revolts during the early phase of Spanish occupation were the Dagami Revolt in Cebu in 1567, the Manila Revolt (also known as Lakandula and Sulayman Revolts) in 1574, the Pampanga Revolt in 1585, Magat Salamat Revolt in 1587-88 in Manila, Magalat Revolt in Cagayan in 1596, Tamblot Revolt in Bohol in 1621-1622, Bankaw Revolt in Leyte in 1621-22, Maniago Revolt in Pampanga in 1660, Sumuroy Revolt in Samar in 1649-50, and many others. Most of these early revolts were directly caused by the exaction of tributes and forced and corvée labour and other forms of abuses by the Spanish colonialists"—Ocay, 2010, p14.

13. J L Phelan, "Some Ideological Aspects of the Conquest of the Philippines", The Americas, vol 13 (3), January 1957, p225.

14. Phelan, 1959, p103.

15. J Le Roy, "The Friars in the Philippines", Political Science Quarterly, vol 18 (4), December 1903, p662.

16. Until "the very end of the Spanish regime no more than 5 percent of the local population had any facility with the colonial language"—B Anderson, "Manila's Cacique Democracy", New Left Review, no 169, May/June 1988, p6.

17   P W Stanley, *A Nation in the Making: The Philippines and the United States 1899-1921* (Harvard, Cambridge, 1974), p43.

18   Feodor Jagor quoted in J Le Roy, *Philippine Life in Town and Country* (GP Putnam's Sons, New York, 1905), p151.

19   J Israel, *Radical Enlightenment* (Oxford University Press, Oxford, 2002), p3.

20   R Constantino, *A History of the Philippines* (Monthly Review Press, New York, 1975), pp147-148.

21   Carlos María de la Torre, letter of 4 January 1870, quoted in J N Schumacher, *Revolutionary Clergy* (Ateneo de Manila University Press, Quezon City, 1981), pp18-19.

22   Constantino, 1978, p123.

23   Schumacher, 1981, p269.

24   Tagalog: Kataastaasang Kagalanggalang na Katipunan ng mga Anak ng Bayan—Highest and Most Respectable Society for the Sons of the People, founded in 1892.

25   Constantino, 1975, pp161-163.

26   L Fernández, *The Philippine Republic* (Columbia University, New York, 1926), p22.

27   And by 1898 the friars controlled fewer than 50 percent of the colony's parishes—M Martinez, *The Philippine Revolution* (International Academy of Management and Economics, Makati City, 2002), p164.

28   Schumacher, 1981, pp81-112.

29   Fernández, 1926, p45.

30   Emilio Aguinaldo, "Filipinos, beloved brothers", proclamation issued 6 December 1898, quoted in J Richardson, *Komunista* (Ateneo de Manila University Press, Quezon City, 2011), p9.

31   S Karnow, *In our Image* (Random House, New York, 1989), pp111-115.

32   Karnow, 1989, p124.

33   Schumacher considers this a biased exaggeration, but not without truth. See Schumacher, 1981, p275.

34   This was not the case everywhere. In some places, such as the island of Negros, the US was welcomed. In Cebu some clergy took a neutral position, both in the initial revolution against Spain—because many parishes were already under secular Filipino control with the blessing of the local friar—and subsequently in the war against the US.

35   Schumacher, 1981, p155.

36   Schumacher, 1981, p144.

37   Richardson, 2011, p13.

38   Anderson, 1988, p11.

39   Sturtevant, 1976, p204.

40   Quoted in B Kerkvliet, *The Huk Rebellion* (Rowman and Littlefield, Oxford, 1977), p6.

41   Taruc, 1953, pp13-15.

42   Constantino, 1978, p70.

43   Richardson, 2011, pp10, 30-31.

44   Tagalog: Katipunan ng mga Anakpawis sa Pilipinas.

45   Richardson, 2011, p195.

46   See A Tan, "The ideology of Pedro Abad Santos' Socialist Party", *Asian Center Occasional Papers*, series 11, no 3 (University of the Philippines, Quezon City, 1984), p2.

47   The article was penned by A V H Hartendorp. Quoted in Sturtevant, 1976, p212.

48   See Richardson, 2011, pp172-179, 197, 211.

49   "Commentaries and prescriptions emanating from the Comintern, respected as embodying the accumulated experience of communists throughout the world, were beyond question the decisive determinants of the PKP's own overall line. Statements issued by the International were frequently echoed and occasionally quoted directly in party documents and were never subjected to open critical appraisal, let alone challenged"—Richardson, 2011, p217.

50   Quoted in K Fuller, *Forcing the Pace* (University of the Philippines Press, Quezon City, 2007), p121. See also A Saulo, *Communism in the Philippines* (Ateneo Publications Office,

Philippines, 1969), pp32-33.

51 E Lachica, *Huk* (Solidaridad Publishing House, Manila, 1971), p89.

52 L Taruc, *He Who Rides the Tiger* (Geoffrey Chapman Ltd, 1967), p17.

53 Richardson, 2011, p252.

54 M Bolasco, "Marxism and Christianity in the Philippines 1930-1983", in Third World Studies (ed), *Marxism in the Philippines* (Third World Studies Center, Quezon, 1984), p106.

55 Crippen, 1947, p99.

56 Richardson, 2011, p164, and fn 155, pp312-313.

57 PKP, "An appeal to our Catholic brothers", 1938. Quoted in Fuller, 2007, p125.

58 M R Henson, *Comfort Woman* (Rowman & Littlefield, New York, 1999), pp28, 30-31.

59 Kerkvliet, 1977, p66.

60 This is apparent in early Huk propaganda and song. Maria Rosa Henson related: "The Huk explained that the Japanese...wanted to free us from American colonialism... But the Japanese failed to do good things in the occupied countries. They were oppressive and abusive." And the final lines of a famous Huk song read: "They blighted our people with misfortune, they killed those who opposed them, yet they say they are not our enemy because we belong to one race." See Henson, 1999, p28.

61 M Thompson, *The Anti-Marcos Struggle* (Yale University Press, New Haven, 1995), p177.

62 W Pomeroy, "The Philippine peasantry and the Huk revolt", *The Journal of Peasant Studies*, vol 5 (4), 1978, p505.

63 Taruc, 1967, p22.

64 Lachica, 1971, p107.

65 For this paragraph and more, see V Lanzona, *Amazons of the Huk Rebellion* (University of Wisconsin Press, Madison, 2009).

66 Taruc, 1953, pp102-103. Liwayway became known as the "Joan of Arc of the Philippines". See Lanzona, 2009, pp151-156

67 L Greenberg, *The Hukbalahap Insurrection* (US Army Center of Military History, Washington DC, 1987), pp18-19.

68 Lachica, 1971, p104.

69 T Agoncillo, *A Short History of the Philippines* (New American Library, New York, 1969), p237, quoted in Fuller, *Forcing the Pace*, pp181-182.

70 Quoted in Fuller, 2007, p169.

71 Taruc, 1953, p117.

72 Taruc, 1953, p127.

73 The Pacific War Online Encyclopedia, pwencycl.kgbudge.com/H/u/Hukbalahap.htm

74 Quoted in Fuller, 2007, p184.

75 Taruc, 1953, p155.

76 N Cullather, *Illusions of Influence* (Stanford University Press, Stanford, 1994), p65.

77 Kerkvliet, 1977, p264.

78 Saulo, 1969, p36.

79 The quote is Lava's. See J Lava, "Reviews", *Journal of Contemporary Asia*, vol 9 (1), 1979, pp75-93; see also Pomeroy, 1978, pp497-517.

80 F Nemenzo, "The millenarian-populist aspects of Filipino Marxism", in Third World Studies (ed), *Marxism in the Philippines* (Third World Studies Center, Quezon, 1984), p9.

81 Taruc, 1953, p105.

82 Taruc, 1953, p33. See also Tan, 1984.

83 Taruc, 1953, p29.

84 Fuller, 2007, p141.

85 Quoted in Saulo, 1969, p24.

86 Quoted in Fuller, 2007, p134.

87 Fuller, 2007, pp141-142.

88 The figures, although not terribly accurate, are at least indicative of the situation. See Richardson, 2011, pp68-72, 220.

89 Fuller, 2007, p177.

90 Quoted in Kerkvliet, 1977, p52; see also pp181-182.

91 Quoted in Karnow, 1989, p42.

92 Kerkvliet, 1977, p182.

93 Nemenzo, 1984, p19.

94 Pomeroy, 1978, p505. See also Taruc, 1953, p61.

95 Nemenzo, 1984, p19.

96 "Our entire propaganda during the war, our leaflets, newspapers, and appeals for action, are testimony to the high regard in which we held our American allies against Japanese fascism"—Taruc, 1953, p194.

97 Quoted in Kerkvliet, 1977, p102.

98 For a useful overview, see Fuller, 2007, ch 6.

99 Taruc, 1953, p212.

100 Tenant farmer, quoted in Kerkvliet, 1977, p110.

101 Taruc, 1953, p196.

102 Luis Taruc admitted this to Kerkvliet. See Kerkvliet, 1977, p114.

103 Quoted in Crippen, 1947, p117.

104 Lachica, 1971, p119.

105 A Lembke, *Lansdale, Magsaysay, America, and the Philippines* (Combat Studies Institute Press, Kansas, 2013), p5.

106 Cullather, 1994, pp64-65.

107 Taruc, 1953, p201.

108 Quoted in Taruc, 1953, p239.

109 Quoted in Kerkvliet, 1977, p160.

110 See Kerkvliet, 1977, pp178-188; Fuller, 2007, pp269-274.

111 Lembke, 2013, p25.

112 Quoted in Kerkvliet, 1977, p161. See W Pomeroy, *The Forest* (University of the Philippines Press, Quezon City, 1963), pp34-35, and Fuller, 2007, pp268-269, for portrayals of the expansion.

113 Quoted in Walter Ladwig, "When the police are the problem", in C Christine Fair and S Ganguly (eds), *Policing Insurgencies* (Oxford University Press, Oxford, 2014), p22.

114 Quoted in Fuller, 2007, p282.

115 Pomeroy, 1963, p62.

116 Pomeroy, 1963, pp152-153.

117 J Vargas and T Rizal, *Communism in Decline* (SEATO, Bangkok, 1957/8).

INDEX

Terms such as Britain, USA, Allies, Germany are not indexed as they occur frequently throughout the text.